FOUR GREAT WRITERS OF COMEDY

The plays in this volume reflect the
drive and vitality of their creators, whose
careers swerved from adventure to misadventure,
from gaiety to misery, often with a speed
and abandon that might seem reckless to more
provident souls.

But these were men of their times, the
product of rebellion against a confining age.
Implicit in the works of Wycherley and Congreve
is a good hard blow at the stultifying Puritanism
of the Cromwell regime; in those of Goldsmith
and Sheridan a loud and defiant shout at the
sentimentality and humorlessness of the House
of Hanover.

Artists and critics, these four men were
lovers of life and living, wells of energy,
mirth and wit. Their riant spirits will
evermore refresh a too sober world.

A BANTAM CLASSIC

FOUR GREAT COMEDIES
OF THE RESTORATION

WYCHERLEY
CONGREVE

AND EIGHTEENTH CENTURY

GOLDSMITH
SHERIDAN

With an introduction by
BROOKS ATKINSON

BANTAM BOOKS / NEW YORK

FOUR GREAT COMEDIES
OF THE RESTORATION AND EIGHTEENTH CENTURY

Published as a Bantam Classic September 1958
2nd printing.....................December 1959
3rd printing.......................October 1961
4th printing.....................September 1962
5th printing.......................August 1963
6th printing
7th printing
8th printing

Contents

Introduction

by
Brooks Atkinson

The four comedies in this volume represent a little more than one century of English manners and English playwriting. Since they are populated with lively characters who speak brisk prose, they can be enjoyed on their own terms as stage literature. But all forms of art—plays, novels, paintings—become most enjoyable when they are looked upon as parts of the life of their times—living relics of societies that have passed into history—and also as portraits of their authors. On both counts these comedies are fascinating. If it were not for Wycherley and Congreve it would be difficult to believe that any society could be as shallow, obscene and decadent as the one mirrored in *The Country Wife* and *The Way of the World;* and if it were not for Goldsmith and Sheridan it would be difficult to appreciate the degree to which national character can change in seventy-five or one hundred years.

When Wycherley's *The Country Wife* appeared in 1673 the fashionable world of London was recklessly revolting against the sanctimonious dullness of the stern Commonwealth of Cromwell. In 1660 the House of Stuart had been restored to the throne in the person of Charles II, a prodigal and profligate monarch who saw no reason why he should not enjoy himself extravagantly. The smart people of London were only too happy to follow his example.

Wycherley was fully equipped by experience and temperament to participate. When he was a lad his father, who disliked the tone of English education under Cromwell, sent Wycherley to school in France. In Paris, Wycherley enjoyed the satirical comedies of Moliére as well as the gilded society of Louis XIV. When he returned to England and to Oxford he was well prepared to chronicle the follies and amorous intrigues of London society.

Since his last play (*The Plain Dealer*, 1674) pours scorn on the immorality and corruption of Restoration society, Wycherley is sometimes portrayed as a reformer. But it is difficult to find in *The Country Wife* anything except a witty and scandalous relish of licentiousness. Borrowing his plot from Terence's *The Eunuch,* he applied it to his own day with racy enthusiasm.

Apparently, Wycherley had more character, sincerity and manliness than the fops of his time—but not enough to make him unacceptable to the court of Charles II. He was a particular favorite of the Duchess of Cleveland, who was one of Charles' mistresses. Nor did he shun intrigue in his personal life. He married a wealthy widow in secret, hoping thus to avoid the displeasure of the king, who liked to control the careers of all his courtiers. After his wife's death, Wycherley exhausted his resources in a long series of court actions to collect the inheritance she had left him. He spent seven years in Fleet Prison for debt, and Charles II did nothing to release him.

The next king, James II, paid Wycherley's debts, got him out of prison and put him on pension. But Wycherley was a man of his times. At the age of seventy-five he married an adventuress—under the erroneous impression that she was wealthy—and he settled a jointure on her. The lady was a fraud. She had beat him at his own game. He died eleven days later, a Restoration man in both wit and folly.

By 1700, the year in which Congreve's *The Way of the World* appeared, London society had recovered from its most odious excesses. The court of William and Mary was more sober than the court of Charles II. In 1698 a militant parson, the Reverend Jeremy Collier, had published a sensational pamphlet entitled *A Short View of the Immorality and Profaneness of the English Stage*. It denounced Shakespeare and Ben Jonson as well as the contemporary Restoration writers, though, curiously enough, not Wycherley.

Congreve was one of the writers who struck back at the parson. He was apparently not intimidated by a tirade based on the hot-headed assumption that the stage was responsible for the decline in public morality—instead of the other way round. But by 1700 London society had lost its taste for the debauchery of Charles II's time. Although the characters of *The Way of the World* are cynical and worldly, they are less ribald than the characters of *The Country Wife*.

The Way of the World is generally regarded as the masterpiece of Restoration drama. It has the polish and brittleness of a sheet of glass. The dialogue is neatly phrased; the figures of speech are intricate and dainty. Since Congreve wrote artificial rather than realistic comedy, the plot is contrived to keep the play in motion, not to reveal the truth of life. But *The Way of the World* is a literary delight; and within the framework of Restoration manners, Millamant is one of the loveliest, most ravishing characters in English drama.

When it opened in 1700 at the Lincoln's Inn Fields Theatre, *The Way of the World* was not a success. Congreve never wrote another play. Having written five he ceased being an author and became a gentleman, like a character out of his own works. When Voltaire came to visit him, Congreve fatuously asked to be regarded not as an author but as a gentleman. The great French iconoclast was furious.

As a frequenter of the coffee houses Congreve enjoyed the society of Pope, Swift, Gay, Addison and Steele. As a gallant he enjoyed the company of Mrs. Bracegirdle, one of the finest and most amiable actresses of her time, but when he rose in society, he forsook her for Henrietta, Duchess of Marlborough. Congreve was either so fascinated by Henrietta or so bemused by her exalted social position that when he died he left the bulk of his estate to her with the exception of two hundred pounds to Mrs. Bracegirdle. Since the Duchess was already fabulously rich and Mrs. Bracegirdle was impoverished, his disposition of his property seems to have been vain on the one hand and heartless on the other. It is as difficult to find nobility in a Restoration dramatist as it is easy to find wit in a Restoration drama.

English playwriting for the next three-quarters of a century generally lacked distinction. The public mood was changing. In Restoration times the theatres had been appendages of the court and were concerned with the amusement of fashionable people. But the rise of the middle class and the new prosperity of the merchants, many of whose daughters married into the aristocracy, brought new audiences into the theatre—people less interested in manners and style. Farquhar and Vanbrugh continued the Restoration tradition, but softened it to please a less sophisticated public. In 1728 John Gay wrote *The Beggar's Opera*—an ironic musical play that satirized Sir Robert Walpole, prime minister, and other officials of state and town. To this day *The Beggar's Opera* remains a notable marriage of dainty melody and mordant satire. Henry Fielding, author of *Tom Jones,* a lively man of letters and an alert citizen, also wrote a few farces, as did Samuel Foote, a celebrated mountebank whom Dr. Johnson regarded as an uproarious comic.

But playwriting as a whole relapsed into sentimental, mawkish drama to suit the taste of the great public. It was a drama of "cautious purity," in the phrase of Hazlitt. This was the period of the House of Hanover—at that time a heavy, humorless line of kings who were more Germanic than English and had undistinguished tastes in literature.

Not every one was satisfied with the pious sobriety of the theatre. In 1772, Oliver Goldsmith, an Irishman who was supporting himself in London by hackwork, attacked the prevailing style with a plea for the return of comedy. *Essay on the Theatre; or A Comparison Between Laughing and Sentimental Comedy,* he called his polemic. He had already tried to do something about it with a humorous, though uneven, comedy entitled *The Good Natur'd Man.* Since it was not solemn or genteel, it was regarded as "low."

But no one could resist his *She Stoops to Conquer; or, The Mistakes of a Night,* which was acted at Covent Garden in 1773. Its natural good temper and drollery, which are still captivating, reflect the Irish temperament of the well-loved author of *The Vicar of Wakefield* and *The Deserted Village. She Stoops to Conquer* owes nothing to the witty world of the Restoration dramatists. Its country humors are closer to Shakespeare.

Goldsmith was an improvident, impulsive, random sort of man whose misadventures were not unlike those found in his play. The plot of *She Stoops to Conquer* is in fact derived from one of his own experiences, for, like Marlow in the play, he once swaggered into a private home under the impression that he had entered an inn and commanded his host after the manner of a paying guest. Much of what we know about Goldsmith's personality comes from Boswell's *Life of Samuel Johnson, LL.D.* Since Boswell was obviously jealous of Goldsmith, we cannot take everything that he says at face value. Dr. Johnson had a high opinion of Goldsmith and more than once straightened out his muddled affairs. In fact, Johnson intervened with the manager of the Covent Garden Theatre to get *She Stoops to Conquer* on the stage after Goldsmith had bungled the transaction by recalling the manuscript and sending it to Garrick.

But Goldsmith was a lovable soul. When he died the next year, of a fever complicated by worry over his enormous debts, his friends in the Literary Club were deeply distressed.

Sir Joshua Reynolds, the portrait painter, threw down his brush when he heard the dismal news, retreated into silence, and remained disconsolate for a long time. *She Stoops to Conquer* preserves the sunniness that attached Goldsmith's friends to him.

The English comedy of manners had one more day of brilliance before an eclipse of more than a century. In 1777 Richard Brinsley Sheridan put on *The School for Scandal*. Like Goldsmith, Sheridan was Irish. (Note, incidentally, that Congreve was educated in Dublin.) Sheridan was an attractive, alert young man with a knack for shining in public, no matter what he was doing. Although he never appeared on the stage, his whole life was a dazzling performance.

When he was twenty-two he concluded a story-book courtship (which included two duels) by marrying the incomparable Elizabeth Linley, a beautiful concert singer who had innumerable admirers, all of whom, except Sheridan, had the means to support her. Two years later, when, as usual, he was desperately in need of money, he wrote *The Rivals*—a comedy only a little less famous than his great one. The next year, when he was twenty-five, he purchased the Drury Lane Theatre, which was worth thirty or forty times his total financial resources. When he was twenty-six he gave it the most ingenious and successful comedy of his time—*The School for Scandal*, which has never long been off the stage in two centuries.

Its form is that of the Restoration comedy of the previous century, but in conformity with the moral tone of the Age of Johnson, and with Sheridan's own tastes in manners, the comedy is decent. Its standards of conduct reflect Sheridan's generous nature. In contrast with the brittleness of Restoration writing, the style has grace, flow and sensibility; and a certain undertone of amiability makes it winning as well as amusing. Sheridan was a fastidious workman. All his public performances, whether as writer or man of the world, had an easy, spontaneous style. But the aptness of the phrasing in *The School for Scandal* and the dexterity of the narrative represent the intensity of his craftsmanship. In addition to *The Rivals* and *The School for Scandal* he wrote one other sparkling work—*The Critic* in 1779. During the four years when he was working in the theatre he also wrote two or three potboilers.

But from 1779 to his death in 1816 he squandered most of his energy on a political career. As a member of Parliament he gave one memorable address, the Begum speech, which resulted in the impeachment of Warren Hastings. It was his last electrifying performance. Bad luck, recklessness about money, amorous entanglements, excessive drinking, and general irresponsibility left him a rather unsavory man in his middle age. During the twilight of Sheridan's career, Byron had this to say about him: "Whatever he tried he did better than anyone else. He wrote the best comedy, *The School for Scandal*, the best opera, *The Duenna*, the best farce, *The Critic*, and the best address, the Monologue on Garrick. And to crown it all, he delivered the very best oration ever conceived or heard in this country, the famous Begum speech."

But his twenties had been his triumphant period. His last years were as distressing as the last panels in Hogarth's *The Rake's Progress*. Sheridan left no successors in the writing of comedy. After *The School for Scandal*, the English comedy of manners took a long sleep until Oscar Wilde roused it with *Lady Windermere's Fan* in 1892.

The Country Wife

by
William Wycherley

❧

*Indignor quidquam reprehendi, non quia crasse.
Compositum illepideve putetur, sed quia nuper:
Nec veniam antiquis, sed honorem et praemia posci.**
HORACE.

**I am indignant when anything is censured,
not because it is believed to be coarsely and
inelegantly composed, but because it is new:
and yet for the ancients, not indulgence for
their faults, but honor and rewards are demand-
ed.* EPISTLES II, i. 76-8

PROLOGUE

Spoken by MR. HORNER

POETS, like cudgelled bullies, never do
At first or second blow submit to you;
But will provoke you still, and ne'er have done,
Till you are weary first with laying on.
The late so baffled scribbler of this day,
Though he stands trembling, bids me boldly say,
What we before most plays are used to do,
For poets out of fear first draw on you;
In a fierce prologue the still pit defy,
And, ere you speak, like Castril[1] give the lie.
But though our Bayes's battle oft I've fought,
And with bruised knuckles their dear conquests bought;
Nay, never yet feared odds upon the stage,
In prologue dare not hector with the age;
But would take quarter from your saving hands,
Though Bayes within all yielding countermands,
Says, you confederate wits no quarter give,
Therefore his play shan't ask your leave to live.
Well, let the vain rash fop, by huffing so,
Think to obtain the better terms of you;
But we, the actors, humbly will submit,
Now, and at any time, to a full pit;
Nay, often we anticipate your rage,
And murder poets for you on our stage:
We set no guards upon our tiring-room,
But when with flying colors there you come,
We patiently, you see, give up to you
Our poets, virgins, nay, our matrons too.

DRAMATIS PERSONÆ

MR. HORNER.
MR. HARCOURT.
MR. DORILANT.
MR. PINCHWIFE.
MR. SPARKISH.
SIR JASPER FIDGET.
QUACK.

MRS. MARGERY PINCHWIFE.
ALITHEA, sister of PINCHWIFE.
LADY FIDGET.
MRS. DAINTY FIDGET, sister of SIR JASPER.
MRS. SQUEAMISH.
OLD LADY SQUEAMISH.
LUCY, ALITHEA's maid.

A Boy, Waiters, Servants, and Attendants.

Scene—LONDON

ACT I

Scene I: Horner's *Lodging*.

Enter Horner, Quack *following him at a distance.*

Horner. (Aside.) A quack is as fit for a pimp, as a midwife for a bawd; they are still but in their way, both helpers of nature.—*(Aloud.)* Well, my dear doctor, hast thou done what I desired?

Quack. I have undone you forever with the women, and reported you throughout the whole town as bad as an eunuch, with as much trouble as if I had made you one in earnest.

Horner. But have you told all the midwives you know, the orange wenches at the playhouses, the city husbands, and old fumbling keepers of this end of the town? for they'll be the readiest to report it.

Quack. I have told all the chambermaids, waiting-women, tire-women, and old women of my acquaintance; nay, and whispered it as a secret to 'em, and to the whisperers of Whitehall; so that you need not doubt 'twill spread, and you will be as odious to the handsome young women as——

Horner. As the small-pox. Well——

Quack. And to the married women of this end of the town, as——

Horner. As the great one, nay, as their own husbands.

Quack. And to the city dames, as aniseed Robin, of filthy and contemptible memory; and they will frighten their children with your name, especially their females.

Horner. And cry, Horner's coming to carry you away. I am only afraid 'twill not be believed. You told 'em it was by an English-French disaster, and an English-French surgeon, who has given me at once not only a cure, but an antidote for the future against that damned malady, and that worse distemper, love, and all other women's evils?

Quack. Your late journey into France has made it the more credible, and your being here a fortnight before you appeared in public, looks as if you apprehended the shame, which I wonder you do not. Well, I have been hired by young gallants to belie 'em t'other way; but you are the first would be thought a man unfit for women.

Horner. Dear Mr. Doctor, let vain rogues be contented only to be thought abler men than they are; generally 'tis all the pleasure they have; but mine lies another way.

Quack. You take, methinks, a very preposterous way to it, and as ridiculous as if we operators in physic should put forth bills to disparage our medicaments, with hopes to gain customers.

Horner. Doctor, there are quacks in love as well as physic, who get but the fewer and worse patients for their boasting; a good name is seldom got by giving it one's self; and women, no more than honor, are compassed by bragging. Come, come, doctor, the wisest lawyer never discovers the merits of his cause till the trial; the wealthiest man conceals his riches, and the cunning gamester his play. Shy husbands and keepers, like old rooks, are not to be cheated but by a new unpractised trick: false friendship will pass now no more than false dice upon 'em; no, not in the city.

Enter BOY.

Boy. There are two ladies and a gentleman coming up. *Exit.*

Horner. A pox! some unbelieving sisters of my former acquaintance, who, I am afraid, expect their sense should be satisfied of the falsity of the report. No—this formal fool and women!

Enter Sir JASPER FIDGET, Lady FIDGET, *and* Mrs. DAINTY FIDGET.

Quack. His wife and sister.

Sir Jasper. My coach breaking just now before your door, sir, I look upon as an occasional reprimand to me, sir, for not kissing your hands, sir, since your coming out of France, sir; and so my disaster, sir, has been my good fortune, sir; and this is my wife and sister, sir.

Horner. What then, sir?

Sir Jasper. My lady, and sister, sir.—Wife, this is Master Horner.

Lady Fidget. Master Horner, husband!

Sir Jasper. My lady, my Lady Fidget, sir.

Horner. So, sir.

Sir Jasper. Won't you be acquainted with her, sir?—*(Aside.)* So, the report is true, I find, by his coldness or aversion to the sex, but I'll play the wag with him.—*(Aloud.)* Pray salute my wife, my lady, sir.

Horner. I will kiss no man's wife, sir, for him, sir; I have taken my eternal leave, sir, of the sex already, sir.

Sir Jasper. (Aside.) Ha! ha! ha! I'll plague him yet.—(Aloud.) Not know my wife, sir?

Horner. I do know your wife, sir; she's a woman, sir, and consequently a monster, sir, a greater monster than a husband, sir.

Sir Jasper. A husband! how, sir?

Horner. So, sir; but I make no more cuckolds, sir. (Makes horns.)

Sir Jasper. Ha! ha! ha! Mercury! Mercury!

Lady Fidget. Pray, Sir Jasper, let us be gone from this rude fellow.

Mrs. Dainty. Who, by his breeding, would think he had ever been in France?

Lady Fidget. Foh! he's but too much a French fellow, such as hate women of quality and virtue for their love to their husbands. Sir Jasper, a woman is hated by 'em as much for loving her husband as for loving their money. But pray let's be gone.

Horner. You do well, madam; for I have nothing that you came for. I have brought over not so much as a bawdy picture, no new postures, nor the second part of the *Ecole des Filles;* nor——

Quack. (Apart to HORNER.) Hold, for shame, sir! What d'ye mean? you'll ruin yourself for ever with the sex——

Sir Jasper. Ha! ha! ha! he hates women perfectly, I find.

Mrs. Dainty. What pity 'tis he should!

Lady Fidget. Ay, he's a base fellow for't. But affectation makes not a woman more odious to them than virtue.

Horner. Because your virtue is your greatest affectation, madam.

Lady Figet. How, you saucy fellow! would you wrong my honor?

Horner. If I could.

Lady Fidget. How d'ye mean, sir?

Sir Jasper. Ha! ha! ha! no, he can't wrong your ladyship's honor, upon my honor. He, poor man—hark you in your ear—(Whispers.) a mere eunuch.

Lady Fidget. O filthy French beast! foh! foh! why do we stay? let's be gone: I can't endure the sight of him.

Sir Jasper. Stay but till the chairs come; they'll be here presently.

Lady Fidget. No!

Sir Jasper. Nor can I stay longer. 'Tis, let me see, a quarter and half quarter of a minute past eleven. The council will be sat; I must away. Business must be preferred always before love and ceremony with the wise, Mr. Horner.

Horner. And the impotent, Sir Jasper.

Sir Jasper. Ay, ay, the impotent, Master Horner; hah! hah! hah!

Lady Fidget. What, leave us with a filthy man alone in his lodgings?

Sir Jasper. He's an innocent man now, you know. Pray stay, I'll hasten the chairs to you.—Mr. Horner, your servant; I should be glad to see you at my house. Pray come and dine with me and play at cards with my wife after dinner; you are fit for women at that game yet, ha! ha!—(*Aside.*) 'Tis as much a husband's prudence to provide innocent diversion for a wife as to hinder her unlawful pleasures; and he had better employ her than let her employ herself.—(*Aloud.*) Farewell.

Horner. Your servant, Sir Jasper.   *Exit* Sir JASPER.

Lady Fidget. I will not stay with him, foh!——

Horner. Nay, madam, I beseech you stay, if it be but to see I can be as civil to ladies yet as they would desire.

Lady Fidget. No, no, foh! you cannot be civil to ladies.

Mrs. Dainty. You as civil as ladies would desire?

Lady Fidget. No, no, no, foh! foh! foh!

Exeunt Lady FIDGET *and* Mrs. DAINTY FIDGET.

Quack. Now, I think, I, or you yourself, rather, have done your business with the women.

Horner. Thou art an ass. Don't you see already, upon the report, and my carriage, this grave man of business leaves his wife in my lodgings, invites me to his house and wife, who before would not be acquainted with me out of jealousy?

Quack. Nay, by this means you may be the more acquainted with the husbands, but the less with the wives.

Horner. Let me alone; if I can but abuse the husbands, I'll soon disabuse the wives. Stay—I'll reckon you up the advantages I am like to have by my stratagem. First, I shall be rid of all my old acquaintances, the most insatiable sort of duns that invade our lodgings in a morning; and next to the pleasure of making a new mistress is that of being rid of an old one, and of all old debts. Love, when it comes to be so, is paid the most unwillingly.

Quack. Well, you may be so rid of your old acquaintances; but how will you get any new ones?

Horner. Doctor, thou wilt never make a good chemist, thou art so incredulous and impatient. Ask but all the young fellows of the town if they do not lose more time, like huntsmen, in starting the game, than in running it down. One knows not where to find 'em; who will or will not. Women of quality are so civil you can hardly distinguish love from good breeding, and a man is often mistaken: but now I can be sure she that shows an aversion to me loves the sport, as those women that are gone, whom I warrant to be right. And then the next thing is, your women of honor, as you call 'em, are only chary of their reputations, not their persons; and 'tis scandal they would avoid, not men. Now may I have, by the reputation of an eunuch, the privileges of one, and be seen in a lady's chamber in a morning as early as her husband; kiss virgins before their parents or lovers; and may be, in short, the *passe-partout*[2] of the town. Now, doctor.

Quack. Nay, now you shall be the doctor; and your process is so new that we do not know but it may succeed.

Horner. Not so new either; *probatum est,*[3] doctor.

Quack. Well, I wish you luck and many patients, whilst I go to mine.   *Exit.*

Enter HARCOURT *and* DORILANT.

Harcourt. Come, your appearance at the play yesterday has, I hope, hardened you for the future against the women's contempt and the men's raillery; and now you'll abroad as you were wont.

Horner. Did I not bear it bravely?

Dorilant. With a most theatrical impudence, nay, more than the orange-wenches[4] show there, or a drunken vizard-mask[5], or a great-bellied actress; nay, or the most impudent of creatures, an ill poet; or what is yet more impudent, a second-hand critic.

Horner. But what say the ladies? have they no pity?

Harcourt. What ladies? The vizard-masks, you know, never pity a man when all's gone, though in their service.

Dorilant. And for the women in the boxes, you'd never pity them when 'twas in your power.

Harcourt. They say 'tis pity but all that deal with common women should be served so.

Dorilant. Nay, I dare swear they won't admit you to play at cards with them, go to plays with 'em, or do the little duties which other shadows of men are wont to do for 'em.

Horner. What do you call shadows of men?

Dorilant. Half-men.

Horner. What, boys?

Dorilant. Ay, your old boys, old *beaux garçons,* who, like superannuated stallions, are suffered to run, feed, and whinny with the mares as long as they live, though they can do nothing else.

Horner. Well, a pox on love and wenching! Women serve but to keep a man from better company. Though I can't enjoy them, I shall you the more. Good fellowship and friendship are lasting, rational, and manly pleasures.

Harcourt. For all that, give me some of those pleasures you call effeminate too; they help to relish one another.

Horner. They disturb one another.

Harcourt. No, mistresses are like books. If you pour upon them too much they doze you and make you unfit for company; but if used discreetly, you are the fitter for conversation by 'em.

Dorilant. A mistress should be like a little country retreat near the town; not to dwell in constantly, but only for a night and away, to taste the town the better when a man returns.

Horner. I tell you, 'tis as hard to be a good fellow, a good friend, and a lover of women, as 'tis to be a good fellow, a good friend, and a lover of money. You cannot follow both, then choose your side. Wine gives you liberty, love takes it away.

Dorilant. Gad, he's in the right on't.

Horner. Wine gives you joy; love, grief and tortures— besides surgeons. Wine makes us witty; love, only sots. Wine makes us sleep; love breaks it.

Dorilant. By the world he has reason, Harcourt.

Horner. Wine makes——

Dorilant. Ay, wine makes us—makes us princes; love makes us beggars, poor rogues, egad—and wine——

Horner. So, there's one converted.—No, no, love and wine, oil and vinegar.

Harcourt. I grant it; love will still be uppermost.

Horner. Come, for my part, I will have only those glorious manly pleasures of being very drunk and very slovenly.

Enter BOY.

Boy. Mr. Sparkish is below, sir.   *Exit.*

Harcourt. What, my dear friend! a rogue that is fond of me only, I think, for abusing him.

Dorilant. No, he can no more think the men laugh at him than that women jilt him; his opinion of himself is so good.

Horner. Well, there's another pleasure by drinking I thought not of. I shall lose his acquaintance because he cannot drink: and you know 'tis a very hard thing to be rid of him; for he's one of those nauseous offerers at wit, who, like the worst fiddlers, run themselves into all companies.

Harcourt. One that, by being in the company of men of sense, would pass for one.

Horner. And may so to the short-sighted world, as a false jewel amongst true ones is not discerned at a distance. His company is as troublesome to us as a cuckold's when you have a mind to his wife's.

Harcourt. No, the rogue will not let us enjoy one another, but ravishes our conversation; though he signifies no more to't than Sir Martin Mar-all's[6] gaping and awkward thrumming upon the lute does to his man's voice and music.

Dorilant. And to pass for a wit in town shows himself a fool every night to us, that are guilty of the plot.

Horner. Such wits as he are, to a company of reasonable men, like rooks to the gamesters; who only fill a room at the table, but are so far from contributing to the play that they only serve to spoil the fancy of those that do.

Dorilant. Nay, they are used like rooks too, snubbed, checked, and abused; yet the rogues will hang on.

Horner. A pox on 'em and all that force nature and would be still what she forbids 'em! Affectation is her greatest monster.

Harcourt. Most men are the contraries to that they would seem. Your bully, you see, is a coward with a long sword; the little humbly fawning physician, with his ebony cane, is he that destroys men.

Dorilant. The usurer, a poor rogue, possessed of moldy bonds and mortgages; and we they call spendthrifts are only wealthy, who lay out his money upon daily new purchases of pleasure.

Horner. Ay, your arrantest cheat is your trustee or executor; your jealous man, the greatest cuckold; your churchman, the greatest atheist; and your noisy, pert rogue of a wit, the greatest fop, dullest ass, and worst company, as you shall see; for here he comes.

Enter SPARKISH.

Sparkish. How is't, sparks? How is't? Well, faith, Harry, I must rally thee a little, ha! ha! ha! upon the report in town of thee, ha! ha! ha! I can't hold i'faith; shall I speak?

Horner. Yes; but you'll be so bitter then.

Sparkish. Honest Dick and Frank here shall answer for me; I will not be extreme bitter, by the universe.

Harcourt. We will be bound in a ten thousand pound bond, he shall not be bitter at all.

Dorilant. Nor sharp, nor sweet.

Horner. What, not downright insipid?

Sparkish. Nay then, since you are so brisk, and provoke me, take what follows. You must know, I was discoursing and rallying with some ladies yesterday, and they happened to talk of the fine new signs in town——

Horner. Very fine ladies, I believe.

Sparkish. Said I, I know where the best new sign is.—— Where? says one of the ladies.—In Covent Garden, I replied. —Said another, In what street?—In Russel Street, answered I. —Lord, says another, I'm sure there was never a fine new

sign there yesterday.—Yes, but there was, said I again; and
it came out of France, and has been there a fortnight.

Dorilant. A pox! I can hear no more, prithee.

Horner. No, hear him out; let him tune his crowd a while.

Harcourt. The worst music, the greatest preparation.

Sparkish. Nay, faith, I'll make you laugh.—It cannot be,
says a third lady.—Yes, yes, quoth I again.—Says a fourth
lady——

Horner. Look to't, we'll have no more ladies.

Sparkish. No—then mark, mark, now. Said I to the fourth,
Did you never see Mr. Horner? he lodges in Russel Street and
he's a sign of a man, you know, since he came out of France;
ha! ha! ha!

Horner. But the devil take me if thine be the sign of a jest.

Sparkish. With that they all fell a-laughing till they bepissed
themselves. What, but it does not move you, methinks? Well,
I see one had as good go to law without a witness, as break
a jest without a laugher on one's side.—Come, come, sparks,
but where do we dine? I have left at Whitehall an earl, to
dine with you.

Dorilant. Why, I thought thou hadst loved a man with a
title better than a suit with a French trimming to't.

Harcourt. Go to him again.

Sparkish. No, sir, a wit to me is the greatest title in the
world.

Horner. But go dine with your earl, sir; he may be exceptious. We are your friends, and will not take it ill to be left,
I do assure you.

Harcourt. Nay, faith, he shall go to him.

Sparkish. Nay, pray, gentlemen.

Dorilant. We'll thrust you out, if you won't; what, disappoint anybody for us?

Sparkish. Nay, dear gentlemen, hear me.

Horner. No, no, sir, by no means; pray go, sir.

Sparkish. Why, dear rogues——

Dorilant. No, no. *(They all thrust him out of the room.)*

All. Ha! ha! ha!

Re-enter SPARKISH.

Sparkish. But, sparks, pray hear me. What, d'ye think I'll
eat then with gay shallow fops and silent coxcombs? I think
wit as necessary at dinner as a glass of good wine; and that's
the reason I never have any stomach when I eat alone.—
Come, but where do we dine?

Horner. Even where you will.

Sparkish. At Chateline's?[7]

Dorilant. Yes, if you will.

Sparkish. Or at the Cock?

Dorilant. Yes, if you please.

Sparkish. Or at the Dog and Partridge?

Horner. Ay, if you have a mind to't; for we shall dine at neither.

Sparkish. Pshaw! with your fooling we shall lose the new play; and I would no more miss seeing a new play the first day, than I would miss sitting in the wit's row. Therefore I'll go fetch my mistress, and away.   *Exit.*

Enter PINCHWIFE.

Horner. Who have we here? Pinchwife?

Pinchwife. Gentlemen, your humble servant.

Horner. Well, Jack, by thy long absence from the town, the grumness of thy countenance, and the slovenliness of thy habit, I should give thee joy, should I not, of marriage?

Pinchwife. (Aside.) Death! does he know I'm married too? I thought to have concealed it from him at least.—*(Aloud.)* My long stay in the country will excuse my dress; and I have a suit of law that brings me up to town, that puts me out of humor. Besides, I must give Sparkish tomorrow five thousand pounds to lie with my sister.

Horner. Nay, you country gentlemen, rather than not purchase, will buy anything; and he is a cracked title, if we may quibble. Well, but am I to give thee joy? I heard thou wert married.

Pinchwife. What then?

Horner. Why, the next thing that is to be heard, is thou'rt a cuckold.

Pinchwife. (Aside.) Insupportable name!

Horner. But I did not expect marriage from such a whoremaster as you; one that knew the town so much and women so well.

Pinchwife. Why, I have married no London wife.

Horner. Pshaw! that's all one. That grave circumspection in marrying a country wife is like refusing a deceitful pampered Smithfield jade, to go and be cheated by a friend in the country.

Pinchwife. (Aside.) A pox on him and his simile!—*(Aloud.)* At least we are a little surer of the breed there, know what her keeping has been, whether foiled or unsound.

Horner. Come, come, I have known a clap gotten in Wales; and there are cousins, justices' clerks, and chaplains in the country—I won't say coachmen. But she's handsome and young?

Pinchwife. (Aside.) I'll answer as I should do.—*(Aloud.)*

No, no; she has no beauty but her youth, no attraction but her modesty: wholesome, homely, and huswifely; that's all.

Dorilant. He talks as like a grazier as he looks.

Pinchwife. She's too awkard, ill-favored, and silly to bring to town.

Harcourt. Then methinks you should bring her to be taught breeding.

Pinchwife. To be taught! no, sir, I thank you. Good wives and private soldiers should be ignorant—I'll keep her from your instructions, I warrant you.

Harcourt. (Aside.) The rogue is as jealous as if his wife were not ignorant.

Horner. Why, if she be ill-favored, there will be less danger here for you than by leaving her in the country. We have such variety of dainties that we are seldom hungry.

Dorilant. But they have always coarse, constant, swinging stomachs in the country.

Harcourt. Foul feeders indeed!

Dorilant. And your hospitality is great there.

Harcourt. Open house; every man's welcome.

Pinchwife. So, so, gentlemen.

Horner. But prithee, why shouldst thou marry her? If she be ugly, ill-bred, and silly, she must be rich then.

Pinchwife. As rich as if she brought me twenty thousand pound out of this town; for she'll be as sure not to spend her moderate portion, as a London baggage would be to spend hers, let it be what it would: so 'tis all one. Then, because she's ugly, she's the likelier to be my own; and being ill-bred, she'll hate conversation; and since silly and innocent, will not know the difference betwixt a man of one-and-twenty and one of forty.

Horner. Nine—to my knowledge. But if she be silly, she'll expect as much from a man of forty-nine, as from him of one-and-twenty. But methinks wit is more necessary than beauty; and I think no young woman ugly that has it, and no handsome woman agreeable without it.

Pinchwife. 'Tis my maxim, he's a fool that marries; but he's a greater that does not marry a fool. What is wit in a wife good for, but to make a man a cuckold?

Horner. Yes, to keep it from his knowledge.

Pinchwife. A fool cannot contrive to make her husband a cuckold.

Horner. No; but she'll club with a man that can: and what is worse, if she cannot make her husband a cuckold; she'll make him jealous, and pass for one: and then 'tis all one.

Pinchwife. Well, well, I'll take care for one. My wife shall make me no cuckold, though she had your help, Mr. Horner. I understand the town, sir.

Dorilant. (*Aside.*) His help!

Harcourt. (*Aside.*) He's come newly to town, it seems, and has not heard how things are with him.

Horner. But tell me, has marriage cured thee of whoring, which it seldom does?

Harcourt. 'Tis more than age can do.

Horner. No, the word is, I'll marry and live honest. But a marriage vow is like a penitent gamester's oath; and entering into bonds and penalties to stint himself to such a particular small sum at play for the future, which makes him but the more eager; and not being able to hold out, loses his money again, and his forfeit to boot.

Dorilant. Ay, ay, a gamester will be a gamester whilst his money lasts, and a whoremaster whilst his vigor.

Harcourt. Nay, I have known 'em when they are broke and can lose no more, keep a fumbling with the box in their hands to fool with only, and hinder other gamesters.

Dorilant. That had wherewithal to make lusty stakes.

Pinchwife. Well, gentlemen, you may laugh at me; but you shall never lie with my wife. I know the town.

Horner. But prithee, was not the way you were in better? is not keeping better than marriage?

Pinchwife. A pox on't! the jades would jilt me; I could never keep a whore to myself.

Horner. So, then you only married to keep a whore to yourself. Well, but let me tell you: women, as you say, are like soldiers—made constant and loyal by good pay, rather than by oaths and covenants. Therefore I'd advise my friends to keep rather than marry; since too I find, by your example, it does not serve one's turn; for I saw you yesterday in the eighteenpenny place with a pretty country-wench.

Pinchwife. (*Aside.*) How the devil! did he see my wife then? I sat there that she might not be seen. But she shall never go to a play again.

Horner. What! dost thou blush, at nine-and-forty, for having been seen with a wench?

Dorilant. No, faith, I warrant 'twas his wife which he seated there out of sight; for he's a cunning rogue and understands the town.

Harcourt. He blushes. Then 'twas his wife; for men are now more ashamed to be seen with them in public than with a wench.

Pinchwife. (*Aside.*) Hell and damnation! I'm undone, since Horner has seen her, and they know 'twas she.

Horner. But prithee, was it thy wife? She was exceeding pretty: I was in love with her at that distance.

Pinchwife. You are like never to be nearer to her. Your servant, gentlemen.   *(Offers to go.)*

Horner. Nay, prithee stay.

Pinchwife. I cannot; I will not.

Horner. Come, you shall dine with us.

Pinchwife. I have dined already.

Horner. Come, I know thou hast not: I'll treat thee, dear rogue; thou sha't spend none of thy Hampshire money today.

Pinchwife. *(Aside.)* Treat me! So, he uses me already like his cuckold.

Horner. Nay, you shall not go.

Pinchwife. I must; I have business at home.   *Exit.*

Harcourt. To beat his wife. He's as jealous of her as a Cheapside husband of a Covent Garden wife.

Horner. Why, 'tis as hard to find an old whoremaster without jealousy and the gout, as a young one without fear, or the pox:—

> As gout in age from pox in youth proceeds,
> So wenching past, then jealousy succeeds;
> The worst disease that love and wenching breeds.

                                                      Exeunt.

ACT II

Scene I: *A Room in* Pinchwife's *House.*

Mrs. Margery Pinchwife *and* Alithea. Pinchwife
peeping behind at the door.

Mrs. Pinchwife. Pray, sister, where are the best fields and woods to walk in, in London?

Alithea. *(Aside.)* A pretty question!—*(Aloud.)* Why, sister, Mulberry Garden and St. James's Park; and, for close walks, the New Exchange.

Mrs. Pinchwife. Pray, sister, tell me why my husband looks so grum here in town, and keeps me up so close, and will not let me go a-walking, nor let me wear my best gown yesterday.

Alithea. Oh, he's jealous, sister.

Mrs. Pinchwife. Jealous! what's that?

Alithea. He's afraid you should love another man.

Mrs. Pinchwife. How should he be afraid of my loving another man when he will not let me see any but himself?

Alithea. Did he not carry you yesterday to a play?

Mrs. Pinchwife. Ay; but we sat amongst ugly people. He would not let me come near the gentry, who sat under us, so that I could not see 'em. He told me none but naughty women sat there, whom they toused and moused. But I would have ventured, for all that.

Alithea. But how did you like the play?

Mrs. Pinchwife. Indeed I was weary of the play; but I liked hugeously the actors. They are the goodliest, properest men, sister!

Alithea. Oh, but you must not like the actors, sister.

Mrs. Pinchwife. Ay, how should I help it, sister? Pray, sister, when my husband comes in will you ask leave for me to go a-walking?

Alithea. (Aside.) A-walking! ha! ha! Lord, a country-gentlewoman's pleasure is the drudgery of a footpost; and she requires as much airing as her husband's horses. But here comes your husband: I'll ask, though I'm sure he'll not grant it.

Mrs. Pinchwife. He says he won't let me go abroad for fear of catching the pox.[8]

Alithea. Fy! the small-pox you should say.

Enter PINCHWIFE.

Mrs. Pinchwife. Oh my dear, dear bud, welcome home! Why dost thou look so fropish? who has nangered thee?

Pinchwife. You're a fool. (Mrs. PINCHWIFE goes aside, and cries.)

Alithea. Faith, so she is, for crying for no fault, poor tender creature!

Pinchwife. What, you would have her as impudent as yourself, as arrant a jilflirt, a gadder, a magpie; and to say all, a mere notorious town-woman?

Alithea. Brother, you are my only censurer; and the honor of your family will sooner suffer in your wife there than in me, though I take the innocent liberty of the town.

Pinchwife. Hark you, mistress, do not talk so before my wife.—The innocent liberty of the town!

Alithea. Why, pray, who boasts of any intrigue with me? what lampoon has made my name notorious? what ill women frequent my lodgings? I keep no company with any women of scandalous reputations.

Pinchwife. No, you keep the men of scandalous reputations company.

Alithea. Where? would you not have me civil? answer 'em in a box at the plays, in the drawing-room at Whitehall, in St. James's Park, Mulberry Garden, or——

Pinchwife. Hold, hold! Do not teach my wife where the men are to be found: I believe she's the worse for your town-documents already. I bid you keep her in ignorance, as I do.

Mrs. Pinchwife. Indeed, be not angry with her, bud, she will tell me nothing of the town, though I ask her a thousand times a day.

Pinchwife. Then you are very inquisitive to know, I find?

Mrs. Pinchwife. Not I indeed, dear; I hate London. Our place-house in the country is worth a thousand of't: would I were there again!

Pinchwife. So you shall, I warrant. But were you not talking of plays and players when I came in?—(*To* ALITHEA.) You are her encourager in such discourses.

Mrs. Pinchwife. No, indeed, dear; she chid me just now for liking the playermen.

Pinchwife. (Aside.) Nay, if she be so innocent as to own to me her liking them, there is no hurt in't.—(*Aloud.*) Come, my poor rogue, but thou likest none better than me?

Mrs. Pinchwife. Yes, indeed, but I do. The playermen are finer folks.

Pinchwife. But you love none better than me?

Mrs. Pinchwife. You are my own dear bud and I know you. I hate a stranger.

Pinchwife. Ay, my dear, you must love me only; and not be like the naughty town-women who only hate their husbands and love every man else; love plays, visits, fine coaches, fine clothes, fiddles, balls, treats, and so lead a wicked town-life.

Mrs. Pinchwife. Nay, if to enjoy all these things be a town-life, London is not so bad a place, dear.

Pinchwife. How! if you love me, you must hate London.

Alithea. (Aside.) The fool has forbid me discovering to her the pleasures of the town, and he is now setting her agog upon them himself.

Mrs. Pinchwife. But, husband, do the town-women love the playermen too?

Pinchwife. Yes, I warrant you.

Mrs. Pinchwife. Ay, I warrant you.

Pinchwife. Why, you do not, I hope?

Mrs. Pinchwife. No, no, bud. But why have we no playermen in the country?

Pinchwife. Ha!—Mrs. Minx, ask me no more to go to a play.

Mrs. Pinchwife. Nay, why, love? I did not care for going: but when you forbid me, you make me, as 'twere, desire it.

Alithea. (Aside.) So 'twill be in other things, I warrant.

Mrs. Pinchwife. Pray let me go to a play, dear.

Pinchwife. Hold your peace, I wo' not.

Mrs. Pinchwife. Why, love?

Pinchwife. Why, I'll tell you.

Alithea. (*Aside.*) Nay, if he tell her, she'll give him more cause to forbid her that place.

Mrs. Pinchwife. Pray why, dear?

Pinchwife. First, you like the actors; and the gallants may like you.

Mrs. Pinchwife. What, a homely country girl! No, bud, no-body will like me.

Pinchwife. I tell you yes, they may.

Mrs. Pinchwife. No, no, you jest—I won't believe you: I will go.

Pinchwife. I tell you then, that one of the lewdest fellows in town, who saw you there, told me he was in love with you.

Mrs. Pinchwife. Indeed! who, who, pray who was't?

Pinchwife. (*Aside.*) I've gone too far, and slipped before I was aware; how overjoyed she is!

Mrs. Pinwife. Was it any Hampshire gallant, any of our neighbors? I promise you, I am beholden to him.

Pinchwife. I promise you, you lie; for he would but ruin you, as he has done hundreds. He has no other love for women but that; such as he look upon women, like basilisks,⁹ but to destroy 'em.

Mrs. Pinchwife. Ay, but if he loves me why should he ruin me? answer me to that. Methinks he should not, I would do him no harm.

Alithea. Ha! ha! ha!

Pinchwife. 'Tis very well; but I'll keep him from doing you any harm, or me either. But here comes company; get you in, get you in.

Mrs. Pinchwife. But, pray, husband, is he a pretty gentle-man that loves me?

Pinchwife. In, baggage, in.

(*Thrusts her in, and shuts the door.*)

Enter Sparkish *and* Harcourt.

What, all the lewd libertines of the town brought to my lodging by this easy coxcomb! 'sdeath, I'll not suffer it.

Sparkish. Here, Harcourt, do you approve my choice?—(*To* Alithea.) Dear little rogue, I told you I'd bring you ac-quainted with all my friends, the wits and——

(Harcourt *salutes her.*)

Pinchwife. Ay, they shall know her, as well as you yourself will, I warrant you.

Sparkish. This is one of those, my pretty rogue, that are to dance at your wedding tomorrow; and him you must bid wel-come ever to what you and I have.

Pinchwife. (Aside.) Monstrous!

Sparkish. Harcourt, how dost thou like her, faith? Nay, dear, do not look down; I should hate to have a wife of mine out of countenance at anything.

Pinchwife. (Aside.) Wonderful!

Sparkish. Tell me, I say, Harcourt, how dost thou like her? Thou hast stared upon her enough to resolve me.

Harcourt. So infinitely well, that I could wish I had a mistress too, that might differ from her in nothing but her love and engagement to you.

Alithea. Sir, Master Sparkish has often told me that his acquaintance were all wits and rallieurs, and now I find it.

Sparkish. No, by the universe, madam, he does not rally now; you may believe him. I do assure you, he is the honestest, worthiest, true-hearted gentleman—a man of such perfect honor, he would say nothing to a lady he does not mean.

Pinchwife. (Aside.) Praising another man to his mistress!

Harcourt. Sir, you are so beyond expectation obliging, that——

Sparkish. Nay, egad, I am sure you do admire her extremely; I see't in your eyes.—He does admire you, madam. —By the world, don't you?

Harcourt. Yes, above the world, or the most glorious part of it—her whole sex: and till now I never thought I should have envied you or any man about to marry, but you have the best excuse for marriage I ever knew.

Alithea. Nay, now, sir, I'm satisfied you are of the society of the wits and rallieurs; since you cannot spare your friend, even when he is but too civil to you. But the surest sign is, since you are an enemy to marriage—for that I hear you hate as much as business or bad wine.

Harcourt. Truly, madam, I was never an enemy to marriage till now, because marriage was never an enemy to me before.

Alithea. But why, sir, is marriage an enemy to you now? because it robs you of your friend here? for you look upon a friend married as one gone into a monastery, that is, dead to the world.

Harcourt. 'Tis indeed because you marry him; I see, madam, you can guess my meaning. I do confess heartily and openly, I wish it were in my power to break the match; by Heavens I would.

Sparkish. Poor Frank!

Alithea. Would you be so unkind to me?

Harcourt. No, no, 'tis not because I would be unkind to you.

Sparkish. Poor Frank! no gad, 'tis only his kindness to me.

Pinchwife. (Aside.) Great kindness to you indeed! Insensible fop; let a man make love to his wife to his face!

Sparkish. Come, dear Frank, for all my wife there, that shall be, thou shalt enjoy me sometimes, dear rogue. By my honor, we men of wit condole for our deceased brother in marriage as much as for one dead in earnest: I think that was prettily said of me, ha, Harcourt?—But come, Frank, be not melancholy for me.

Harcourt. No, I assure you, I am not melancholy for you.

Sparkish. Prithee, Frank, dost think my wife that shall be there, a fine person?

Harcourt. I could gaze upon her till I became as blind as you are.

Sparkish. How as I am? how?

Harcourt. Because you are a lover, and true lovers are blind, stock blind.

Sparkish. True, true; but by the world she has wit too, as well as beauty: go, go with her into a corner and try if she has wit; talk to her anything, she's bashful before me.

Harcourt. Indeed, if a woman wants wit in a corner she has it nowhere.

Alithea. (Aside to SPARKISH.*)* Sir, you dispose of me a little before your time——

Sparkish. Nay, nay, madam, let me have an earnest of your obedience, or—go, go, madam——

(HARCOURT *courts* ALITHEA *aside.*)

Pinchwife. How, sir! if you are not concerned for the honor of a wife, I am for that of a sister; he shall not debauch her. Be a pander to your own wife! bring men to her! let 'em make love before your face! thrust 'em into a corner together then leave 'em in private! is this your town wit and conduct?

Sparkish. Ha! ha! ha! a silly wise rogue would make one laugh more than a stark fool; ha! ha! I shall burst. Nay, you shall not disturb 'em; I'll vex thee, by the world.

(*Struggles with* PINCHWIFE *to keep him from* HARCOURT *and* ALITHEA.*)

Alithea. The writings are drawn, sir, settlements made; 'tis too late, sir, and past all revocation.

Harcourt. Then so is my death.

Alithea. I would not be unjust to him.

Harcourt. Then why to me so?

Alithea. I have no obligation to you.

Harcourt. My love.

Alithea. I had his before.

Harcourt. You never had it; he wants, you see, jealousy, the only infallible sign of it.

Alithea. Love proceeds from esteem; he cannot distrust my virtue: besides, he loves me, or he would not marry me.

Harcourt. Marrying you is no more sign of his love than bribing your woman, that he may marry you, is a sign of his generosity. Marriage is rather a sign of interest than love; and he that marries a fortune covets a mistress, not loves her. But if you take marriage for a sign of love, take it from me immediately.

Alithea. No, now you have put a scruple in my head; but in short, sir, to end our dispute, I must marry him. My reputation would suffer in the world else.

Harcourt. No; if you do marry him, with your pardon, madam, your reputation suffers in the world, and you would be thought in necessity for a cloak.

Alithea. Nay, now you are rude, sir.—Mr. Sparkish, pray come hither, your friend here is very troublesome, and very loving.

Harcourt. (Aside to ALITHEA.) Hold! hold!——

Pinchwife. D'ye hear that?

Sparkish. Why, d'ye think I'll seem to be jealous, like a country bumpkin?

Pinchwife. No, rather be a cuckold, like a credulous cit.

Harcourt. Madam, you would not have been so little generous as to have told him.

Alithea. Yes, since you could be so little generous to wrong him.

Harcourt. Wrong him! no man can do't. He's beneath an injury: a bubble, a coward, a senseless idiot, a wretch so contemptible to all the world but you, that——

Alithea. Hold, do not rail at him, for since he is like to be my husband, I am resolved to like him: nay, I think I am obliged to tell him you are not his friend.—Master Sparkish, Master Sparkish!

Sparkish. What, what?—*(To* HARCOURT.) Now, dear rogue, has not she wit?

Harcourt. (Speaks surlily.) Not so much as I thought, and hoped she had.

Alithea. Mr. Sparkish, do you bring people to rail at you?

Harcourt. Madam——

Sparkish. How! no; but if he does rail at me, 'tis but in jest, I warrant: what we wits do for one another, and never take any notice of it.

Alithea. He spoke so scurrilously of you, I had no patience to hear him; besides, he has been making love to me.

Harcourt. (Aside.) True, damned tell-tale woman!

Sparkish. Pshaw! to show his parts—we wits rail and make

love often, but to show our parts: as we have no affections, so
we have no malice, we——

Alithea. He said you were a wretch below an injury——

Sparkish. Pshaw!

Harcourt. (*Aside.*) Damned, senseless, impudent, virtuous
jade! Well, since she won't let me have her, she'll do as good,
she'll make me hate her.

Alithea. A common bubble——

Sparkish. Pshaw!

Alithea. A coward——

Sparkish. Pshaw, pshaw!

Alithea. A senseless, drivelling idiot——

Sparkish. How! did he disparage my parts? Nay, then, my
honor's concerned, I can't put up that, sir, by the world—
brother, help me to kill him—(*Aside*) I may draw now, since
we have the odds of him:—'tis a good occasion, too, before
my mistress——   (*Offers to draw.*)

Alithea. Hold, hold!

Sparkish. What, what?

Alithea. (*Aside.*) I must not let 'em kill the gentleman
neither, for his kindness to me: I am so far from hating him,
that I wish my gallant had his person and understanding.
Nay, if my honor——

Sparkish. I'll be thy death.

Alithea. Hold, hold! Indeed, to tell the truth, the gentleman
said after all, that what he spoke was but out of friendship to
you.

Sparkish. How! say! I am—I am a fool, that is, no wit, out
of friendship to me?

Alithea. Yes, to try whether I was concerned enough for
you; and made love to me only to be satisfied of my virtue,
for your sake.

Harcourt. (*Aside.*) Kind, however.

Sparkish. Nay, if it were so, my dear rogue, I ask thee
pardon; but why would not you tell me so, faith?

Harcourt. Because I did not think on't, faith.

Sparkish. Come, Horner does not come; Harcourt, let's be
gone to the new play.—Come, madam.

Alithea. I will not go, if you intend to leave me alone in
the box and run into the pit, as you use to do.

Sparkish. Pshaw! I'll leave Harcourt with you in the box
to entertain you, and that's as good; if I sat in the box, I
should be thought no judge but of trimmings.—Come away,
Harcourt, lead her down.

                      (*Exeunt* SPARKISH, HARCOURT, *and* ALITHEA.)

Pinchwife. Well, go thy ways, for the flower of the true

town fops, such as spend their estates before they come to
'em, and are cuckolds before they're married. But let me go
look to my own freehold.—How!

Enter Lady FIDGET, Mrs. DAINTY FIDGET, *and* Mrs.
SQUEAMISH.

Lady Fidget. Your servant, sir: where is your lady? We are
come to wait upon her to the new play.
Pinchwife. New play!
Lady Fidget. And my husband will wait upon you presently.
Pinchwife. (Aside.) Damn your civility.—*(Aloud.)* Madam,
by no means; I will not see Sir Jasper here till I have waited
upon him at home; nor shall my wife see you till she has
waited upon your ladyship at your lodgings.
Lady Fidget. Now we are here, sir?
Pinchwife. No, Madam.
Mrs. Dainty. Pray, let us see her.
Mrs. Squeamish. We will not stir till we see her.
Pinchwife. (Aside.) A pox on you all!—*(Goes to the door,
and returns.)* She has locked the door and is gone abroad.
Lady Fidget. No, you have locked the door and she's within.
Mrs. Dainty. They told us below she was here.
Pinchwife. (Aside.) Will nothing do?—*(Aloud.)* Well, it
must out then. To tell you the truth, ladies, which I was
afraid to let you know before, lest it might endanger your
lives. My wife has just now the small-pox come out upon her;
do not be frightened; but pray be gone, ladies; you shall not
stay here in danger of your lives; pray get you gone, ladies.
Lady Fidget. No, no, we have all had 'em.
Mrs. Squeamish. Alack, alack!
Mrs. Dainty. Come, come, we must see how it goes with
her; I understand the disease.
Lady Fidget. Come!
Pinchwife. (Aside.) Well, there is no being too hard for
women at their own weapon—lying; therefore I'll quit the
field.   *Exit.*
Mrs. Squeamish. Here's an example of jealousy!
Lady Fidget. Indeed, as the world goes, I wonder there are
no more jealous, since wives are so neglected.
Mrs. Dainty. Pshaw! as the world goes, to what end should
they be jealous?
Lady Fidget. Foh! 'tis a nasty world.
Mrs. Squeamish. That men of parts, great acquaintance,
and quality, should take up with and spend themselves and
fortunes in keeping little playhouse creatures, foh!
Lady Fidget. Nay, that women of understanding, great

acquaintance, and good quality, should fall a-keeping too of little creatures, foh!

Mrs. Squeamish. Why, 'tis the men of quality's fault: they never visit women of honor and reputation as they used to do; and have not so much as common civility for ladies of our rank, but use us with the same indifferency and ill-breeding as if we were all married to 'em.

Lady Fidget. She says true; 'tis an arrant shame women of quality should be so slighted; methinks birth—birth should go for something; I have known men admired, courted, and followed for their titles only.

Mrs. Squeamish. Ay, one would think men of honor should not love, no more than marry, out of their own rank.

Mrs. Dainty. Fy, fy, upon 'em! they are come to think cross breeding for themselves best, as well as for their dogs and horses.

Lady Fidget. They are dogs and horses for't.

Mrs. Squeamish. One would think, if not for love, for vanity a little.

Mrs. Dainty. Nay, they do satisfy their vanity upon us sometimes; and are kind to us in their report—tell all the world they lie with us.

Lady Fidget. Damned rascals, that we should be only wronged by 'em! To report a man has had a person, when he has not had a person, is the greatest wrong in the whole world that can be done to a person.

Mrs. Squeamish. Well, 'tis an arrant shame noble persons should be so wronged and neglected.

Lady Fidget. But still 'tis an arranter shame for a noble person to neglect her own honor, and defame her own noble person with little inconsiderable fellows, foh!

Mrs. Dainty. I suppose the crime against our honor is the same with a man of quality as with another.

Lady Fidget. How! no sure; the man of quality is likest one's husband, and therefore the fault should be the less.

Mrs. Dainty. But then the pleasure should be the less.

Lady Fidget. Fy, fy, fy, for shame, sister! whither shall we ramble? Be continent in your discourse or I shall hate you.

Mrs. Dainty. Besides, an intrigue is so much the more notorious for the man's quality.

Mrs. Squeamish. 'Tis true that nobody takes notice of a private man, and therefore with him 'tis more secret; and the crime's the less when 'tis not known.

Lady Fidget. You say true; i'faith, I think you are in the right on't: 'tis not an injury to a husband till it be an injury to our honors; so that a woman of honor loses no honor with a private person; and to say truth——

Mrs. Dainty. (Apart to Mrs. Squeamish.) So, the little fellow is grown a private person——with her——

Lady Fidget. But still my dear, dear honor——

Enter Sir Jasper Fidget, Horner, *and* Dorilant.

Sir Jasper. Ay, my dear, dear of honor, thou hast still so much honor in thy mouth——

Horner. (Aside.) That she has none elsewhere.

Lady Fidget. Oh, what d'ye mean to bring in these upon us?

Mrs. Dainty. Foh! these are as bad as wits.

Mrs. Squeamish. Foh!

Lady Fidget. Let us leave the room.

Sir Jasper. Stay, stay; faith, to tell you the naked truth——

Lady Fidget. Fy, Sir Jasper! do not use that word naked.

Sir Jasper. Well, well, in short I have business at Whitehall and cannot go to the play with you; therefore would have you go——

Lady Fidget. With those two to a play?

Sir Jasper. No, not with t'other, but with Mr. Horner; there can be no more scandal to go with him than with Mr. Tattle, or Master Limberham.

Lady Fidget. With that nasty fellow! no—no.

Sir Jasper. (Whispers to Lady Fidget.) Nay, prithee, dear, hear me.

Horner. Ladies——

(Horner *and* Dorilant *draw near* Mrs. Squeamish *and* Mrs. Dainty Fidget.)

Mrs. Dainty. Stand off.

Mrs. Squeamish. Do not approach us.

Mrs. Dainty. You herd with the wits; you are obscenity all over.

Mrs. Squeamish. And I would as soon look upon a picture of Adam and Eve, without fig-leaves, as any of you, if I could help it; therefore keep off, and do not make us sick.

Dorilant. What a devil are these?

Horner. Why, these are pretenders to honor, as critics to wit, only by censuring others; and as every raw, peevish, out-of-humored, affected, dull, tea-drinking, arithmetical fop, sets up for a wit by railing at men of sense, so these for honor, by railing at the court, and ladies of as great honor as quality.

Sir Jasper. Come, Mr. Horner, I must desire you to go with these ladies to the play, sir.

Horner. I, sir?

Sir Jasper. Ay, ay, come, sir.

Horner. I must beg your pardon, sir, and theirs; I will not be seen in women's company in public again for the world.

Sir Jasper. Ha, ha, strange aversion!

Mrs. Squeamish. No, he's for women's company in private.

Sir Jasper. He—poor man—he—ha! ha! ha!

Mrs. Dainty. 'Tis a greater shame amongst lewd fellows to be seen in virtuous women's company, than for the women to be seen with them.

Horner. Indeed, madam, the time was I only hated virtuous women, but now I hate the other too; I beg your pardon, ladies.

Lady Fidget. You are very obliging, sir, because we would not be troubled with you.

Sir Jasper. In sober sadness, he shall go.

Dorilant. Nay, if he wo' not, I am ready to call upon the ladies, and I think I am the fitter man.

Sir Jasper. You, sir! no, I thank you for that. Master Horner is a privileged man amongst the virtuous ladies; 'twill be a great while before you are so. He! he! he! he's my wife's gallant; he! he! he! No, pray withdraw, sir, for as I take it, the virtuous ladies have no business with you.

Dorilant. And I am sure he can have none with them. 'Tis strange a man can't come amongst virtuous women now, but upon the same terms as men are admitted into the Great Turk's seraglio. But heavens keep me from being an ombre player with 'em!—But where is Pinchwife?   *Exit.*

Sir Jasper. Come, come, man; what, avoid the sweet society of womankind? that sweet, soft, gentle, tame, noble creature, woman made for man's companion——

Horner. So is that soft, gentle, tame, and more noble creature a spaniel, and has all their tricks; can fawn, lie down, suffer beating, and fawn the more; barks at your friends when they come to see you, makes your bed hard, gives you fleas, and the mange sometimes. And all the difference is, the spaniel's the more faithful animal, and fawns but upon one master.

Sir Jasper. He! he! he!

Mrs. Squeamish. Oh the rude beast!

Mrs. Dainty. Insolent brute!

Lady Fidget. Brute! stinking, mortified, rotten French wether,[10] to dare——

Sir Jasper. Hold, an't please your ladyship.—For shame, Master Horner! your mother was a woman—*(Aside.)* Now shall I never reconcile 'em.—*(Aside to* Lady Fidget.*)* Hark you, madam, take my advice in your anger. You know you often want one to make up your drolling pack of ombre players, and you may cheat him easily; for he's an ill gamester, and consequently loves play. Besides, you know you have but two old civil gentlemen (with stinking breaths too) to wait upon you abroad; take in the third into your service. The other are but crazy; and a lady should have a supernumerary gentleman-usher as a supernumerary coach-horse, lest sometimes you should be forced to stay at home.

Lady Fidget. But are you sure he loves play, and has money?

Sir Jasper. He loves play as much as you, and has money as much as I.

Lady Fidget. (Aside.) Then I am contented to make him pay for his scurrility. Money makes up in a measure all other wants in men.—Those whom we cannot make hold for gallants, we make fine.

Sir Jasper. (Aside.) So, so; now to mollify, wheedle him.— *(Aside to* HORNER.) Master Horner, will you never keep civil company? methinks 'tis time now, since you are only fit for them. Come, come, man, you must e'en fall to visiting our wives, eating at our tables, drinking tea with our virtuous relations after dinner, dealing cards to 'em, reading plays and gazettes to 'em, picking fleas out of their smocks for 'em, collecting receipts, new songs, women, pages, and footmen for 'em.

Horner. I hope they'll afford me better employment, sir.

Sir Jasper. He! he! he! 'tis fit you know your work before you come into your place. And since you are unprovided of a lady to flatter, and a good house to eat at, pray frequent mine, and call my wife mistress, and she shall call you gallant, according to the custom.

Horner. Who, I?

Sir Jasper. Faith, thou sha't for my sake; come, for my sake only.

Horner. For your sake——

Sir Jasper. Come, come, here's a gamester for you; let him be a little familiar sometimes; nay, what if a little rude? Gamesters may be rude with ladies, you know.

Lady Fidget. Yes; losing gamesters have a privilege with women.

Horner. I always thought the contrary—that the winning gamester had most privilege with women; for when you have lost your money to a man, you'll lose anything you have, all you have, they say, and he may use you as he pleases.

Sir Jasper. He! he! he! well, win or lose, you shall have your liberty with her.

Lady Fidget. As he behaves himself; and for your sake I'll give him admittance and freedom.

Horner. All sorts of freedom, madam?

Sir Jasper. Ay, ay, ay, all sorts of freedom thou canst take. And so go to her; begin thy new employment; wheedle her, jest with her, and be better acquainted one with another.

Horner. (Aside.) I think I know her already; therefore may venture with her my secret for hers.

(HORNER *and* Lady FIDGET *whisper.*)

Sir Jasper. Sister cuz, I have provided an innocent play-fellow for you there.

Mrs. Dainty. Who, he?

Mrs. Squeamish. There's a playfellow, indeed!

Sir Jasper. Yes sure.—What, he is good enough to play at cards, blindman's-buff, or the fool with, sometimes!

Mrs. Squeamish. Foh! we'll have no such playfellows.

Mrs. Dainty. No, sir; you shan't choose playfellows for us, we thank you.

Sir Jasper. Nay, pray hear me.   *(Whispering to them.)*

Lady Fidget. But, poor gentleman, could you be so generous, so truly a man of honor, as for the sakes of us women of honor, to cause yourself to be reported no man? No man! and to suffer yourself the greatest shame that could fall upon a man, that none might fall upon us women by your conversation? but, indeed, sir, as perfectly, perfectly the same man as before your going into France, sir? as perfectly, perfectly, sir?

Horner. As perfectly, perfectly, madam. Nay, I scorn you should take my word; I desire to be tried only, madam.

Lady Fidget. Well, that's spoken again like a man of honor: all men of honor desire to come to the test. But, indeed, generally you men report such things of yourselves, one does not know how or whom to believe; and it is come to that pass, we dare not take your words no more than your tailor's, without some staid servant of yours be bound with you. But I have so strong a faith in your honor, dear, dear, noble sir, that I'd forfeit mine for yours, at any time, dear sir.

Horner. No, madam, you should not need to forfeit it for me; I have given you security already to save you harmless, my late reputation being so well known in the world, madam.

Lady Fidget. But if upon any future falling-out, or upon a suspicion of my taking the trust out of your hands, to employ some other, you yourself should betray your trust, dear sir? I mean, if you'll give me leave to speak obscenely, you might tell, dear sir.

Horner. If I did, nobody would believe me. The reputation of impotency is as hardly recovered again in the world as that of cowardice, dear madam.

Lady Fidget. Nay, then, as one may say, you may do your worst, dear, dear sir.

Sir Jasper. Come, is your ladyship reconciled to him yet? have you agreed on matters? for I must be gone to Whitehall.

Lady Fidget. Why, indeed, Sir Jasper, Master Horner is a

thousand, thousand times a better man than I thought him.
Cousin Squeamish, sister Dainty, I can name him now. Truly,
not long ago, you know, I thought his very name obscenity;
and I would as soon have lain with him as have named him.

Sir Jasper. Very likely, poor madam.

Mrs. Dainty. I believe it.

Mrs. Squeamish. No doubt on't.

Sir Jasper. Well, well—that your ladyship is as virtuous as
any she, I know, and him all the town knows—he! he! he!
therefore now you like him, get you gone to your business
together, go, go to your business, I say, pleasure, whilst I go
to my pleasure, business.

Lady Fidget. Come, then, dear gallant.

Horner. Come away, my dearest mistress.

Sir Jasper. So, so; why 'tis as I'd have it.   *Exit.*

Horner. And as I'd have it.

Lady Fidget. Who for his business from his wife will run,
            Takes the best care to have her business done.
                                                    Exeunt.

ACT III

Scene I: *A Room in* Pinchwife's *House.*

Enter Alithea *and* Mrs. Pinchwife.

Alithea. Sister, what ails you? you are grown melancholy.

Mrs. Pinchwife. Would it not make any one melancholy to
see you go every day fluttering about abroad, whilst I must
stay at home like a poor lonely sullen bird in a cage?

Alithea. Ay, sister; but you came young, and just from the
nest to your cage: so that I thought you liked it, and could
be as cheerful in't as others that took their flight themselves
early, and are hopping abroad in the open air.

Mrs. Pinchwife. Nay, I confess I was quiet enough till my
husband told me what pure lives the London ladies live abroad,
with their dancing, meetings, and junketings, and dressed
every day in their best gowns; and I warrant you, play at
nine-pins every day of the week, so they do.

Enter Pinchwife.

Pinchwife. Come, what's here to do? you are putting the
town-pleasures in her head, and setting her a-longing.

Alithea. Yes, after nine-pins. You suffer none to give her
those longings you mean but yourself.

Pinchwife. I tell her of the vanities of the town like a confessor.

Alithea. A confessor! just such a confessor as he that, by forbidding a silly ostler to grease the horse's teeth, taught him to do't.

Pinchwife. Come, Mrs. Flippant, good precepts are lost when bad examples are still before us: the liberty you take abroad makes her hanker after it, and out of humor at home. Poor wretch! she desired not to come to London; I would bring her.

Alithea. Very well.

Pinchwife. She has been this week in town, and never desired till this afternoon to go abroad.

Alithea. Was she not at a play yesterday?

Pinchwife. Yes; but she ne'er asked me; I was myself the cause of her going.

Alithea. Then if she ask you again, you are the cause of her asking, and not my example.

Pinchwife. Well, tomorrow night I shall be rid of you; and the next day, before 'tis light, she and I'll be rid of the town and my dreadful apprehensions.—Come, be not melancholy; for thou sha't go into the country after tomorrow, dearest.

Alithea. Great comfort!

Mrs. Pinchwife. Pish! what d'ye tell me of the country for?

Pinchwife. How's this! what! pish at the country?

Mrs. Pinchwife. Let me alone; I am not well.

Pinchwife. Oh, if that be all—what ails my dearest?

Mrs. Pinchwife. Truly, I don't know: but I have not been well since you told me there was a gallant at the play in love with me.

Pinchwife. Ha!——

Alithea. That's by my example too!

Pinchwife. Nay, if you are not well, but are so concerned because a lewd fellow chanced to lie and say he liked you, you'll make me sick too.

Mrs. Pinchwife. Of what sickness?

Pinchwife. Oh, of that which is worse than the plague, jealousy.

Mrs. Pinchwife. Pish, you jeer! I'm sure there's no such disease in our receipt-book at home.

Pinchwife. No, thou never met'st with it, poor innocent.— (*Aside.*) Well, if thou cuckold me, 'twill be my own fault— for cuckolds and bastards are generally makers of their own fortune.

Mrs. Pinchwife. Well, but pray, bud, let's go to a play tonight.

Pinchwife. 'Tis just done, she comes from it. But why are you so eager to see a play?

Mrs. Pinchwife. Faith, dear, not that I care one pin for their talk there; but I like to look upon the player-men, and would see, if I could, the gallant you say loves me: that's all, dear bud.

Pinchwife. Is that all, dear bud?

Alithea. This proceeds from my example!

Mrs. Pinchwife. But if the play be done, let's go abroad, however, dear bud.

Pinchwife. Come, have a little patience and thou shalt go into the country on Friday.

Mrs. Pinchwife. Therefore I would see first some sights to tell my neighbors of. Nay, I will go abroad, that's once.

Alithea. I'm the cause of this desire too!

Pinchwife. But now I think on't, who, who was the cause of Horner's coming to my lodgings today? That was you.

Alithea. No, you, because you would not let him see your handsome wife out of your lodging.

Mrs. Pinchwife. Why, O Lord! did the gentleman come hither to see me indeed?

Pinchwife. No, no.—You are not the cause of that damned question too, Mistress Alithea?—(*Aside.*) Well, she's in the right of it. He is in love with my wife—and comes after her —'tis so—but I'll nip his love in the bud; lest he should follow us into the country and break his chariot-wheel near our house, on purpose for an excuse to come to't. But I think I know the town.

Mrs. Pinchwife. Come, pray, bud, let's go abroad before 'tis late; for I will go, that's flat and plain.

Pinchwife. (*Aside.*) So! the obstinacy already of the town-wife; and I must, whilst she's here, humor her like one.—(*Aloud.*) Sister, how shall we do, that may not be seen or known?

Alithea. Let her put on her mask.

Pinchwife. Pshaw! a mask makes people but the more inquisitive and is as ridiculous a disguise as a stage-beard: her shape, stature, habit will be known. And if we should meet with Horner, he would be sure to take acquaintance with us, must wish her joy, kiss her, talk to her, leer upon her, and the devil and all. No, I'll not use her to a mask, 'tis dangerous; for masks have made more cuckolds than the best faces that ever were known.

Alithea. How will you do then?

Mrs. Pinchwife. Nay, shall we go? The Exchange will be shut, and I have a mind to see that.

Pinchwife. So—I have it—I'll dress her up in the suit we

are to carry down to her brother, little Sir James; nay, I understand the town-tricks. Come, let's go dress her. A mask! no—a woman masked, like a covered dish, gives a man curiosity and appetite; when, it may be, uncovered, 'twould turn his stomach: no, no.

Alithea. Indeed your comparison is something a greasy one: but I had a gentle gallant used to say, A beauty masked, like the sun in eclipse, gathers together more gazers than if it shined out.

Exeunt.

SCENE II: *The New Exchange.*[11]

Enter HORNER, HARCOURT, *and* DORILANT.

Dorilant. Engaged to women, and not sup with us!

Horner. Ay, a pox on 'em all!

Harcourt. You were much a more reasonable man in the morning, and had as noble resolutions against 'em as a widower of a week's liberty.

Dorilant. Did I ever think to see you keep company with women in vain?

Horner. In vain: no—'tis since I can't love 'em, to be revenged on 'em.

Harcourt. Now your sting is gone, you looked in the box amongst all those women like a drone in the hive; all upon you, shoved and ill-used by 'em all, and thrust from one side to t'other.

Dorilant. Yet he must be buzzing amongst 'em still, like other beetle-headed liquorish drones. Avoid 'em, and hate 'em, as they hate you.

Horner. Because I do hate 'em, and would hate 'em yet more, I'll frequent 'em. You may see by marriage, nothing makes a man hate a woman more than her constant conversation. In short, I converse with 'em, as you do with rich fools, to laugh at 'em and use 'em ill.

Dorilant. But I would no more sup with women, unless I could lie with 'em, than sup with a rich coxcomb, unless I could cheat him.

Horner. Yes, I have known thee sup with a fool for his drinking; if he could set out your hand that way only, you were satisfied, and if he were a wine-swallowing mouth, 'twas enough.

Harcourt. Yes, a man drinks often with a fool, as he tosses with a marker, only to keep his hand in use. But do the ladies drink?

Horner. Yes, sir; and I shall have the pleasure at least of laying 'em flat with a bottle, and bring as much scandal that way upon 'em as formerly t'other.

Harcourt. Perhaps you may prove as weak a brother among 'em that way as t'other.

Dorilant. Foh! drinking with women is as unnatural as scolding with 'em. But 'tis a pleasure of decayed fornicators, and the basest way of quenching love.

Harcourt. Nay, 'tis drowning love, instead of quenching it. But leave us for civil women too!

Dorilant. Ay, when he can't be the better for 'em. We hardly pardon a man that leaves his friend for a wench, and that's a pretty lawful call.

Horner. Faith, I would not leave you for 'em, if they would not drink.

Dorilant. Who would disappoint his company at Lewis's for a gossiping?

Harcourt. Foh! Wine and women, good apart, together are as nauseous as sack and sugar. But hark you, sir, before you go, a little of your advice; an old maimed general, when unfit for action, is fittest for counsel. I have other designs upon women than eating and drinking with them; I am in love with Sparkish's mistress, whom he is to marry tomorrow: now how shall I get her?

Enter SPARKISH, *looking about.*

Horner. Why, here comes one will help you to her.

Harcourt. He! he, I tell you, is my rival, and will hinder my love.

Horner. No; a foolish rival and a jealous husband assist their rival's designs; for they are sure to make their women hate them, which is the first step to their love for another man.

Harcourt. But I cannot come near his mistress but in his company.

Horner. Still the better for you; for fools are most easily cheated when they themselves are accessories: and he is to be bubbled[12] of his mistress as of his money, the common mistress, by keeping him company.

Sparkish. Who is that that is to be bubbled? Faith, let me snack; I han't met with a bubble since Christmas. 'Gad, I think bubbles are like their brother woodcocks, go out with the cold weather.

Harcourt. (*Apart to* HORNER.) A pox! he did not hear all, I hope.

Sparkish. Come, you bubbling rogues you, where do we sup?—Oh, Harcourt, my mistress tells me you have been

making fierce love to her all the play long: ha! ha!—But
I——

Harcourt. I make love to her!

Sparkish. Nay, I forgive thee, for I think I know thee, and
I know her; but I am sure I know myself.

Harcourt. Did she tell you so? I see all women are like
these of the Exchange; who, to enhance the prize of their
commodities, report to their fond customers offers which were
never made 'em.

Horner. Ay, women are apt to tell before the intrigue, as
men after it, and so show themselves the vainer sex. But hast
thou a mistress, Sparkish? 'Tis as hard for me to believe it,
as that thou ever hadst a bubble, as you bragged just now.

Sparkish. Oh, your servant, sir: are you at your raillery,
sir? But we are some of us beforehand with you today at the
play. The wits were something bold with you, sir; did you not
hear us laugh?

Horner. Yes; but I thought you had gone to plays to laugh
at the poet's wit, not at your own.

Sparkish. Your servant, sir: no, I thank you. 'Gad, I go to
a play as to a country treat; I carry my own wine to one, and
my own wit to t'other, or else I'm sure I should not be merry
at either. And the reason why we are so often louder than the
players is because we think we speak more wit, and so become the poet's rivals in his audience: for to tell you the
truth, we hate the silly rouges; nay, so much, that we find
fault even with their bawdy upon the stage, whilst we talk
nothing else in the pit as loud.

Horner. But why shouldst thou hate the silly poets? Thou
hast too much wit to be one: and they, like whores, are only
hated by each other: and thou dost scorn writing, I'm sure.

Sparkish. Yes; I'd have you to know I scorn writing: but
women, women, that make men do all foolish things, make
'em write songs too. Everybody does it. 'Tis even as common
with lovers as playing with fans; and you can no more help
rhyming to your Phyllis, than drinking to your Phyllis.

Harcourt. Nay, poetry in love is no more to be avoided
than jealousy.

Dorilant. But the poets damned your songs, did they?

Sparkish. Damn the poets! they have turned 'em into burlesque, as they call it. That burlesque is a hocus-pocus trick
they have got, which, by the virtue of *Hictius doctius topsy
turvy*,[13] they make a wise and witty man in the world, a fool
upon the stage you know not how: and 'tis therefore I hate
'em too, for I know not but it may be my own case; for
they'll put a man into a play for looking asquint. Their pre-
decessors were contented to make serving-men only their

stage-fools: but these rogues must have gentlemen, with a pox to 'em, nay, knights; and, indeed, you shall hardly see a fool upon the stage but he's a knight. And to tell you the truth, they have kept me these six years from being a knight in earnest, for fear of being knighted in a play, and dubbed a fool.

Dorilant. Blame 'em not, they must follow their copy, the age.

Harcourt. But why shouldst thou be afraid of being in a play, who expose yourself every day in the play-houses, and at public places?

Horner. 'Tis but being on the stage, instead of standing on a bench in the pit.

Dorilant. Don't you give money to painters to draw you like? and are you afraid of your pictures at length in a play-house, where your mistresses may see you?

Sparkish. A pox! painters don't draw the small-pox or pimples in one's face. Come, damn all your silly authors whatever, all books and booksellers, by the world; and all readers, courteous or uncourteous!

Harcourt. But who comes here, Sparkish?

Enter PINCHWIFE *and* Mrs. PINCHWIFE *in man's clothes,*
ALITHEA *and* LUCY.

Sparkish. Oh, hide me! There's my mistress too.
                    (SPARKISH *hides himself behind* HARCOURT.)

Harcourt. She sees you.

Sparkish. But I will not see her. 'Tis time to go to White-hall and I must not fail the drawing-room.

Harcourt. Pray, first carry me, and reconcile me to her.

Sparkish. Another time. Faith, the king will have supped.

Harcourt. Not with the worse stomach for thy absence. Thou art one of those fools that think their attendance at the king's meals as necessary as his physicians, when you are more troublesome to him than his doctors or his dogs.

Sparkish. Pshaw! I know my interest, sir. Prithee hide me.

Horner. Your servant, Pinchwife.—What, he knows us not!

Pinchwife. (*To his* Wife *aside.*) Come along.

Mrs. Pinchwife. Pray, have you any ballads? give me six-penny worth.

Bookseller. We have no ballads.

Mrs. Pinchwife. Then give me *Covent Garden Drollery,* and a play or two—Oh, here's *Tarugo's Wiles,* and *The Slighted Maiden;*[14] I'll have them.

Pinchwife. (*Apart to her.*) No; plays are not for your reading. Come along; will you discover yourself?

Horner. Who is that pretty youth with him, Sparkish?

Sparkish. I believe his wife's brother, because he's something like her: but I never saw her but once.

Horner. Extremely handsome; I have seen a face like it too. Let us follow 'em.

Exeunt PINCHWIFE, MRS. PINCHWIFE, ALITHEA, *and* LUCY; HORNER *and* DORILANT *following them.*

Harcourt. Come, Sparkish, your mistress saw you, and will be angry you go not to her. Besides, I would fain be reconciled to her, which none but you can do, dear friend.

Sparkish. Well, that's a better reason, dear friend. I would not go near her now for hers or my own sake; but I can deny you nothing: for though I have known thee a great while, never go, if I do not love thee as well as a new acquaintance.

Harcourt. I am obliged to you indeed, dear friend. I would be well with her, only to be well with thee still; for these ties to wives usually dissolve all ties to friends. I would be contented she should enjoy you a-nights, but I would have you to myself a-days as I have had, dear friend.

Sparkish. And thou shalt enjoy me a-days, dear, dear friend, never stir: and I'll be divorced from her, sooner than from thee. Come along.

Harcourt. (*Aside.*) So, we are put to't, when we make our rival our procurer; but neither she nor her brother would let me come near her now. When all's done, a rival is the best cloak to steal to a mistress under, without suspicion; and when we have once got to her as we desire, we throw him off like other cloaks.

Exit SPARKISH, HARCOURT *following him.*

Enter PINCHWIFE, MRS. PINCHWIFE.

Pinchwife. (*To* ALITHEA, *behind.*) Sister, if you will not go, we must leave you.—(*Aside.*) The fool her gallant and she will muster up all the young saunterers of this place, and they will leave their dear seamstresses to follow us. What a swarm of cuckolds and cuckold-makers are here!—Come, let's be gone, Mistress Margery.

Mrs. Pinchwife. Don't you believe that; I han't half my bellyful of sights yet.

Pinchwife. Then walk this way.

Mrs. Pinchwife. Lord, what a power of brave signs are here! stay—the Bull's-Head, the Ram's-Head, and the Stag's-Head, dear——

Pinchwife. Nay, if every husband's proper sign here were visible, they would be all alike.

Mrs. Pinchwife. What d'ye mean by that, bud?

Pinchwife. 'Tis no matter—no matter, bud.

Mrs. Pinchwife. Pray tell me: nay, I will know.

Pinchwife. They would be all Bulls, Stags, and Rams-heads.

              Exeunt PINCHWIFE *and* Mrs. PINCHWIFE.

    Enter SPARKISH, HARCOURT, ALITHEA, *and* LUCY,
              at the other side.

Sparkish. Come, dear madam, for my sake you shall be reconciled to him.

Alithea. For your sake I hate him.

Harcourt. That's something too cruel, madam, to hate me for his sake.

Sparkish. Ay indeed, madam, too, too cruel to me, to hate my friend for my sake.

Alithea. I hate him because he is your enemy; and you ought to hate him too, for making love to me, if you love me.

Sparkish. That's a good one! I hate a man for loving you! If he did love you, 'tis but what he can't help; and 'tis your fault, not his, if he admires you. I hate a man for being of my opinion! I'll n'er do't, by the world.

Alithea. Is it for your honor, or mine, to suffer a man to make love to me, who am to marry you tomorrow?

Sparkish. Is it for your honor, or mine, to have me jealous? That he makes love to you is a sign you are handsome; and that I am not jealous is a sign you are virtuous. That I think is for your honor.

Alithea. But 'tis your honor too I am concerned for.

Harcourt. But why, dearest madam, will you be more concerned for his honor than he is himself? Let his honor alone, for my sake and his. He! he has no honor——

Sparkish. How's that?

Harcourt. But what my dear friend can guard himself.

Sparkish. Oh, ho—that's right again.

Harcourt. Your care of his honor argues his neglect of it, which is no honor to my dear friend here. Therefore once more, let his honor go which way it will, dear madam.

Sparkish. Ay, ay; were it for my honor to marry a woman whose virtue I suspected, and could not trust her in a friend's hands?

Alithea. Are you not afraid to lose me?

Harcourt. He afraid to lose you, madam! No, no—you

may see how the most estimable and most glorious creature in the world is valued by him. Will you not see it?

Sparkish. Right, honest Frank, I have that noble value for her that I cannot be jealous of her.

Alithea. You mistake him. He means, you care not for me, nor who has me.

Sparkish. Lord, madam, I see you are jealous! Will you wrest a poor man's meaning from his words?

Alithea. You astonish me, sir, with your want of jealousy.

Sparkish. And you make me giddy, madam, with your jealousy and fears, and virtue and honor. 'Gad, I see virtue makes a woman as troublesome as a little reading or learning.

Alithea. Monstrous!

Lucy. (*Aside*.) Well, to see what easy husbands these women of quality can meet with! a poor chambermaid can never have such ladylike luck. Besides, he's thrown away upon her. She'll make no use of her fortune, her blessing none to a gentleman, for a pure cuckold; for it requires good breeding to be a cuckold.

Alithea. I tell you then plainly, he pursues me to marry me.

Sparkish. Pshaw!

Harcourt. Come, madam, you see you strive in vain to make him jealous of me. My dear friend is the kindest creature in the world to me.

Sparkish. Poor fellow!

Harcourt. But his kindness only is not enough for me, without your favor, your good opinion, dear madam: 'tis that must perfect my happiness. Good gentleman, he believes all I say: would you would do so! Jealous of me! I would not wrong him nor you for the world.

Sparkish. Look you there. Hear him, hear him, and do not walk away so.   (ALITHEA *walks carelessly to and fro*.)

Harcourt. I love you, madam, so——

Sparkish. How's that? Nay, now you begin to go too far indeed.

Harcourt. So much, I confess, I say, I love you, that I would not have you miserable, and cast yourself away upon so unworthy and inconsiderable a thing as what you see here.

(*Clapping his hand on his breast, points at* SPARKISH.)

Sparkish. No, faith, I believe thou wouldst not: now his meaning is plain: but I knew before thou wouldst not wrong me, nor her.

Harcourt. No, no,. Heavens forbid the glory of her sex should fall so low, as into the embraces of such a contemptible wretch, the least of mankind—my friend here—I injure him!   (*Embracing* SPARKISH.)

Alithea. Very well.

Sparkish. No, no, dear friend, I knew it.—Madam, you see he will rather wrong himself than me, in giving himself such names.

Alithea. Do not you understand him yet?

Sparkish. Yes: how modestly he speaks of himself, poor fellow!

Alithea. Methinks he speaks impudently of yourself, since —before yourself too; insomuch that I can no longer suffer his scurrilous abusiveness to you, no more than his love to me.   *(Offers to go.)*

Sparkish. Nay, nay, madam, pray stay—his love to you! Lord, madam, has he not spoke yet plain enough?

Alithea. Yes, indeed, I should think so.

Sparkish. Well then, by the world, a man can't speak civilly to a woman now, but presently she says he makes love to her. Nay. madam, you shall stay, with your pardon, since you have not yet understood him, till he has made an *eclaircissement*[15] of his love to you; that is—what kind of love it is. Answer to thy catechism, friend; do you love my mistress here?

Harcourt. Yes, I wish she would not doubt it.

Sparkish. But how do you love her?

Harcourt. With all my soul.

Alithea. I thank him. Methinks he speaks plain enough now.

Sparkish. (To ALITHEA.*)* You are out still.—But with what kind of love, Harcourt?

Harcourt. With the best and truest love in the world.

Sparkish. Look you there then, that is with no matrimonial love, I'm sure.

Alithea. How's that? do you say matrimonial love is not best?

Sparkish. 'Gad, I went too far ere I was aware. But speak for thyself, Harcourt; you said you would not wrong me nor her.

Harcourt. No, no, madam, e'en take him for Heaven's sake—

Sparkish. Look you there, madam.

Harcourt. Who should in all justice be yours: he that loves you most.   *(Claps his hand on his breast.)*

Alithea. Look you there, Mr. Sparkish, who's that?

Sparkish. Who should it be?—Go on, Harcourt.

Harcourt. Who loves you more than women, titles; or fortune, fools.   *(Points at* SPARKISH.*)*

Sparkish. Look you there, he means me still, for he points at me.

Alithea. Ridiculous!

Harcourt. Who can only match your faith and constancy in love.

Sparkish. Ay.

Harcourt. Who knows, if it be possible, how to value so much beauty and virtue.

Sparkish. Ay.

Harcourt. Whose love can no more be equalled in the world, than that heavenly form of yours.

Sparkish. No.

Harcourt. Who could no more suffer a rival, than your absence; and yet could no more suspect your virtue, than his own constancy in his love to you.

Sparkish. No.

Harcourt. Who, in fine, loves you better than his eyes, that first made him love you.

Sparkish. Ay—Nay, madam, faith, you shan't go till——

Alithea. Have a care, lest you make me stay too long.

Sparkish. But till he has saluted you; that I may be assured you are friends, after his honest advice and declaration. Come, pray, madam, be friends with him.

Enter PINCHWIFE *and* Mrs. PINCHWIFE.

Alithea. You must pardon me, sir, that I am not yet so obedient to you.

Pinchwife. What, invite your wife to kiss men? Monstrous! are you not ashamed? I will never forgive you.

Sparkish. Are you not ashamed, that I should have more confidence in the chastity of your family than you have? You must not teach me; I am a man of honor, sir, though I am frank and free; I am frank, sir——

Pinchwife. Very frank, sir, to share your wife with your friends.

Sparkish. He is an humble, menial friend, such as reconciles the differences of the marriage bed; you know man and wife do not always agree; I design him for that use, therefore would have him well with my wife.

Pinchwife. A menial friend!—you will get a great many menial friends by showing your wife as you do.

Sparkish. What then? It may be I have a pleasure in't, as I have to show fine clothes at a play-house the first day, and count money before poor rogues.

Pinchwife. He that shows his wife or money will be in danger of having them borrowed sometimes.

Sparkish. I love to be envied and would not marry a wife that I alone could love; loving alone is as dull as eating alone.

Is it not a frank age? and I am a frank person; and to tell you the truth, it may be, I love to have rivals in a wife—they make her seem to a man still but as a kept mistress; and so good night, for I must to Whitehall.—Madam, I hope you are now reconciled to my friend; and so I wish you a good night, madam, and sleep if you can: for to-morrow you know I must visit you early with a canonical gentleman. Good night, dear Harcourt.   *Exit.*

Harcourt. Madam, I hope you will not refuse my visit to-morrow, if it should be earlier with a canonical gentleman than Mr. Sparkish's.

Pinchwife. This gentlewoman is yet under my care, therefore you must yet forbear your freedom with her, sir.

> (*Coming between* ALITHEA *and* HARCOURT.)

Harcourt. Must, sir?

Pinchwife. Yes, sir, she is my sister.

Harcourt. 'Tis well she is, sir—for I must be her servant, sir.—Madam——

Pinchwife. Come away, sister, we had been gone, if it had not been for you, and so avoided these lewd rake-hells who seem to haunt us.

Enter HORNER *and* DORILANT.

Horner. How now, Pinchwife!

Pinchwife. Your servant.

Horner. What! I see a little time in the country makes a man turn wild and unsociable, and only fit to converse with his horses, dogs, and his herds.

Pinchwife. I have business, sir, and must mind it; your business is pleasure, therefore you and I must go different ways.

Horner. Well, you may go on, but this pretty young gentleman——   (*Takes hold of* Mrs. PINCHWIFE.)

Harcourt. The lady——

Dorilant. And the maid——

Horner. Shall stay with us; for I suppose their business is the same with ours, pleasure.

Pinchwife. (*Aside.*) 'Sdeath, he knows her, she carries it so sillily! yet if he does not, I should be more silly to discover it first.

Alithea. Pray, let us go, sir.

Pinchwife. Come, come——

Horner. (*To* Mrs. PINCHWIFE.) Had you not rather stay with us?—Prithee, Pinchwife, who is this pretty young gentleman?

Pinchwife. One to whom I'm a guardian.—(*Aside.*) I wish I could keep her out of your hands.

Horner. Who is he? I never saw anything so pretty in all my life.

Pinchwife. Pshaw! do not look upon him so much, he's a poor bashful youth, you'll put him out of countenance.— Come away, brother. (*Offers to take her away.*)

Horner. Oh, your brother!

Pinchwife. Yes, my wife's brother.—Come, come, she'll stay supper for us.

Horner. I thought so, for he is very like her I saw you at the play with, whom I told you I was in love with.

Mrs. Pinchwife. (*Aside.*) Oh, jeminy! is that he that was in love with me? I am glad on't, I vow, for he's a curious fine gentleman, and I love him already, too.—(*To* PINCHWIFE.) Is this he, bud?

Pinchwife. (*To his* Wife.) Come away, come away.

Horner. Why, what haste are you in? why won't you let me talk with him?

Pinchwife. Because you'll debauch him; he's yet young and innocent, and I would not have him debauched for anything in the world.—(*Aside.*) How she gazes on him! the devil!

Horner. Harcourt, Dorilant, look you here, this is the likeness of that dowdy he told us of, his wife; did you ever see a lovelier creature? The rogue has reason to be jealous of his wife, since she is like him, for she would make all that see her in love with her.

Harcourt. And, as I remember now, she is as like him here as can be.

Dorilant. She is indeed very pretty, if she be like him.

Horner. Very pretty? a very pretty commendation!—she is a glorious creature, beautiful beyond all things I ever beheld.

Pinchwife. So, so.

Harcourt. More beautiful than a poet's first mistress of imagination.

Horner. Or another man's last mistress of flesh and blood.

Mrs. Pinchwife. Nay, now you jeer, sir; pray don't jeer me.

Pinchwife. Come, come.—(*Aside.*) By Heavens, she'll discover herself!

Horner. I speak of your sister, sir.

Pinchwife. Ay, but saying she was handsome, if like him, made him blush.—(*Aside.*) I am upon a rack!

Horner. Methinks he is so handsome he should not be a man.

Pinchwife. (*Aside.*) Oh there 'tis out! he has discovered her! I am not able to suffer any longer.—(*To his* Wife.) Come, come away, I say.

Horner. Nay, by your leave, sir, he shall not go yet.— (*Aside to them.*) Harcourt, Dorilant, let us torment this jealous rogue a little.

Harcourt. Dorilant. How?

Horner. I'll show you.

Pinchwife. Come, pray let him go, I cannot stay fooling any longer; I tell you his sister stays supper for us.

Horner. Does she? Come then, we'll all go to sup with he and thee.

Pinchwife. No, now I think on't, having stayed so long for us, I warrant she's gone to bed.—(*Aside.*) I wish she and I were well out of their hands.—(*To his* Wife.) Come, I must rise early tomorrow, come.

Horner. Well then, if she be gone to bed, I wish her and you a good night. But pray, young gentleman, present my humble service to her.

Mrs. Pinchwife. Thank you heartily, sir.

Pinchwife. (*Aside.*) 'Sdeath, she will discover herself yet in spite of me.—(*Aloud.*) He is something more civil to you, for your kindness to his sister, than I am, it seems.

Horner. Tell her, dear sweet little gentleman, for all your brother there, that you have revived the love I had for her at first sight in the playhouse.

Mrs. Pinchwife. But did you love her indeed, and indeed?

Pinchwife. (*Aside.*) So, so.—(*Aloud.*) Away, I say.

Horner. Nay, stay.—Yes, indeed, and indeed, pray do you tell her so, and give her this kiss from me.   (*Kisses her.*)

Pinchwife. (*Aside.*) Oh Heavens! what do I suffer? Now 'tis too plain he knows her, and yet——

Horner. And this, and this——   (*Kisses her again.*)

Mrs. Pinchwife. What do you kiss me for? I am no woman.

Pinchwife. (*Aside.*) So, there, 'tis out.—(*Aloud.*) Come, I cannot, nor will stay any longer.

Horner. Nay, they shall send your lady a kiss too. Here Harcourt, Dorilant, will you not?   (*They kiss her.*)

Pinchwife. (*Aside.*) How! do I suffer this? Was I not accusing another just now for this rascally patience, in permitting his wife to be kissed before his face? Ten thousand ulcers gnaw away their lips.—(*Aloud.*) Come, come.

Horner. Good night, dear little gentleman; madam, good night; farewell, Pinchwife.—(*Apart to* HARCOURT *and* DORILANT). Did not I tell you I would raise his jealous gall?

Exeunt HORNER, HARCOURT, *and* DORILANT.

Pinchwife. So, they are gone at last; stay, let me see first if the coach be at this door. *Exit.*

Enter HORNER, HARCOURT, *and* DORILANT.

Horner. What, not gone yet? Will you be sure to do as I desired you, sweet sir?

Mrs. Pinchwife. Sweet sir, but what will you give me then?

Horner. Anything. Come away into the next walk.

(*Exit, haling away* Mrs. PINCHWIFE.)

Alithea. Hold! hold! what d'ye do?

Lucy. Stay, stay, hold——

Harcourt. Hold, madam, hold, let him present him—he'll come presently; nay, I will never let you go till you answer my question.

Lucy. For God's sake, sir, I must follow 'em.

(ALITHEA *and* LUCY, *struggling with* HARCOURT *and* DORILANT.)

Dorilant. No, I have something to present you with too; you shan't follow them.

Enter PINCHWIFE.

Pinchwife. Where?—how—what's become of?—gone!—whither?

Lucy. He's only gone with the gentleman, who will give him something, an't please your worship.

Pinchwife. Something!—give him something, with a pox! —where are they?

Alithea. In the next walk only, brother.

Pinchwife. Only, only! where, where?

(*Exit and returns presently, then goes out again.*)

Harcourt. What's the matter with him? why so much concerned? But, dearest madam——

Alithea. Pray let me go, sir; I have said and suffered enough already.

Harcourt. Then you will not look upon, nor pity, my sufferings?

Alithea. To look upon 'em, when I cannot help 'em, were cruelty, not pity; therefore, I will never see you more.

Harcourt. Let me then, madam, have my privilege of a banished lover, complaining or railing, and giving you but a farewell reason why, if you cannot condescend to marry me, you should not take that wretch, my rival.

Alithea. He only, not you, since my honor is engaged so far to him, can give me a reason why I should not marry

him; but if he be true, and what I think him to me, I must
be so to him. Your servant, sir.

Harcourt. Have women only constancy when 'tis a vice,
and are, like Fortune, only true to fools?

Dorilant. (To LUCY, *who struggles to get from him.)* Thou
sha't not stir, thou robust creature; you see I can deal with
you, therefore you should stay the rather, and be kind.

Enter PINCHWIFE.

Pinchwife. Gone, gone, not to be found! quite gone! ten
thousand plagues go with 'em! Which way went they?

Alithea. But into t'other walk, brother.

Lucy. Their business will be done presently sure, an't
please your worship; it can't be long in doing, I'm sure on't.

Alithea. Are they not there?

Pinchwife. No, you know where they are, you infamous
wretch, eternal shame of your family, which you do not dis-
honor enough yourself you think, but you must help her to
do it too, thou legion of bawds!

Alithea. Good brother——

Pinchwife. Damned, damned sister!

Alithea. Look you here, she's coming.

Enter Mrs. PINCHWIFE *running, with her hat full of oranges and dried fruit under her arm,* HORNER *following.*

Mrs. Pinchwife. Oh dear bud, look you here what I have
got, see!

Pinchwife. (Aside, rubbing his forehead.) And what I have
got here too, which you can't see.

Mrs. Pinchwife. The fine gentleman has given me better
things yet.

Pinchwife. Has he so?—*(Aside.)* Out of breath and col-
ored!—I must hold yet.

Horner. I have only given your little brother an orange,
sir.

Pinchwife. (To HORNER.) Thank you, sir.—*(Aside.)* You
have only squeezed my orange, I suppose, and given it me
again; yet I must have a city patience.—*(To his* Wife.)
Come, come away.

Mrs. Pinchwife. Stay, till I have put up my fine things, bud.

Enter Sir JASPER FIDGET.

Sir Jasper. Oh, Master Horner, come, come, the ladies stay for you; your mistress, my wife, wonders you make not more haste to her.

Horner. I have stayed this half hour for you here, and 'tis your fault I am not now with your wife.

Sir Jasper. But, pray, don't let her know so much; the truth on't is, I was advancing a certain project to his majesty about—I'll tell you.

Horner. No, let's go, and hear it at your house. Good night, sweet little gentleman; one kiss more, you'll remember me now, I hope. *(Kisses her.)*

Dorilant. What, Sir Jasper, will you separate friends? He promised to sup with us, and if you take him to your house, you'll be in danger of our company too.

Sir Jasper. Alas! gentlemen, my house is not fit for you; there are none but civil women there, which are not for your turn. He, you know, can bear with the society of civil women now, ha! ha! ha! besides, he's one of my family—he's—he! he! he!

Dorilant. What is he?

Sir Jasper. Faith, my eunuch, since you'll have it; he! he!
                    Exeunt Sir JASPER FIDGET *and* HORNER.

Dorilant. I rather wish thou wert his or my cuckold. Harcourt, what a good cuckold is lost there for want of a man to make him one? Thee and I cannot have Horner's privilege, who can make use of it.

Harcourt. Ay, to poor Horner 'tis like coming to an estate at three-score, when a man can't be the better for't.

Pinchwife. Come.

Mrs. Pinchwife. Presently, bud.

Dorilant. Come, let us go too.—(*To* ALITHEA.) Madam, your servant.—(*To* LUCY.) Good night, strapper.

Harcourt. Madam, though you will not let me have a good day or night, I wish you one; but dare not name the other half of my wish.

Alithea. Good night, sir, for ever.

Mrs. Pinchwife. I don't know where to put this here, dear bud, you shall eat it; nay, you shall have part of the fine gentleman's good things, or treat, as you call it, when we come home.

Pinchwife. Indeed, I deserve it, since I furnished the best part of it. *(Strikes away the orange.)*

> The gallant treats presents, and gives the ball;
> But 'tis the absent cuckold pays for all. *Exeunt.*

ACT IV

SCENE I: PINCHWIFE'S *House in the morning.*

Enter ALITHEA *dressed in new clothes, and* LUCY.

Lucy. Well—madam, now have I dressed you, and set you out with so many ornaments and spent upon you ounces of essence and pulvillio;[16] and all this for no other purpose but as people adorn and perfume a corpse for a stinking second-hand grave: such, or as bad, I think Master Sparkish's bed.

Alithea. Hold your peace.

Lucy. Nay, madam, I will ask you the reason why you would banish poor Master Harcourt for ever from your sight; how could you be so hard-hearted?

Alithea. 'Twas because I was not hard-hearted.

Lucy. No, no; 'twas stark love and kindness, I warrant.

Alithea. It was so; I would see him no more because I love him.

Lucy. Hey day, a very pretty reason!

Alithea. You do not understand me.

Lucy. I wish you may yourself.

Alithea. I was engaged to marry, you see, another man, whom my justice will not suffer me to deceive or injure.

Lucy. Can there be a greater cheat or wrong done to a man than to give him your person without your heart? I should make a conscience of it.

Alithea. I'll retrieve it for him after I am married a while.

Lucy. The woman that marries to love better, will be as much mistaken as the wencher that marries to live better. No, madam, marrying to increase love is like gaming to become rich; alas! you only lose what little stock you had before.

Alithea. I find by your rhetoric you have been bribed to betray me.

Lucy. Only by his merit, that has bribed your heart, you see, against your word and rigid honor. But what a devil is this honor! 'tis sure a disease in the head, like the megrim[17] or falling-sickness, that always hurries people away to do themselves mischief. Men lose their lives by it; women, what's dearer to 'em, their love, the life of life.

Alithea. Come, pray talk you no more of honor, nor Master Harcourt; I wish the other would come to secure my fidelity to him and his right in me.

Lucy. You will marry him then?

Alithea. Certainly. I have given him already my word, and will my hand too, to make it good, when he comes.

Lucy. Well, I wish I may never stick pin more, if he be not an arrant natural, to t'other fine gentleman.

Alithea. I own he wants the wit of Harcourt, which I will dispense withal for another want he has, which is want of jealousy, which men of wit seldom want.

Lucy. Lord, madam, what should you do with a fool to your husband? You intend to be honest, don't you? then that husbandly virtue, credulity, is thrown away upon you.

Alithea. He only that could suspect my virtue should have cause to do it; 'tis Sparkish's confidence in my truth that obliges me to be so faithful to him.

Lucy. You are not sure his opinion may last.

Alithea. I am satisfied; 'tis impossible for him to be jealous after the proofs I have had of him. Jealousy in a husband— Heaven defend me from it! it begets a thousand plagues to a poor woman, the loss of her honor, her quiet, and her——

Lucy. And her pleasure.

Alithea. What d'ye mean, impertinent?

Lucy. Liberty is a great pleasure, madam.

Alithea. I say, loss of her honor, her quiet, nay, her life sometimes; and what's as bad almost, the loss of this town; that is, she is sent into the country, which is the last ill-usage of a husband to a wife, I think.

Lucy. (*Aside.*) Oh, does the wind lie there?—(*Aloud.*) Then of necessity, madam, you think a man must carry his wife into the country, if he be wise. The country is as terrible, I find, to our young English ladies, as a monastery to those abroad; and on my virginity, I think they would rather marry a London jailer, than a high sheriff of a county, since neither can stir from his employment. Formerly women of wit married fools for a great estate, a fine seat, or the like; but now 'tis for a pretty seat only in Lincoln's Inn Fields, St. James's Fields, or the Pall Mall.[18]

Enter SPARKISH, *and* HARCOURT, *dressed like a* Parson.

Sparkish. Madam, your humble servant, a happy day to you, and to us all.

Harcourt. Amen.

Alithea. Who have we here?

Sparkish. My chaplain, faith—Oh madam, poor Harcourt

remembers his humble service to you; and, in obedience to your last commands, refrains coming into your sight.

Alithea. Is not that he?

Sparkish. No, fy, no; but to show that he ne'er intended to hinder our match, has sent his brother here to join our hands. When I get me a wife, I must get her a chaplain, according to the custom; that is his brother, and my chaplain.

Alithea. His brother!

Lucy. (Aside.) And your chaplain, to preach in your pulpit then——

Alithea. His brother!

Sparkish. Nay, I knew you would not believe it.—I told you, sir, she would take you for your brother Frank.

Alithea. Believe it!

Lucy. (Aside.) His brother! ha! ha! he! He has a trick left still, it seems.

Sparkish. Come, my dearest, pray let us go to church before the canonical hour[19] is past.

Alithea. For shame, you are abused still.

Sparkish. By the world, 'tis strange now you are so incredulous.

Alithea. 'Tis strange you are so credulous.

Sparkish. Dearest of my life, hear me. I tell you this is Ned Harcourt of Cambridge, by the world; you see he has a sneaking college look. 'Tis true he's something like his brother Frank; and they differ from each other no more than in their age, for they were twins.

Lucy. Ha! ha! ha!

Alithea. Your servant, sir; I cannot be so deceived, though you are. But come, let's hear, how do you know what you affirm so confidently?

Sparkish. Why I'll tell you all. Frank Harcourt coming to me this morning to wish me joy, and present his service to you, I asked him if he could help me to a parson. Whereupon he told me, he had a brother in town who was in orders; and he went straight away, and sent him, you see there, to me.

Alithea. Yes, Frank goes and put on a black coat, then tells you he is Ned; that's all you have for't.

Sparkish. Pshaw! pshaw! I tell you, by the same token, the midwife put her garter about Frank's neck to know 'em asunder, they were so like.

Alithea. Frank tells you this too?

Sparkish. Ay, and Ned there too; nay, they are both in a story.

Alithea. So, so; very foolish.

Sparkish. Lord, if you won't believe one, you had best try him by your chambermaid there; for chambermaids must

needs know chaplains from other men, they are so used to
'em.

Lucy. Let's see: nay, I'll be sworn he has the canonical
smirk, and the filthy clammy palm of a chaplain.

Alithea. Well, most reverend doctor, pray let us make an
end of this fooling.

Harcourt. With all my soul, divine heavenly creature, when
you please.

Alithea. He speaks like a chaplain indeed.

Sparkish. Why, was there not soul, divine, heavenly, in
what he said?

Alithea. Once more, most impertinent black coat, cease
your persecution, and let us have a conclusion of this ridiculous love.

Harcourt. (Aside.) I had forgot, I must suit my style to my
coat, or I wear it in vain.

Alithea. I have no more patience left; let us make once an
end of this troublesome love, I say.

Harcourt. So be it, seraphic lady, when your honor shall
think it meet and convenient so to do.

Sparkish. 'Gad, I'm sure none but a chaplain could speak
so, I think.

Alithea. Let me tell you, sir, this dull trick will not serve
your turn; though you delay our marriage, you shall not
hinder it.

Harcourt. Far be it from me, munificent patroness, to delay your marriage; I desire nothing more than to marry you
presently, which I might do, if you yourself would; for my
noble, good-natured, and thrice generous patron here would
not hinder it.

Sparkish. No, poor man, not I, faith.

Harcourt. And now, madam, let me tell you plainly nobody
else shall marry you; by Heavens! I'll die first, for I'm sure
I should die after it.

Lucy. How his love has made him forget his function, as I
have seen it in real parsons!

Alithea. That was spoken like a chaplain too? now you
understand him, I hope.

Sparkish. Poor man, he takes it heinously to be refused; I
can't blame him, 'tis putting an indignity upon him, not to be
suffered; but you'll pardon me, madam, it shan't be; he shall
marry us; come away, pray, madam.

Lucy. Ha! ha! he! more ado! 'tis late.

Alithea. Invincible stupidity! I tell you, he would marry
me as your rival, not as your chaplain.

Sparkish. (Pulling her away.) Come, come, madam.

Lucy. I pray, madam, do not refuse this reverend divine

the honor and satisfaction of marrying you; for dare I say, he has set his heart upon't, good doctor.

Alithea. What can you hope or design by this?

Harcourt. (Aside.) I could answer her, a reprieve for a day only, oftener revokes a hasty doom. At worst, if she will not take mercy on me and let me marry her, I have at least the lover's second pleasure—hindering my rival's enjoyment, though but for a time.

Sparkish. Come, madam, 'tis e'en twelve o'clock, and my mother charged me never to be married out of the canonical hours. Come, come; Lord, here's such a deal of modesty, I warrant, the first day.

Lucy. Yes, an't please your worship, married women show all their modesty the first day, because married men show all their love the first day.   *Exeunt.*

SCENE II: *A Bedchamber in* PINCHWIFE'S *House.*

PINCHWIFE *and* Mrs. PINCHWIFE *discovered.*

Pinchwife. Come, tell me, I say.

Mrs. Pinchwife. Lord! han't I told it a hundred times over?

Pinchwife. (Aside.) I would try, if in the repetition of the ungrateful tale, I could find her altering it in the least circumstance; for if her story be false, she is so too.—*(Aloud.)* Come, how was't, baggage?

Mrs. Pinchwife. Lord, what pleasure you take to hear it sure!

Pinchwife. No, you take more in telling it I find; but speak, how was't?

Mrs. Pinchwife. He carried me up into the house next to the Exchange.

Pinchwife. So, and you two were only in the room!

Mrs. Pinchwife. Yes, for he sent away a youth that was there, for some dried fruit, and China oranges.

Pinchwife. Did he so? Damn him for it—and for——

Mrs. Pinchwife. But presently came up the gentlewoman of the house.

Pinchwife. Oh, 'twas well she did; but what did he do whilst the fruit came?

Mrs. Pinchwife. He kissed me a hundred times, and told me he fancied he kissed my fine sister, meaning me, you know, whom he said he loved with all his soul, and bid me to be sure to tell her so, and to desire her to be at her window by eleven of the clock this morning, and he would walk under it at that time.

Pinchwife. (Aside.) And he was as good as his word, very punctual; a pox reward him for't.

Mrs. Pinchwife. Well, and he said if you were not within, he would come up to her, meaning me, you know, bud, still.

Pinchwife. (Aside.) So—he knew her certainly; but for this confession, I am obliged to her simplicity.—*(Aloud.)* But what, you stood very still when he kissed you?

Mrs. Pinchwife. Yes, I warrant you; would you have had me discovered myself?

Pinchwife. But you told me he did some beastliness to you, as you call it; what was't?

Mrs. Pinchwife. Why, he put——

Pinchwife. What?

Mrs. Pinchwife. Why, he put the tip of his tongue between my lips, and so mousled me—and I said, I'd bite it.

Pinchwife. An eternal canker seize it, for a dog!

Mrs. Pinchwife. Nay, you need not be so angry with him neither, for to say the truth, he has the sweetest breath I ever knew.

Pinchwife. The devil! you were satisfied with it then, and would do it again.

Mrs. Pinchwife. Not unless he should force me.

Pinchwife. Force you, changeling! I tell you, no woman can be forced.

Mrs. Pinchwife. Yes, but she may sure, by such a one as he, for he's a proper, goodly, strong man; 'tis hard, let me tell you, to resist him.

Pinchwife. (Aside.) So, 'tis plain she loves him, yet she has not love enough to make her conceal it from me; but the sight of him will increase her aversion for me and love for him; and that love instruct her how to deceive me and satisfy him, all idiot as she is. Love! 'twas he gave women first their craft, their art of deluding. Out of Nature's hands they came plain, open, silly, and fit for slaves, as she and Heaven intended 'em; but damned Love—well—I must strangle that little monster whilst I can deal with him.—*(Aloud.)* Go fetch pen, ink, and paper out of the next room.

Mrs. Pinchwife. Yes, bud.   *Exit.*

Pinchwife. Why should women have more invention in love than men? It can only be because they have more desires, more soliciting passions, more lust, and more of the devil.

Enter Mrs. PINCHWIFE.

Come, minx, sit down and write.

Mrs. Pinchwife. Ay, dear bud, but I can't do't very well.

Pinchwife. I wish you could not at all.

Mrs. Pinchwife. But what should I write for?

Pinchwife. I'll have you write a letter to your lover.

Mrs. Pinchwife. Oh lord, to the fine gentleman a letter!

Pinchwife. Yes, to the fine gentleman.

Mrs. Pinchwife. Lord, you do but jeer: sure you jest.

Pinchwife. I am not so merry: come, write as I bid you.

Mrs. Pinchwife. What, do you think I am a fool?

Pinchwife. (Aside.) She's afraid I would not dictate any love to him, therefore she's unwilling.—*(Aloud.)* But you had best begin.

Mrs. Pinchwife. Indeed, and indeed, but I won't, so I won't.

Pinchwife. Why?

Mrs. Pinchwife. Because he's in town; you may send for him if you will.

Pinchwife. Very well, you would have him brought to you; is it come to this? I say, take the pen and write, or you'll provoke me.

Mrs. Pinchwife. Lord, what d'ye make a fool of me for? Don't I know that letters are never writ but from the country to London, and from London into the country? Now he's in town, and I am in town too; therefore I can't write to him, you know.

Pinchwife. (Aside.) So, I am glad it is no worse; she is innocent enough yet.—*(Aloud.)* Yes, you may, when your husband bids you, write letters to people that are in town.

Mrs. Pinchwife. Oh, may I so? then I'm satisfied.

Pinchwife. Come, begin: *(Dictates.)*—"Sir"——

Mrs. Pinchwife. Shan't I say, "Dear Sir?"—You know one says always something more than bare "Sir."

Pinchwife. Write as I bid you, or I will write whore with this penknife in your face.

Mrs. Pinchwife. Nay, good bud *(Writes.)*—"Sir"——

Pinchwife. "Though I suffered last night your nauseous, loathed kisses and embraces"—Write!

Mrs. Pinchwife. Nay, why should I say so? You know I told you he had a sweet breath.

Pinchwife. Write!

Mrs. Pinchwife. Let me but put out "loathed."

Pinchwife. Write, I say!

Mrs. Pinchwife. Well then.   *(Writes.)*

Pinchwife. Let's see, what have you writ?—*(Takes the paper and reads.)* "Though I suffered last night your kisses and embraces"—Thou impudent creature! where is "nauseous" and "loathed?"

Mrs. Pinchwife. I can't abide to write such filthy words.

Pinchwife. Once more write as I'd have you, and question

it not, or I will spoil thy writing with this. I will stab out those eyes that cause my mischief. *(Holds up the penknife.)*

Mrs. Pinchwife. Oh lord! I will.

Pinchwife. So—so—let's see now.—*(Reads.)* "Though I suffered last night your nauseous, loathed kisses and embraces"—go on—"yet I would not have you presume that you shall ever repeat them"—so—— *(She writes.)*

Mrs. Pinchwife. I have writ it.

Pinchwife. On, then—"I then concealed myself from your knowledge, to avoid your insolencies."—— *(She writes.)*

Mrs. Pinchwife. So——

Pinchwife. "The same reason, now I am out of your hands"—— *(She writes.)*

Mrs. Pinchwife. So——

Pinchwife. "Makes me own to you my unfortunate, though innocent frolic, of being in man's clothes"——*(She writes.)*

Mrs. Pinchwife. So——

Pinchwife. "That you may for evermore cease to pursue her, who hates and detests you"—— *(She writes on.)*

Mrs. Pinchwife. So—heigh! *(Sighs.)*

Pinchwife. What, do you sigh?—"detests you—as much as she loves her husband and her honor."

Mrs. Pinchwife. I vow, husband, he'll ne'er believe I should write such a letter.

Pinchwife. What, he'd expect a kinder from you? Come, now your name only.

Mrs. Pinchwife. What, shan't I say "Your most faithful humble servant till death?"

Pinchwife. No, tormenting fiend!—*(Aside.)* Her style, I find, would be very soft.—*(Aloud.)* Come, wrap it up now, whilst I go fetch wax and a candle; and write on the backside, "For Mr. Horner." *Exit.*

Mrs. Pinchwife. "For Mr. Horner."—So, I am glad he has told me his name. Dear Mr. Horner! but why should I send thee such a letter that will vex thee, and make thee angry with me?—Well, I will not send it.—Ay, but then my husband will kill me—for I see plainly he won't let me love Mr. Horner—but what care I for my husband?—I won't, so I won't, send poor Mr. Horner such a letter—But then my husband—but oh, what if I writ at bottom my husband made me write it?—Ay, but then my husband would see't—Can one have no shift? ah, a London woman would have had a hundred presently. Stay—what if I should write a letter, and wrap it up like this, and write upon't too? Ay, but then my husband would see't—I don't know what to do.—But yet evads I'll try, so I will—for I will not send this letter to poor Mr. Horner, come what will on't.

"Dear sweet Mr. Horner"—*(Writes and repeats what she writes.)*—so—"my husband would have me send you a base, rude, unmannerly letter; but I won't"—so—"and would have me forbid you loving me; but I won't"—so—"and would have me say to you, I hate you, poor Mr. Horner; but I won't tell a lie for him"—there—"for I'm sure if you and I were in the country at cards together"—so—"I could not help treading on your toe under the table"—so—"or rubbing knees with you, and staring in your face, till you saw me"—very well—"and then looking down, and blushing for an hour together"—so—"but I must make haste before my husband comes: and now he has taught me to write letters, you shall have longer ones from me, who am, dear, dear, poor, dear Mr. Horner, your most humble friend, and servant to command till death,—Margery Pinchwife."

Stay, I must give him a hint at bottom—so—now wrap it up just like t'other—so—now write "For Mr. Horner"—But oh now, what shall I do with it? for here comes my husband.

Enter PINCHWIFE.

Pinchwife. (Aside.) I have been detained by a sparkish coxcomb who pretended a visit to me; but I fear 'twas to my wife—*(Aloud.)* What, have you done?

Mrs. Pinchwife. Ay, ay, bud, just now.

Pinchwife. Let's see't: what d'ye tremble for? what, you would not have it go?

Mrs. Pinchwife. Here—*(Aside.)* No, I must not give him that: so I had been served if I had given him this.

                    (He opens and reads the first letter.)
Pinchwife. Come, where's the wax and seal?

Mrs. Pinchwife. (Aside.) Lord, what shall I do now? Nay, then I have it—*(Aloud.)* Pray let me see't. Lord, you will think me so arrant a fool, I cannot seal a letter; I will do't, so I will.

        (Snatches the letter from him, changes it for the other, seals it, and delivers it to him.)
Pinchwife. Nay, I believe you will learn that, and other things too, which I would not have you.

Mrs. Pinchwife. So, han't I done it curiously?—*(Aside.)* I think I have; there's my letter going to Mr. Horner, since he'll needs have me send letters to folks.

Pinchwife. 'Tis very well; but I warrant, you would not have it go now?

Mrs. Pinchwife. Yes, indeed, but I would, bud, now.

Pinchwife. Well, you are a good girl then. Come, let me

lock you up in your chamber, till I come back; and be sure you come not within three strides of the window when I am gone, for I have a spy in the street.—*(Exit* Mrs. PINCHWIFE, PINCHWIFE *locks the door.)* At least, 'tis fit she thinks so. If we do not cheat women, they'll cheat us, and fraud may be justly used with secret enemies, of which a wife is the most dangerous; and he that has a handsome one to keep, and a frontier town, must provide against treachery, rather than open force. Now I have secured all within, I'll deal with the foe without, with false intelligence. *Holds up the letter. Exit.*

SCENE III: HORNER'S *Lodging.*

Enter HORNER *and* QUACK.

Quack. Well, sir, how fadges[20] the new design? have you not the luck of all your brother projectors, to deceive only yourself at last?

Horner. No, good domine doctor, I deceive you, it seems, and others too; for the grave matrons, and old, rigid husbands think me as unfit for love, as they are; but their wives, sisters, and daughters know, some of 'em, better things already.

Quack. Already!

Horner. Already, I say. Last night I was drunk with half-a-dozen of your civil persons, as you call 'em, and people of honor, and so was made free of their society and dressing-rooms forever hereafter; and am already come to the privileges of sleeping upon their pallets, warming smocks, tying shoes and garters, and the like, doctor, already, already, doctor.

Quack. You have made good use of your time, sir.

Horner. I tell thee, I am now no more interruption to 'em, when they sing, or talk bawdy, than a little squab French page who speaks no English.

Quack. But do civil persons and women of honor drink, and sing bawdy songs?

Horner. Oh, amongst friends, amongst friends. For your bigots in honor are just like those in religion; they fear the eye of the world more than the eye of Heaven; and think there is no virtue, but railing at vice, and no sin, but giving scandal. They rail at a poor, little, kept player, and keep themselves some young, modest pulpit comedian to be privy to their sins in their closets, not to tell 'em of them in their chapels.

Quack. Nay, the truth on't is, priests, amongst the women now, have quite got the better of us lay-confessors, physicians.

Horner. And they are rather their patients; but——

        Enter Lady FIDGET, *looking about her.*

Now we talk of women of honor, here comes one. Step behind the screen there, and but observe, if I have not particular privileges with the women of reputation already, doctor, already.   (QUACK *retires.*)
    Lady Fidget. Well, Horner, am not I a woman of honor? you see, I'm as good as my word.
    Horner. And you shall see, madam, I'll not be behindhand with you in honor; and I'll be as good as my word too, if you please but to withdraw into the next room.
    Lady Fidget. But first, my dear sir, you must promise to have a care of my dear honor.
    Horner. If you talk a word more of your honor, you'll make me incapable to wrong it. To talk of honor in the mysteries of love, is like talking of Heaven or the Diety, in an operation of witchcraft, just when you are employing the devil: it makes the charm impotent.
    Lady Fidget. Nay, fy! let us not be smutty. But you talk of mysteries and bewitching to me; I don't understand you.
    Horner. I tell you, madam, the word money in a mistress's mouth, at such a nick of time, is not a more disheartening sound to a younger brother, than that of honor to an eager lover like myself.
    Lady Fidget. But you can't blame a lady of my reputation to be chary.
    Horner. Chary! I have been chary of it already, by the report I have caused of myself.
    Lady Fidget. Ay, but if you should ever let other women know that dear secret, it would come out. Nay, you must have a great care of your conduct; for my acquaintance are so censorious (oh, 'tis a wicked, censorious world, Mr. Horner!), I say, are so censorious, and detracting, that perhaps they'll talk to the prejudice of my honor, though you should not let them know the dear secret.
    Horner. Nay, madam, rather than they shall prejudice your honor, I'll prejudice theirs; and, to serve you, I'll lie with 'em all, make the secret their own, and then they'll keep it. I am a Machiavel in love, madam.
    Lady Fidget. Oh, no, sir, not that way.
    Horner. Nay, the devil take me, if censorious women are to be silenced any other way.
    Lady Fidget. A secret is better kept, I hope, by a single person than a multitude; therefore pray do not trust anybody else with it, dear, dear Mr. Horner.   (*Embracing him.*)

Enter Sir JASPER FIDGET.

Sir Jasper. How now!

Lady Fidget. (Aside.) Oh my husband!—prevented—and what's almost as bad, found with my arms about another man —that will appear too much—what shall I say?—*(Aloud.)* Sir Jasper, come hither: I am trying if Mr. Horner were ticklish, and he's as ticklish as can be. I love to torment the confounded toad; let you and I tickle him.

Sir Jasper. No, your ladyship will tickle him better without me I suppose. But is this your buying china? I thought you had been at the china-house.

Horner (Aside.) China-house! that's my cue, I must take it. —*(Aloud.)* A pox! can't you keep your impertinent wives at home? Some men are troubled with the husbands, but I with the wives; but I'd have you to know, since I cannot be your journeyman by night, I will not be your drudge by day, to squire your wife about, and be your man of straw, or scarecrow only to pies and jays, that would be nibbling at your forbidden fruit; I shall be shortly the hackney gentleman-usher of the town.

Sir Jasper. (Aside.) He! he! he! poor fellow, he's in the right on't, faith. To squire women about for other folks is as ungrateful an employment, as to tell money for other folks. —*(Aloud.)* He! he! he! be'n't angry, Horner.

Lady Fidget. No, 'tis I have more reason to be angry, who am left by you to go abroad indecently alone; or, what is more indecent, to pin myself upon such ill-bred people of your acquaintance as this is.

Sir Jasper. Nay, prithee, what has he done?

Lady Fidget. Nay, he has done nothing.

Sir Jasper. But what d'ye take ill, if he has done nothing?

Lady Fidget. Ha! ha! ha! faith, I can't but laugh however; why, d'ye think the unmannerly toad would come down to me to the coach? I was fain to come up to fetch him, or go without him, which I was resolved not to do; for he knows china very well, and has himself very good, but will not let me see it, lest I should beg some; but I will find it out, and have what I came for yet.

Horner. (Apart to Lady FIDGET, *as he follows her to the door.)* Lock the door, madam.—*(Exit* Lady FIDGET, *and locks the door.)*—*(Aloud.)* So, she has got into my chamber and locked me out. Oh the impertinency of woman-kind! Well, Sir Jasper, plain-dealing is a jewel; if ever you suffer your wife to trouble me again here, she shall carry you home a pair of horns; by my lord mayor she shall; though I cannot furnish you myself, you are sure, yet I'll find a way.

Sir Jasper. Ha! ha! he!—(*Aside.*) At my first coming in, and finding her arms about him, tickling him it seems, I was half jealous, but now I see my folly.—(*Aloud.*) He! he! he! poor Horner.

Horner. Nay, though you laugh now, 'twill be my turn ere long. Oh women, more impertinent, more cunning, and more mischievous than their monkeys, and to me almost as ugly! —Now is she throwing my things about and rifling all I have; but I'll get in to her the back way, and so rifle her for it.

Sir Jasper. Ha! ha! ha! poor angry Horner.

Horner. Stay here a little, I'll ferret her out to you presently, I warrant.   *Exit at the other door.*
    (Sir JASPER *talks through the door to his* Wife, *she answers from within.*)

Sir Jasper. Wife! my Lady Fidget! wife! he is coming into you the back way.

Lady Fidget. Let him come, and welcome, which way he will.

Sir Jasper. He'll catch you, and use you roughly, and be too strong for you.

Lady Fidget. Don't you trouble yourself, let him if he can.

Quack. (*Aside.*) This indeed I could not have believed from him, nor any but my own eyes.

Enter Mrs. SQUEAMISH.

Mrs. Squeamish. Where's this woman-hater, this toad, this ugly, greasy, dirty sloven?

Sir Jasper. (*Aside.*) So, the women all will have him ugly: methinks he is a comely person, but his wants make his form contemptible to 'em; and 'tis e'en as my wife said yesterday, talking of him, that a proper handsome eunuch was as ridiculous a thing as a gigantic coward.

Mrs. Squeamish. Sir Jasper, your servant: where is the odious beast?

Sir Jasper. He's within in his chamber, with my wife; she's playing the wag with him.

Mrs. Squeamish. Is she so? and he's a clownish beast; he'll give her no quarter, he'll play the wag with her again, let me tell you: come, let's go help her.—What, the door's locked?

Sir Jasper. Ay, my wife locked it.

Mrs. Squeamish. Did she so? let's break it open then.

Sir Jasper. No, no, he'll do her no hurt.

Mrs. Squeamish. (*Aside.*) But is there no other way to get in to 'em? wither goes this? I will disturb 'em.
                     Exit at another door.

Enter Old Lady SQUEAMISH.

Lady Squeamish. Where is this harlotry, this impudent baggage, this rambling tomrigg? Oh Sir Jasper, I'm glad to see you here; did you not see my vile grandchild come in hither just now?

Sir Jasper. Yes.

Lady Squeamish. Ay, but where is she then? where is she? Lord, Sir Jasper, I have e'en rattled myself to pieces in pursuit of her: but can you tell what she makes here? they say below, no woman lodges here.

Sir Jasper. No.

Lady Squeamish. No! what does she here then? say, if it be not a woman's lodging, what makes she here? But are you sure no woman lodges here?

Sir Jasper. No, nor no man neither, this is Mr. Horner's lodging.

Lady Squeamish. Is it so, are you sure?

Sir Jasper. Yes, yes.

Lady Squeamish. So; then there's no hurt in't, I hope. But where is he?

Sir Jasper. He's in the next room with my wife.

Lady Squeamish. Nay, if you trust him with your wife, I may with my Biddy. They say, he's a merry harmless man now, e'en as harmless a man as ever came out of Italy with a good voice,[21] and as pretty, harmless company for a lady, as a snake without his teeth.

Sir Jasper. Ay, ay, poor man.

Enter MRS. SQUEAMISH.

Mrs. Squeamish. I can't find 'em.—Oh, are you here, grandmother? I followed, you must know, my Lady Fidget hither; 'tis the prettiest lodging, and I have been staring on the prettiest pictures——

Enter Lady FIDGET *with a piece of china in her hand, and* HORNER *following.*

Lady Fidget. And I have been toiling and moiling for the prettiest piece of china, my dear.

Horner. Nay, she has been too hard for me, do what I could.

Mrs. Squeamish. Oh, lord, I'll have some china too. Good Mr. Horner, don't think to give other people china, and me none; come in with me too.

Horner. Upon my honor, I have none left now.

Mrs. Squeamish. Nay, nay, I have known you deny your china before now, but you shan't put me off so. Come.

Horner. This lady had the last there.

Lady Fidget. Yes indeed, madam, to my certain knowledge, he has no more left.

Mrs. Squeamish. Oh, but it may be he may have some you could not find.

Lady Fidget. What, d'ye think if he had had any left I would not have had it too? for we women of quality never think we have china enough.

Horner. Do not take it ill, I cannot make china for you all, but I will have a roll-waggon[22] for you too, another time.

Mrs. Squeamish. Thank you, dear toad.

Lady Fidget. (Aside to HORNER.*)* What do you mean by that promise?

Horner. (Aside to Lady FIDGET.*)* Alas, she has an innocent, literal understanding.

Lady Squeamish. Poor Mr. Horner! he has enough to do to please you all, I see.

Horner. Ay, madam, you see how they use me.

Lady Squeamish. Poor gentleman, I pity you.

Horner. I thank you, madam: I could never find pity, but from such reverend ladies as you are; the young ones will never spare a man.

Mrs. Squeamish. Come, come, beast, and go dine with us; for we shall want a man at ombre after dinner.

Horner. That's all their use of me, madam, you see.

Mrs. Squeamish. Come, sloven, I'll lead you, to be sure of you.   *(Pulls him by the cravat.)*

Lady Squeamish. Alas, poor man, how she tugs him! Kiss, kiss her; that's the way to make such nice women quiet.

Horner. No, madam, that remedy is worse than the torment; they know I dare suffer anything rather than do it.

Lady Squeamish. Prithee kiss her, and I'll give you her picture in little, that you admired so last night; prithee do.

Horner. Well, nothing but that could bribe me: I love a woman only in effigy, and good painting as much as I hate them.—I'll do't, for I could adore the devil well painted.

                           (Kisses Mrs. SQUEAMISH.*)*

Mrs. Squeamish. Foh, you filthy toad! nay, now I've done jesting.

Lady Squeamish. Ha! ha! ha! I told you so.

Mrs. Squeamish. Foh! a kiss of his——

Sir Jasper. Has no more hurt in't than one of my spaniel's.

Mrs. Squeamish. Nor no more good neither.

Quack. (Aside.) I will now believe anything he tells me.

Enter PINCHWIFE.

Lady Fidget. Oh lord, here's a man! Sir Jasper, my mask, my mask! I would not be seen here for the world.

Sir Jasper. What, not when I am with you?

Lady Fidget. No, no, my honor—let's be gone.

Mrs. Squeamish. Oh grandmother, let's be gone; make haste, make haste, I know not how he may censure us.

Lady Fidget. Be found in the lodging of anything like a man!—Away.

> *Exeunt* Sir JASPER FIDGET, Lady FIDGET, Old Lady
> SQUEAMISH, *and* Mrs. SQUEAMISH.

Quack. (Aside.) What's here? another cuckold? he looks like one, and none else sure have any business with him.

Horner. Well, what brings my dear friend hither?

Pinchwife. Your impertinency.

Horner. My impertinency!—why, you gentlemen that have got handsome wives, think you have a privilege of saying anything to your friends, and are as brutish as if you were our creditors.

Pinchwife. No, sir, I'll ne'er trust you any way.

Horner. But why not, dear Jack? why diffide in me thou know'st so well?

Pinchwife. Because I do know you so well.

Horner. Han't I been always thy friend, honest Jack, always ready to serve thee, in love or battle, before thou wert married, and am so still?

Pinchwife. I believe so, you would be my second now, indeed.

Horner. Well then, dear Jack, why so unkind, so grum, so strange to me? Come, prithee kiss me, dear rogue: gad, I was always, I say, and am still as much thy servant as——

Pinchwife. As I am yours, sir. What, you would send a kiss to my wife, is that it?

Horner. So, there 'tis—a man can't show his friendship to a married man, but presently he talks of his wife to you. Prithee, let thy wife alone, and let thee and I be all one, as we were wont. What, thou art as shy of my kindness as a Lombard Street alderman of a courtier's civility at Locket's![23]

Pinchwife. But you are overkind to me, as kind as if I were your cuckold already; yet I must confess you ought to be kind and civil to me, since I am so kind, so civil to you, as to bring you this; look you there, sir.   *(Delivers him a letter.)*

Horner. What is't?

Pinchwife. Only a love letter, sir.

Horner. From whom?—how! this is from your wife—hum —and hum—   *(Reads.)*

Pinchwife. Even from my wife, sir: am I not wondrous kind and civil to you now too?—*(Aside.)* But you'll not think her so.

Horner. (Aside.) Ha! is this a trick of his or hers?

Pinchwife. The gentleman's surprised I find.—What, you expected a kinder letter?

Horner. No faith, not I, how could I?

Pinchwife. Yes, yes, I'm sure you did. A man so well made as you are, must needs be disappointed, if the women declare not their passion at first sight or opportunity.

Horner. (*Aside.*) But what should this mean? Stay, the postscript. (*Reads aside.*) "Be sure you love me, whatsoever my husband says to the contrary, and let him not see this, lest he should come home and pinch me, or kill my squirrel." —It seems he knows not what the letter contains.

Pinchwife. Come, ne'er wonder at it so much.

Horner. Faith, I can't help it.

Pinchwife. Now, I think I have deserved your infinite friendship and kindness, and have showed myself sufficiently an obliging kind friend and husband; am I not so, to bring a letter from my wife to her gallant?

Horner. Ay, the devil take me, art thou, the most obliging, kind friend and husband in the world, ha! ha!

Pinchwife. Well, you may be merry, sir; but in short I must tell you, sir, my honor will suffer no jesting.

Horner. What dost thou mean?

Pinchwife. Does the letter want a comment? Then, know, sir, though I have been so civil a husband, as to bring you a letter from my wife, to let you kiss and court her to my face, I will not be a cuckold, sir, I will not.

Horner. Thou art mad with jealousy. I never saw thy wife in my life but at the play yesterday, and I know not if it were she or no. I court her, kiss her!

Pinchwife. I will not be a cuckold, I say; there will be danger in making me a cuckold.

Horner. Why, wert thou not well cured of thy last clap?

Pinchwife. I wear a sword.

Horner. It should be taken from thee, less thou should'st do thyself a mischief with it; thou art mad, man.

Pinchwife. As mad as I am, and as merry as you are, I must have more reason from you ere we part. I say again, though you kissed and courted last night my wife in man's clothes, as she confesses in her letter——

Horner. (*Aside.*) Ha!

Pinchwife. Both she and I say, you must not design it again, for you have mistaken your woman, as you have done your man.

Horner. (*Aside.*) Oh—I understand something now— (*Aloud.*) Was that thy wife! Why would'st thou not tell me 'twas she? Faith, my freedom with her was your fault, not mine.

Pinchwife. (Aside.) Faith, so 'twas.

Horner. Fy! I'd never do't to a woman before her husband's face, sure.

Pinchwife. But I had rather you should do't to my wife before my face, than behind my back; and that you shall never do.

Horner. No—you will hinder me.

Pinchwife. If I would not hinder you, you see by her letter she would.

Horner. Well, I must e'en acquiesce then, and be contented with what she writes.

Pinchwife. I'll assure you 'twas voluntarily writ; I had no hand in't you may believe me.

Horner. I do believe thee, faith.

Pinchwife. And I believe her too, for she's an innocent creature, has no dissembling in her: and so fare you well, sir.

Horner. Pray, however, present my humble service to her, and tell her I will obey her letter to a tittle, and fulfil her desires, be what they will, or with what difficulty soever I do't; and you shall be no more jealous of me, I warrant her, and you.

Pinchwife. Well then, fare you well; and play with any man's honor but mine, kiss any man's wife but mine, and welcome.   *Exit.*

Horner. Ha! ha! ha! doctor.

Quack. It seems, he has not heard the report of you, or does not believe it.

Horner. Ha! ha!—now, doctor, what think you?

Quack. Pray let's see the letter—hum—"for—dear—love you——"   *(Reads the letter.)*

Horner. I wonder how she could contrive it! What say'st thou to't? 'tis an original.

Quack. So are your cuckolds too originals: for they are like no other common cuckolds, and I will henceforth believe it not impossible for you to cuckold the Grand Signior amidst his guards of eunuchs, that I say.

Horner. And I say for the letter, 'tis the first love-letter that ever was without flames, darts, fates, destinies, lying and dissembling in't.

Enter SPARKISH *pulling in* PINCHWIFE.

Sparkish. Come back, you are a pretty brother-in-law, neither go to church nor to dinner with your sister bride!

Pinchwife. My sister denies her marriage, and you see is gone away from you dissatisfied.

Sparkish. Pshaw! upon a foolish scruple, that our parson

was not in lawful orders, and did not say all the common-prayer; but 'tis her modesty only I believe. But let all women be never so modest the first day, they'll be sure to come to themselves by night, and I shall have enough of her then. In the meantime, Harry Horner, you must dine with me: I keep my wedding at my aunt's in the Piazza.

Horner. Thy wedding! what stale maid has lived to despair of a husband, or what young one of a gallant?

Sparkish. Oh, your servant, sir—this gentleman's sister then,—no stale maid.

Horner. I'm sorry for't.

Pinchwife. (*Aside*.) How comes he so concerned for her?

Sparkish. You sorry for't? why, do you know any ill by her?

Horner. No, I know none but by thee; 'tis for her sake, not yours, and another man's sake that might have hoped, I thought.

Sparkish. Another man! another man! what is his name?

Horner. (*Aside*.) Nay, since 'tis past, he shall be nameless. —Poor Harcourt! I am sorry thou hast missed her.

Pinchwife. (*Aside*.) He seems to be much troubled at the match.

Sparkish. Prithee, tell me—Nay, you shan't go, brother.

Pinchwife. I must of necessity, but I'll come to you to dinner.   *Exit*.

Sparkish. But, Harry, what, have I a rival in my wife already? But with all my heart, for he may be of use to me hereafter; for though my hunger is now my sauce, and I can fall on heartily without, the time will come when a rival will be as good sauce for a married man to a wife, as an orange to veal.

Horner. Oh thou damned rogue! thou hast set my teeth on edge with thy orange.

Sparkish. Then let's to dinner—there I was with you again. Come.

Horner. But who dines with thee?

Sparkish. My friends and relations, my brother Pinch-wife, you see, of your acquaintance.

Horner. And his wife?

Sparkish. No, 'gad, he'll ne'er let her come amongst us good fellows; your stingy country coxcomb keeps his wife from his friends as he does his little firkin of ale for his own drinking, and a gentleman can't get a smack on't; but his servants, when his back is turned, broach it at their pleasures, and dust it away, ha! ha! ha!—'Gad, I am witty, I think, considering I was married today, by the world; but come——

Horner. No, I will not dine with you, unless you can fetch her too.

Sparkish. Pshaw! what pleasure canst thou have with women now, Harry?

Horner. My eyes are not gone; I love a good prospect yet, and will not dine with you unless she does too; go fetch her therefore, but do not tell her husband 'tis for my sake.

Sparkish. Well, I'll go try what I can do; in the meantime, come away to my aunt's lodging, 'tis in the way to Pinchwife's.

Horner. The poor woman has called for aid, and stretched forth her hand, doctor; I cannot but help her over the pale out of the briars.   *Exeunt.*

SCENE IV: *A Room in* Pinchwife's *House.*

Mrs. Pinchwife *alone, leaning on her elbow.—A table, pen, ink, and paper.*

Mrs. Pinchwife. Well, 'tis e'en so, I have got the London disease they call love; I am sick of my husband, and for my gallant. I have heard this distemper called a fever, but methinks 'tis like an ague; for when I think of my husband, I tremble, and am in a cold sweat, and have inclinations to vomit; but when I think of my gallant, dear Mr. Horner, my hot fit comes, and I am all in a fever indeed; and, as in other fevers, my own chamber is tedious to me, and I would fain be removed to his, and then methinks I should be well. Ah, poor Mr. Horner! Well, I cannot, will not stay here; therefore I'll make an end of my letter to him, which shall be a finer letter than my last, because I have studied it like anything. Oh sick, sick!   *(Takes the pen and writes.)*

Enter Pinchwife, *who seeing her writing, steals softly behind her and looking over her shoulder, snatches the paper from her.*

Pinchwife. What, writing more letters?

Mrs. Pinchwife. Oh lord, bud, why d'ye fright me so?

         (She offers to run out; he stops her, and reads.)

Pinchwife. How's this? nay, you shall not stir, madam:— "Dear, dear, dear Mr. Horner"—very well—I have taught you to write letters to good purpose—but let us see't. "First, I am to beg your pardon for my boldness in writing to you, which I'd have you to know I would not have done, had not you said first you loved me so extremely, which if you do,

you will suffer me to lie in the arms of another man whom I
loathe, nauseate, and detest."——Now you can write these
filthy words. But what follows?——"Therefore, I hope you will
speedily find some way to free me from this unfortunate
match, which was never, I assure you, of my choice, but I'm
afraid 'tis already too far gone; however, if you love me, as
I do you, you will try what you can do; but you must help
me away before tomorrow, or else, alas! I shall be forever
out of your reach, for I can defer no longer our—our——"
what is to follow "our"?—speak, what—our journey into the
country I suppose—Oh woman, damned woman! and Love,
damned Love, their old tempter! for this is one of his mir-
acles; in a moment he can make those blind that could see,
and those see that were blind, those dumb that could speak,
and those prattle who were dumb before; nay, what is more
than all, make these dough-baked, senseless, indocile animals,
women, too hard for us their politic lords and rulers, in a
moment. But make an end to your letter, and then I'll make
an end of you thus, and all my plagues together.

(Draws his sword.)

Mrs. Pinchwife. Oh lord, Oh lord, you are such a passionate man, bud!

Enter SPARKISH.

Sparkish. How now, what's here to do?
Pinchwife. This fool here now!
Sparkish. What! drawn upon your wife? You should never
do that, but at night in the dark, when you can't hurt her.
This is my sister-in-law, is it not? ay, faith, e'en our country
Margery *(pulls aside her handkerchief);* one may know her.
Come, she and you must go dine with me; dinner's ready,
come. But where's my wife? is she not come home yet? where
is she?
Pinchwife. Making you a cuckold; 'tis that they all do, as
soon as they can.
Sparkish. What, the wedding-day? no, a wife that designs
to make a cully of her husband will be sure to let him win
the first stake of love, by the world. But come, they stay din-
ner for us: come, I'll lead down our Margery.
Pinchwife. No—sir, go, we'll follow you.
Sparkish. I will not wag without you.
Pinchwife. (Aside.) This coxcomb is a sensible torment to
me amidst the greatest in the world.
Sparkish. Come, come, Madam Margery.
Pinchwife. No; I'll lead her my way: what, would you
treat your friends with mine, for want of your own wife?—

(Leads her to the other door, and locks her in and returns.)
I am contented my rage should take breath——

Sparkish. (Aside.) I told Horner this.

Pinchwife. Come now.

Sparkish. Lord, how shy you are of your wife! but let me tell you, brother, we men of wit have amongst us a saying, that cuckolding, like the small-pox, comes with a fear; and you may keep your wife as much as you will out of danger of infection, but if her constitution incline her to't, she'll have it sooner or later, by the world, say they.

Pinchwife. (Aside.) What a thing is a cuckold, that every fool can make him ridiculous!——*(Aloud.)* Well, sir—but let me advise you, now you are come to be concerned, because you suspect the danger, not to neglect the means to prevent it, especially when the greatest share of the malady will light upon your own head, for

> Hows'e'er the kind wife's belly comes to swell,
> The husband breeds for her, and first is ill.

Exeunt.

ACT V

SCENE I: PINCHWIFE'S *House.*

Enter PINCHWIFE *and* Mrs. PINCHWIFE. *A table and candle.*

Pinchwife. Come, take the pen and make an end of the letter, just as you intended; if you are false in a tittle, I shall soon perceive it, and punish you as you deserve.—*(Lays his hand on his sword.)* Write what was to follow—let's see— "You must make haste, and help me away before to-morrow, or else I shall be for ever out of your reach, for I can defer no longer our"—What follows "our"?

Mrs. Pinchwife. Must all out, then, bud?—Look you there, then.   *(Mrs.* PINCHWIFE *takes the pen and writes.)*

Pinchwife. Let's see—"For I can defer no longer our— wedding—Your slighted Alithea."—What's the meaning of this? my sister's name to't? speak, unriddle.

Mrs. Pinchwife. Yes, indeed, bud.

Pinchwife. But why her name to't? speak—speak, I say.

Mrs. Pinchwife. Ay, but you'll tell her then again. If you would not tell her again——

Pinchwife. I will not:—I am stunned, my head turns round.—Speak.

Mrs. Pinchwife. Won't you tell her, indeed, and indeed?

Pinchwife. No; speak, I say.

Mrs. Pinchwife. She'll be angry with me; but I had rather she should be angry with me than you, bud; and, to tell you the truth, 'twas she made me write the letter, and taught me what I should write.

Pinchwife. (Aside.) Ha! I thought the style was somewhat better than her own.—*(Aloud.)* Could she come to teach you, since I had locked you up alone?

Mrs. Pinchwife. Oh, through the key-hole, bud.

Pinchwife. But why should she make you write a letter for her to him, since she can write herself?

Mrs. Pinchwife. Why, she said because—for I was unwilling to do it——

Pinchwife. Because what—because?

Mrs. Pinchwife. Because, lest Mr. Horner should be cruel, and refuse her; or be vain afterwards, and show the letter, she might disown it, the hand not being hers.

Pinchwife. (Aside.) How's this? Ha!—then I think I shall come to myself again.—This changeling could not invent this lie: but if she could, why should she? she might think I should soon discover it.—Stay—now I think on't too, Horner said he was sorry she had married Sparkish; and her disowning her marriage to me makes me think she has evaded it for Horner's sake: yet why should she take this course? But men in love are fools; women may well be so—*(Aloud.)* But hark you, madam, your sister went out in the morning, and I have not seen her within since.

Mrs. Pinchwife. Alack-a-day, she has been crying all day above, it seems, in a corner.

Pinchwife. Where is she? let me speak with her.

Mrs. Pinchwife. (Aside.) Oh lord, then she'll discover all! —*(Aloud.)* Pray hold, bud; what, d'ye mean to discover me? she'll know I have told you then. Pray, bud, let me talk with her first.

Pinchwife. I must speak with her, to know whether Horner ever made her any promise, and whether she be married to Sparkish or no.

Mrs. Pinchwife. Pray, dear bud, don't till I have spoken with her and told her that I have told you all; for she'll kill me else.

Pinchwife. Go then, and bid her come out to me.

Mrs. Pinchwife. Yes, yes, bud.

Pinchwife. Let me see——

Mrs. Pinchwife. (Aside.) I'll go, but she is not within to come to him: I have just got time to know of Lucy her maid, who first set me on work, what lie I shall tell next; for I am e'en at my wit's end.   *Exit.*

Pinchwife. Well, I resolve it, Horner shall have her: I'd rather give him my sister than lend him my wife; and such an alliance will prevent his pretensions to my wife, sure. I'll make him of kin to her, and then he won't care for her.

Enter Mrs. PINCHWIFE.

Mrs. Pinchwife. Oh lord, bud! I told you what anger you would make me with my sister.

Pinchwife. Won't she come hither?

Mrs. Pinchwife. No, no. Lack-a-day, she's ashamed to look you in the face: and she says, if you go in to her, she'll run away downstairs, and shamefully go herself to Mr. Horner, who has promised her marriage, she says; and she will have no other, so she won't.

Pinchwife. Did he so?—promise her marriage!—then she shall have no other. Go tell her so; and if she will come and discourse with me a little concerning the means, I will about it immediately. Go.—(*Exit* Mrs. PINCHWIFE.) His estate is equal to Sparkish's, and his extraction much better than his, as his parts are; but my chief reason is, I'd rather be akin to him by the name of brother-in-law than that of cuckold.

Enter Mrs. PINCHWIFE.

Well, what says she now?

Mrs. Pinchwife. Why, she says she would only have you lead her to Horner's lodging; with whom she first will discourse the matter before she talks with you, which yet she cannot do; for alack, poor creature, she says she can't so much as look you in the face, therefore, she'll come to you in a mask. And you must excuse her, if she make you no answer to any question of yours, till you have brought her to Mr. Horner; and if you will not chide her, nor question her, she'll come out to you immediately.

Pinchwife. Let her come: I will not speak a word to her, nor require a word from her.

Mrs. Pinchwife. Oh, I forgot: besides, she says she cannot look you in the face, though through a mask; therefore would desire you to put out the candle.

Pinchwife. I agree to all. Let her make haste.—There, 'tis out.—(*Puts out the candle. Exit* Mrs. PINCHWIFE.) My case is something better: I'd rather fight with Horner for not lying with my sister, than for lying with my wife; and of the two, I had rather find my sister too forward than my wife. I expected no other from her free education, as she calls it, and her passion for the town. Well, wife and sister are names

which make us expect love and duty, pleasure and comfort;
but we find 'em plagues and torments, and are equally,
though differently, troublesome to their keeper; for we have as
much ado to get people to lie with our sisters as to keep 'em
from lying with our wives.

Enter Mrs. PINCHWIFE *masked, and in hoods and scarfs, and
a nightgown and petticoat of* ALITHEA'S.

What, are you come, sister? let us go then.—But first, let me
lock up my wife. Mrs. Margery, where are you?

   Mrs. Pinchwife. Here, bud.

   Pinchwife. Come hither, that I may lock you up: get you
in.—(*Locks the door.*) Come, sister, where are you now?

   (Mrs. PINCHWIFE *give him her hand; but when he lets her
   go, she steals softly on to the other side of him, and
   is led away by him for his sister,* ALITHEA.)

SCENE II: HORNER'S *Lodging.*

HORNER *and* QUACK.

   Quack. What, all alone? not so much as one of your cuckolds here, nor one of their wives! They use to take their
turns with you, as if they were to watch you.

   Horner. Yes, it often happens that a cuckold is but his
wife's spy, and is more upon family duty when he is with
her gallant abroad, hindering his pleasure, than when he is
at home with her playing the gallant. But the hardest duty a
married woman imposes upon a lover is keeping her husband
company always.

   Quack. And his fondness wearies you almost as soon as
hers.

   Horner. A pox! keeping a cuckold company, after you
have had his wife, is as tiresome as the company of a country squire to a witty fellow of the town, when he has got all
his money.

   Quack. And as at first a man makes a friend of the husband to get the wife, so at last you are fain to fall out with
the wife to be rid of the husband.

   Horner. Ay, most cuckold-makers are true courtiers; when
once a poor man has cracked his credit for 'em, they can't
abide to come near him.

   Quack. But at first, to draw him in, are so sweet, so kind,
so dear! just as you are to Pinchwife. But what becomes of
that intrigue with his wife?

   Horner. A pox! he's as surly as an alderman that has been

bit; and since he's so coy, his wife's kindness is in vain, for she's a silly innocent.

Quack. Did she not send you a letter by him?

Horner. Yes; but that's a riddle I have not yet solved. Allow the poor creature to be willing, she is silly too, and he keeps her up so close——

Quack. Yes, so close, that he makes her but the more willing, and adds but revenge to her love; which two, when met, seldom fail of satisfying each other one way or another.

Horner. What! here's the man we are talking of, I think.

Enter PINCHWIFE, *leading in* Mrs. PINCHWIFE, *masked, muffled, and in her sister's gown.*

Pshaw!

Quack. Bringing his wife to you is the next thing to bringing a love-letter from her.

Horner. What means this?

Pinchwife. The last time, you know, sir, I brought you a love-letter; now, you see, a mistress; I think you'll say I am a civil man to you.

Horner. Ay, the devil take me, will I say thou art the civilest man I ever met with; and I have known some. I fancy I understand thee now better than I did the letter. But, hark thee, in thy ear——

Pinchwife. What?

Horner. Nothing but the usual question, man: is she sound, on thy word?

Pinchwife. What, you take her for a wench, and me for a pimp?

Horner. Pshaw! wench and pimp, paw[24] words; I know thou art an honest fellow, and hast a great acquaintance among the ladies, and perhaps hast made love for me, rather than let me make love to thy wife.

Pinchwife. Come, sir, in short, I am for no fooling.

Horner. Nor I neither: there prithee, let's see her face presently. Make her show, man: art thou sure I don't know her?

Pinchwife. I am sure you do know her.

Horner. A pox! why dost thou bring her to me then?

Pinchwife. Because she's a relation of mine——

Horner. Is she, faith, man? then thou art still more civil and obliging, dear rogue.

Pinchwife. Who desired me to bring her to you.

Horner. Then she is obliging, dear rogue.

Pinchwife. You'll make her welcome for my sake, I hope.

Horner. I hope she is handsome enough to make herself welcome. Prithee let her unmask.

Pinchwife. Do you speak to her; she would never be ruled by me.

Horner. Madam—— (Mrs. PINCHWIFE *Whispers to* HORNER.) She says she must speak with me in private. Withdraw, prithee.

Pinchwife. *(Aside.)* She's unwilling, it seems, I should know all her indecent conduct in this business.—*(Aloud.)* Well then, I'll leave you together, and hope when I am gone, you'll agree; if not, you and I shan't agree, sir.

Horner. What means the fool? if she and I agree 'tis no matter what you and I do.

(Whispers to Mrs. PINCHWIFE, *who makes signs with her hand for him to be gone.)*

Pinchwife. In the meantime I'll fetch a parson, and find out Sparkish, and disabuse him. You would have me fetch a parson, would you not? Well then—now I think I am rid of her and shall have no more trouble with her—our sisters and daughters, like userers' money, are safest when put out; but our wives, like their writings, never safe, but in our closets under lock and key.   *Exit.*

Enter BOY.

Boy. Sir Jasper Fidget, sir, is coming up.   *Exit.*

Horner. Here's the trouble of a cuckold now we are talking of. A pox on him! has he not enough to do to hinder his wife's sport, but he must other women's too?—Step in here, madam.   *(Exit Mrs.* PINCHWIFE.)*

Enter Sir JASPER FIDGET.

Sir Jasper. My best and dearest friend.

Horner. *(Aside to* QUACK.*)* The old style, doctor.—*(Aloud.)* Well, be short, for I am busy. What would your impertinent wife have now?

Sir Jasper. Well guessed, i'faith; for I do come from her.

Horner. To invite me to supper! Tell her, I can't come: go.

Sir Jasper. Nay, now you are out, faith; for my lady, and the whole knot of the virtuous gang, as they call themselves, are resolved upon a frolic of coming to you tonight in masquerade, and are all dressed already.

Horner. I shan't be at home.

Sir Jasper. *(Aside.)* Lord, how churlish he is to women!—*(Aloud.)* Nay, prithee don't disappoint 'em; they'll think 'tis my fault: prithee don't. I'll send in the banquet and the fiddles. But make no noise on't; for the poor virtuous rogues would not have it known, for the world, that they go a-masquerading; and they would come to no man's ball but yours.

Horner. Well, well—get you gone; and tell 'em, if they come, 'will be at the peril of their honor and yours.

Sir Jasper. He! he! he!—we'll trust you for that: farewell.

Exit.

Horner. Doctor, anon you too shall be my guest,
But now I'm going to a private feast.   *Exeunt.*

SCENE III: *The Piazza of Covent Garden.*

Enter SPARKISH *with a letter in his hand,* PINCHWIFE *following.*

Sparkish. But who would have thought a woman could have been false to me? By the world, I could not have thought it.

Pinchwife. You were for giving and taking liberty: she has taken it only, sir, now you find in that letter. You were a frank person, and so is she, you see there.

Sparkish. Nay, if this be her hand—for I never saw it.

Pinchwife. 'Tis no matter whether that be her hand or no; I am sure this hand, at her desire, led her to Mr. Horner, with whom I left her just now, to go fetch a parson to 'em at their desire too, to deprive you of her for ever; for it seems yours was but a mock marriage.

Sparkish. Indeed, she would needs have it that 'twas Harcourt himself, in a parson's habit, that married us; but I'm sure he told me 'twas his brother Ned.

Pinchwife. Oh, there 'tis out; and you were deceived, not she: for you are such a frank person. But I must be gone.— You'll find her at Mr. Horner's. Go, and believe your eyes.

Exit.

Sparkish. Nay, I'll to her, and call her as many crocodiles, sirens, harpies, and other heathenish names, as a poet would do a mistress who had refused to hear his suit; nay more, his verses on her.—But stay, is not that she following a torch at t'other end of the Piazza? and from Horner's certainly— 'tis so.

Enter ALITHEA *following a torch, and* LUCY *behind.*

You are well met, madam, though you don't think so. What, you have made a short visit to Mr. Horner? but I suppose you'll return to him presently, by that time the parson can be with him.

Alithea. Mr. Horner and the parson, sir!

Sparkish. Come, madam, no more dissembling, no more jilting; for I am no more a frank person.

Alithea. How's this?

Lucy. (*Aside.*) So. 'twill work, I see.

Sparkish. Could you find out no easy country fool to abuse? none but me, a gentleman of wit and pleasure about the town? But it was your pride to be too hard for a man of parts, unworthy false woman! false as a friend that lends a man money to lose; false as dice, who undo those that trust all they have to 'em.

Lucy. (*Aside.*) He has been a great bubble, by his similes, as they say.

Alithea. You have been too merry, sir, at your wedding-dinner, sure.

Sparkish. What, d'ye mock me too?

Alithea. Or you have been deluded.

Sparkish. By you.

Alithea. Let me understand you.

Sparkish. Have you the confidence (I should call it something else, since you know your guilt) to stand my just reproaches? you did not write an impudent letter to Mr. Horner? who I find now has clubbed with you in deluding me with his aversion for women, that I might not, forsooth, suspect him for my rival.

Lucy. (*Aside.*) D'ye think the gentleman can be jealous now, madam?

Alithea. I write a letter to Mr. Horner!

Sparkish. Nay, madam, do not deny it. Your brother showed it me just now; and told me likewise, he left you at Horner's lodging to fetch a parson to marry you to him: and I wish you joy, madam, joy, joy; and to him too, much joy; and to myself more joy, for not marrying you.

Alithea. (*Aside.*) So, I find my brother would break off the match; and I can consent to't, since I see this gentleman can be made jealous.—(*Aloud.*) Oh Lucy, by his rude usage and jealousy, he makes me almost afraid I am married to him. Art thou sure 'twas Harcourt himself, and no parson, that married us?

Sparkish. No, madam, I thank you. I suppose, that was a contrivance too of Mr. Horner's and yours, to make Harcourt play the parson; but I would as little as you have him one now, no, not for the world. For, shall I tell you another truth? I never had any passion for you till now, for now I hate you. 'Tis true, I might have married your portion, as other men of parts of the town do sometimes: and so, your servant. And to show my unconcernedness, I'll come to your wedding and resign you with as much joy as I would a stale wench to a new cully; nay, with as much joy as I would after the first night, if I had been married to you. There's for you; and so your servant, servant. *Exit.*

Alithea. How was I deceived in a man!

Lucy. You'll believe then a fool may be made jealous now? for that easiness in him that suffers him to be led by a wife, will likewise permit him to be persuaded against her by others.

Alithea. But marry Mr. Horner! my brother does not intend it, sure: if I thought he did, I would take thy advice, and Mr. Harcourt for my husband. And now I wish, that if there be any overwise woman of the town, who, like me, would marry a fool for fortune, liberty, or title, first, that her husband may love play, and be a cully to all the town but her, and suffer none but Fortune to be mistress of his purse; then, if for liberty, that he may send her into the country, under the conduct of some huswifely mother-in-law; and if for title, may the world give 'em none but that of cuckold.

Lucy. And for her greater curse, madam, may he not deserve it.

Alithea. Away, impertinent! Is not this my old Lady Lanterlu's?

Lucy. Yes, madam.—(*Aside.*) And here I hope we shall find Mr. Harcourt. *Exeunt.*

SCENE IV: HORNER'S *Lodging: a table, banquet, and bottles.*

Enter HORNER, Lady FIDGET, Mrs. DAINTY FIDGET, *and* Mrs. SQUEAMISH.

Horner. (*Aside.*) A pox! they are come too soon—before I have sent back my new mistress. All that I have now to do is to lock her in, that they may not see her.

Lady Fidget. That we may be sure of our welcome, we have brought our entertainment with us, and are resolved to treat thee, dear toad.

Mrs. Dainty. And that we may be merry to purpose, have left Sir Jasper and my old Lady Squeamish quarrelling at home at backgammon.

Mrs. Squeamish. Therefore let us make use of our time, lest they should chance to interrupt us.

Lady Fidget. Let us sit then.

Horner. First, that you may be private, let me lock this door and that, and I'll wait upon you presently.

Lady Fidget. No, sir, shut 'em only, and your lips for ever; for we must trust you as much as our women.

Horner. You know all vanity's killed in me; I have no occasion for talking.

Lady Fidget. Now, ladies, supposing we had drank each of us two bottles, let us speak the truth of our hearts.

Mrs. Dainty and Mrs. Squeamish. Agreed.

Lady Fidget. By this brimmer, for truth is nowhere else to be found—(*aside to* HORNER.) not in thy heart, false man!

Horner. (*Aside to* Lady FIDGET.) You have found me a true man, I'm sure.

Lady Fidget. (*Aside to* HORNER.) Not every way.—But let us sit and be merry.   (*Sings.*)

> Why should our damned tyrants oblige us to live
> On the pittance of pleasure which they only give?
>   We must not rejoice
>   With wine and with noise:
> In vain we must wake in a dull bed alone,
> Whilst to our warm rival the bottle they're gone.
>   Then lay aside charms,
>   And take up these arms.
> 'Tis wine only gives 'em their courage and wit;
> Because we live sober, to men we submit.
>   If for beauties you'd pass,
>   Take a lick of the glass,
> 'Twill mend your complexions, and when they are gone,
>   The best red we have is the red of the grape:
> Then, sisters, lay't on,
>   And damn a good shape.

Mrs. Dainty. Dear brimmer! Well, in token of our openness and plain-dealing, let us throw our masks over our heads.

Horner. (*Aside.*) So, 'twill come to the glasses anon.

Mrs. Squeamish. Lovely brimmer! let me enjoy him first.

Lady Fidget. No, I never part with a gallant till I've tried him. Dear brimmer! that makest our husbands short-sighted.

Mrs. Dainty. And our bashful gallants bold.

Mrs. Squeamish. And, for want of a gallant, the butler lovely in our eyes.—Drink, eunuch.

Lady Fidget. Drink, thou representative of a husband. Damn a husband!

Mrs. Dainty. And, as it were a husband, an old keeper.

Mrs. Squeamish. And an old grandmother.

Horner. And an English bawd, and a French surgeon.

Lady Fidget. Ay, we have all reason to curse 'em.

Horner. For my sake, ladies?

Lady Fidget. No, for our own; for the first spoils all young gallants' industry.

Mrs. Dainty. And the other's art makes 'em bold only with common women.

Mrs. Squeamish. And rather run the hazard of the vile distemper amongst them, than of a denial amongst us.

Mrs. Dainty. The filthy toads choose mistresses now as they do stuffs, for having been fancied and worn by others.

Mrs. Squeamish. For being common and cheap.

Lady Fidget. Whilst women of quality, like the richest stuffs, lie untumbled, and unasked for.

Horner. Ay, neat, and cheap, and new, often they think best.

Mrs. Dainty. No, sir, the beasts will be known by a mistress longer than by a suit.

Mrs. Squeamish. And 'tis not for cheapness neither.

Lady Fidget. No; for the vain fops will take up druggets and embroider 'em. But I wonder at the depraved appetites of witty men; they used to be out of the common road, and hate imitation. Pray tell me, beast, when you were a man, why you rather chose to club with a multitude in a common house for an entertainment, than to be the only guest at a good table.

Horner. Why, faith, ceremony and expectation are unsufferable to those that are sharp bent. People always eat with the best stomach at an ordinary, where every man is snatching for the best bit.

Lady Fidget. Though he get a cut over the fingers.—But I have heard, that people eat most heartily of another man's meat, that is, what they do not pay for.

Horner. When they are sure of their welcome and freedom; for ceremony in love and eating is as ridiculous as in fighting: falling on briskly is all should be done on those occasions.

Lady Fidget. Well, then, let me tell you, sir, there is nowhere more freedom than in our houses; and we take freedom, from a young person as a sign of good breeding, and a person may be as free as he pleases with us, as frolic, as gamesome, as wild as he will.

Horner. Han't I heard you all declaim against wild men?

Lady Fidget. Yes, but for all that, we think wildness in a man as desirable a quality as in a duck or rabbit; a tame man! foh!

Horner. I know not, but your reputations frightened me as much as your faces invited me.

Lady Fidget. Our reputation! Lord, why should you not think that we women make use of our reputation, as you men of yours, only to deceive the world with less suspicion? Our virtue is like the statesman's religion, the quaker's word, the gamester's oath, and the great man's honor; but to cheat those that trust us.

Mrs. Squeamish. And that demureness, coyness, and modesty, that you see in our faces in the boxes at plays, is as much a sign of a kind woman, as a vizard-mask in the pit.

Mrs. Dainty. For, I assure you, women are least masked when they have the velvet vizard on.

Lady Fidget. You would have found us modest women in our denials only.

Mrs. Squeamish. Our bashfulness is only the reflection of the men's.

Mrs. Dainty. We blush when they are shamefaced.

Horner. I beg your pardon, ladies, I was deceived in you devilishly. But why that mighty pretence to honor?

Lady Fidget. We have told you; but sometimes 'twas for the same reason you men pretend business often, to avoid ill company, to enjoy the better and more privately those you love.

Horner. But why would you ne'er give a friend a wink then?

Lady Fidget. Faith, your reputation frightened us, as much as ours did you, you were so notoriously lewd.

Horner. And you so seemingly honest.

Lady Fidget. Was that all that deterred you?

Horner. And so expensive—you allow freedom, you say.

Lady Fidget. Ay, ay.

Horner. That I was afraid of losing my little money, as well as my little time, both which my other pleasures required.

Lady Fidget. Money! foh! you talk like a little fellow now: do such as we expect money?

Horner. I beg your pardon, madam, I must confess, I have heard that great ladies, like great merchants, set but the higher prices upon what they have, because they are not in necessity of taking the first offer.

Mrs. Dainty. Such as we make sale of our hearts?

Mrs. Squeamish. We bribed for our love? foh!

Horner. With your pardon, ladies, I know, like great men in offices, you seem to exact flattery and attendance only from your followers; but you have receivers about you, and such fees to pay, a man is afraid to pass your grants. Besides, we must let you win at cards, or we lose your hearts; and if you make an assignation, 'tis at a goldsmith's, jeweler's, or china-house; where for your honor you deposit to him, he must pawn his to the punctual cit, and so paying for what you take up, pays for what he takes up.

Mrs. Dainty. Would you not have us assured of our gallants' love?

Mrs. Squeamish. For love is better known by liberality than by jealousy.

Lady Fidget. For one may be dissembled, the other not.—(*Aside.*) But my jealousy can be no longer dissembled, and they are telling ripe.—(*Aloud.*)—Come, here's to our gallants in waiting, whom we must name, and I'll begin. This is my false rogue. (*Claps him on the back.*)

Mrs. Squeamish. How!

Horner. (*Aside.*) So, all will out now.

Mrs. Squeamish. (*Aside to* HORNER.) Did you not tell me, 'twas for my sake only you reported yourself no man?

Mrs. Dainty. (*Aside to* HORNER.) Oh, wretch! did you not swear to me, 'twas for my love and honor you passed for that thing you do?

Horner. So, so.

Lady Fidget. Come, speak, ladies: this is my false villain.

Mrs. Squeamish. And mine too.

Mrs. Dainty. And mine.

Horner. Well then, you are all three my false rogues too, and there's an end on't.

Lady Fidget. Well then, there's no remedy; sister sharers, let us not fall out, but have a care of our honor. Though we get no presents, no jewels of him, we are savers of our honor, the jewel of most value and use, which shines yet to the world unsuspected, though it be counterfeit.

Horner. Nay, and is e'en as good as if it were true, provided the world think so; for honor, like beauty now, only depends on the opinion of others.

Lady Fidget. Well, Harry Common, I hope you can be true to three. Swear; but 'tis to no purpose to require your oath, for you are as often forsworn as you swear to new women.

Horner. Come, faith, madam, let us e'en pardon one another; for all the difference I find betwixt we men and you women, we forswear ourselves at the beginning of an amour, you as long as it lasts.

Enter Sir JASPER FIDGET, *and* Old Lady SQUEAMISH.

Sir Jasper. Oh, my Lady Fidget, was this your cunning, to come to Mr. Horner without me? but you have been nowhere else, I hope.

Lady Fidget. No, Sir Jasper.

Lady Squeamish. And you came straight hither, Biddy?

Mrs. Squeamish. Yes, indeed, lady grandmother.

Sir Jasper. 'Tis well, 'tis well; I knew when once they were thoroughly acquainted with poor Horner, they'd ne'er be from him: you may let her masquerade it with my wife and Horner, and I warrant her reputation safe.

Enter BOY.

Boy. Oh, sir, here's the gentleman come, whom you bid me not suffer to come up, without giving you notice, with a lady too, and other gentlemen.

Horner. Do you all go in there, whilst I send 'em away; and, boy, do you desire 'em to stay below till I come, which shall be immediately.

(*Exeunt* Sir JASPER FIDGET, Lady FIDGET, Lady SQUEAMISH, Mrs. SQUEAMISH, *and* Mrs. DAINTY FIDGET.)

Boy. Yes, sir.   *Exit*.

(*Exit* HORNER *at the other door, and returns with* Mrs. PINCHWIFE.)

Horner. You would not take my advice, to be gone home before your husband came back. He'll now discover all; yet pray, my dearest, be persuaded to go home and leave the rest to my management; I'll let you down the back way.

Mrs. Pinchwife. I don't know the way home, so I don't.

Horner. My man shall wait upon you.

Mrs. Pinchwife. No, don't you believe that I'll go at all; what, are you weary of me already?

Horner. No, my life, 'tis that I may love you long, 'tis to secure my love, and your reputation with your husband; he'll never receive you again else.

Mrs. Pinchwife. What care I? d'ye think to frighten me with that? I don't intend to go to him again; you shall be my husband now.

Horner. I cannot be your husband, dearest, since you are married to him.

Mrs. Pinchwife. Oh, would you make me believe that? Don't I see every day at London here, women leave their first husbands and go and live with other men as their wives? pish, pshaw! you'd make me angry, but that I love you so mainly.

Horner. So, they are coming up—In again, in, I hear 'em. —(*Exit* Mrs. PINCHWIFE.) Well, a silly mistress is like a weak place, soon got, soon lost—a man has scarce time for plunder; she betrays her husband first to her gallant, and then her gallant to her husband.

Enter PINCHWIFE, ALITHEA, HARCOURT, SPARKISH, LUCY, *and a* PARSON.

Pinchwife. Come, madam, 'tis not the sudden change of

your dress, the confidence of your asseverations, and your false witness there shall persuade me I did not bring you hither just now; here's my witness, who cannot deny it, since you must be confronted.—Mr. Horner, did not I bring this lady to you just now?

Horner. (*Aside.*) Now must I wrong one woman for another's sake,—but that's no new thing with me, for in these cases I am still on the criminal's side against the innocent.

Alithea. Pray speak, sir.

Horner. (*Aside.*) It must be so. I must be impudent, and try my luck; impudence uses to be too hard for truth.

Pinchwife. What, you are studying an evasion or excuse for her! Speak, sir.

Horner. No, faith; I am something backward only to speak in women's affairs or disputes.

Pinchwife. She bids you speak.

Alithea. Ah, pray, sir, do, pray satisfy him.

Horner. Then truly, you did bring that lady to me just now.

Pinchwife. Oh ho!

Alithea. How, sir?

Harcourt. How, Horner?

Alithea. What mean you, sir? I always took you for a man of honor.

Horner. (*Aside.*) Ay, so much a man of honor, that I must save my mistress, I thank you, come what will on't.

Sparkish. So, if I had had her, she'd have made me believe the moon had been made of a Christmas pie.

Lucy. (*Aside.*) Now could I speak, if I durst, and solve the riddle, who am the author of it.

Alithea. Oh unfortunate woman! A combination against my honor! which most concerns me now, because you share in my disgrace, sir, and it is your censure, which I must now suffer, that troubles me, not theirs.

Harcourt. Madam, then have no trouble, you shall now see 'tis possible for me to love too, without being jealous; I will not only believe your innocence myself, but make all the world believe it.—(*Aside to* HORNER.) Horner, I must now be concerned for this lady's honor.

Horner. And I must be concerned for a lady's honor too.

Harcourt. This lady has her honor, and I will protect it.

Horner. My lady has not her honor, but has given it me to keep, and I will preserve it.

Harcourt. I understand you not.

Horner. I would not have you.

Mrs. Pinchwife. What's the matter with 'em all?

(*Peeping in behind.*)

Pinchwife. Come, come, Mr. Horner, no more disputing; here's the parson, I brought him not in vain.

Harcourt. No, sir, I'll employ him, if this lady please.

Pinchwife. How! what d'ye mean?

Sparkish. Ay, what does he mean?

Horner. Why, I have resigned your sister to him, he has my consent.

Pinchwife. But he has not mine, sir; a woman's injured honor, no more than a man's, can be repaired or satisfied by any but him that first wronged it; and you shall marry her presently, or——   *(Lays his hand on his sword.)*

Enter Mrs. PINCHWIFE.

Mrs. Pinchwife. Oh lord, they'll kill poor Mr. Horner! besides, he shan't marry her whilst I stand by, and look on; I'll not lose my second husband so.

Pinchwife. What do I see?

Alithea. My sister in my clothes!

Sparkish. Ha!

Mrs. Pinchwife. (*To* PINCHWIFE.) Nay, pray now don't quarrel about finding work for the parson, he shall marry me to Mr. Horner; for now, I believe, you have enough of me.

Horner. (*Aside.*) Damned, damned loving changeling!

Mrs. Pinchwife. Pray, sister, pardon me for telling so many lies of you.

Horner. I suppose the riddle is plain now.

Lucy. No, that must be my work.—Good sir, hear me.
      (Kneels to PINCHWIFE, *who stands doggedly with his hat over his eyes.)*

Pinchwife. I will never hear woman again, but make 'em all silent thus——   *(Offers to draw upon his* Wife.)*

Horner. No, that must not be.

Pinchwife. You then shall go first, 'tis all one to me.
      (Offers to draw on HORNER, *but is stopped by* HARCOURT.)*

Harcourt. Hold!

Enter Sir JASPER FIDGET, Lady FIDGET, Lady SQUEAMISH, Mrs. DAINTY FIDGET, *and* Mrs. SQUEAMISH.

Sir Jasper. What's the matter? what's the matter? pray, what's the matter, sir? I beseech you communicate, sir.

Pinchwife. Why, my wife has communicated, sir, as your wife may have done too, sir, if she knows him, sir.

Sir Jasper. Pshaw, with him! ha! ha! he!

Pinchwife. D'ye mock me, sir? a cuckold is a kind of a wild beast; have a care, sir.

Sir Jasper. No, sure, you mock me, sir. He cuckold you! it can't be, ha! ha! he! why, I'll tell you, sir——
(Offers to whisper.)

Pinchwife. I tell you again, he has whored my wife, and yours too, if he knows her, and all the women he comes near; 'tis not his dissembling, his hypocrisy, can wheedle me.

Sir Jasper. How! does he dissemble! is he a hypocrite? Nay, then—how—wife—sister, is he a hypocrite?

Lady Squeamish. A hypocrite! a dissembler! Speak, young harlotry, speak, how?

Sir Jasper. Nay, then—Oh my head too!—Oh thou libidinous lady!

Lady Squeamish. Oh thou harloting harlotry! hast thou done't then?

Sir Jasper. Speak, good Horner, art thou a dissembler, a rogue? hast thou——

Horner. So!

Lucy. (*Apart to* HORNER.) I'll fetch you off, and her too, if she will but hold her tongue.

Horner. (*Apart to* LUCY.) Canst thou? I'll give thee——

Lucy. (*To* PINCHWIFE.) Pray have but patience to hear me, sir, who am the unfortunate cause of all this confusion. Your wife is innocent, I only culpable; for I put her upon telling you all these lies concerning my mistress, in order to the breaking off the match between Mr. Sparkish and her, to make way for Mr. Harcourt.

Sparkish. Did you so, ternal rotten tooth? Then, it seems, my mistress was not false to me, I was only deceived by you. Brother, that should have been, now man of conduct, who is a frank person now, to bring your wife to her lover, ha?

Lucy. I assure you, sir, she came not to Mr. Horner out of love, for she loves him no more——

Mrs. Pinchwife. Hold, I told lies for you, but you shall tell none for me, for I do love Mr. Horner with all my soul, and nobody shall say me nay; pray, don't you go to make poor Mr. Horner believe to the contrary; 'tis spitefully done of you, I'm sure.

Horner. (*Aside to* Mrs. PINCHWIFE.) Peace, dear idiot.

Mrs. Pinchwife. Nay, I will not peace.

Pinchwife. Not till I make you.

Enter DORILANT *and* QUACK.

Dorilant. Horner, your servant; I am the doctor's guest, he must excuse our intrusion.

Quack. But what's the matter, gentlemen? for Heaven's sake, what's the matter?

Horner. (*Whispers.*) Oh, 'tis well you are come. 'Tis a censorious world we live in; you may have brought me a reprieve, or else I had died for a crime I never committed, and these innocent ladies had suffered with me; therefore, pray satisfy these worthy, honorable, jealous gentlemen— that——

Quack. Oh, I understand you, is that all?—Sir Jasper, by Heavens, and upon the word of a physician, sir——

(*Whispers to* Sir JASPER.)

Sir Jasper. Nay, I do believe you truly.—Pardon me, my virtuous lady, and dear of honor.

Lady Squeamish. What, then all's right again?

Sir Jasper. Ay, ay, and now let us satisfy him too.

(*They whisper with* PINCHWIFE.)

Pinchwife. An eunuch! Pray, no fooling with me.

Quack. I'll bring half the surgeons in town to swear it.

Pinchwife. They!—they'll swear a man that bled to death through his wounds died of an apoplexy.

Quack. Pray, hear me, sir—why, all the town has heard the report of him.

Pinchwife. But does all the town believe it?

Quack. Pray, inquire a little, and first of all these.

Pinchwife. I'm sure when I left the town, he was the lewdest fellow in't.

Quack. I tell you, sir, he has been in France since; pray, ask but these ladies and gentlemen, your friend Mr. Dorilant. Gentlemen and ladies, han't you all heard the late sad report of poor Mr. Horner?

All the Ladies. Ay, ay, ay.

Dorilant. Why, thou jealous fool, dost thou doubt it? he's an arrant French capon.

Mrs. Pinchwife. 'Tis false, sir, you shall not disparage poor Mr. Horner, for to my certain knowledge——

Lucy. Oh, hold!

Mrs. Squeamish. (*Aside to* LUCY.) Stop her mouth!

Lady Fidget. (*To* PINCHWIFE.) Upon my honor, sir, 'tis as true——

Mrs. Dainty. D'ye think we would have been seen in his company?

Mrs. Squeamish. Trust our unspotted reputations with him?

Lady Fidget. (*Aside to* HORNER.) This you get, and we too, by trusting your secret to a fool.

Horner. Peace, madam.—(*Aside to* QUACK.) Well, doctor, is not this a good design, that carries a man on unsuspected, and brings him off safe?

Pinchwife. (*Aside.*) Well, if this were true—but my wife—— (DORILANT *whispers with* Mrs. PINCHWIFE.)

Alithea. Come, brother, your wife is yet innocent, you see; but have a care of too strong an imagination, lest, like an over-concerned timorous gamester, by fancying an unlucky cast, it should come. Women and fortune are truest still to those that trust 'em.

Lucy. And any wild thing grows but the more fierce and hungry for being kept up, and more dangerous to the keeper.

Alithea. There's doctrine for all husbands, Mr. Harcourt.

Harcourt. I edify, madam, so much, that I am impatient till I am one.

Dorilant. And I edify so much by example, I will never be one.

Sparkish. And because I will not disparage my parts, I'll ne'er be one.

Horner. And I, alas! can't be one.

Pinchwife. But I must be one—against my will to a country wife, with a country murrain to me!

Mrs. Pinchwife. (*Aside.*) And I must be a country wife still too, I find; for I can't, like a city one, be rid of my musty husband, and do what I list.

Horner. Now, sir, I must pronounce your wife innocent, though I blush whilst I do it; and I am the only man by her now exposed to shame which I will straight drown in wine, as you shall your suspicion; and the ladies' troubles we'll divert with a ballad.——Doctor, where are your maskers?

Lucy. Indeed, she's innocent, sir, I am her witness; and her end of coming out was but to see her sister's wedding; and what she has said to your face of her love to Mr. Horner, was but the usual innocent revenge on a husband's jealousy—was it not, madam, speak?

Mrs. Pinchwife. (*Aside to* LUCY *and* HORNER.) Since you'll have me tell more lies—(*Aloud.*) Yes, indeed, bud.

Pinchwife. For my own sake fain I would all believe;
　Cuckolds, like lovers, should themselves deceive.
　But—— (*Sighs.*)
　His honor is least safe (too late I find)
　Who trusts it with a foolish wife or friend.

A Dance of Cuckolds.

Horner. Vain fops but court and dress, and keep a
　　pother,[25]
　To pass for women's men with one another;
　But he who aims by women to be prized,
　First by the men, you see, must be despised. *Exeunt.*

EPILOGUE

Spoken by LADY FIDGET.

Now you the vigorous, who daily here
O'er vizard-mask in public domineer,
And what you'd do to her, if in place where;
Nay, have the confidence to cry, "Come out!"
Yet when she says, "Lead on!" you are not stout;
But to your well-dressed brother straight turn round,
And cry, "Pox on her, Ned, she can't be sound!"
Then slink away, a fresh one to engage,
With so much seeming heat and loving rage,
You'd frighten listening actress on the stage;
Till she at last has seen you huffing come,
And talk of keeping in the tiring-room,
Yet cannot be provoked to lead her home.
Next, you Falstaffs of fifty, who beset
Your buckram maidenheads, which your friends get;
And whilst to them you of achievements boast,
They share the booty, and laugh at your cost.
In fine, you essenced boys, both old and young,
Who would be thought so eager, brisk, and strong,
Yet do the ladies, not their husbands wrong;
Whose purses for your manhood make excuse,
And keep your Flanders mares for show not use;
Encouraged by our woman's man today,
A Horner's part may vainly think to play;
And may intrigues so bashfully disown,
That they may doubted be by few or none;
May kiss the cards at picquet, ombre, loo,[26]
And so be taught to kiss the lady too;
But, gallants, have a care, faith, what you do.
The world, which to no man his due will give,
You by experience know you can deceive,
And men may still believe you vigorous,
But then we women—there's no cozening us.

To the Right Honorable

RALPH, EARL OF MONTAGUE, &c.

MY LORD,

Whether the world will arraign me of vanity or not, that I have presumed to dedicate this comedy to your Lordship, I am yet in doubt; though, it may be, it is some degree of vanity even to doubt of it. One who has at any time had the honor of your Lordship's conversation, cannot be supposed to think very meanly of that which he would prefer to your perusal; yet it were to incur the imputation of too much sufficiency, to pretend to such a merit as might abide the test of your Lordship's censure.

Whatever value may be wanting to this play while yet it is mine, will be sufficiently made up to it when it is once become your Lordship's; and it is my security that I cannot have overrated it more by my dedication, than your Lordship will dignify it by your patronage.

That it succeeded on the stage, was almost beyond my expectation; for but little of it was prepared for that general taste which seems now to be predominant in the palates of our audience.

Those characters which are meant to be ridiculed in most of our comedies, are of fools so gross, that, in my humble opinion, they should rather disturb than divert the well-natured and reflecting part of an audience; they are rather objects of charity than contempt; and instead of moving our mirth, they ought very often to excite our compassion.

This reflection moved me to design some characters which should appear ridiculous, not so much through a natural folly (which is incorrigible, and therefore not proper for the stage) as through an affected wit; a wit, which at the same time that it is affected, is also false. As there is some difficulty in the formation of a character of this nature, so there is some hazard which attends the progress of its success upon the stage; for many come to a play so overcharged with criticism, that they very often let fly their censure, when through their rashness they have mistaken their aim. This I had occasion lately to observe; for this play had been acted two or three days before some of these hasty judges could find the leisure to distinguish betwixt the character of a Witwoud and a Truewit.

I must beg your Lordship's pardon for this digression from the true course of this epistle; but that it may not seem altogether impertinent, I beg that I may 'plead the occasion of it, in part of that excuse of which I stand in need, for recommending this comedy to your protection. It is only by the countenance of your Lordship, and the *few* so qualified, that such who write with care and pains can hope to be distinguished; for the prostituted name of *poet* promiscuously levels all that bear it.

Terence, the most correct writer in the world, had a Scipio and a Lælius, if not to assist him, at least to support him in his reputation; and notwithstanding his extraordinary merit, it may be their countenance was not more than necessary.

The purity of his style, the delicacy of his turns, and the justness of his characters, were all of them beauties which the greater part of his audience were incapable of tasting; some of the coarsest strokes of Plautus, so severely censured by Horace, were more likely to affect the multitude; such who come with expectation to laugh at the last act of a play, and are better entertained with two or three unseasonable jests, than with the artful solution of the *fable*.

As Terence excelled in his performances, so had he great advantages to encourage his undertakings; for he built most on the foundations of Menander; his plots were generally modelled, and his characters ready drawn to his hand. He copied Menander, and Menander had no less light in the formation of his characters, from the observations of Theophrastus, of whom he was a disciple; and Theophrastus, it is known, was not only the disciple, but the immediate successor of Aristotle, the first and greatest judge of poetry. These were great models to design by; and the further advantage which Terence possessed, towards giving his plays the due ornaments of purity of style and justness of manners, was not less considerable, from the freedom of conversation which was permitted him with Lælius and Scipio, two of the greatest and most polite men of his age. And indeed the privilege of such a conversation is the only certain means of attaining to the perfection of dialogue.

If it has happened in any part of this comedy, that I have gained a turn of style or expression more correct, or at least, more corrigible than in those which I have formerly written, I must, with equal pride and gratitude, ascribe it to the honor of your Lordship's admitting me into your conversation, and that of a society where everybody else was so well worthy of you, in your retirement last summer from the town; for it was immediately after that this comedy was written. If I have failed in my performance, it is only to be regretted, where there were so many, not inferior either to a Scipio or a Lælius, that there should be one wanting equal in capacity to a Terence.

If I am not mistaken, poetry is almost the only art which has not yet laid claim to your Lordship's patronage. Architecture and painting, to the great honor of our country, have flourished under your influence and protection. In the meantime, poetry, the eldest sister of all arts, and parent of most, seems to have resigned her birthright, by having neglected to pay her duty to your Lordship, and by permitting others of a later extraction, to prepossess that place in your esteem to which none can pretend a better title. Poetry, in its nature, is sacred to the good and great; the relation between them is reciprocal, and they are ever propitious to it. It is the privilege of poetry to address to them, and it is their prerogative alone to give it protection.

This received maxim is a general apology for all writers who consecrate their labors to great men; but I could wish at this time, that this address were exempted from the common pretence of all dedications; and that I can distinguish your Lordship even among the most deserving, so this offering might become remarkable by some particular instance of respect which should assure your Lordship, that I am, with all due sense of your extreme worthiness and humanity, my Lord, your Lordship's most obedient, and most obliged humble servant.

WILL. CONGREVE.

PROLOGUE

Spoken by MR. FAINALL.

Of those few fools who with ill stars are cursed,
Sure scribbling fools, called poets, fare the worst:
For they're a sort of fools which Fortune makes,
And after she has made 'em fools, forsakes.
With Nature's oafs 'tis quite a different case,
For Fortune favors all her idiot-race.
In her own nest the cuckoo-eggs we find,
O'er which she broods to hatch the changeling-kind.
No portion for her own she has to spare,
So much she dotes on her adopted care.

    Poets are bubbles, by the town drawn in,
Suffered at first some trifling stakes to win;
But what unequal hazards do they run!
Each time they write they venture all they've won:
The squire that's buttered[1] still, is sure to be undone.
This author heretofore has found your favor,
But pleads no merit from his past behavior.
To build on that might prove a vain presumption,
Should grants, to poets made, admit resumption;
And in Parnassus he must lose his seat
If that be found a forfeited estate.

    He owns with toil he wrought the following scenes;
But, if they're naught, ne'er spare him for his pains.
Damn him the more: have no commiseration
For dullness on mature deliberation.
He swears he'll not resent one hissed-off scene;
Nor, like those peevish wits, his play maintain,
Who, to assert their sense, your taste arraign.
Some plot we think he has, and some new thought;
Some humor too, no farce—but that's a fault.
Satire, he thinks, you ought not to expect;
For so reformed a town who dares correct?
To please, this time, has been his sole pretence;
He'll not instruct, lest it should give offence.

Should he by chance a knave or fool expose,
That hurts none here; sure here are none of those.
In short, our play shall (with your leave to show it)
Give you one instance of a passive poet,
Who to your judgments yields all resignation;
So save or damn, after your own discretion.

DRAMATIS PERSONÆ

FAINALL, in love with MRS. MARWOOD.
MIRABELL, in love with MRS. MILLAMANT.
WITWOUD }
PETULANT } followers of MRS. MILLAMANT.
SIR WILFULL WITWOUD, half brother to WITWOUD, and
    nephew to LADY WISHFORT.
WAITWELL, servant to MIRABELL.

LADY WISHFORT, enemy to MIRABELL, for having falsely
    pretended love to her.
MRS. MILLAMANT, a fine lady, niece to LADY WISHFORT, and
    loves MIRABELL.
MRS. MARWOOD, friend to MR. FAINALL, and likes MIRABELL.
MRS. FAINALL, daughter to LADY WISHFORT, and wife to
    FAINALL, formerly friend to MIRABELL.
FOIBLE, woman to LADY WISHFORT.
MINCING, woman to MRS. MILLAMENT.
BETTY, waiting-maid at a chocolate-house.
PEG, maid to LADY WISHFORT.

Coachmen, Dancers, Footmen, and Attendants.

Scene—LONDON.

ACT I

SCENE I: *A Chocolate House.*

MIRABELL *and* FAINALL, *rising from cards,* BETTY *waiting.*

Mirabell. You are a fortunate man, Mr. Fainall!

Fainall. Have we done?

Mirabell. What you please. I'll play on to entertain you.

Fainall. No, I'll give you your revenge another time, when you are not so indifferent; you are thinking of something else now, and play too negligently. The coldness of a losing gamester lessens the pleasure of the winner. I'd no more play with a man that slighted his ill fortune than I'd make love to a woman who undervalued the loss of her reputation.

Mirabell. You have a taste extremely delicate, and are for refining on your pleasures.

Fainall. Prithee, why so reserved? Something has put you out of humor.

Mirabell. Not at all. I happen to be grave today, and you are gay; that's all.

Fainall. Confess, Millamant and you quarrelled last night after I left you. My fair cousin has some humors that would tempt the patience of a stoic. What, some coxcomb came in, and was well received by her, while you were by?

Mirabell. Witwoud and Petulant; and what was worse, her aunt, your wife's mother, my evil genius; or to sum up all in her own name, my old Lady Wishfort came in.

Fainall. Oh, there it is then! She has a lasting passion for you, and with reason.—What, then my wife was there?

Mirabell. Yes, and Mrs. Marwood, and three or four more, whom I never saw before. Seeing me, they all put on their grave faces, whispered one another; then complained aloud of the vapors, and after fell into a profound silence.

Fainall. They had a mind to be rid of you.

Mirabell. For which reason I resolved not to stir. At last the good old lady broke through her painful taciturnity with an invective against long visits. I would not have understood her, but Millamant joining in the argument, I rose, and with a constrained smile, told her I thought nothing was so easy as to know when a visit began to be troublesome. She reddened, and I withdrew without expecting her reply.

Fainall. You were to blame to resent what she spoke only in compliance with her aunt.

Mirabell. She is more mistress of herself than to be under the necessity of such a resignation.

Fainall. What! though half her fortune depends upon her marrying with my lady's approbation?

Mirabell. I was then in such a humor, that I should have been better pleased if she had been less discreet.

Fainall. Now I remember, I wonder not they were weary of you. Last night was one of their cabal nights. They have 'em three times a week, and meet by turns at one another's apartments, where they come together like the coroner's inquest, to sit upon the murdered reputations of the week. You and I are excluded; and it was once proposed that all the male sex should be excepted; but somebody moved that, to avoid scandal, there might be one man of the community; upon which motion Witwoud and Petulant were enrolled members.

Mirabell. And who may have been the foundress of this sect? My Lady Wishfort, I warrant, who publishes her detestation of mankind; and full of the vigour of fifty-five, declares for a friend and ratafia;[2] and let posterity shift for itself, she'll breed no more.

Fainall. The discovery of your sham addresses to her, to conceal your love to her niece, has provoked this separation; had you dissembled better, things might have continued in the state of nature.

Mirabell. I did as much as man could, with any reasonable conscience; I proceeded to the very last act of flattery with her, and was guilty of a song in her commendation. Nay, I got a friend to put her into a lampoon and compliment her with the imputation of an affair with a young fellow, which I carried so far that I told her the malicious town took notice that she was grown fat of a sudden; and when she lay in of a dropsy, persuaded her she was reported to be in labor. The devil's in't, if an old woman is to be flattered further, unless a man should endeavor downright personally to debauch her; and that my virtue forbade me. But for the discovery of this amour I am indebted to your friend, or your wife's friend, Mrs. Marwood.

Fainall. What should provoke her to be your enemy unless she has made you advances which you have slighted? Women do not easily forgive omissions of this nature.

Mirabell. She was always civil to me till of late. I confess I am not one of those coxcombs who are apt to interpret a woman's good manners to her prejudice, and think that she who does not refuse 'em everything, can refuse 'em nothing.

Fainall. You are a gallant man, Mirabell; and though you may have cruelty enough not to satisfy a lady's longing, you have too much generosity not to be tender of her honor. Yet you speak with an indifference which seems to be affected and confesses you are conscious of a negligence.

Mirabell. You pursue the argument with a distrust that seems to be unaffected and confesses you are conscious of a concern for which the lady is more indebted to you than is your wife.

Fainall. Fy, fy, friend! if you grow censorious I must leave you. I'll look upon the gamesters in the next room.

Mirabell. Who are they?

Fainall. Petulant and Witwoud. (*To* BETTY.) Bring me some chocolate.   *Exit.*

Mirabell. Betty, what says your clock?

Betty. Turned of the last canonical hour,[3] sir.   *Exit.*

Mirabell. How pertinently the jade answers me! (*Looking on his watch.*) Ha! almost one o'clock! Oh, y'are come!

Enter FOOTMAN.

Well, is the grand affair over? You have been something tedious.

Footman. Sir, there's such coupling at Pancras[4] that they stand behind one another, as 'twere in a country dance. Ours was the last couple to lead up; and no hopes appearing of dispatch; besides, the parson growing hoarse, we were afraid his lungs would have failed before it came to our turn; so we drove round to Duke's place; and there they were riveted in a trice.

Mirabell. So, so, you are sure they are married?

Footman. Married and bedded, sir; I am witness.

Mirabell. Have you the certificate?

Footman. Here it is, sir.

Mirabell. Has the tailor brought Waitwell's clothes home, and the new liveries?

Footman. Yes, sir.

Mirabell. That's well. Do you go home again, d'ye hear, and adjourn the consummation till further orders. Bid Waitwell shake his ears, and Dame Partlet[5] rustle up her feathers and meet me at one o'clock by Rosamond's Pond,[6] that I may see her before she returns to her lady; and as you tender your ears be secret.   *Exit* FOOTMAN.

Enter FAINALL, *followed shortly by* BETTY.

Fainall. Joy of your success, Mirabell; you look pleased.

Mirabell. Ay; I have been engaged in a matter of some sort

of mirth, which is not yet ripe for discovery. I am glad this
is not a cabal night. I wonder, Fainall, that you who are married and of consequence should be discreet, will suffer your
wife to be of such a party.

Fainall. Faith, I am not jealous. Besides, most who are engaged are women and relations; and for the men, they are of
a kind too contemptible to give scandal.

Mirabell. I am of another opinion. The greater the coxcomb, always the more the scandal: for a woman who is not
a fool, can have but one reason for associating with a man
who is one.

Fainall. Are you jealous as often as you see Witwoud entertained by Millamant?

Mirabell. Of her understanding I am, if not of her person.

Fainall. You do her wrong; for, to give her her due, she
has wit.

Mirabell. She has beauty enough to make any man think
so; and complaisance enough not to contradict him who shall
tell her so.

Fainall. For a passionate lover, methinks you are a man
somewhat too discerning in the failings of your mistress.

Mirabell. And for a discerning man, somewhat too passionate a lover; for I like her with all her faults; nay, like
her for her faults. Her follies are so natural, or so artful,
that they become her; and those affectations which in another woman would be odious, serve but to make her more
agreeable. I'll tell thee, Fainall, she once used me with that
insolence, that in revenge I took her to pieces; sifted her, and
separated her failings; I studied 'em, and got 'em by rote. The
catalogue was so large that I was not without hopes one day
or other to hate her heartily: to which end I so used myself
to think of 'em, that at length, contrary to my design and expectation, they gave me every hour less and less disturbance;
till in a few days it became habitual to me to remember 'em
without being displeased. They are now grown as familiar to
me as my own frailties; and in all probability, in a little time
longer I shall like 'em as well.

Fainall. Marry her, marry her! be half as well acquainted
with her charms as you are with her defects, and my life on't,
you are your own man again.

Mirabell. Say you so?

Fainall. Ay, ay, I have experience: I have a wife, and so
forth.

Enter MESSENGER.

Messenger. Is one Squire Witwoud here?

Betty. Yes, what's your business?

Messenger. I have a letter for him from his brother Sir Wilfull, which I am charged to deliver into his own hands.

Betty. He's in the next room, friend—that way.

Exit MESSENGER.

Mirabell. What, is the chief of that noble family in town—Sir Wilfull Witwoud?

Fainall. He is expected today. Do you know him?

Mirabell. I have seen him. He promises to be an extraordinary person. I think you have the honor to be related to him.

Fainall. Yes; he is half brother to this Witwoud by a former wife, who was sister to my Lady Wishfort, my wife's mother. If you marry Millamant, you must call cousins too.

Mirabell. I had rather be his relation than his acquaintance.

Fainall. He comes to town in order to equip himself for travel.

Mirabell. For travel! why, the man that I mean is above forty.

Fainall. No matter for that; 'tis for the honor of England, that all Europe should know we have blockheads of all ages.

Mirabell. I wonder there is not an act of Parliament to save the credit of the nation, and prohibit the exportation of fools.

Fainall. By no means; 'tis better as 'tis. 'Tis better to trade with a little loss, than to be quite eaten up with being overstocked.

Mirabell. Pray, are the follies of this knight-errant, and those of the squire his brother anything related?

Fainall. Not at all; Witwoud grows by the knight, like a medlar[7] grafted on a crab. One will melt in your mouth, and t'other set your teeth on edge; one is all pulp, and the other all core.

Mirabell. So one will be rotten before he be ripe, and the other will be rotten without ever being ripe at all.

Fainall. Sir Wilfull is an odd mixture of bashfulness and obstinancy. But when he's drunk he's as loving as the monster in *The Tempest*,[8] and much after the same manner. To give t'other his due, he has something of good-nature, and does not always want wit.

Mirabell. Not always: but as often as his memory fails him, and his commonplace[9] of comparisons. He is a fool with a good memory and some few scraps of other folks' wit. He is one whose conversation can never be approved; yet it is now and then to be endured. He has indeed one good quality, he is not exceptious; for he so passionately affects the reputation of understanding raillery, that he will construe an affront into a jest; and call downright rudeness and ill language, satire and fire.

Fainall. If you have a mind to finish his picture, you have an opportunity to do it at full length. Behold the original!

Enter WITWOUD.

Witwoud. Afford me your compassion, my dears! pity me, Fainall! Mirabell, pity me!

Mirabell. I do from my soul.

Fainall. Why, what's the matter?

Witwoud. No letters for me, Betty?

Betty. Did not a messenger bring you one but now, sir?

Witwoud. Ay, but no other?

Betty. No, sir.

Witwoud. That's hard, that's very hard.—A messenger! a mule, a beast of burden! he has brought me a letter from the fool my brother, as heavy as a panegyric in a funeral sermon, or a copy of commendatory verses from one poet to another: and what's worse, 'tis as sure a forerunner of the author, as an epistle dedicatory.

Mirabell. A fool, and your brother, Witwoud!

Witwoud. Ay, ay, my half-brother. My half-brother he is, no nearer upon honor.

Mirabell. Then 'tis possible he may be but half a fool.

Witwoud. Good, good, Mirabell, *le drôle!*[10] good, good; hang him, don't let's talk of him.—Fainall, how does your lady? Gad, I say anything in the world to get this fellow out of my head. I beg pardon that I should ask a man of pleasure and the town a question at once so foreign and domestic. But I talk like an old maid at a marriage; I don't know what I say. But she's the best woman in the world.

Fainall. 'Tis well you don't know what you say, or else your commendation would go near to make me either vain or jealous.

Witwoud. No man in town lives well with a wife but Fainall.—Your judgment, Mirabell.

Mirabell. You had better step and ask his wife, if you would be credibly informed.

Witwoud. Mirabell?

Mirabell. Ay.

Witwoud. My dear, I ask ten thousand pardons—gad, I have forgot what I was going to say to you!

Mirabell. I thank you heartily, heartily.

Witwoud. No, but prithee excuse me—my memory is such a memory.

Mirabell. Have a care of such apologies, Witwoud; for I never knew a fool but he affected to complain, either of the spleen or his memory.

Fainall. What have you done with Petulant?

Witwoud. He's reckoning his money—my money it was. I have no luck today.

Fainall. You may allow him to win of you at play, for you are sure to be too hard for him at repartee. Since you monopolise the wit that is between you, the fortune must be his of course.

Mirabell. I don't find that Petulant confesses the superiority of wit to be your talent, Witwoud.

Witwoud. Come, come, you are malicious now, and would breed debates. Petulant's my friend, and a very honest fellow, and a very pretty fellow, and has a smattering—faith and troth, a pretty deal of an odd sort of a small wit. Nay, I'll do him justice. I'm his friend, I won't wrong him neither. And if he had any judgment in the world, he would not be altogether contemptible. Come, come, don't detract from the merits of my friend.

Fainall. You don't take your friend to be over-nicely bred?

Witwoud. No, no, hang him, the rogue has no manners at all, that I must own—no more breeding than a bum-baily,[11] that I grant you—'tis pity, faith; the fellow has fire and life.

Mirabell. What, courage?

Witwoud. Hum, faith I don't know as to that, I can't say as to that—Yes, faith, in a controversy, he'll contradict anybody.

Mirabell. Though 'twere a man whom he feared, or a woman whom he loved?

Witwoud. Well, well, he does not always think before he speaks—we have all our failings. You are too hard upon him, you are, faith. Let me excuse him—I can defend most of his faults, except one or two. One he has, that's the truth on't; if he were my brother, I could not acquit him—that, indeed, I could wish were otherwise.

Mirabell. Ay, marry, what's that, Witwoud?

Witwoud. Oh, pardon me!—expose the infirmities of my friend!—No, my dear, excuse me there.

Fainall. What! I warrant he's unsincere, or 'tis some such trifle.

Witwoud. No, no; what if he be? 'Tis no matter for that, his wit will excuse that. A wit should no more be sincere than a woman constant; one argues a decay of parts, as t'other of beauty.

Mirabell. Maybe you think him too positive?

Witwoud. No, no, his being positive is an incentive to argument, and keeps up conversation.

Fainall. Too illiterate?

Witwoud. That! that's his happiness—his want of learning

gives him the more opportunities to show his natural parts.

Mirabell. He wants words?

Witwoud. Ay: but I like him for that now; for his want of words gives me the pleasure very often to explain his meaning.

Fainall. He's impudent?

Witwoud. No, that's not it.

Mirabell. Vain?

Witwoud. No.

Mirabell. What! he speaks unseasonable truths sometimes, because he has not wit enough to invent an evasion?

Witwoud. Truths! ha! ha! ha! no, no; since you will have it,—I mean, he never speaks truth at all—that's all. He will lie like a chambermaid, or a woman of quality's porter. Now that is a fault.

Enter COACHMAN.

Coachman. Is Master Petulant here, mistress?

Betty. Yes.

Coachman. Three gentlewomen in a coach would speak with him.

Fainall. Oh brave Petulant! three!

Betty. I'll tell him.

Coachman. You must bring two dishes of chocolate and a glass of cinnamon-water.   *Exeunt* BETTY *and* COACHMAN.

Witwoud. That should be for two fasting strumpets, and a bawd troubled with wind. Now you may know what the three are.

Mirabell. You are very free with your friend's acquaintance.

Witwoud. Ay, ay, friendship without freedom is as dull as love without enjoyment, or wine without toasting. But to tell you a secret, these are trulls whom he allows coach-hire, and something more, by the week, to call on him once a day at public places.

Mirabell. How!

Witwoud. You shall see he won't go to 'em, because there's no more company here to take notice of him. Why this is nothing to what he used to do—before he found out this way, I have known him call for himself.

Fainall. Call for himself! what dost thou mean?

Witwoud. Mean! why he would slip out of this chocolate-house, just when you had been talking to him—as soon as your back was turned—whip he was gone!—then trip to his lodging, clap on a hood and scarf and a mask, slap into a hackney-coach, and drive hither to the door again in a trice, where he would send in for himself; that I mean, call for himself, wait for himself; nay, and what's more, not finding himself, sometimes leave a letter for himself.

Mirabell. I confess this is something extraordinary.—I believe he waits for himself now, he is so long a-coming: Oh! I ask his pardon.

Enter PETULANT *and* BETTY.

Betty. Sir, the coach stays.

Petulant. Well, well—I come. 'Sbud, a man had as good be a professed midwife as a professed whoremaster, at this rate! to be knocked up and raised at all hours, and in all places. Pox on 'em, I won't come!—D'ye hear, tell 'em I won't come—let 'em snivel and cry their hearts out.

Fainall. You are very cruel, Petulant.

Petulant. All's one, let it pass—I have a humor to be cruel.

Mirabell. I hope they are not persons of condition that you use at this rate.

Petulant. Condition! condition's a dried fig, if I am not in humor!—By this hand, if they were your—a—a—your what d'ye-call-'ems themselves, they must wait or rub off,[12] if I want appetite.

Mirabell. What d'ye-call-'ems! what are they, Witwoud?

Witwoud. Empresses, my dear—by your what-d'ye-call-'ems he means sultana queens.

Petulant. Ay, Roxolanas.[13]

Mirabell. Cry you mercy!

Fainall. Witwoud says they are—

Petulant. What does he say th'are?

Witwoud. I? fine ladies, I say.

Petulant. Pass on, Witwoud.—Hark'ee, by this light his relations—two co-heiresses his cousins, and an old aunt who loves caterwauling better than a conventicle.[14]

Witwoud. Ha! ha! ha! I had a mind to see how the rogue would come off.—Ha! ha! ha! gad, I can't be angry with him if he had said they were my mother and my sisters.

Mirabell. No!

Witwoud. No; the rogue's wit and readiness of invention charm me. Dear Petulant!

Betty. They are gone, sir, in great anger.

Petulant. Enough, let 'em trundle. Anger helps complexion, saves paint.

Fainall. This continence is all dissembled; this is in order to have something to brag of the next time he makes court to Millamant and swear he has abandoned the whole sex for her sake.

Mirabell. Have you not left off your impudent pretensions there yet? I shall cut your throat some time or other, Petulant, about that business.

Petulant. Ay, ay, let that pass—there are other throats to be cut.

Mirabell. Meaning mine, sir?

Petulant. Not I—I mean nobody—I know nothing. But there are uncles and nephews in the world—and they may be rivals—what then! All's one for that.

Mirabell. How! hark'ee, Petulant, come hither—explain, or I shall call your interpreter.

Petulant. Explain! I know nothing. Why, you have an uncle, have you not, lately come to town, and lodges by my Lady Wishfort's?

Mirabell. True.

Petulant. Why, that's enough—you and he are not friends; and if he should marry and have a child you may be disinherited, ha?

Mirabell. Where hast thou stumbled upon all this truth?

Petulant. All's one for that, why, then, say I know something.

Mirabell. Come, thou art an honest fellow, Petulant, and shalt make love to my mistress; thou sha't, faith. What hast thou heard of my uncle?

Petulant. I? Nothing, I. If throats are to be cut, let swords clash! snug's the word, I shrug and am silent.

Mirabell. Oh, raillery, raillery! Come, I know thou art in the woman's secrets. What, you're a cabalist; I know you stayed at Millamant's last night after I went. Was there any mention made of my uncle or me? Tell me. If thou hadst but good-nature equal to thy wit, Petulant, Tony Witwoud, who is now thy competitor in fame, would show as dim by thee as a dead whiting's eye by a pearl of orient; he would no more be seen by thee, than Mercury is by the sun. Come, I'm sure thou wo't tell me.

Petulant. If I do, will you grant me common sense then for the future?

Mirabell. Faith, I'll do what I can for thee, and I'll pray that Heaven may grant it thee in the meantime.

Petulant. Well, hark'ee.

(MIRABELL *and* PETULANT *talk apart.*)

Fainall. Petulant and you both will find Mirabell as warm a rival as a lover.

Witwoud. Pshaw! pshaw! that she laughs at Petulant is plain. And for my part, but that it is almost a fashion to admire her, I should—hark'ee—to tell you a secret, but let it go no further—between friends, I shall never break my heart for her.

Fainall. How!

Witwoud. She's handsome; but she's a sort of an uncertain woman.

Fainall. I thought you had died for her.

Witwoud. Umh—no—

Fainall. She has wit.

Witwoud. 'Tis what she will hardly allow anybody else. Now, demme, I should hate that, if she were as handsome as Cleopatra. Mirabell is not so sure of her as he thinks for.

Fainall. Why do you think so?

Witwoud. We stayed pretty late there last night, and heard something of an uncle to Mirabell, who is lately come to town—and is between him and the best part of his estate. Mirabell and he are at some distance, as my Lady Wishfort has been told; and you know she hates Mirabell worse than a quaker hates a parrot, or than a fishmonger hates a hard frost. Whether this uncle has seen Mrs. Millamant or not, I cannot say, but there were items of such a treaty being in embryo; and if it should come to life, poor Mirabell would be in some sort unfortunately fobbed,[15] i'faith.

Fainall. 'Tis impossible Millamant should hearken to it.

Witwoud. Faith, my dear, I can't tell; she's a woman, and a kind of humorist.

Mirabell. And this is the sum of what you could collect last night?

Petulant. The quintessence. Maybe Witwoud knows more, he stayed longer. Besides, they never mind him; they say anything before him.

Mirabell. I thought you had been the greatest favorite.

Petulant. Ay, *tête-à-tête*, but not in public, because I make remarks.

Mirabell. You do?

Petulant. Ay, ay; pox, I'm malicious, man! Now he's soft you know; they are not in awe of him—the fellow's well-bred; he's what you call a what-d'ye-call-'em, a fine gentleman—but he's silly withal.

Mirabell. I thank you. I know as much as my curiosity requires. Fainall, are you for the Mall?[16]

Fainall. Ay, I'll take a turn before dinner.

Witwoud. Ay, we'll all walk in the Park; the ladies talked of being there.

Mirabell. I thought you were obliged to watch for your brother Sir Wilfull's arrival.

Witwoud. No, no; he comes to his aunt's, my Lady Wishfort. Pox on him! I shall be troubled with him too; what shall I do with the fool?

Petulant. Beg him for his estate, that I may beg you afterwards: and so have but one trouble with you both.

Witwoud. Oh rare Petulant! Thou art as quick as fire in a frosty morning. Thou shalt to the Mall with us, and we'll be very severe.

Petulant. Enough! I'm in a humor to be severe.

Mirabell. Are you? Pray then walk by yourselves: let not us be accessory to your putting the ladies out of countenance with your senseless ribaldry, which you roar out aloud as often as they pass by you; and when you have made a handsome woman blush, then you think you have been severe.

Petulant. What, what! then let 'em either show their innocence by not understanding what they hear, or else show their discretion by not hearing what they would not be thought to understand.

Mirabell. But hast thou then sense enough to know that thou oughtest to be most ashamed thyself, when thou hast put another out of countenance?

Petulant. Not I, by this hand!—I always take blushing either for a sign of guilt, or ill breeding.

Mirabell. I confess you ought to think so. You are in the right, that you may plead the error of your judgment in defence of your practice.

> Where modesty's ill manners, 'tis but fit
> That impudence and malice pass for wit.

Exeunt.

ACT II

Scene I: *St. James's Park.*

Mrs. Fainall *and* Mrs. Marwood.

Mrs. Fainall. Ay, ay, dear Marwood, if we will be happy, we must find the means in ourselves and among ourselves. Men are ever in extremes: either doting or averse. While they are lovers, if they have fire and sense, their jealousies are insupportable; and when they cease to love (we ought to think at least) they loath; they look upon us with horror and distaste; they meet us like the ghosts of what we were, and as such, fly from us.

Mrs. Marwood. True, 'tis an unhappy circumstance of life, that love should ever die before us; and that the man so often should outlive the lover. But say what you will, 'tis better to be left than never to have been loved. To pass our youth in dull indifference, to refuse the sweets of life because they once must leave us, is as preposterous as to wish to have been born old because we one day must be old. For my part, my youth may wear and waste, but it shall never rust in my possession.

Mrs. Fainall. Then it seems you dissemble an aversion to mankind only in compliance to my mother's humor?

Mrs. Marwood. Certainly. To be free; I have no taste of those insipid dry discourses with which our sex of force must entertain themselves apart from men. We may affect endearments to each other, profess eternal friendships, and seem to dote like lovers; but 'tis not in our natures long to persevere. Love will resume his empire in our breasts; and every heart, or soon or late, receive and re-admit him as its lawful tyrant.

Mrs. Fainall. Bless me, how have I been deceived! why you profess a libertine.

Mrs. Marwood. You see my friendship by my freedom. Come, be as sincere, acknowledge that your sentiments agree with mine.

Mrs. Fainall. Never!

Mrs. Marwood. You hate mankind?

Mrs. Fainall. Heartily, inveterately.

Mrs. Marwood. Your husband?

Mrs. Fainall. Most transcendently; ay, though I say it, meritoriously.

Mrs. Marwood. Give me your hand upon it.

Mrs. Fainall. There.

Mrs. Marwood. I join with you; what I have said has been to try you.

Mrs. Fainall. Is it possible? dost thou hate those vipers, men?

Mrs. Marwood. I have done hating 'em, and am now come to despise 'em; the next thing I have to do, is eternally to forget 'em.

Mrs. Fainall. There spoke the spirit of an Amazon, a Penthesilea![17]

Mrs. Marwood. And yet I am thinking sometimes to carry my aversion further.

Mrs. Fainall. How?

Mrs. Marwood. Faith, by marrying; if I could but find one that loved me very well, and would be thoroughly sensible of ill usage, I think I should do myself the violence of undergoing the ceremony.

Mrs. Fainall. You would not make him a cuckold?

Mrs. Marwood. No; but I'd make him believe I did and that's as bad.

Mrs. Fainall. Why had not you as good do it?

Mrs. Marwood. Oh! if he should ever discover it, he would then know the worst and be out of his pain; but I would have him ever to continue upon the rack of fear and jealousy.

Mrs. Fainall. Ingenious mischief! would thou wert married to Mirabell.

Mrs. Marwood. Would I were!

Mrs. Fainall. You change color.

Mrs. Marwood. Because I hate him.

Mrs. Fainall. So do I; but I can hear him named. But what reason have you to hate him in particular?

Mrs. Marwood. I never loved him; he is, and always was, insufferably proud.

Mrs. Fainall. By the reason you give for your aversion, one would think it dissembled; for you have laid a fault to his charge, of which his enemies must acquit him.

Mrs. Marwood. Oh! then it seems you are one of his favorable enemies! Methinks you look a little pale—and now you flush again.

Mrs. Fainall. Do I? I think I am a little sick o' the sudden.

Mrs. Marwood. What ails you?

Mrs. Fainall. My husband. Don't you see him? He turned short upon me unawares, and has almost overcome me.

Enter FAINALL *and* MIRABELL.

Mrs. Marwood. Ha! ha! ha! he comes opportunely for you.

Mrs. Fainall. For you, for he has brought Mirabell with him.

Fainall. My dear!

Mrs. Fainall. My soul!

Fainall. You don't look well today, child.

Mrs. Fainall. D'ye think so?

Mirabell. He is the only man that does, madam.

Mrs. Fainall. The only man that would tell me so at least; and the only man from whom I could hear it without mortification.

Fainall. Oh my dear, I am satisfied of your tenderness; I know you cannot resent anything from me, especially what is an effect of my concern.

Mrs. Fainall. Mr. Mirabell, my mother interrupted you in a pleasant relation last night; I would fain hear it out.

Mirabell. The persons concerned in that affair have yet a

tolerable reputation. I am afraid Mr. Fainall will be censorious.

Mrs. Fainall. He has a humor more prevailing than his curiosity, and will willingly dispense with the hearing of one scandalous story, to avoid giving an occasion to make another by being seen to walk with his wife. This way, Mr. Mirabell, and I dare promise you will oblige us both.

Exeunt Mrs. FAINALL *and* MIRABELL.

Fainall. Excellent creature! Well, sure if I should live to be rid of my wife, I should be a miserable man.

Mrs. Marwood. Ay?

Fainall. For having only that one hope, the accomplishment of it, of consequence, must put an end to all my hopes; and what a wretch is he who must survive his hopes! Nothing remains when that day comes, but to sit down and weep like Alexander when he wanted other worlds to conquer.

Mrs. Marwood. Will you not follow 'em?

Fainall. Faith, I think not.

Mrs. Marwood. Pray let us; I have a reason.

Fainall. You are not jealous?

Mrs. Marwood. Of whom?

Fainall. Of Mirabell.

Mrs. Marwood. If I am, is it consistent with my love to you that I am tender of your honor?

Fainall. You would intimate, then, as if there were a fellow-feeling between my wife and him.

Mrs. Marwood. I think she does not hate him to that degree she would be thought.

Fainall. But he, I fear, is too insensible.

Mrs. Marwood. It may be you are deceived.

Fainall. It may be so. I do now begin to apprehend it.

Mrs. Marwood. What?

Fainall. That I have been deceived, madam, and you are false.

Mrs. Marwood. That I am false! what mean you?

Fainall. To let you know I see through all your little arts. —Come, you both love him; and both have equally dissembled your aversion. Your mutual jealousies of one another have made you clash till you have both struck fire. I have seen the warm confession reddening on your cheeks and sparkling from your eyes.

Mrs. Marwood. You do me wrong.

Fainall. I do not. 'Twas for my ease to oversee and wilfully neglect the gross advances made him by my wife; that by permitting her to be engaged, I might continue unsuspected in my pleasures and take you oftener to my arms in full security. But could you think, because the nodding husband would not wake, that e'er the watchful lover slept?

Mrs. Marwood. And wherewithal can you reproach me?

Fainall. With infidelity, with loving another, with love of Mirabell.

Mrs. Marwood. 'Tis false! I challenge you to show an instance that can confirm your groundless accusation. I hate him.

Fainall. And wherefore do you hate him? He is insensible and your resentment follows his neglect. An instance! the injuries you have done him are a proof: your interposing in his love. What cause had you to make discoveries of his pretended passion? to undeceive the credulous aunt, and be the officious obstacle of his match with Millamant?

Mrs. Marwood. My obligations to my lady urged me. I had professed a friendship to her and could not see her easy nature so abused by that dissembler.

Fainall. What, was it conscience then? Professed a friendship! O the pious friendships of the female sex!

Mrs. Marwood. More tender, more sincere, and more enduring, than all the vain and empty vows of men, whether professing love to us, or mutual faith to one another.

Fainall. Ha! ha! ha! you are my wife's friend too.

Mrs. Marwood. Shame and ingratitude! do you reproach me? you, you upbraid me? Have I been false to her, through strict fidelity to you, and sacrificed my friendship to keep my love inviolate? And have you the baseness to charge me with the guilt, unmindful of the merit? To you it should be meritorious, that I have been vicious: and do you reflect that guilt upon me which should lie buried in your bosom?

Fainall. You misinterpret my reproof. I meant but to remind you of the slight account you once could make of strictest ties when set in competition with your love to me.

Mrs. Marwood. 'Tis false; you urged it with deliberate malice! 'twas spoken in scorn, and I never will forgive it.

Fainall. Your guilt, not your resentment, begets your rage. If yet you loved, you could forgive a jealousy; but you are stung to find you are discovered.

Mrs. Marwood. It shall be all discovered. You too shall be discovered; be sure you shall. I can but be exposed.—If I do it myself I shall prevent your baseness.

Fainall. Why, what will you do?

Mrs. Marwood. Disclose it to your wife; own what has passed between us.

Fainall. Frenzy!

Mrs. Marwood. By all my wrongs I'll do't!—I'll publish to the world the injuries you have done me, both in my fame and fortune! With both I trusted you, you bankrupt in honor, as indigent of wealth.

Fainall. Your fame I have preserved. Your fortune has been bestowed as the prodigality of your love would have it, in pleasures which we both have shared. Yet, had not you been false, I had ere this repaid it—'tis true. Had you permitted Mirabell with Millamant to have stolen their marriage, my lady had been incensed beyond all means of reconcilement: Millamant had forfeited the moiety of her fortune, which then would have descended to my wife—and wherefore did I marry, but to make lawful prize of a rich widow's wealth, and squander it on love and you?

Mrs. Marwood. Deceit and frivolous pretence!

Fainall. Death, am I not married? What's pretence? Am I not imprisoned, fettered? Have I not a wife? nay a wife that was a widow, a young widow, a handsome widow; and would be again a widow, but that I have a heart of proof, and something of a constitution to bustle through the ways of wedlock and this world! Will you yet be reconciled to truth and me?

Mrs. Marwood. Impossible. Truth and you are inconsistent; I hate you and shall for ever.

Fainall. For loving you?

Mrs. Marwood. I loathe the name of love after such usage; and next to the guilt with which you would asperse me, I scorn you most. Farewell!

Fainall. Nay, we must not part thus.

Mrs. Marwood. Let me go.

Fainall. Come, I'm sorry.

Mrs. Marwood. I care not—let me go—break my hands, do—I'd leave 'em to get loose.

Fainall. I would not hurt you for the world. Have I no other hold to keep you here?

Mrs. Marwood. Well, I have deserved it all.

Fainall. You know I love you.

Mrs. Marwood. Poor dissembling!—Oh, that—well, it is not yet—

Fainall. What? what is it not? what is it not yet? It is not yet too late—

Mrs. Marwood. No, it is not yet too late—I have that comfort.

Fainall. It is, to love another.

Mrs. Marwood. But not to loathe, detest, abhor mankind, myself, and the whole treacherous world.

Fainall. Nay, this is extravagance.—Come, I ask your pardon—no tears—I was to blame, I could not love you and be easy in my doubts. Pray forbear—I believe you; I'm convinced I've done you wrong; and any way, every way will make amends. I'll hate my wife yet more, damn her! I'll part with her, rob her of all she's worth, and we'll retire somewhere, anywhere, to another world. I'll marry thee—be pacified.—'Sdeath, they come. Hide your face, your tears—you have a mask, wear it a moment. This way, this way—be persuaded.   *Exeunt.*

Enter MIRABELL *and* MRS. FAINALL.

Mrs. Fainall. They are here yet.

Mirabell. They are turning into the other walk.

Mrs. Fainall. While I only hated my husband, I could bear to see him; but since I have despised him, he's too offensive.

Mirabell. Oh, you should hate with prudence.

Mrs. Fainall. Yes, for I have loved with indiscretion.

Mirabell. You should have just so much disgust for your husband as may be sufficient to make you relish your lover.

Mrs. Fainall. You have been the cause that I have loved without bounds, and would you set limits to that aversion of which you have been the occasion? Why did you make me marry this man?

Mirabell. Why do we daily commit disagreeable and dangerous actions? To save that idol, reputation. If the familiarities of our loves had produced that consequence of which you were apprehensive, where could you have fixed a father's name with credit, but on a husband? I knew Fainall to be a man lavish of his morals, an interested and professing friend, a false and designing lover; yet one on whose wit and outward fair behavior have gained a reputation with the town enough to make that woman stand excused who has suffered herself to be won by his addresses. A better man ought not to have been sacrificed to the occasion; a worse had not answered to the purpose. When you are weary of him you know your remedy.

Mrs. Fainall. I ought to stand in some degree of credit with you, Mirabell.

Mirabell. In justice to you, I have made you privy to my whole design, and put it in your power to ruin or advance my fortune.

Mrs. Fainall. Whom have you instructed to represent your pretended uncle?

Mirabell. Waitwell, my servant.

Mrs. Fainall. He is an humble servant[18] to Foible my mother's woman, and may win her to your interest

Mirabel. Care is taken for that—she is won and worn by this time. They were married this morning.

Mrs. Fainall. Who?

Mirabell. Waitwell and Foible. I would not tempt my servant to betray me by trusting him too far. If your mother, in
hopes to ruin me, should consent to marry my pretended
uncle, he might, like Mosca in the *Fox*,[19] stand upon terms;
so I made him sure beforehand.

Mrs. Fainall. So if my poor mother is caught in a contract,
you will discover the imposture betimes; and release her by
producing a certificate of her gallant's former marriage?

Mirabell. Yes, upon condition that she consent to my marriage with her niece, and surrender the moiety of her fortune in her possession.

Mrs. Fainall. She talked last night of endeavoring at a
match between Millamant and your uncle.

Mirabell. That was by Foible's direction and my instruc-
tion, that she might seem to carry it more privately.

Mrs. Fainall. Well, I have an opinion of your success; for
I believe my lady will do anything to get a husband; and
when she has this, which you have provided for her, I suppose she will submit to anything to get rid of him.

Mirabell. Yes, I think the good lady would marry anything that resembled a man, though 'twere no more than
what a butler could pinch out of a napkin.

Mrs. Fainall. Female frailty! we must all come to it, if
we live to be old, and feel the craving of a false appetite
when the true is decayed.

Mirabell. An old woman's appetite is depraved like that of
a girl—'tis the green sickness of a second childhood; and,
like the faint offer of a latter spring, serves but to usher in
the fall and withers in an affected bloom.

Mrs. Fainall. Here's your mistress.

Enter Mrs. MILLAMANT, WITWOUD, *and* MINCING.

Mirabell. Here she comes, i'faith, full sail, with her fan
spread and her streamers out, and a shoal of fools for ten-
ders. Ha, no, I cry her mercy!

Mrs. Fainall. I see but one poor empty sculler, and he
tows her woman after him.

Mirabell. (*To* Mrs. MILLAMANT.) You seem to be unat-
tended, madam—you used to have the *beau monde* throng
after you; and a flock of gay fine perukes hovering round
you.

Witwoud. Like moths about a candle.—I had like to have
lost my comparison for want of breath.

Mrs. Millamant. Oh, I have denied myself airs today. I
have walked as fast through the crowd—

Witwoud. As a favorite just disgraced; and with as few followers.

Mrs. Millamant. Dear Mr. Witwoud, truce with your similitudes; for I'm as sick of 'em—

Witwoud. As a physician of a good air.—I cannot help it, madam, though 'tis against myself.

Mrs. Millamant. Yet, again! Mincing, stand between me and his wit.

Witwoud. Do, Mrs. Mincing, like a screen before a great fire.—I confess I do blaze today, I am too bright.

Mrs. Fainall. But, dear Millamant, why were you so long?

Mrs. Millamant. Long! Lord, have I not made violent haste? I have asked every living thing I met for you; I have inquired after you, as after a new fashion.

Witwoud. Madam, truce with your similitudes.—No, you met her husband, and did not ask him for her.

Mrs. Millamant. By your leave, Witwoud, that were like inquiring after an old fashion, to ask a husband for his wife.

Witwoud. Hum, a hit! a hit! a palpable hit! I confess it.

Mrs. Fainall. You were dressed before I came abroad.

Mrs. Millamant. Ay, that's true.—Oh, but then I had— Mincing, what had I? Why was I so long?

Mincing. O mem, you la'ship stayed to peruse a packet of letters.

Mrs. Millamant. Oh, ay, letters—I had letters—I am persecuted with letters—I hate letters—Nobody knows how to write letters, and yet one has 'em, one does not know why. They serve one to pin up one's hair.

Witwoud. Is that the way? Pray, madam, do you pin up your hair with all your letters? I find I must keep copies.

Mrs. Millamant. Only with those in verse, Mr. Witwoud. I never pin up my hair with prose. I think I tried once, Mincing.

Mincing. O mem, I shall never forget it.

Mrs. Millamant. Ay, poor Mincing tift[20] and tift all the morning.

Mincing. Till I had the cramp in my fingers, I'll vow, mem; and all to no purpose. But when your la'ship pins it up with poetry it sits so pleasant the next day as anything, and is so pure and so crips.

Witwoud. Indeed, so *crips*?

Mincing. You're such a critic, Mr. Witwoud.

Mrs. Millamant. Mirabell, did you take exceptions last night? Oh, ay, and went away.—Now I think on't I'm angry —no, now I think on't I'm pleased—for I believe I gave you some pain.

Mirabell. Does that please you?

Mrs. Millamant. Infinitely; I love to give pain.

Mirabell. You would affect a cruelty which is not your nature; your true vanity is in the power of pleasing.

Mrs. Millamant. Oh, I ask you pardon for that—one's cruelty is one's power; and when one parts with one's cruelty, one parts with one's power; and when one has parted with that, I fancy one's old and ugly.

Mirabell. Ay, ay, suffer your cruelty to ruin the object of your power, to destroy your lover—and then how vain, how lost a thing you'll be! Nay, 'tis true: you are no longer handsome when you've lost your lover; your beauty dies upon the instant; for beauty is the lover's gift. 'Tis he bestows your charms—your glass is all a cheat. The ugly and the old, whom the looking-glass mortifies, yet after commendation can be flattered by it, and discover beauties in it; for that reflects our praises, rather than your face.

Mrs. Millamant. O the vanity of these men!—Fainall, d'ye hear him? If they did not commend us, we were not handsome! Now you must know they could not commend one, if one was not handsome. Beauty the lover's gift!—Lord, what is a lover, that it can give? Why, one makes lovers as fast as one pleases, and they live as long as one pleases, and they die as soon as one pleases; and then, if one pleases, one makes more.

Witwoud. Very pretty. Why, you make no more of making of lovers, madam, than of making so many card-matches.

Mrs. Millamant. One no more owes one's beauty to a lover, than one's wit to an echo. They can but reflect what we look and say: vain empty things if we are silent or unseen, and want a being.

Mirabell. Yet to those two vain empty things you owe the two greatest pleasures of your life.

Mrs. Millamant. How so?

Mirabell. To your lover you owe the pleasure of hearing yourselves praised; and to an echo the pleasure of hearing yourselves talk.

Witwoud. But I know a lady that loves talking so incessantly, she won't give an echo fair play; she has that everlasting rotation of tongue, that an echo must wait till she dies, before it can catch her last words.

Mrs. Millamant. O fiction!—Fainall, let us leave these men.

Mirabell. Draw off Witwoud.   (*Aside to* Mrs. FAINALL.)

Mrs. Fainall. Immediately.—I have a word or two for Mr. Witwoud.   *Exeunt* Mrs. FAINALL *and* WITWOUD.

Mirabell. I would beg a little private audience too.—You had the tyranny to deny me last night; though you knew I came to impart a secret to you that concerned my love.

Mrs. Millamant. You saw I was engaged.

Mirabell. Unkind! You had the leisure to entertain a herd of fools; things who visit you from their excessive idleness; bestowing on your easiness that time which is the incumbrance of their lives. How can you find delight in such society? It is impossible they should admire you, they are not capable: or if they were, it should be to you as a mortification; for sure to please a fool is some degree of folly.

Mrs. Millamant. I please myself—besides, sometimes to converse with fools is for my health.

Mirabell. Your health! is there a worse disease than the conversation of fools?

Mrs. Millamant. Yes, the vapors; fools are physic for it, next to assafœtida.

Mirabell. You are not in a course of fools?

Mrs. Millamant. Mirabell, if you persist in this offensive freedom, you'll displease me.—I think I must resolve, after all, not to have you: we shan't agree.

Mirabell. Not in our physic, it may be.

Mrs. Millamant. And yet our distemper, in all likelihood, will be the same; for we shall be sick of one another. I shan't endure to be reprimanded nor instructed; 'tis so dull to act always by advice, and so tedious to be told of one's faults—I can't bear it. Well, I won't have you, Mirabell—I'm resolved—I think—you may go.—Ha! ha! ha! what would you give, that you could help loving me?

Mirabell. I would give something that you did not know I could not help it.

Mrs. Millamant. Come, don't look grave then. Well, what do you say to me?

Mirabell. I say that a man may as soon make a friend by his wit, or a fortune by his honesty, as win a woman by plain-dealing and sincerity.

Mrs. Millamant. Sententious Mirabell! Prithee, don't look with that violent and inflexible wise face, like Solomon at the dividing of the child in an old tapestry hanging.

Mirabell. You are merry, madam, but I would persuade you for a moment to be serious.

Mrs. Millamant. What, with that face? no, if you keep your countenance, 'tis impossible I should hold mine. Well, after all, there is something very moving in a love-sick face. Ha! ha! ha!—well, I won't laugh, don't be peevish—Heigho! now I'll be melancholy, as melancholy as a watch-light.[21] Well, Mirabell, if ever you will win me, woo me now.—Nay, if you are so tedious, fare you well—I see they are walking away.

Mirabell. Can you not find in the variety of your disposition one moment—

Mrs. Millamant. To hear you tell me Foible's married, and your plot like to speed? No.

Mirabell. But how came you to know it?

Mrs. Millamant. Without the help of the devil, you can't imagine—unless she should tell me herself. Which of the two it may have been I will leave you to consider; and when you have done thinking of that, think of me.   *Exit.*

Mirabell. I have something more.—Gone!—Think of you? to think of a whirlwind, though 'twere in a whirlwind, were a case of more steady contemplation; a very tranquillity of mind and mansion. A fellow that lives in a windmill, has not a more whimsical dwelling than the heart of a man that is lodged in a woman. There is no point of the compass to which they cannot turn, and by which they are not turned; and by one as well as another. For motion, not method, is their occupation. To know this, and yet continue to be in love, is to be made wise from the dictates of reason, and yet persevere to play the fool by the force of instinct.—Oh, here come my pair of turtles!—What, billing so sweetly! is not Valentine's day over with you yet?

Enter WAITWELL and FOIBLE.

Sirrah Waitwell, why sure you think you were married for your own recreation, and not for my conveniency.

Waitwell. Your pardon, sir. With submission, we have indeed been solacing in lawful delights; but still with an eye to business, sir. I have instructed her as well as I could. If she can take your directions as readily as my instructions, sir, your affairs are in a prosperous way.

Mirabell. Give you joy, Mrs. Foible.

Foible. O las, sir, I'm so ashamed!—I'm afraid my lady has been in a thousand inquietudes for me. But I protest, sir, I made as much haste as I could.

Waitwell. That she did indeed, sir. It was my fault that she did not make more.

Mirabell. That I believe.

Foible. But I told my lady as you instructed me, sir, that I had a prospect of seeing Sir Rowland, your uncle; and that I would put her ladyship's picture in my pocket to show him; which I'll be sure to say has made him so enamored of her beauty, that he burns with impatience to lie at her ladyship's feet and worship the original.

Mirabell. Excellent Foible! Matrimony has made you eloquent in love.

Waitwell. I think she has profited, sir, I think so.

Foible. You have seen Madam Millamant, sir?

Mirabell. Yes.

Foible. I told her, sir, because I did not know that you might find an opportunity; she had so much company last night.

Mirabell. Your diligence will merit more—in the mean time—   *(Gives money)*

Foible. O dear, sir, your humble servant!

Waitwell. Spouse!

Mirabell. Stand off, sir, not a penny!—Go on and prosper, Foible—the lease shall be made good, and the farm stocked, if we succeed.

Foible. I don't question your generosity, sir: and you need not doubt of success. If you have no more commands, sir, I'll be gone; I'm sure my lady is at her toilet, and can't dress till I come—Oh, dear, I'm sure that *(Looking out.)* was Mrs. Marwood that went by in a mask! If she has seen me with you I'm sure she'll tell my lady. I'll make haste home and prevent her. Your servant, sir.—B'w'y, Waitwell.   *Exit.*

Waitwell. Sir Rowland, if you please.—The jade's so pert upon her preferment she forgets herself.

Mirabell. Come, sir, will you endeavor to forget yourself, and transform into Sir Rowland?

Waitwell. Why, sir, it will be impossible I should remember myself.—Married, knighted, and attended all in one day! 'Tis enough to make any man forget himself. The difficulty will be how to recover my acquaintance and familiarity with my former self, and fall from my transformation to a reformation into Waitwell. Nay, I shan't be quite the same Waitwell neither; for now, I remember me, I'm married and can't be my own man again.

Ay there's my grief; that's the sad change of life,
To lose my title, and yet keep my wife.   *Exeunt.*

ACT III

SCENE I: *A Room in* Lady WISHFORT'S *House.*

Lady WISHFORT *at her toilet*, PEG *waiting.*

Lady Wishfort. Merciful! No news of Foible yet?

Peg. No, madam.

Lady Wishfort. I have no more patience.—If I have not fretted myself till I am pale again, there's no veracity in me! Fetch me the red—the red, do you hear, sweetheart?—An arrant ash-color, as I am a person! Look you how this wench stirs! Why dost thou not fetch me a little red? didst thou not hear me, Mopus?

Peg. The red ratafia does your ladyship mean, or the cherry-brandy?

Lady Wishfort. Ratafia, fool! No, fool. Not the ratafia, fool—grant me patience!—I mean the Spanish paper,[22] idiot —complexion, darling. Paint! paint! paint! dost thou understand that, changeling, dangling thy hands like bobbins before thee? Why dost thou not stir, puppet? thou wooden thing upon wires!

Peg. Lord, madam, your ladyship is so impatient!—I cannot come at the paint, madam; Mrs. Foible has locked it up and carried the key with her.

Lady Wishfort. A pox take you both!—fetch me the cherry-brandy then. (*Exit* PEG.) I'm as pale and as faint, I look like Mrs. Qualmsick, the curate's wife, that's always breeding.—Wench, come, come, wench, what art thou doing? sipping, tasting?—Save thee, dost thou not know the bottle?

Re-enter PEG *with a bottle and china cup.*

Peg. Madam, I was looking for a cup.

Lady Wishfort. A cup, save thee! and what a cup hast thou brought!—Dost thou take me for a fairy, to drink out of an acorn? Why didst thou not bring thy thimble? Hast thou ne'er a brass thimble clinking in thy pocket with a bit of nutmeg?—I warrant thee. Come, fill, fill!—So—again.—(*Knocking at the door.*)—See who that is.—Set down the bottle first—here, here, under the table.—What, wouldst thou go with the bottle in thy hand, like a tapster? As I am a person, this wench has lived in an inn upon the road before she came to me, like Maritornes the Asturian in *Don Quixote!* —No Foible yet?

Peg. No, madam; Mrs. Marwood.

Lady Wishfort. Oh, Marwood; let her come in.—Come in, good Marwood.

Enter MRS. MARWOOD.

Mrs. Marwood. I'm surprised to find your ladyship in dishabille at this time of day.

Lady Wishfort. Foible's a lost thing—has been abroad since morning, and never heard of since.

Mrs. Marwood. I saw her but once, as I came masked through the park, in conference with Mirabell.

Lady Wishfort. With Mirabell!—You call my blood into

my face, with mentioning that traitor. She durst not have the confidence! I sent her to negotiate an affair in which, if I'm detected, I'm undone. If that wheedling villain has wrought upon Foible to detect me, I'm ruined. O my dear friend, I'm a wretch of wretches if I'm detected.

Mrs. Marwood. O madam, you cannot suspect Mrs. Foible's integrity!

Lady Wishfort. Oh, he carries poison in his tongue that would corrupt integrity itself! If she has given him an opportunity, she has as good as put her integrity into his hands. Ah, dear Marwood, what's integrity to an opportunity?— Hark! I hear her!—dear friend, retire into my closet, that I may examine her with more freedom.—You'll pardon me, dear friend; I can make bold with you.—There are books over the chimney.—Quarles and Prynne, and *The Short View of the Stage,* with Bunyan's works, to entertain you—(*To* Peg.)—Go, you thing, and send her in.

Exeunt Mrs. Marwood *and* Peg.

Enter Foible.

Lady Wishfort. O Foible, where has thou been? what hast thou been doing?

Foible. Madam, I have seen the party.

Lady Wishfort. But what hast thou done?

Foible. Nay, 'tis your ladyship has done, and are to do; I have only promised. But a man so enamored—so transported!—Well, here it is, all that is left; all that is not kissed away.—Well, if worshipping of pictures be a sin——poor Sir Rowland, I say.

Lady Wishfort. The miniature has been counted like—but hast thou not betrayed me, Foible? Hast thou not detected me to that faithless Mirabell?—What hadst thou to do with him in the Park? Answer me, has he got nothing out of thee?

Foible. (*Aside.*) So the devil has been beforehand with me. What shall I say?—(*Aloud.*)—Alas, madam, could I help it, if I met that confident thing? was I in fault? If you had heard how he used me, and all upon your ladyship's account, I'm sure you would not suspect my fidelity. Nay, if that had been the worst, I could have borne; but he had a fling at your ladyship too; and then I could not hold, but i'faith I gave him his own.

Lady Wishfort. Me? what did the filthy fellow say?

Foible. O madam! 'tis a shame to say what he said—with his taunts and his fleers, tossing up his nose. Humph! (says he) what, you are hatching some plot (says he), you are so

early abroad, or catering (says he), ferreting some disbanded
officer, I warrant.—Half-pay is but thin subsistence (says he)
—well, what pension does your lady propose? Let me see
(says he), what, she must come down pretty deep now, she's
superannuated (says he) and—

Lady Wishfort. Odds my life, I'll have him, I'll have him
murdered! I'll have him poisoned! Where does he eat?—I'll
marry a drawer to have him poisoned in his wine. I'll send
for Robin[23] from Locket's[24] immediately.

Foible. Poison him! poisoning's too good for him. Starve
him, madam, starve him; marry Sir Rowland, and get him
disinherited. Oh you would bless yourself to hear what he
said!

Lady Wishfort. A villain! superannuated!

Foible. Humph (says he), I hear you are laying designs
against me too (says he), and Mrs. Millamant is to marry
my uncle (he does not suspect a word of your ladyship);
but (says he) I'll fit you for that. I warrant you (says he)
I'll hamper you for that (says he); you and your old frippery[25] too (says he); I'll handle you—

Lady Wishfort. Audacious villain! handle me; would he
durst!—Frippery! old frippery! was there ever such a foul-
mouthed fellow? I'll be married tomorrow; I'll be contracted
tonight.

Foible. The sooner the better, madam.

Lady Wishfort. Will Sir Rowland be here, sayest thou?
when, Foible?

Foible. Incontinently, madam. No new sheriff's wife expects the return of her husband after knighthood with that
impatience in which Sir Rowland burns for the dear hour of
kissing your ladyship's hand after dinner.

Lady Wishfort. Frippery! superannuated frippery! I'll frippery the villain; I'll reduce him to frippery and rags! a tat-
terdemalion! I hope to see him hung with tatters, like a
Long-lane pent-house[26] or a gibbet thief. A slander-mouthed
railer! I warrant the spendthrift prodigal's in debt as much
as the million lottery, or the whole court upon a birthday.
I'll spoil his credit with his tailor. Yes, he shall have my niece
with her fortune, he shall.

Foible. He! I hope to see him lodge in Ludgate[27] first, and
angle into Blackfriars for brass farthings with an old mitten.

Lady Wishfort. Ay, dear Foible; thank thee for that, dear
Foible. He has put me all out of patience. I shall never re-
compose my features to receive Sir Rowland with any economy of face. This wretch has fretted me that I am absolutely
decayed. Look, Foible.

Foible. Your ladyship has frowned a little too rashly, indeed, madam. There are some cracks discernible in the white varnish.

Lady Wishfort. Let me see the glass.—Cracks, sayest thou?—why, I am arrantly flayed—I look like an old peeled wall. Thou must repair me, Foible, before Sir Rowland comes, or I shall never keep up to my picture.

Foible. I warrant you, madam, a little art once made your picture like you; and now a little of the same art must make you like your picture. Your picture must sit for you, madam.

Lady Wishfort. But art thou sure Sir Rowland will not fail to come? Or will he not fail when he does come? Will he be importunate, Foible, and push? For if he should not be importunate, I shall never break decorums—I shall die with confusion, if I am forced to advance.—Oh, no, I can never advance!—I shall swoon if he should expect advances. No, I hope Sir Rowland is better bred than to put a lady to the necessity of breaking her forms. I won't be too coy, neither. —I won't give him despair—but a little disdain is not amiss; a little scorn is alluring.

Foible. A little scorn becomes your ladyship.

Lady Wishfort. Yes, but tenderness becomes me best—a sort of dyingness—you see that picture has a sort of a—ha, Foible? a swimmingness in the eye—yes, I'll look so—my niece affects it; but she wants features. Is Sir Rowland handsome? Let my toilet be removed—I'll dress above. I'll receive Sir Rowland here: Is he handsome? Don't answer me. I won't know: I'll be surprised, I'll be taken by surprise.

Foible. By storm, madam, Sir Rowland's a brisk man.

Lady Wishfort. Is he! O then he'll importune, if he's a brisk man. I shall save decorums if Sir Rowland importunes. I have a mortal terror at the apprehension of offending against decorums. Oh, I'm glad he's a brisk man. Let my things be removed, good Foible.   *Exit.*

Enter Mrs. Fainall.

Mrs. Fainall. O Foible. I have been in a fright, lest I should come too late! That devil Marwood saw you in the Park with Mirabell, and I'm afraid will discover it to my lady.

Foible. Discover what, madam!

Mrs. Fainall. Nay, nay, put not on that strange face. I am privy to the whole design, and know that Waitwell, to whom thou wert this morning married, is to personate Mirabell's uncle, and as such, winning my lady, to involve her in those difficulties from which Mirabell only must release her, by his making his conditions to have my cousin and her fortune left to her own disposal.

Foible. O dear madam, I beg your pardon. It was not my confidence in your ladyship that was deficient; but I thought the former good correspondence between your ladyship and Mr. Mirabell might have hindered his communicating this secret.

Mrs. Fainall. Dear Foible, forget that.

Foible. O dear madam, Mr. Mirabell is such a sweet, winning gentleman—but your ladyship is the pattern of generosity.—Sweet lady, to be so good! Mr. Mirabell cannot choose but be grateful. I find your ladyship has his heart still. Now, madam, I can safely tell your ladyship our success: Mrs. Marwood had told my lady; but I warrant I managed myself. I turned it all for the better. I told my lady that Mr. Mirabell railed at her; I laid horrid things to his charge, I'll vow; and my lady is so incensed that she'll be contracted to Sir Rowland tonight, she says; I warrant I worked her up, that he may have her for asking for, as they say of a Welsh maidenhead.

Mrs. Fainall. O rare Foible!

Foible. I beg your ladyship to acquaint Mr. Mirabell of his success. I would be seen as little as possible to speak to him—besides, I believe Madam Marwood watches me.—She has a month's mind;[28] but I know Mr. Mirabell can't abide her.—John!—*(Calls.)* remove my lady's toilet.—Madam, your servant: my lady is so impatient I fear she'll come for me if I stay.

Mrs. Fainall. I'll go with you up the back-stairs, lest I should meet her.　　　　　　　　　　　　　　　　*Exeunt.*

Enter Mrs. MARWOOD.

Mrs. Marwood. Indeed, Mrs. Engine, is it thus with you? are you become a go-between of this importance? yes, I shall watch you. Why this wench is the *passe-partout*, a very master-key to everybody's strong-box. My friend Fainall, have you carried it so swimmingly? I thought there was something in it; but it seems 'tis over with you. Your loathing is not from a want of appetite, then, but from a surfeit. Else you could never be so cool to fall from a principal to be an assistant; to procure for him! a pattern of generosity, that, I confess. Well, Mr. Fainall, you have met with your match. —O man, man! woman, woman! the devil's an ass: if I were a painter, I would draw him like an idiot, a driveller with a bib and bells. Man should have his head and horns, and woman the rest of him. Poor simple fiend!—"Madam Marwood has a month's mind, but he can't abide her."—'Twere better for him you had not been his confessor in that affair, without you could have kept his counsel closer. I shall not prove another pattern of generosity; he has not obliged me to that with those excesses of himself! and now I'll have none of him. Here comes the good lady, panting ripe; with a heart full of hope, and a head full of care, like any chemist upon the day of projection.[29]

Enter Lady WISHFORT.

Lady Wishfort. O dear, Marwood, what shall I say for this rude forgetfulness?—but my dear friend is all goodness.

Mrs. Marwood. No apologies, dear madam; I have been very well entertained.

Lady Wishfort. As I'm a person, I am in a very chaos to think I should so forget myself:—but I have such an olio[30] of affairs, really I know not what to do.—Foible!—*(Calls.)* I expect my nephew, Sir Wilfull, every moment too.—Why, Foible!—He means to travel for improvement.

Mrs. Marwood. Methinks Sir Wilfull should rather think of marrying than travelling at his years. I hear he is turned of forty.

Lady Wishfort. Oh, he's in less danger of being spoiled by his travels—I am against my nephew's marrying too young. It will be time enough when he comes back, and has acquired discretion to choose for himself.

Mrs. Marwood. Methinks Mrs. Millamant and he would make a very fit match. He may travel afterwards. 'Tis a thing very usual with young gentlemen.

Lady Wishfort. I promise you I have thought on't—and since 'tis your judgment, I'll think on't again. I assure you I will; I value your judgment extremely. On my word, I'll propose it.

Enter FOIBLE.

Lady Wishfort. Come, come, Foible—I had forgot my nephew will be here before dinner—I must make haste.

Foible. Mr. Witwoud and Mr. Petulant are come to dine with your ladyship.

Lady Wishfort. O dear, I can't appear till I'm dressed.— Dear Marwood, shall I be free with you again, and beg you to entertain 'em? I'll make all imaginable haste. Dear friend, excuse me.   *Exeunt* Lady WISHFORT *and* FOIBLE.

Enter Mrs. MILLAMANT, *and* MINCING.

Mrs. Millamant. Sure never anything was so unbred as that odious man!—Marwood, your servant.

Mrs. Marwood. You have a color; what's the matter?

Mrs. Millamant. That horrid fellow, Petulant, has provoked me into a flame: I have broken my fan.—Mincing, lend me yours. Is not all the powder out of my hair?

Mrs. Marwood. No. What has he done?

Mrs. Millamant. Nay, he has done nothing; he has only talked—nay, he has said nothing neither; but he has contradicted everything that has been said. For my part, I thought Witwoud and he would have quarrelled.

Mincing. I vow, mem, I thought once they would have fit.

Mrs. Millamant. Well, 'tis a lamentable thing, I swear, that one has not the liberty of choosing one's acquaintance as one does one's clothes.

Mrs. Marwood. If we had that liberty, we should be as weary of one set of acquaintance, though never so good, as we are of one suit though never so fine. A fool and a doily stuff[31] would now and then find days of grace, and be worn for variety.

Mrs. Millamant. I could consent to wear 'em, if they would wear alike; but fools never wear out—they are such *drap de Berri*[32] things! Without one could give 'em to one's chambermaid after a day or two.

Mrs. Marwood. 'Twere better so indeed. Or what think you of the playhouse? A fine, gay, glossy fool should be given there, like a new masking habit, after the masquerade is over and we have done with the disguise. For a fool's visit is always a disguise; and never admitted by a woman of wit, but to blind her affair with a lover of sense. If you would but appear barefaced now, and own Mirabell, you might as easily put off Petulant and Witwoud as your hood and scarf. And indeed, 'tis time, for the town has found it; the secret is grown too big for the pretence. 'Tis like Mrs. Primly's great belly; she may lace it down before, but it burnishes on her hips. Indeed, Millamant, you can no more conceal it than my Lady Strammel can her face; that goodly face, which in defiance of her Rhenish wine tea,[33] will not be comprehended in a mask.

Mrs. Millamant. I'll take my death, Marwood, you are more censorious than a decayed beauty or a discarded toast. —Mincing, tell the men they may come up.—My aunt is not dressing here; their folly is less provoking than your malice. (*Exit* MINCING.) The town has found it! what has it found? That Mirabell loves me is no more a secret than it is a secret that you discovered it to my aunt, or than the reason why you discovered it is a secret.

Mrs. Marwood. You are nettled.

Mrs. Millamant. You are mistaken. Ridiculous!

Mrs. Marwood. Indeed, my dear, you'll tear another fan, if you don't mitigate those violent airs.

Mrs. Millamant. O silly! ha! ha! ha! I could laugh immoderately. Poor Mirabell! his constancy to me has quite destroyed his complaisance for all the world beside. I swear, I never enjoined it him to be so coy. If I had the vanity to think he would obey me, I would command him to show more gallantry—'tis hardly well-bred to be so particular on one hand, and so insensible on the other. But I despair to prevail, and so let him follow his own way. Ha! ha! ha! pardon me, dear creature, I must laugh, ha! ha! ha! though I grant you 'tis a little barbarous, ha! ha! ha!

Mrs. Marwood. What pity 'tis so much fine raillery and delivered with so significant gesture, should be so unhappily directed to miscarry!

Mrs. Millamant. Ha! dear creature, I ask your pardon—I swear I did not mind you.

Mrs. Marwood. Mr. Mirabell and you both may think it a thing impossible, when I shall tell him by telling you—

Mrs. Millamant. O dear, what? for it is the same thing if I hear it—ha! ha! ha!

Mrs. Marwood. That I detest him, hate him, madam.

Mrs. Millamant. O madam, why so do I—and yet the creature loves me—ha! ha! ha! How can one forbear laughing to think of it.—I am a sibyl if I am not amazed to think what he can see in me. I'll take my death, I think you are handsomer—and within a year or two as young—if you could but stay for me, I should overtake you, but that cannot be.—Well, that thought makes me melancholic.—Now, I'll be sad.

Mrs. Marwood. Your merry note may be changed sooner than you think.

Mrs. Millamant. D'ye say so? Then I'm resolved I'll have a song to keep up my spirits.

Enter MINCING.

Mincing. The gentlemen stay but to comb, madam, and will wait on you.

Mrs. Millamant. Desire Mrs.—— that is in the next room to sing the song I would have learned yesterday.—You shall hear it, madam—not that there's any great matter in it—but 'tis agreeable to my humor.

Song.

Love's but the frailty of the mind,
  When 'tis not with ambition joined;
A sickly flame, which, if not fed, expires,
And feeding, wastes in self-consuming fires.

  'Tis not to wound a wanton boy
  Or amorous youth, that gives the joy;
But 'tis the glory to have pierced a swain,
For whom inferior beauties sighed in vain.

  Then I alone the conquest prize,
  When I insult a rival's eyes:
If there's delight in love, 'tis when I see
That heart, which others bleed for, bleed for me.

Enter PETULANT *and* WITWOUD.

Mrs. Millamant. Is your animosity composed, gentlemen?

Witwoud. Raillery, raillery, madam; we have no animosity —we hit off a little wit now and then, but no animosity. The falling out of wits is like the falling out of lovers: we agree in the main, like treble and bass.—Ha, Petulant?

Petulant. Ay, in the main—but when I have a humor to contradict—

Witwoud. Ay, when he has a humor to contradict, then I contradict too. What, I know my cue. Then we contradict one another like two battledores; for contradictions beget one another like Jews.

Petulant. If he says black's black—if I have a humor to say 'tis blue—let that pass—all's one for that. If I have a humor to prove it, it must be granted.

Witwoud. Not positively must—but it may—it may.

Petulant. Yes, it positively must, upon proof positive.

Witwoud. Ay, upon proof positive it must; but upon proof presumptive it only may.—That's a logical distinction now, madam.

Mrs. Marwood. I perceive your debates are of importance and very learnedly handled.

Petulant. Importance is one thing, and learning's another; but a debate's a debate, that I assert.

Witwoud. Petulant's an enemy to learning; he relies altogether on his parts.

Petulant. No, I'm no enemy to learning; it hurts not me.

Mrs. Marwood. That's a sign indeed it's no enemy to you.

Petulant. No, no, it's no enemy to anybody but them that have it.

Mrs. Millamant. Well, an illiterate man's my aversion. I wonder at the impudence of any illiterate man to offer to make love.

Witwoud. That I confess I wonder at too.

Mrs. Millamant. Ah! to marry an ignorant that can hardly read or write!

Petulant. Why should a man be any further from being married, though he can't read, than he is from being hanged? The ordinary's[34] paid for setting the psalm, and the parish-priest for reading the ceremony. And for the rest which is to follow in both cases, a man may do it without book—so all's one for that.

Mrs. Millamant. D'ye hear the creature?—Lord, here's company, I'll be gone.

Exeunt Mrs. MILLAMANT *and* MINCING.

Enter Sir WILFULL WITWOUD *in a riding dress, followed by* FOOTMAN.

Witwoud. In the name of Bartlemew and his fair,[35] what have we here?

Mrs. Marwood. 'Tis your brother, I fancy. Don't you know him?

Witwoud. Not I.—Yes, I think it is he—I've almost forgot him; I have not seen him since the Revolution.[36]

Footman. (*To* Sir WILFULL.) Sir, my lady's dressing. Here's company; if you please to walk in, in the mean time.

Sir Wilfull. Dressing! what, it's but morning here, I warrant, with you in London; we should count it towards afternoon in our parts, down in Shropshire.—Why, then, belike, my aunt han't dined yet, ha, friend?

Footman. Your aunt, sir?

Sir Wilfull. My aunt, sir! yes, my aunt, sir, and your lady, sir; your lady is my aunt, sir.—Why, what dost thou not know me, friend? why then send somebody hither that does. How long hast thou lived with thy lady, fellow, ha?

Footman. A week, sir; longer than anybody in the house, except my lady's woman.

Sir Wilfull. Why then belike thou dost not know thy lady, if thou seest her—ha, friend?

Footman. Why, truly, sir, I cannot safely swear to her face in a morning, before she is dressed. 'Tis like I may give a shrewd guess at her by this time.

Sir Wilfull. Well, prithee try what thou canst do; if thou canst not guess, inquire her out, dost hear, fellow? and tell her, her nephew, Sir Wilfull Witwoud, is in the house.

Footman. I shall, sir.

Sir Wilfull. Hold ye; hear me, friend; a word with you in your ear; prithee who are these gallants?

Footman. Really, sir, I can't tell; here come so many here, 'tis hard to know 'em all.   *Exit.*

Sir Wilfull. Oons, this fellow knows less than a starling; I don't think a' knows his own name.

Mrs. Marwood. Mr. Witwoud, your brother is not be-hindhand in forgetfulness—I fancy he has forgot you too.

Witwoud. I hope so—the devil take him that remembers first, I say.

Sir Wilfull. Save you, gentlemen and lady!

Mrs. Marwood. For shame, Mr. Witwoud; why don't you speak to him?—And you, sir.

Witwoud. Petulant, speak.

Petulant. And you, sir.

Sir Wilfull. No offence, I hope. (*Salutes* Mrs. MARWOOD.)

Mrs. Marwood. No, sure, sir.

Witwoud. This is a vile dog, I see that already. No offence! ha! ha! ha! To him; to him, Petulant, smoke him.[37]

Petulant. It seems as if you had come a journey, sir; hem, hem.   (*Surveying him round.*)

Sir Wilfull. Very likely, sir, that it may seem so.

Petulant. No offence, I hope, sir.

Witwoud. Smoke the boots, the boots; Petulant, the boots: ha! ha! ha!

Sir Wilfull. May be not, sir; thereafter, as 'tis meant, sir.

Petulant. Sir, I presume upon the information of your boots.

Sir Wilfull. Why, 'tis like you may, sir: if you are not satisfied with the information of my boots, sir, if you will step to the stable, you may inquire further of my horse, sir.

Petulant. Your horse, sir! your horse is an ass, sir!

Sir Wilfull. Do you speak by way of offence, sir?

Mrs. Marwood. The gentleman's merry, that's all sir.—(*Aside.*) S'life, we shall have a quarrel betwixt an horse and an ass before they find one another out.—(*Aloud.*) You must not take anything amiss from your friends, sir. You are among your friends here, though it may be you don't know it.—If I am not mistaken, you are Sir Wilfull Witwoud.

Sir Wilfull. Right, lady; I am Sir Wilfull Witwoud, so I write myself; no offence to anybody, I hope; and nephew to the Lady Wishfort of this mansion.

Mrs. Marwood. Don't you know this gentleman, sir?

Sir Wilfull. Hum! what, sure 'tis not—yea by'r Lady, but 'tis—s'heart, I know not whether 'tis or no—yea, but 'tis, by the Wrekin.[38] Brother Anthony! what, Tony, i'faith! what, dost thou not know me? By'r Lady, nor I thee, thou art so becravated, and so beperiwigged.—S'heart, why dost not speak? art thou overjoyed?

Witwoud. Odso, brother, is it you? your servant, brother.

Sir Wilfull. Your servant! why yours, sir. Your servant again— s'heart, and your friend and servant to that—and a —and a—flap-dragon[39] for your service, sir! and a hare's foot and a hare's scut[40] for your service, sir! an you be so cold and so courtly.

Witwoud. No offence, I hope, brother.

Sir Wilfull. S'heart, sir, but there is, and much offence!— A pox, is this your Inns o' Court[41] breeding, not to know your friends and your relations, your elders and your betters?

Witwoud. Why, brother Wilfull of Salop,[42] you may be as short as a Shrewsbury-cake,[43] if you please. But I tell you 'tis not modish to know relations in town: you think you're in the country, where great lubberly brothers slabber and kiss one another when they meet, like a call of sergeants[44] —'tis not the fashion here; 'tis not indeed, dear brother.

Sir Wilfull. The fashion's a fool; and you're a fop, dear brother. S'heart, I've suspected this—by'r Lady, I conjectured you were a fop, since you began to change the style of your letters, and write on a scrap of paper gilt round the edges, no bigger than a *subpœna.* I might expect this when you left off, "Honored brother," and "hoping you are in good health," and so forth—to begin with a "Rat me, knight, I'm so sick of a last night's debauch"—'ods heart, and then tell a familiar tale of a cock and a bull, and a whore and a bottle, and so conclude.—You could write news before you were out of your time,[45] when you lived with honest Pumple Nose, the attorney of Furnival's Inn—you could entreat to be remembered then to your friends round the Wrekin. We could have gazettes, then, and Dawks's Letter, and the Weekly Bill,[46] till of late days.

Petulant. S'life, Witwoud, were you ever an attorney's clerk? of the family of the Furnivals? Ha! ha! ha!

Witwoud. Ay, ay, but that was but for a while: not long, not long. Pshaw! I was not in my own power then; an orphan, and this fellow was my guardian. Ay, ay, I was glad to consent to that man to come to London: he had the disposal of me then. If I had not agreed to that, I might have been bound 'prentice to a felt-maker in Shrewsbury; this fellow would have bound me to a maker of felts.

Sir Wilfull. S'heart, and better than to be bound to a maker of fops; where, I suppose, you have served your time; and now you may set up for yourself.

Mrs. Marwood. You intend to travel, sir, I am informed.

Sir Wilfull. Belike I may, madam. I may chance to sail upon the salt seas, if my mind hold.

Petulant. And the wind serve.

Sir Wilfull. Serve or not serve, I shan't ask licence of you, sir; nor the weathercock your companion: I direct my discourse to the lady, sir.—'Tis like my aunt may have told you, madam—yes, I have settled my concerns, I may say now, and am minded to see foreign parts. If an' how that the peace holds, whereby that is, taxes abate.

Mrs. Marwood. I thought you had designed for France at all adventures.

Sir Wilfull. I can't tell that; 'tis like I may, and 'tis like I may not. I am somewhat dainty in making a resolution—because when I make it I keep it. I don't stand shill I, shall I,[47] then; if I say't, I'll do't. But I have thoughts to tarry a small matter in town, to learn somewhat of your lingo first, before I cross the seas. I'd gladly have a spice of your French, as they say, whereby to hold discourse in foreign countries.

Mrs. Marwood. Here's an academy in town for that use.

Sir Wilfull. There is? 'Tis like there may.

Mrs. Marwood. No doubt you will return very much improved.

Witwoud. Yes, refined, like a Dutch skipper from a whale-fishing.

Enter Lady WISHFORT *and* FAINALL.

Lady Wishfort. Nephew, you are welcome.

Sir Wilfull. Aunt, your servant.

Fainall. Sir Wilfull, your most faithful servant.

Sir Wilfull. Cousin Fainall, give me your hand.

Lady Wishfort. Cousin Witwoud, your servant; Mr. Petulant, your servant; nephew, you are welcome again. Will you drink anything after your journey, nephew, before you eat? Dinner's almost ready.

Sir Wilfull. I'm very well, I thank you, aunt—however, I thank you for your courteous offer. S'heart, I was afraid you would have been in the fashion too, and have remembered to have forgot your relations. Here's your cousin Tony; belike, I mayn't call him brother, for fear of offence.

Lady Wishfort. Oh, he's a ralliur, nephew—my cousin's a wit: and your great wits always rally their best friends to

choose. When you have been abroad, nephew, you'll understand raillery better.

(FAINALL *and* Mrs. MARWOOD *talk apart.*)
Sir Wilfull. Why then, let him hold his tongue in the mean
time, and rail when that day comes.

Enter MINCING.

Mincing. Mem, I am come to acquaint your la'ship that
dinner is impatient.
Sir Wilfull. Impatient! why then belike it won't stay till I
pull off my boots.—Sweetheart, can you help me to a pair
of slippers?—My man's with his horses, I warrant.
Lady Wishfort. Fy, fy, nephew! you would not pull off
your boots here?—Go down into the hall—dinner shall stay
for you.—My nephew's a little unbred, you'll pardon him,
madam.—Gentlemen, will you walk?—Marwood—
Mrs. Marwood. I'll follow you, madam—before Sir Wilfull
is ready.   *Exeunt all but* Mrs. MARWOOD *and* FAINALL.
Fainall. Why then, Foible's a bawd, an arrant, rank,
match-making bawd. And I, it seems, am a husband, a rank
husband; and my wife's a very errant, rank wife—all in the
way of the world. 'Sdeath, to be a cuckold by anticipation,
a cuckold in embryo! sure I was born with budding antlers,
like a young satyr, or a citizen's child.[48] 'Sdeath! to be out-
witted—to be out-jilted—out-matrimonied!—If I had kept
my speed like a stag, 'twere somewhat—but to crawl after,
with my horns, like a snail, and be outstripped by my wife—
'tis scurvy wedlock.
Mrs. Marwood. Then shake it off; you have often wished
for an opportunity to part—and now you have it. But first
prevent their plot—the half of Millamant's fortune is too
considerable to be parted with to a foe, to Mirabell.
Fainall. Damn him! that had been mine—had you not
made that fond discovery—that had been forfeited, had they
been married. My wife had added lustre to my horns by that
increase of fortune; I could have worn 'em tipped with gold,
though my forehead had been furnished like a deputy-lieutenant's hall.[49]
Mrs. Marwood. They may prove a cap of maintenance[50]
to you still, if you can away with your wife. And she's no
worse than when you had her—I dare swear she had given
up her game before she was married.
Fainall. Hum! that may be. She might throw up her cards,
but I'll be hanged if she did not put pam in her pocket.[51]
Mrs. Marwood. You married her to keep you; and if you

can contrive to have her keep you better than you expected, why should you not keep her longer than you intended.

Fainall. The means, the means!

Mrs. Marwood. Discover to my lady your wife's conduct; threaten to part with her!—my lady loves her, and will come to any composition to save her reputation. Take the opportunity of breaking it just upon the discovery of this imposture. My lady will be enraged beyond bounds, and sacrifice niece, and fortune, and all, at that conjuncture. And let me alone to keep her warm; if she should flag in her part, I will not fail to prompt her.

Fainall. Faith, this has an appearance.

Mrs. Marwood. I'm sorry I hinted to my lady to endeavor a match between Millamant and Sir Wilfull; that may be an obstacle.

Fainall. Oh, for that matter, leave me to manage him: I'll disable him for that; he will drink like a Dane; after dinner I'll set his hand in.[52]

Mrs. Marwood. Well, how do you stand affected towards your lady?

Fainall. Why, faith, I'm thinking of it.—Let me see—I am married already, so that's over. My wife has played the jade with me—well, that's over too. I never loved her, or if I had, why that would have been over too by this time. Jealous of her I cannot be, for I am certain; so there's an end of jealousy: Weary of her I am, and shall be—no, there's no end of that—no, no, that were too much to hope. Thus far concerning my repose; now for my reputation. As to my own, I married not for it, so that's out of the question; and as to my part in my wife's—why, she had parted with hers before; so bringing none to me, she can take none from me. 'Tis against all rule of play, that I should lose to one who has not wherewithal to stake.

Mrs. Marwood. Besides, you forget, marriage is honorable.

Fainall. Hum, faith, and that's well thought on; marriage is honorable as you say; and if so, wherefore should cuckoldom be a discredit, being derived from so honorable a root?

Mrs. Marwood. Nay, I know not; if the root be honorable, why not the branches?

Fainall. So, so, why this point's clear—well, how do we proceed?

Mrs. Marwood. I will contrive a letter which shall be delivered to my lady at the time when that rascal who is to act Sir Rowland is with her. It shall come as from an unknown hand—for the less I appear to know of the truth, the better

I can play the incendiary. Besides, I would not have Foible provoked if I could help it—because you know she knows some passages—nay, I expect all will come out. But let the mine be sprung first, and then I care not if I am discovered.

Fainall. If the worst come to the worst—I'll turn my wife to grass. I have already a deed of settlement of the best part of her estate which I wheedled out of her; and that you shall partake at least.

Mrs. Marwood. I hope you are convinced that I hate Mirabell now; you'll be no more jealous?

Fainall. Jealous! no—by this kiss—let husbands be jealous; but let the lover still believe; or if he doubt, let it be only to endear his pleasure, and prepare the joy that follows when he proves his mistress true. But let husbands' doubts convert to endless jealousy; or if they have belief, let it corrupt to superstition and blind credulity. I am single, and will herd no more with 'em. True, I wear the badge, but I'll disown the order. And since I take my leave of 'em, I care not if I leave 'em a common motto to their common crest:—

> All husbands must or pain or shame endure;
> The wise too jealous are, fools too secure.

                                  Exeunt.

ACT IV

SCENE I: *A Room in* LADY WISHFORT'S *House*.

LADY WISHFORT *and* FOIBLE.

Lady Wishfort. Is Sir Rowland coming, sayest thou, Foible? and are things in order?

Foible. Yes, madam, I have put wax lights in the sconces, and placed the footmen in a row in the hall, in their best liveries, and the coachman and postillion to fill up the equipage.

Lady Wishfort. Have you pulvilled[53] the coachman and postillion, that they may not stink of the stable when Sir Rowland comes by?

Foible. Yes, madam.

Lady Wishfort. And are the dancers and the music ready, that he may be entertained in all points with correspondence to his passion?

Foible. All is ready, madam.

Lady Wishfort. And—well—and how do I look, Foible?

Foible. Most killing well, madam.

Lady Wishfort. Well, and how shall I receive him? in what figure shall I give his heart the first impression? There is a great deal in the first impression. Shall I sit?—no, I won't sit —I'll walk—ay, I'll walk from the door upon his entrance; and then turn full upon him—no, that will be too sudden. I'll lie—ay, I'll lie down—I'll receive him in my little dressing-room, there's a couch—yes, yes, I'll give the first impression on a couch.—I won't lie neither, but loll and lean upon one elbow with one foot a little dangling off, jogging in a thoughtful way—yes—and then as soon as he appears, start, ay, start and be surprised, and rise to meet him in a pretty disorder—yes—Oh, nothing is more alluring than a levee[54] from a couch, in some confusion—it shows the foot to advantage, and furnishes with blushes, and recomposing airs beyond comparison. Hark! there's a coach.

Foible. 'Tis he, madam.

Lady Wishfort. O dear!—Has my nephew made his addresses to Millamant? I ordered him.

Foible. Sir Wilfull is set in to drinking, madam, in the parlor.

Lady Wishfort. Odds my life, I'll send him to her. Call her down, Foible; bring her hither. I'll send him as I go—when they are together, then come to me, Foible, that I may not be too long alone with Sir Rowland.   *Exit.*

Enter Mrs. MILLAMANT *and* Mrs. FAINALL.

Foible. Madam, I stayed here, to tell your ladyship that Mr. Mirabell has waited this half-hour for an opportunity to talk with you: though my lady's orders were to leave you and Sir Wilfull together. Shall I tell Mr. Mirabell that you are at leisure?

Mrs. Millamant. No—what would the dear man have? I am thoughtful, and would amuse myself—bid him come another time.

> "There never yet was woman made
> Nor shall but to be cursed."[55]

> *(Repeating, and walking about.)*

That's hard.

Mrs. Fainall. You are very fond of Sir John Suckling today, Millamant, and the poets.

Mrs. Millamant. He? Ay, and filthy verses—so I am.

Foible. Sir Wilfull is coming, madam. Shall I send Mr. Mirabell away?

Mrs. Millamant. Ay, if you please, Foible, send him away —or send him hither—just as you will, dear Foible. I think

I'll see him—shall I? ay, let the wretch come.   *Exit* Foible.
    "Thyrsis, a youth of the inspired train."[56]
                                                        (Repeating.)
Dear Fainall, entertain Sir Wilfull—thou has philosophy to
undergo a fool, thou art married and hast patience—I would
confer with my own thoughts.

Mrs. Fainall. I am obliged to you that you would make me
your proxy in this affair, but I have business of my own.

                    Enter Sir Wilfull.

Mrs. Fainall. O Sir Wilfull, you are come at the critical
instant. There's your mistress up to the ears in love and contemplation; pursue your point now or never.

Sir Wilfull. Yes; my aunt will have it so—I would gladly
have been encouraged with a bottle or two, because I'm
somewhat wary at first before I am acquainted.—*(This while*
Millamant *walks about repeating to herself.)*—But I hope,
after a time, I shall break my mind—that is, upon further
acquaintance—so for the present, cousin, I'll take my leave—
if so be you'll be so kind to make my excuse, I'll return to
my company—

Mrs. Mainall. O fy, Sir Wilfull! what, you must not be
daunted.

Sir Wilfull. Daunted! no, that's not it; it is not so much for
that—for if so be that I set on't, I'll do't. But only for the
present, 'tis sufficient till further acquaintance, that's all—
your servant.

Mrs. Fainall. Nay, I'll swear you shall never lose so favorable an opportunity if I can help it. I'll leave you together,
and lock the door.   *Exit.*

Sir Wilfull. Nay, nay, cousin—I have forgot my gloves—
what d'ye do?—S'heart, a'has locked the door indeed, I think
—nay, Cousin Fainall, open the door—pshaw, what a vixen
trick is this?—Nay, now a'has seen me too.—Cousin, I made
bold to pass through as it were—I think this door's en-
chanted!

Mrs. Millamant. (Repeating.)
            "I prithee spare me, gentle boy,
                Press me no more for that slight toy."[57]

Sir Wilfull. Anan?[58] Cousin, your servant.

Mrs. Millamant (Repeating.)
            "That foolish trifle of a heart."

Sir Wilfull!

Sir Wilfull. Yes—your servant. No offense, I hope, cousin.

Mrs. Millamant (Repeating.)

"I swear it will not do its part,
Though thou dost thine, employest thy power and art."

Natural, easy Suckling!

Sir Wilfull. Anan? Suckling! no such suckling neither, cousin, nor stripling: I thank Heaven, I'm no minor.

Mrs. Millamant. Ah, rustic, ruder than Gothic!

Sir Wilfull. Well, well, I shall understand your lingo one of these days, cousin; in the meanwhile I must answer in plain English.

Mrs. Millamant. Have you any business with me, Sir Wilfull?

Sir Wilfull. Not at present, cousin—yes I make bold to see, to come and know if that how you were disposed to fetch a walk this evening; if so be that I might not be troublesome, I would have sought a walk with you.

Mrs. Millamant. A walk! what then?

Sir Wilfull. Nay, nothing—only for the walk's sake, that's all.

Mrs. Millamant. I nauseate walking; 'tis a country diversion; I loathe the country, and everything that relates to it.

Sir Wilfull. Indeed! ha! look ye, look ye, you do? Nay, 'tis like you may—here are choice of pastimes here in town, as plays and the like; that must be confessed indeed.

Mrs. Millamant. Ah l'étourdi![59] I hate the town too.

Sir Wilfull. Dear heart, that's much—ha! that you should hate 'em both! ha! 'tis like you may; there are some can't relish the town, and others can't away with the country—'tis like you may be one of those, cousin.

Mrs. Millamant. Ha! ha! ha! yes, 'tis like I may.—You have nothing further to say to me?

Sir Wilfull. Not at present, cousin.—'Tis like when I have an opportunity to be more private—I may break my mind in some measure—I conjecture you partly guess—however, that's as time shall try—but spare to speak and spare to speed, as they say.

Mrs. Millamant. If it is of no great importance, Sir Wilfull, you will oblige me to leave me; I have just now a little business—

Sir Wilfull. Enough, enough, cousin: yes, yes, all a case—when you're disposed. Now's as well as another time, and another time as well as now. All's one for that—yes, yes, if your concerns call you, there's no haste; it will keep cold, as they say. Cousin, your servant—I think this door's locked.

Mrs. Millamant. You may go this way, sir.

Sir Wilfull. Your servant; then with your leave I'll return to my company. *Exit.*

Mrs. Millamant. Ay, ay; ha! ha! ha!
  "Like Phœbus sung the no less amorous boy."[60]

Enter MIRABELL.

Mirabell.   "Like Daphne she, as lovely and as coy."
Do you lock yourself up from me, to make my search more
curious? or is this pretty artifice contrived to signify that here
the chase must end, and my pursuits be crowned? For you
can fly no further.

Mrs. Millamant. Vanity! no—I'll fly, and be followed to
the last moment. Though I am upon the very verge of matrimony, I expect you should solicit me as much as if I were
wavering at the grate of a monastery, with one foot over the
threshold. I'll be solicited to the very last, nay, and afterwards.

Mirabell. What, after the last?

Mrs. Millamant. Oh, I should think I was poor and had
nothing to bestow, if I were reduced to an inglorious ease
and freed from the agreeable fatigues of solicitation.

Mirabell. But do not you know that when favors are con-
ferred upon instant and tedious solicitation, that they di-
minish in their value, and that both the giver loses the grace,
and the receiver lessens his pleasure?

Mrs. Millamant. It may be in things of common application; but never sure in love. Oh, I hate a lover that can dare
to think he draws a moment's air, independent of the bounty
of his mistress. There is not so impudent a thing in nature as
the saucy look of an assured man, confident of success. The
pedantic arrogance of a very husband has not so pragmatical[61] an air. Ah! I'll never marry, unless I am first made sure
of my will and pleasure.

Mirabell. Would you have 'em both before marriage? or
will you be contented with the first now, and stay for the
other till after grace?

Mrs. Millamant. Ah! don't be impertinent.—My dear liberty, shall I leave thee? my faithful solitude, my darling
contemplation, must I bid you then adieu? Ay-h adieu—my
morning thoughts, agreeable wakings, indolent slumbers, all
ye *douceurs,* ye *sommeils du matin*[62], *adieu?*—I can't do't,
'tis more than impossible—positively, Mirabell, I'll lie abed
in a morning as long as I please.

Mirabell. Then I'll get up in a morning as early as I
please.

Mrs. Millamant. Ah! idle creature, get up when you will—
and d'ye hear, I won't be called names after I'm married;
positively I won't be called names.

horrid fright—Fainall, I shall never say it—well—I think—
I'll endure you.

Mrs. Fainall. Fy! fy! have him, have him, and tell him so
in plain terms; for I am sure you have a mind to him.

Mrs. Millamant. Are you? I think I have—and the horrid
man looks as if he thought so too—well, you ridiculous thing
you, I'll have you—I won't be kissed, nor I won't be thanked
—here kiss my hand though.—So, hold your tongue now;
don't say a word.

Mrs. Fainall. Mirabell, there's a necessity for your obedience;— you have neither time to talk nor stay. My mother
is coming; and in my conscience if she should see you, would
fall into fits, and maybe not recover time enough to return
to Sir Rowland, who, as Foible tells me, is in a fair way to
succeed. Therefore spare your ecstacies for another occasion,
and slip down the back-stairs, where Foible waits to consult
you.

Mrs. Millamant. Ay, go, go. In the meantime I suppose
you have said something to please me.

Mirabell. I am all obedience. *Exit.*

Mrs. Fainall. Yonder Sir Wilfull's drunk, and so noisy
that my mother has been forced to leave Sir Rowland to
appease him; but he answers her only with singing and
drinking—what they may have done by this time I know not;
but Petulant and he were upon quarrelling as I came by.

Mrs. Millamant. Well, if Mirabell should not make a good
husband, I am a lost thing,—for I find I love him violently.

Mrs. Fainall. So it seems; for you mind not what's said to
you.—If you doubt him, you had best take up with Sir
Wilfull.

Mrs. Millamant. How can you name that superannuated
lubber? foh!

Enter WITWOUD.

Mrs. Fainall. So, is the fray made up, that you have left
'em?

Witwoud. Left 'em? I could stay no longer—I have laughed
like ten christ'nings—I am tipsy with laughing—if I had
stayed any longer I should have burst,—I must have been let
out and pieced in the sides like an unsized camlet[68].—Yes,
yes, the fray is composed; my lady came in like a *noli
prosequi*[69], and stopped the proceedings.

Mrs. Millamant. What was the dispute?

Witwoud. That's the jest; there was no dispute. They could
neither of 'em speak for rage, and so fell a sputtering at one
another like two roasting apples.

Enter PETULANT, *drunk.*

Witwoud. Now, Petulant, all's over, all's well. Gad, my head begins to whim it about—why dost thou not speak? thou art both as drunk and as mute as a fish.

Petulant. Look you, Mrs. Millamant—if you can love me, dear nymph—say it—and that's the conclusion—pass on, or pass off—that's all.

Witwoud. Thou hast uttered volumes, folios, in less than *decimo sexto*[70], my dear Lacedemonian[71]. Sirrah Petulant, thou art an epitomiser of words.

Petulant. Witwoud—you are an annihilator of sense.

Witwoud. Thou art a retailer of phrases; and dost deal in remnants of remnants, like a maker of pincushions—thou art in truth (metaphorically speaking) a speaker of shorthand.

Petulant. Thou art (without a figure) just one-half of an ass, and Baldwin[72] yonder, thy half-brother, is the rest.—A Gemini[73] of asses split would make just four of you.

Witwoud. Thou dost bite, my dear mustard-seed; kiss me for that.

Petulant. Stand off!—I'll kiss no more males—I have kissed your twin yonder in a humor of reconciliation, till he (*Hiccups*) rises upon my stomach like a radish.

Mrs. Millamant. Eh! filthy creature! what was the quarrel?

Petulant. There was no quarrel—there might have been a quarrel.

Witwoud. If there had been words enow between 'em to have expressed provocation, they had gone together by the ears like a pair of castanets.

Petulant. You were the quarrel.

Mrs. Millamant. Me!

Petulant. If I have a humor to quarrel, I can make less matters conclude premises.—If you are not handsome, what then, if I have a humor to prove it? If I shall have my reward, say so; if not, fight for your face the next time yourself—I'll go sleep.

Witwoud. Do; wrap thyself up like a wood-louse, and dream revenge—and hear me, if thou canst learn to write by to-morrow morning, pen me a challenge.—I'll carry it for thee.

Petulant. Carry your mistress's monkey a spider!—Go flea dogs, and read romances!—I'll go to bed to my maid. *Exit.*

Mrs. Fainall. He's horridly drunk.—How came you all in this pickle?

Witwoud. A plot! a plot! to get rid of the night—your husband's advice; but he sneaked off.

Enter Sir WILFULL *drunk, and* Lady WISHFORT.

Lady Wishfort. Out upon't, out upon't! At years of discretion, and comport yourself at this rantipole[74] rate!

Sir Wilfull. No offense, aunt.

Lady Wishfort. Offense! as I'm a person, I'm ashamed of you—foh! how you stink of wine! D'ye think my niece will ever endure such a Borachio! you're an absolute Borachio[75].

Sir Wilfull. Borachio?

Lady Wishfort. At a time when you should commence an amour, and put your best foot foremost—

Sir Wilfull. S'heart, an you grutch me your liquor, make a bill—give me more drink, and take my purse—   *(Sings.)*

> "Prithee fill me the glass,
>   Till it laugh in my face,
> With ale that is potent and mellow;
>   He that whines for a lass,
>   Is an ignorant ass,
> For a bumper has not its fellow."

But if you would have me marry my cousin—say the word, and I'll do't—Wilfull will do't, that's the word—Wilfull will do't, that's my crest—my motto I have forgot.

Lady Wishfort. My nephew's a little overtaken, cousin—but 'tis with drinking your health.—O' my word you are obliged to him.

Sir Wilfull. In vino veritas[76], aunt.—If I drink your health today, cousin—I am a Borachio. But if you have a mind to be married, say the word, and send for the piper; Wilfull will do't. If not, dust it away, and let's have t'other round.—Tony!—Odds heart, where's Tony!—Tony's an honest fellow; but he spits after a bumper, and that's a fault.—   *(Sings.)*

> "We'll drink, and we'll never ha' done, boys,
>   Put the glass then around with the sun, boys,
> Let Apollo's example invite us;
>   For he's drunk every night,
>   And that makes him so bright,
> That he's able next morning to light us."

The sun's a good pimple[77], an honest soaker; he has a cellar at your Antipodes. If I travel, aunt, I touch at your Antipodes[78].—Your Antipodes are a good, rascally sort of topsyturvy fellows: If I had a bumper, I'd stand upon my head and drink a health to 'em—A match or no match, cousin with the hard name?—Aunt, Wilfull will do't. If she has her

maidenhead, let her look to't; if she has not, let her keep her
own counsel in the meantime, and cry out at the nine months'
end.

Mrs. Millamant. Your pardon, madam, I can stay no
longer—Sir Wilfull grows very powerful. Eh! how he smells!
I shall be overcome if I stay.—Come, cousin.

                Exeunt Mrs. MILLAMANT *and* Mrs. FAINALL.

Lady Wishfort. Smells! he would poison a tallow-chandler
and his family! Beastly creature, I know not what to do with
him!—Travel, quotha! aye, travel, travel, get thee gone, get
thee gone; get thee but far enough, to the Saracens, or the
Tartars, or the Turks!—for thou art not fit to live in a
Christian commonwealth, thou beastly pagan!

Sir Wilfull. Turks, no; no Turks, aunt: your Turks are in-
fidels, and believe not in the grape. Your Mahometan, your
Mussulman, is a dry stinkard—no offence, aunt. My map
says that your Turk is not so honest a man as your Christian.
I cannot find by the map that your Mufti is orthodox—
whereby it is a plain case that orthodox is a hard word, aunt,
and *(Hiccups)* Greek for claret.—   *(Sings.)*

> "To drink is a Christian diversion,
>   Unknown to the Turk or the Persian:
>   Let Mahometan fools
>   Live by heathenish rules,
> And be damned over tea-cups and coffee.
>   But let British lads sing,
>   Crown a health to the king,
> And a fig for your sultan and sophy!"[79]

Ah Tony!

    Enter FOIBLE, *who whispers to* Lady WISHFORT.

Lady Wishfort. (aside to FOIBLE.) Sir Rowland impatient?
Good lack! what shall I do with this beastly tumbril?—
(Aloud.) Go lie down and sleep, you sot!—or, as I'm a person, I'll have you bastinadoed with broomsticks.—Call up
the wenches.   *Exit* FOIBLE.

Sir Wilfull. Ahey! wenches, where are the wenches?

Lady Wishfort. Dear Cousin Witwoud, get him away, and
you will bind me to you inviolably. I have an affair of moment that invades me with some precipitation—you will
oblige me to all futurity.

Witwoud. Come, knight.—Pox on him, I don't know what
to say to him.—Will you go to a cock-match?

Sir Wilfull. With a wench, Tony! Is she a shakebag, sirrah? Let me bite your cheek for that.

Witwoud. Horrible! he has a breath like a bag-pipe! Ay, ay; come, will you march, my Salopian?

Sir Wilfull. Lead on, little Tony—I'll follow thee, my Anthony, my Tantony. Sirrah, thou shalt be my Tantony, and I'll be thy pig.[80]

"And a fig for your sultan and sophy."

Exeunt Sir WILFULL *and* WITWOUD.

Lady Wishfort. This will never do. It will never make a match—at least before he has been abroad.

Enter WAITWELL, *disguised as* Sir ROWLAND.

Lady Wishfort. Dear Sir Rowland, I am confounded with confusion at the retrospection of my own rudeness!—I have more pardons to ask than the pope distributes in the year of jubilee. But I hope, where there is likely to be so near an alliance, we may unbend the severity of decorums and dispense with a little ceremony.

Waitwell. My impatience, madam, is the effect of my transport; and till I have the possession of your adorable person, I am tantalised on the rack; and do but hang, madam, on the tenter of expectation.

Lady Wishfort. You have an excess of gallantry, Sir Rowland, and press things to a conclusion with a most prevailing vehemence.—But a day or two for decency of marriage—

Waitwell. For decency of funeral, madam! The delay will break my heart—or, if that should fail, I shall be poisoned. My nephew will get an inkling of my designs, and poison me —and I would willingly starve him before I die—I would gladly go out of the world with that satisfaction.—That would be some comfort to me, if I could but live so long as to be revenged on that unnatural viper!

Lady Wishfort. Is he so unnatural, say you? Truly I would contribute much both to the saving of your life, and the accomplishment of your revenge. Not that I respect myself, though he has been a perfidious wretch to me.

Waitwell. Perfidious to you!

Lady Wishfort. O Sir Rowland, the hours he has died away at my feet, the tears that he has shed, the oaths that he has sworn, the palpitations that he has felt, the trances and the tremblings, the ardors and the ecstacies, the kneelings and the risings, the heart-heavings and the hand-gripings, the pangs and the pathetic regards of his protesting eyes! Oh, no memory can register!

Waitwell. What, my rival! is the rebel my rival?—a' dies!

Lady Wishfort. No, don't kill him at once, Sir Rowland, starve him gradually, inch by inch.

Waitwell. I'll do't. In three weeks he shall be barefoot; in a month out at knees with begging an alms.—He shall starve upward and upward, till he has nothing living but his head, and then go out in a stink like a candle's end upon a save-all.[81]

Lady Wishfort. Well, Sir Rowland, you have the way—you are no novice in the labyrinth of love—you have the clue. But as I am a person, Sir Rowland, you must not attribute my yielding to any sinister appetite, or indigestion of widowhood; nor impute my complacency to any lethargy of continence. I hope you do not think me prone to any iteration of nuptials—

Waitwell. Far be it from me—

Lady Wishfort. If you do, I protest I must recede—or think that I have made a prostitution of decorums; but in the vehemence of compassion, and to save the life of a person of so much importance—

Waitwell. I esteem it so.

Lady Wishfort. Or else you wrong my condescension.

Waitwell. I do not, I do not!

Lady Wishfort. Indeed you do.

Waitwell. I do not, fair shrine of virtue!

Lady Wishfort. If you think the least scruple of carnality was an ingredient—

Waitwell. Dear madam, no. You are all camphor and frankincense, all chastity and odor.

Lady Wishfort. Or that—

Enter FOIBLE.

Foible. Madam, the dancers are ready; and there's one with a letter, who must deliver it into your own hands.

Lady Wishfort. Sir Rowland, will you give me leave? Think favorably, judge candidly, and conclude you have found a person who would suffer racks in honor's cause, dear Sir Rowland, and will wait on you incessantly.   *Exit.*

Waitwell. Fy, fy!—What a slavery have I undergone! Spouse, hast thou any cordial? I want spirits.

Foible. What a washy rogue art thou, to pant thus for a quarter of an hour's lying and swearing to a fine lady!

Waitwell. Oh, she is the antidote to desire! Spouse, thou wilt fare the worse for't—I shall have no appetite to iteration of nuptials this eight-and-forty hours.—By this hand I'd rather be a chairman in the dog-days—than act Sir Rowland till this time tomorrow!

Re-enter Lady WISHFORT, *with a letter.*

Lady Wishfort. Call in the dancers.—Sir Rowland, we'll sit, if you please, and see the entertainment. *(A Dance.)* Now, with your permission, Sir Rowland, I will peruse my letter.— I would open it in your presence, because I would not make you uneasy. If it should make you uneasy, I would burn it. Speak, if it does—but you may see the superscription is like a woman's hand.

Foible. (Aside to WAITWELL.) By Heaven! Mrs. Marwood's, I know it.—My heart aches—get it from her.

Waitwell. A woman's hand! no, madam, that's no woman's hand, I see that already. That's somebody whose throat must be cut.

Lady Wishfort. Nay, Sir Rowland, since you give me a proof of your passion by your jealousy, I promise you I'll make a return by a frank communication.—You shall see it —we'll open it together—look you here.—*(Reads.)*—"Madam, though unknown to you"—Look you here, 'tis from nobody that I know—"I have that honor for your character, that I think myself obliged to let you know you are abused. He who pretends to be Sir Rowland, is a cheat and a rascal."—Oh, heavens! what's this?

Foible. (Aside.) Unfortunate! all's ruined!

Waitwell. How, how, let me see, let me see!—*(Reads.)* "A rascal, and disguised and suborned for that imposture,"—O villainy! O villainy!—"by the contrivance of—"

Lady Wishfort. I shall faint, I shall die, oh!

Foible. (Aside to WAITWELL.) Say 'tis your nephew's hand —quickly, his plot, swear it, swear it!

Waitwell. Here's a villain! madam, don't you perceive it, don't you see it?

Lady Wishfort. Too well, too well! I have seen too much.

Waitwell. I told you at first I knew the hand.—A woman's hand! The rascal writes a sort of a large hand; your Roman hand—I saw there was a throat to be cut presently. If he were my son, as he is my nephew, I'd pistol him!

Foible. O treachery!—But are you sure, Sir Rowland, it is his writing?

Waitwell. Sure! am I here? do I live? do I love this pearl of India? I have twenty letters in my pocket from him in the same character.

Lady Wishfort. How!

Foible. O what luck it is, Sir Rowland, that you were pres-

ent at this juncture! This was the business that brought Mr.
Mirabell disguised to Madam Millamant this afternoon. I
thought something was contriving when he stole by me and
would have hid his face.

Lady Wishfort. How, how!—I heard the villain was in the
house indeed; and now I remember, my niece went away
abruptly when Sir Wilfull was to have made his addresses.

Foible. Then, then, madam, Mr. Mirabell waited for her
in her chamber! but I would not tell your ladyship to discompose you when you were to receive Sir Rowland.

Waitwell. Enough, his date is short.

Foible. No, good Sir Rowland, don't incur the law.

Waitwell. Law! I care not for law. I can but die, and 'tis
in a good cause.—My lady shall be satisfied of my truth and
innocence, though it cost me my life.

Lady Wishfort. No, dear Sir Rowland, don't fight; if you
should be killed I must never show my face; or hanged—
Oh, consider my reputation, Sir Rowland!—No, you shan't
fight—I'll go in and examine my niece; I'll make her confess.
I conjure you, Sir Rowland, by all your love, not to fight.

Waitwell. I am charmed, madam; I obey. But some proof
you must let me give you; I'll go for a black box which contains the writings of my whole estate, and deliver that into
your hands.

Lady Wishfort. Ay, dear Sir Rowland, that will be some
comfort; bring the black box.

Waitwell. And may I presume to bring a contract to be
signed this night? may I hope so far?

Lady Wishfort. Bring what you will; but come alive, pray
come alive. Oh, this is a happy discovery!

Waitwell. Dead or alive I'll come—and married we will
be in spite of treachery; ay, and get an heir that shall defeat
the last remaining glimpse of hope in my abandoned nephew.
Come, my buxom widow:

> Ere long you shall substantial proofs receive,
> That I'm an errant knight—

Foible. (*Aside.*)   Or arrant knave.

Exeunt.

ACT V

SCENE I: *A Room in* Lady WISHFORT'S *House.*

Lady WISHFORT *and* FOIBLE.

Lady Wishfort. Out of my house, out of my house, thou
viper! thou serpent, that I have fostered! thou bosom traitress,

that I raised from nothing!—Begone! begone! begone!—go! go!—That I took from washing of old gauze and weaving of dead hair,[82] with a bleak blue nose over a chafing-dish of starved embers, and dining behind a traverse rag, in a shop no bigger than a birdcage!—Go, go! starve again, do, do!

Foible. Dear madam, I'll beg pardon on my knees.

Lady Wishfort. Away! out! out!—Go, set up for yourself again!—Do, drive a trade, do, with your three-pennyworth of small ware, flaunting upon a packthread, under a brandy-seller's bulk, or against a dead wall by a ballad-monger! Go, hang out an old Frisoneer gorget,[83] with a yard of yellow colberteen again. Do; an old gnawed mask, two rows of pins, and a child's fiddle; a glass necklace with the beads broken, and a quilted nightcap with one ear. Go, go, drive a trade!—These were your commodities, you treacherous trull! this was the merchandise you dealt in when I took you into my house, placed you next myself, and made you governante of my whole family! You have forgot this, have you, now you have feathered your nest?

Foible. No, no, dear madam. Do but hear me; have but a moment's patience, I'll confess all. Mr. Mirabell seduced me; I am not the first that he has wheedled with his dissembling tongue; your ladyship's own wisdom has been deluded by him; then how should I, a poor ignorant, defend myself? O madam, if you knew but what he promised me, and how he assured me your ladyship should come to no damage!—Or else the wealth of the Indies should not have bribed me to conspire against so good, so sweet, so kind a lady as you have been to me.

Lady Wishfort. No damage! What, to betray me, and marry me to a cast-servingman! to make me a receptacle, an hospital for a decayed pimp! No damage! O thou frontless impudence, more than a big-bellied actress!

Foible. Pray, do but hear me, madam; he could not marry your ladyship, madam.—No, indeed, his marriage was to have been void in law, for he was married to me first, to secure your ladyship. He could not have bedded your ladyship; for if he had consummated with your ladyship, he must have run the risk of the law, and been put upon his clergy.[84] —Yes, indeed, I inquired of the law in that case before I would meddle or make.

Lady Wishfort. What, then. I have been your property, have I? I have been convenient to you, it seems!—While you were catering for Mirabell, I have been broker for you! What, have you made a passive bawd of me?—This exceeds all precedent; I am brought to fine uses, to become a botcher of second-hand marriages between Abigails and Andrews![85]

—I'll couple you!—Yes, I'll baste you together, you and your Philanderer! I'll Duke's Place you, as I am a person! Your turtle is in custody already: you shall coo in the same cage if there be a constable or warrant in the parish.   *Exit.*

Foible. Oh, that ever I was born! Oh, that I was ever married!—A bride!—ay, I shall be a Bridewell-bride.[86]—Oh!

Enter Mrs. FAINALL.

Mrs. Fainall. Poor Foible, what's the matter?

Foible. O madam, my lady's gone for a constable. I shall be had to a justice and put to Bridewell to beat hemp. Poor Waitwell's gone to prison already.

Mrs. Fainall. Have a good heart, Foible; Mirabell's gone to give security for him. This is all Marwood's and my husband's doing.

Foible. Yes, yes; I know it, madam. She was in my lady's closet, and overheard all that you said to me before dinner. She sent the letter to my lady; and that missing effect, Mr. Fainall laid this plot to arrest Waitwell when he pretended to go for the papers; and in the meantime Mrs. Marwood declared all to my lady.

Mrs. Fainall. Was there no mention made of me in the letter? My mother does not suspect my being in the confederacy? I fancy Marwood has not told her, though she has told my husband.

Foible. Yes, madam; but my lady did not see that part; we stifled the letter before she read so far—Has that mischievous devil told Mr. Fainall of your ladyship then?

Mrs. Fainall. Ay, all's out—my affair with Mirabell—everything discovered. This is the last day of our living together, that's my comfort.

Foible. Indeed, madam; and so 'tis a comfort if you knew all—he has been even with your ladyship, which I could have told you long enough since, but I love to keep peace and quietness by my goodwill. I had rather bring friends together than set 'em at distance. But Mrs. Marwood and he are nearer related than ever their parents thought for.

Mrs. Fainall. Sayest thou so, Foible? canst thou prove this?

Foible. I can take my oath of it, madam; so can Mrs. Mincing. We have had many a fair word from Madam Marwood, to conceal something that passed in our chamber one evening when you were at Hyde Park; and we were thought to have gone a-walking, but we went up unawares—though we were sworn to secrecy too. Madam Marwood took a book and swore us upon it, but it was but a book of poems.

So long as it was not a bible-oath, we may break it with a safe conscience.

Mrs. Fainall. This discovery is the most opportune thing I could wish.—Now, Mincing!

Enter MINCING.

Mincing. My lady would speak with Mrs. Foible, mem. Mr. Mirabell is with her; he has set your spouse at liberty, Mrs. Foible, and would have you hide yourself in my lady's closet till my old lady's anger is abated. Oh, my old lady is in a perilous passion at something Mr. Fainall has said; he swears, and my old lady cries. There's a fearful hurricane, I vow. He says, mem, how that he'll have my lady's fortune made over to him, or he'll be divorced.

Mrs. Fainall. Does your lady or Mirabell know that?

Mincing. Yes, mem; they have sent me to see if Sir Wilfull be sober, and to bring him to them. My lady is resolved to have him, I think, rather than lose such a vast sum as six thousand pounds.—O come, Mrs. Foible, I hear my old lady.

Mrs. Fainall. Foible, you must tell Mincing that she must prepare to vouch when I call her.

Foible. Yes, yes, madam.

Mincing. O yes, mem, I'll vouch anything for your ladyship's service, be what it will.

Exeunt MINCING *and* FOIBLE.

Enter Lady WISHFORT *and* Mrs. MARWOOD.

Lady Wishfort. O my dear friend, how can I enumerate the benefits that I have received from your goodness! To you I owe the timely discovery of the false vows of Mirabell; to you I owe the detection of the impostor Sir Rowland. And now you are become an intercessor with my son-in-law, to save the honor of my house and compound for the frailties of my daughter. Well, friend, you are enough to reconcile me to the bad world, or else I would retire to deserts and solitudes, and feed harmless sheep by groves and purling streams. Dear Marwood, let us leave the world, and retire by ourselves and be shepherdesses.

Mrs. Marwood. Let us first despatch the affair in hand, madam. We shall have leisure to think of retirement afterwards. Here is one who is concerned in the treaty.

Lady Wishfort. Oh, daughter, daughter! is it possible thou shouldst be my child, bone of my bone, and flesh of my flesh, and, as I may say, another me, and yet transgress the most minute particle of severe virtue? Is it possible you should lean aside to iniquity, who have been cast in the direct mould of virtue? I have not only been a mould but a pattern for you, and a model for you, after you were brought into the world.

Mrs. Fainall. I don't understand your ladyship.

Lady Wishfort. Not understand! Why, have you not been naught?[87] have you not been sophisticated? Not understand! here I am ruined to compound for your caprices and your cuckoldoms. I must pawn my plate and my jewels, and ruin my niece, and all little enough——

Mrs. Fainall. I am wronged and abused, and so are you. 'Tis a false accusation, as false as hell, as false as your friend there, aye, or your friend's friend, my false husband.

Mrs. Marwood. My friend, Mrs. Fainall! your husband my friend! what do you mean?

Mrs. Fainall. I know what I mean, madam, and so do you; and so shall the world at a time convenient.

Mrs. Marwood. I am sorry to see you so passionate, madam. More temper would look more like innocence. But I have done. I am sorry my zeal to serve your ladyship and family should admit of misconstruction, or make me liable to affronts. You will pardon me, madam, if I meddle no more with an affair in which I am not personally concerned.

Lady Wishfort. O dear friend, I am so ashamed that you should meet with such returns!—(*To* Mrs. FAINALL.) You ought to ask pardon on your knees, ungrateful creature! she deserves more from you than all your life can accomplish. —(*To* Mrs. MARWOOD.) Oh, don't leave me destitute in this perplexity!—no, stick to me, my good genius.

Mrs. Fainall. I tell you, madam, you are abused.—Stick to you! ay, like a leech, to suck your best blood—she'll drop off when she's full. Madam, you shan't pawn a bodkin, nor part with a brass counter, in composition for me. I defy 'em all. Let 'em prove their aspersions; I know my own innocence, and dare stand a trial.   *Exit.*

Lady Wishfort. Why, if she should be innocent, if she should be wronged after all, ha?—I don't know what to think —and I promise you her education has been unexceptionable —I may say it; for I chiefly made it my own care to initiate her very infancy in the rudiments of virtue, and to impress upon her tender years a young odium and aversion to the very sight of men. Ay, friend, she would ha' shrieked if she had but seen a man till she was in her teens. As I am a person 'tis true—she was never suffered to play with a male child, though but in coats; nay, her very babies[88] were of the feminine gender. Oh, she never looked a man in the face but her own father, or the chaplain, and him we made a shift to put upon her for a woman, by the help of his long garments and his sleek face, till she was going in her fifteen.

Mrs. Marwood. 'Twas much she should be deceived so long.

Lady Wishfort. I warrant you, or she would never have borne to have been catechised by him; and have heard his long lectures against singing and dancing, and such debaucheries; and going to filthy plays, and profane music-meetings, where the lewd trebles squeak nothing but bawdy, and the basses roar blasphemy. Oh, she would have swooned at the sight or name of an obscene play-book!—and can I think, after all this, that my daughter can be naught? What, a whore? and thought it excommunication to set her foot within the door of a playhouse! O dear friend, I can't believe it, no, no! as she says, let him prove it, let him prove it.

Mrs. Marwood. Prove it, madam! What, and have your name prostituted in a public court! yours and your daughter's reputation worried at the bar by a pack of bawling lawyers! To be ushered in with an "Oyez" of scandal; and have your case opened by an old fumbling lecher in a quoif like a man-midwife; to bring your daughters' infamy to light; to be a theme for legal punsters and quibblers by the statute; and become a jest against a rule of court, where there is no precedent for a jest in any record—not even in Doomsday Book; to discompose the gravity of the bench, and provoke naughty interrogatories in more naughty law Latin; while the good judge, tickled with the proceeding, simpers under a grey beard, and fidgets off and on his cushion as if he had swallowed cantharides,[89] or sat upon cow-itch![90]—

Lady Wishfort. Oh, 'tis very hard!

Mrs. Marwood. And then to have my young revellers of the Temple take notes, like 'prentices at a conventicle; and after talk it over again in commons, or before drawers in an eating-house.

Lady Wishfort. Worse and worse!

Mrs. Marwood. Nay, this is nothing; if it would end here 'twere well. But it must, after this, be consigned by the shorthand writers to the public press; and from thence be transferred to the hands, nay into the throats and lungs of hawkers, with voices more licentious than the loud flounderman's or the woman that cries grey peas. And this you must hear till you are stunned; nay, you must hear nothing else for some days.

Lady Wishfort. Oh, 'tis insupportable! No, no, dear friend, make it up, make it up; ay, ay, I'll compound. I'll give up all, myself and my all, my niece and her all—anything, everything for composition.

Mrs. Marwood. Nay, madam, I advise nothing, I only lay before you, as a friend, the inconveniences which perhaps you have overseen. Here comes Mr. Fainall; if he will be satisfied to huddle up all in silence, I shall be glad. You must think I would rather congratulate than condole with you.

Enter FAINALL.

Lady Wishfort. Ay, ay, I do not doubt it, dear Marwood; no, no, I do not doubt it.

Fainall. Well, madam, I have suffered myself to be overcome by the importunity of this lady, your friend; and am content you shall enjoy your own proper estate during life, on condition you oblige yourself never to marry, under such penalty as I think convenient.

Lady Wishfort. Never to marry!

Fainall. No more Sir Rowlands; the next imposture may not be so timely detected.

Mrs. Marwood. That condition, I dare answer, my lady will consent to without difficulty; she has already but too much experienced the perfidiousness of men.—Besides, madam, when we retire to our pastoral solitude we shall bid adieu to all other thoughts.

Lady Wishfort. Ay, that's true; but in case of necessity, as of health, or some such emergency——

Fainall. Oh, if you are prescribed marriage, you shall be considered; I will only reserve to myself the power to choose for you. If your physic be wholesome, it matters not who is your apothecary. Next, my wife shall settle on me the remainder of her fortune not made over already; and for her maintenance depend entirely on my discretion.

Lady Wishfort. This is most inhumanly savage; exceeding the barbarity of a Muscovite husband.

Fainall. I learned it from his Czarish majesty's retinue, in a winter evening's conference over brandy and pepper, amongst other secrets of matrimony and policy as they are at present practised in the northern hemisphere. But this must be agreed unto, and that positively. Lastly, I will be endowed, in right of my wife, with that six thousand pounds which is the moiety of Mrs. Millamant's fortune in your possession; and which she has forfeited (as will appear by the last will and testament of your deceased husband, Sir Jonathan Wishfort) by her disobedience in contracting herself against your consent or knowledge; and by refusing the offered match with Sir Wilfull Witwoud, which you, like a careful aunt, had provided for her.

Lady Wishfort. My nephew was *non compos,*[91] and could not make his addresses.

Fainall. I come to make demands—I'll hear no objections.

Lady Wishfort. You will grant me time to consider?

Fainall. Yes, while the instrument is drawing, to which you must set your hand till more sufficient deeds can be perfected: which I will take care shall be done with all possible speed. In the meantime I'll go for the said instrument, and till my return you may balance this matter in your own discretion. *Exit.*

Lady Wishfort. This insolence is beyond all precedent, all parallel; must I be subject to this merciless villain?

Mrs. Marwood. 'Tis severe indeed, madam, that you should smart for your daughter's wantonness.

Lady Wishfort. 'Twas against my consent that she married this barbarian, but she would have him, though her year was not out.—Ah! her first husband, my son Languish, would not have carried it thus. Well, that was my choice, this is hers: she is matched now with a witness.—I shall be mad! —Dear friend, is there no comfort for me? must I live to be confiscated at this rebel-rate?—Here come two more of my Egyptian plagues too.

Enter Mrs. MILLAMANT, *and* Sir WILFULL WITWOUD.

Sir Wilfull. Aunt, your servant.

Lady Wishfort. Out, caterpillar, call not me aunt! I know thee not!

Sir Wilfull. I confess I have been a little in disguise, as they say.—S'heart, and I'm sorry for't. What would you have? I hope I have committed no offence, aunt—and if I did I am willing to make satisfaction; and what can a man say fairer? If I have broke anything I'll pay for't, an it cost a pound. And so let that content for what's past, and make no more words. For what's to come, to pleasure you I'm willing to marry my cousin. So pray let's all be friends; she and I are agreed upon the matter before a witness.

Lady Wishfort. How's this, dear niece? have I any comfort? can this be true?

Mrs. Millamant. I am content to be a sacrifice to your repose, madam; and to convince you that I had no hand in the plot, as you were misinformed. I have laid my commands on Mirabell to come in person, and be a witness that I give my hand to the flower of knighthood: and for the contract that passed between Mirabell and me, I have obliged him to make a resignation of it in your ladyship's presence. He is without, and waits your leave for admittance.

Lady Wishfort. Well, I'll swear I am something revived at this testimony of your obedience; but I cannot admit that traitor. I fear I cannot fortify myself to support his appearance. He is as terrible to me as a gorgon; if I see him I fear I shall turn to stone, and petrify incessantly.

Mrs. Millamant. If you disoblige him, he may resent your refusal and insist upon the contract still. Then 'tis the last time he will be offensive to you.

Lady Wishfort. Are you sure it will be the last time?—If I were sure of that—shall I never see him again?

Mrs. Millamant. Sir Wilfull, you and he are to travel together, are you not?

Sir Wilfull. S'heart, the gentleman's a civil gentleman, aunt; let him come in. Why, we are sworn brothers and fellow-travellers.—We are to be Pylades and Orestes,[92] he and I.—He is to be my interpreter in foreign parts. He has been overseas once already; and with proviso that I marry my cousin, will cross 'em once again only to bear me company. —S'heart, I'll call him in—an I set on't once, he shall come in; and see who'll hinder him.   *Exit*.

Mrs. Marwood. This is precious fooling, if it would pass; but I'll know the bottom of it.

Lady Wishfort. O dear Marwood, you are not going.

Mrs. Marwood. Not far, madam; I'll return immediately.
                                                                Exit.

Enter Sir WILFULL *and* MIRABELL.

Sir Wilfull. Look up, man, I'll stand by you; 'sbud an she do frown, she can't kill you;—besides—harkee, she dare not frown desperately, because her face is none of her own. S'heart, an she should, her forehead would wrinkle like the coat of a cream-cheese; but mum for that, fellow-traveller.

Mirabell. If a deep sense of the many injuries I have offered to so good a lady, with a sincere remorse, and a hearty contrition, can but obtain the least glance of compassion, I am too happy. Ah, madam, there was a time!—but let it be forgotten—I confess I have deservedly forfeited the high place I once held of sighing at your feet. Nay, kill me not, by turning from me in disdain. I come not to plead for favor —nay, not for pardon; I am a suppliant only for your pity —I am going where I never shall behold you more—

Sir Wilfull. How, fellow-traveller! you shall go by yourself then.

Mirabell. Let me be pitied first, and afterwards forgotten. —I ask no more.

Sir Wilfull. By'r Lady, a very reasonable request, and will cost you nothing, aunt! Come, come, forgive and forget, aunt; why you must, an you are a Christian.

Mirabell. Consider, madam, in reality, you could not receive much prejudice. It was an innocent device; though I confess it had a face of guiltiness, it was at most an artifice which love contrived—and errors which love produces have even been accounted venial. At least think it is punishment enough that I have lost what in my heart I hold most dear, that to your cruel indignation I have offered up this beauty, and with her my peace and quiet; nay, all my hopes of future comfort.

Sir Wilfull. An he does not move me, would I may never be o' the quorum!—an it were not as good a deed as to drink, to give her to him again, I would I might never take shipping!—Aunt, if you don't forgive quickly, I shall melt, I can tell you that. My contract went no farther than a little mouth-glue,[93] and that's hardly dry—one doleful sigh more from my fellow-traveller, and 'tis dissolved.

Lady Wishfort. Well, nephew, upon your account—Ah, he has a false insinuating tongue!—Well, sir, I will stifle my just resentment at my nephew's request. I will endeavor what I can to forget, but on proviso that you resign the contract with my niece immediately.

Mirabell. It is in writing, and with papers of concern; but I have sent my servant for it, and will deliver it to you, with all acknowledgments for your transcendent goodness.

Lady Wishfort. (Aside.) Oh, he has witchcraft in his eyes and tongue!—When I did not see him, I could have bribed a villain to his assassination; but his appearance rakes the embers which have so long lain smothered in my breast.

Enter FAINALL, *and* MRS. MARWOOD.

Fainall. Your date of deliberation, madam, is expired. Here is the instrument; are you prepared to sign?

Lady Wishfort. If I were prepared, I am not impowered. My niece exerts a lawful claim, having matched herself by my direction to Sir Wilfull.

Fainall. That sham is too gross to pass on me—though 'tis imposed on you, madam.

Mrs. Millamant. Sir, I have given my consent.

Mirabell. And, sir, I have resigned my pretensions.

Sir Wilfull. And, sir, I assert my right and will maintain it in defiance of you, sir, and of your instrument. S'heart, an you talk of an instrument, sir. I have an old fox[94] by my thigh shall hack your instrument of ram vellum[95] to shreds, sir!—it shall not be sufficient for a mittimus[96] or a tailor's measure. Therefore withdraw your instrument, sir, or by'r Lady, I shall draw mine.

Lady Wishfort. Hold, nephew, hold!

Mrs. Millamant. Good Sir Wilfull, respite your valor.

Fainall. Indeed! Are you provided of your guard, with your single beef-eater there? but I'm prepared for you, and insist upon my first proposal. You shall submit your own estate to my management, and absolutely make over my wife's to my sole use, as pursuant to the purport and tenor of this other covenant.—I suppose, madam, your consent is not requisite in this case; nor, Mr. Mirabell, your resignation; nor, Sir Wilfull, your right.—You may draw your fox if you please, sir, and make a bear-garden flourish somewhere else; for here it will not avail. This, my Lady Wishfort, must be subscribed, or your darling daughter's turned adrift, like a leaky hulk, to sink or swim, as she and the current of this lewd town can agree.

Lady Wishfort. Is there no means, no remedy to stop my ruin? Ungrateful wretch! dost thou not owe thy being, thy subsistence, to my daughter's fortune?

Fainall. I'll answer you when I have the rest of it in my possession.

Mirabell. But that you would not accept of a remedy from my hands—I own I have not deserved you should owe any obligation to me; or else perhaps I could advise—

Lady Wishfort. Oh, what? what? to save me and my child from ruin, from want, I'll forgive all that's past; nay, I'll consent to anything to come, to be delivered from this tyranny.

Mirabell. Aye, madam; but that is too late; my reward is intercepted. You have disposed of her who only could have made me a compensation for all my services; but be it as it may, I am resolved I'll serve you! you shall not be wronged in this savage manner.

Lady Wishfort. How! dear Mr. Mirabell, can you be so generous at last! But it is not possible. Harkee, I'll break my nephew's match; you shall have my niece yet, and all her fortune, if you can but save me from this imminent danger.

Mirabell. Will you? I'll take you at your word. I ask no. more. I must have leave for two criminals to appear.

Lady Wishfort. Aye, aye, anybody, anybody!

Mirabell. Foible is one, and a penitent.

Enter Mrs. Fainall, Foible, *and* Mincing.

Mrs. Marwood. (*To* Fainall.) O my shame! (Mirabell

and Lady WISHFORT *go to* Mrs. FAINALL *and* FOIBLE.) These corrupt things are brought hither to expose me.

Fainall. If it must all come out, why let 'em know it; 'tis but the way of the world. That shall not urge me to relinquish or abate one tittle of my terms; no, I will insist the more.

Foible. Yes, indeed, madam, I'll take my Bible oath of it.

Mincing. And so will I, mem.

Lady Wishfort. O Marwood, Marwood, art thou false? my friend deceive me! hast thou been a wicked accomplice with that profligate man?

Mrs. Marwood. Have you so much ingratitude and injustice to give credit against your friend, to the aspersions of two such mercenary trulls?

Mincing. Mercenary, mem? I scorn your words. 'Tis true we found you and Mr. Fainall in the blue garret; by the same token, you swore us to secrecy upon Messalina's[97] poems. Mercenary! No, if we would have been mercenary, we should have held our tongues; you would have bribed us sufficiently.

Fainall. Go, you are an insignificant thing!—Well, what are you the better for this; is this Mr. Mirabell's expedient? I'll be put off no longer.—You, thing that was a wife, shall smart for this! I will not leave thee wherewithall to hide thy shame; your body shall be naked as your reputation.

Mrs. Fainall. I despise you, and defy your malice—you have aspersed me wrongfully—I have proved your falsehood —go, you and your treacherous—I will not name it, but starve together—perish!

Fainall. Not while you are worth a groat, indeed, my dear. —Madam, I'll be fooled no longer.

Lady Wishfort. Ah, Mr. Mirabell, this is small comfort, the detection of this affair.

Mirabell. Oh, in good time—your leave for the other offender and penitent to appear, madam.

Enter WAITWELL *with a box of writings.*

Lady Wishfort. O ~~Sir~~ Rowland!—Well, rascal!

Waitwell. What your ladyship pleases. I have brought the black box at last, madam.

Mirabell. Give it me.—Madam, you remember your promise?

Lady Wishfort. Ay, dear sir.

Mirabell. Where are the gentlemen?

Waitwell. At hand, sir, rubbing their eyes—just risen from sleep.

Fainall. 'Sdeath, what's this to me? I'll not wait your private concerns.

Enter PETULANT *and* WITWOUD.

Petulant. How now? What's the matter? whose hand's out?

Witwoud. Heyday! what, are you all got together like players at the end of the last act?

Mirabell. You may remember, gentlemen, I once requested your hands as witnesses to a certain parchment.

Witwoud. Ay, I do, my hand I remember—Petulant set his mark.

Mirabell. You wrong him; his name is fairly written, as shall appear.—You do not remember, gentlemen, anything of what that parchment contained?   *(Undoing the box.)*

Witwoud. No.

Petulant. Not I; I writ, I read nothing.

Mirabell. Very well, now you shall know.—Madam, your promise.

Lady Wishfort. Ay, ay, sir, upon my honor.

Mirabell. Mr. Fainall, it is now time that you should know that your lady, while she was at her own disposal, and before you had by your insinuations wheedled her out of a pretended settlement of the greatest part of her fortune—

Fainall. Sir! pretended!

Mirabell. Yes, sir, I say that this lady while a widow, having, it seems, received some cautions respecting your inconstancy and tyranny of temper, which from her own partial opinion and fondness of you she could never have suspected —she did, I say, by the wholesome advice of friends, and of sages learned in the laws of this land, deliver this same as her act and deed to me in trust, and to the uses within mentioned. You may read if you please—*(Holding out the parchment)* though perhaps what is written on the back may serve your occasions.

Fainall. Very likely, sir. what's here?—Damnation! *(Reads.)* "A deed of conveyance of the whole estate real of Arabella Languish, widow, in trust to Edward Mirabell."—Confusion!

Mirabell. Even so, sir; 'tis the *Way of the World*, sir, of the widows of the world. I suppose this deed may bear an elder date than what you have obtained from your lady?

Fainall. Perfidious fiend! then thus I'll be revenged.

                              (Offers to run at Mrs. FAINALL.)

Sir Wilfull. Hold, sir! now you make your bear-garden flourish somewhere else, sir.

Fainall. Mirabell, you shall hear of this, sir, be sure you shall.—Let me pass, oaf!   *Exit.*

Mrs. Fainall. Madam, you seem to stifle your resentment; you had better give it vent.

Mrs. Marwood. Yes, it shall have vent—and to your confusion; or I'll perish in the attempt. *Exit.*

Lady Wishfort. O daughter, daughter! 'tis plain thou hast inherited thy mother's prudence.

Mrs. Fainall. Thank Mr. Mirabell, a cautious friend, to whose advice all is owing.

Lady Wishfort. Well, Mr. Mirabell, you have kept your promise—and I must perform mine.—First, I pardon, for your sake, Sir Rowland there, and Foible. The next thing is to break the matter to my nephew—and how to do that—

Mirabell. For that, madam, give yourself no trouble; let me have your consent. Sir Wilfull is my friend; he has had compassion upon lovers, and generously engaged a volunteer in this action for our service; and now designs to prosecute his travels.

Sir Wilfull. S'heart, aunt, I have no mind to marry. My cousin's a fine lady, and the gentleman loves her, and she loves him, and they deserve one another; my resolution is to see foreign parts—I have set on't—and when I'm set on't I must do't. And if these two gentlemen would travel too, I think they may be spared.

Petulant. For my part, I say little—I think things are best off or on.

Witwoud. I'gad, I understand nothing of the matter; I'm in a maze yet, like a dog in a dancing-school.

Lady Wishfort. Well, sir, take her, and with her all the joy I can give you.

Mrs. Millamant. Why does not the man take me? would you have me give myself to you over again?

Mirabell. Ay, and over and over again; *(Kisses her hand.)* I would have you as often as possibly I can. Well, Heaven grant I love you not too well; that's all my fear.

Sir Wilfull. S'heart, you'll have time enough to toy after you're married; or if you will toy now, let us have a dance in the mean time, that we who are not lovers may have some other employment besides looking on.

Mirabell. With all my heart, dear Sir Wilfull. What shall we do for music?

Foible. O sir, some that were provided for Sir Rowland's entertainment are yet within call. *(A Dance.)*

Lady Wishfort. As I am a person, I can hold out no longer; —I have wasted my spirits so today already, that I am ready to sink under the fatigue; and I cannot but have some fears upon me yet, that my son Fainall will pursue some desperate course.

Mirabell. Madam, disquiet not yourself on that account; to my knowledge his circumstances are such he must of force comply. For my part, I will contribute all that in me lies to a reunion; in the mean time, madam,—(*To* Mrs. FAINALL.) let me before these witnesses restore to you this deed of trust; it may be a means, well-managed, to make you live easily together.

> From hence let those be warned who mean to wed;
> Lest mutual falsehood stain the bridal bed;
> For each deceiver to his cost may find,
> That marriage-frauds too oft are paid in kind.   *Exeunt*.

EPILOGUE

After our Epilogue this crowd dismisses,
I'm thinking how this play'll be pulled to pieces.
But pray consider, ere you doom its fall,
How hard a thing 'twould be to please you all.
There are some critics so with spleen diseased,
They scarcely come inclining to be pleased:
And sure he must have more than mortal skill,
Who pleases any one against his will.
Then, all bad poets we are sure are foes,
And how their number's swelled, the town well knows:
In shoals I've marked 'em judging in the pit;
Though they're on no pretence for judgment fit,
But that they have been damned for want of wit.
Since when, by their own offences taught,
Set up for spies on plays and finding fault.
Others there are whose malice we'd prevent;
Such who watch plays with scurrilous intent
To mark out who by characters are meant.
And though no perfect likeness they can trace,
Yet each pretends to know the copied face.
Those with false glosses feed their own ill-nature,
And turn to libel what was meant a satire.
May such malicious fops this fortune find,
To think themselves alone the fools designed!
If any are so arrogantly vain,
To think they singly can support a scene,
And furnish fool enough to entertain.
For well the learned and the judicious know
That satire scorns to stoop so meanly low
As any one abstracted fop to show.
For, as when painters form a matchless face,
They from each fair one catch some different grace;
And shining features in one portrait blend,
To which no single beauty must pretend;
So poets oft do in one piece expose
Whole *belles assemblées* of coquettes and beaux.

She Stoops to Conquer

or, The Mistakes of a Night

by
Oliver Goldsmith

To SAMUEL JOHNSON, L.L.D.

Dear Sir,

By inscribing this slight performance to you, I do not mean so much to compliment you as myself. It may do me some honor to inform the public that I have lived many years in intimacy with you. It may serve the interests of mankind also to inform them that the greatest wit may be found in a character without impairing the most unaffected piety.

I have, particularly, reason to thank you for your partiality to this performance. The undertaking a comedy, not merely sentimental, was very dangerous; and Mr. Colman, who saw this piece in its various stages, always thought it so. However, I ventured to trust it to the public; and though it was necessarily delayed till late in the season, I have every reason to be grateful.

I am, Dear Sir,
Your most sincere friend,
And admirer,
OLIVER GOLDSMITH.

PROLOGUE

By David Garrick, Esq.

Enter Mr. Woodward,[1] *Dressed in black, and holding a handkerchief to his eyes.*

Excuse me, sirs, I pray—I can't yet speak—
I'm crying now—and have been all the week!
'Tis not alone this mourning suit, good masters;
I've that within—for which there are no plasters!
Pray would you know the reason why I'm crying?
The Comic Muse, long sick, is now a-dying!
And if she goes, my tears will never stop;
For as a player, I can't squeeze out one drop.
I am undone, that's all—shall lose my bread—
I'd rather, but that's nothing—lose my head.
When the sweet maid is laid upon the bier,
Shuter[2] and I shall be chief mourners here.
To her a mawkish drab of spurious breed,
Who deals in sentimentals will succeed!
Poor Ned and I are dead to all intents,
We can as soon speak Greek as sentiments!
Both nervous grown, to keep our spirits up,
We now and then take down a hearty cup.
What shall we do?—If comedy forsake us!
They'll turn us out, and no one else will take us;
But why can't I be moral?—Let me try—
My heart thus pressing—fixed my face and eye—
With a sententious look, that nothing means,
(Faces are blocks, in sentimental scenes)
Thus I begin—*All is not gold that glitters,
Pleasure seems sweet, but proves a glass of bitters.
When ignorance enters, folly is at hand;
Learning is better far than house and land.
Let not your virtue trip; who trips may stumble,
And virtue is not virtue, if she tumble.*
I give it up—morals won't do for me;
To make you laugh I must play tragedy.
One hope remains—hearing the maid was ill,
A *doctor* comes this night to show his skill.

To cheer her heart, and give your muscles motion,
He in *five draughts* prepared, presents a potion:
A kind of magic charm—for be assured,
If you will *swallow* it, the maid is cured:
But desperate the doctor, and her case is,
If you reject the dose, and make wry faces!
This truth he boasts, will boast it while he lives,
No *poisonous drugs* are mixed in what he gives;
Should he succeed, you'll give him his degree;
If not, within he will receive no fee!
The college, *you,* must his pretensions back,
Pronounce him *regular,* or dub him *quack.*

DRAMATIS PERSONÆ

SIR CHARLES MARLOW.
YOUNG MARLOW, his son.
HARDCASTLE.
HASTINGS.
TONY LUMPKIN.
DIGGORY.

MRS. HARDCASTLE.
MISS HARDCASTLE.
MISS NEVILLE.
MAID.
Landlord, Servants, &c., &c.

ACT I

SCENE I: *A Chamber in an old-fashioned House.*

Enter MRS. HARDCASTLE *and* MR. HARDCASTLE.

Mrs. Hardcastle. I vow, Mr. Hardcastle, you're very particular. Is there a creature in the whole country but ourselves that does not take a trip to town now and then to rub off the rust a little? There's the two Miss Hoggs and our neighbour, Mrs. Grigsby, go to take a month's polishing every winter.

Hardcastle. Ay, and bring back vanity and affectation to last them the whole year. I wonder why London cannot keep its own fools at home. In my time, the follies of the town crept slowly among us, but now they travel faster than a stage-coach. Its fopperies come down, not only as inside passengers, but in the very basket.

Mrs. Hardcastle. Ay, *your* times were fine times, indeed; you have been telling us of *them* for many a long year. Here we live in an old rumbling mansion that looks for all the world like an inn, but that we never see company. Our best visitors are old Mrs. Oddfish, the curate's wife, and little Cripplegate, the lame dancing-master. And all our entertainment your old stories of Prince Eugene and the Duke of Marlborough. I hate such old-fashioned trumpery.

Hardcastle. And I love it. I love every thing that's old: old friends, old times, old manners, old books, old wine; and, I believe, Dorothy, *(taking her hand)* you'll own I have been pretty fond of an old wife.

Mrs. Hardcastle. Lord, Mr. Hardcastle, you're for ever at your Dorothy's and your old wife's. You may be a Darby, but I'll be no Joan,[3] I promise you. I'm not so old as you'd make me, by more than one good year. Add twenty to twenty, and make money of that.

Hardcastle. Let me see; twenty added to twenty, makes just fifty and seven.

Mrs. Hardcastle. It's false, Mr. Hardcastle: I was but twenty when I was brought to bed of Tony, that I had by Mr. Lumpkin, my first husband; and he's not come to years of discretion yet.

171

Hardcastle. Nor ever will, I dare answer for him. Ay, you have taught him finely!

Mrs. Hardcastle. No matter, Tony Lumpkin has a good fortune. My son is not to live by his learning. I don't think a boy wants too much learning to spend fifteen-hundred a year.

Hardcastle. Learning, quotha! A mere composition of tricks and mischief.

Mrs. Hardcastle. Humor, my dear: nothing but humor. Come, Mr. Hardcastle, you must allow the boy a little humor.

Hardcastle. I'd sooner allow him an horse-pond. If burning the footmen's shoes, frighting the maids, and worrying the kittens, be humor, he has it. It was but yesterday he fastened my wig to the back of my chair, and when I went to make a bow I popped my bald head in Mrs. Frizzle's face.

Mrs. Hardcastle. And am I to blame? The poor boy was always too sickly to do any good. A school would be his death. When he comes to be a little stronger, who knows what a year or two's Latin may do for him?

Hardcastle. Latin for him! A cat and fiddle. No, no, the ale-house and the stable are the only schools he'll ever go to.

Mrs. Hardcastle. Well, we must not snub the poor boy now, for I believe we shan't have him long among us. Anybody that looks in his face may see he's consumptive.

Hardcastle. Ay, if growing too fat be one of the symptoms.

Mrs. Hardcastle. He coughs sometimes.

Hardcastle. Yes, when his liquor goes the wrong way.

Mrs. Hardcastle. I'm actually afraid of his lungs.

Hardcastle. And truly, so am I; for he sometimes whoops like a speaking trumpet—(Tony *hallooing behind the Scenes.*)—Oh, there he goes—A very consumptive figure, truly.

Enter Tony, *crossing the Stage.*

Mrs. Hardcastle. Tony, where are you going, my charmer? Won't you give papa and I a little of your company, lovee?

Tony. I'm in haste, mother, I cannot stay.

Mrs. Hardcastle. You shan't venture out this raw evening, my dear. You look most shockingly.

Tony. I can't stay, I tell you. The Three Pigeons expects me down every moment. There's some fun going forward.

Hardcastle. Ay; the ale-house, the old place. I thought so.

Mrs. Hardcastle. A low, paltry set of fellows.

Tony. Not so low neither. There's Dick Muggins the exciseman, Jack Slang the horse doctor, Little Aminadab that grinds the music box, and Tom Twist that spins the pewter platter.

Mrs. Hardcastle. Pray, my dear, disappoint them for one night at least.

Tony. As for disappointing *them,* I should not so much mind; but I can't abide to disappoint *myself*.

Mrs. Hardcastle. (Detaining him.) You shan't go.

Tony. I will, I tell you.

Mrs. Hardcastle. I say you shan't.

Tony. We'll see which is strongest, you or I.

Exit hauling her out.

HARDCASTLE, *solus.*

Hardcastle. Ay, there goes a pair that only spoil each other. But is not the whole age in a combination to drive sense and discretion out of doors? There's my pretty darling, Kate; the fashions of the times have almost infected her too. By living a year or two in town, she is as fond of gauze, and French frippery, as the best of them.

Enter MISS HARDCASTLE.

Hardcastle. Blessings on my pretty innocence! Dressed out as usual, my Kate. Goodness! What a quantity of superfluous silk hast thou got about thee, girl! I could never teach the fools of this age, that the indigent world could be clothed out of the trimmings of the vain.

Miss Hardcastle. You know our agreement, sir. You allow me the morning to receive and pay visits and to dress in my own manner; and in the evening, I put on my housewife's dress to please you.

Hardcastle. Well, remember, I insist on the terms of our agreement; and, by the bye, I believe I shall have occasion to try your obedience this very evening.

Miss Hardcastle. I protest, sir, I don't comprehend your meaning.

Hardcastle. Then, to be plain with you, Kate, I expect the young gentleman I have chosen to be your husband from town this very day. I have his father's letter in which he informs me his son is set out and that he intends to follow himself shortly after.

Miss Hardcastle. Indeed! I wish I had known something of this before. Bless me, how shall I behave? It's a thousand to one I shan't like him. Our meeting will be so formal and so like a thing of business that I shall find no room for friendship or esteem.

Hardcastle. Depend upon it, child, I'll never controul your choice; but Mr. Marlow, whom I have pitched upon, is the son of my old friend, Sir Charles Marlow, of whom you have heard me talk so often. The young gentleman has been bred a scholar, and is designed for an employment in the service of his country. I am told he's a man of excellent understanding.

Miss Hardcastle. Is he?

Hardcastle. Very generous.

Miss Hardcastle. I believe I shall like him.

Hardcastle. Young and brave.

Miss Hardcastle. I'm sure I shall like him.

Hardcastle. And very handsome.

Miss Hardcastle. My dear papa, say no more; (*kissing his hand.*) he's mine, I'll have him.

Hardcastle. And to crown all, Kate, he's one of the most bashful and reserved young fellows in all the world.

Miss Hardcastle. Eh! you have frozen me to death again. That word "reserved" has undone all the rest of his accomplishments. A reserved lover, it is said, always makes a suspicious husband.

Hardcastle. On the contrary, modesty seldom resides in a breast that is not enriched with nobler virtues. It was the very feature in his character that first struck me.

Miss Hardcastle. He must have more striking features to catch me, I promise you. However, if he be so young, so handsome, and so everything, as you mention, I believe he'll do still. I think I'll have him.

Hardcastle. Ay, Kate, but there is still an obstacle. It's more than an even wager he may not have *you*.

Miss Hardcastle. My dear Papa, why will you mortify one so?—Well, if he refuses, instead of breaking my heart at his indifference, I'll only break my glass for its flattery, set my cap to some newer fashion, and look out for some less difficult admirer.

Hardcastle. Bravely resolved! In the mean time I'll go prepare the servants for his reception; as we seldom see company they want as much training as a company of recruits, the first day's muster.   *Exit.*

Miss Hardcastle, *sola*.

Miss Hardcastle. Lud, this news of Papa's puts me all in a flutter. Young, handsome; these he put last; but I put them foremost. Sensible, good-natured; I like all that. But then reserved, and sheepish, that's much against him. Yet, can't he be cured of his timidity by being taught to be proud of his wife? Yes, and can't I—But I vow I'm disposing of the husband, before I have secured the lover.

Enter Miss Neville.

Miss Hardcastle, I'm glad you're come, Neville, my dear. Tell me, Constance, how do I look this evening? Is there any thing whimsical about me? Is it one of my well looking days, child? Am I in face today?

Miss Neville. Perfectly, my dear. Yet now I look again—bless me!—sure no accident has happened among the canary birds or the gold-fishes. Has your brother or the cat been meddling? Or has the last novel been too moving?

Miss Hardcastle. No; nothing of all this. I have been threatened—I can scarce get it out—I have been threatened with a lover.

Miss Neville. And his name—

Miss Hardcastle. Is Marlow.

Miss Neville. Indeed!

Miss Hardcastle. The son of Sir Charles Marlow.

Miss Neville. As I live, the most intimate friend of Mr. Hastings, *my* admirer. They are never asunder. I believe you must have seen him when we lived in town.

Miss Hardcastle. Never.

Miss Neville. He's a very singular character, I assure you. Among women of reputation and virtue, he is the modestest man alive; but his acquaintance give him a very different character among creatures of another stamp: you understand me.

Miss Hardcastle. An odd character, indeed. I shall never be able to manage him. What shall I do? Pshaw, think no more of him, but trust to occurrences for success. But how goes on your own affair, my dear? has my mother been courting you for my brother Tony, as usual?

Miss Neville. I have just come from one of our agreeable *tête-à-têtes*. She has been saying a hundred tender things and setting off her pretty monster as the very pink of perfection.

Miss Hardcastle. And her partiality is such that she actually thinks him so. A fortune like yours is no small temptation. Besides, as she has the sole management of it, I'm not surprised to see her unwilling to let it go out of the family.

Miss Neville. A fortune like mine, which chiefly consists in jewels, is no such mighty temptation. But at any rate, if my dear Hastings be but constant, I make no doubt to be too hard for her at last. However, I let her suppose that I am in love with her son, and she never once dreams that my affections are fixed upon another.

Miss Hardcastle. My good brother holds out stoutly. I could almost love him for hating you so.

Miss Neville. It is a good natured creature at bottom, and I'm sure would wish to see me married to anybody but himself. But my aunt's bell rings for our afternoon's walk round the improvements. *Allons*. Courage is necessary as our affairs are critical.

Miss Hardcastle. Would it were bed time and all were well.

                                                        Exeunt.

SCENE II: *An Ale-house Room. Several shabby fellows with Punch and Tobacco*. TONY *at the head of the Table, a little higher than the rest: A mallet in his hand*.

Omnes. Hurrea, hurrea, hurrea, bravo!

First fellow. Now, gentlemen, silence for a song. The Squire is going to knock himself down for a song.

Omnes. Ay, a song, a song.

Tony. Then I'll sing you, gentlemen, a song I made upon this ale-house, The Three Pigeons.

SONG

Let school-masters puzzle their brain
   With grammar, and nonsense, and learning;
Good liquor, I stoutly maintain,
   Gives genius a better discerning.
Let them brag of their Heathenish Gods,
   Their Lethes, their Styxes, and Stygians;
Their Quis, and their Quæs, and their Quods,
   They're all but a parcel of Pigeons.
            Toroddle, toroddle, toroll!

When Methodist preachers come down,
   A-preaching that drinking is sinful,
I'll wager the rascals a crown,
   They always preach best with a skinful.
But when you come down with your pence,
   For a slice of their scurvy religion,
I'll leave it to all men of sense,
   But you, my good friend, are the pigeon.
            Toroddle, toroddle, toroll!

Then come, put the jorum[4] about,
   And let us be merry and clever,
Our hearts and our liquors are stout,
   Here's the Three Jolly Pigeons for ever.
Let some cry up woodcock or hare,
   Your bustards, your ducks, and your widgeons;
But of all the birds in the air,
   Here's a health to the Three Jolly Pigeons.
            Toroddle, toroddle, toroll!

Omnes. Bravo, bravo.

First Fellow. The squire has got spunk in him.

Second Fellow. I loves to hear him sing, bekeays he never gives us nothing that's *low*.

Third Fellow. O damn anything that's *low*, I cannot bear it.

Fourth Fellow. The genteel thing is the genteel thing at any time. If so be that a gentleman bees in a concatenation accordingly.

Third Fellow. I like the maxum of it, Master Muggins. What, though I am obliged to dance a bear, a man may be a gentleman for all that. May this be my poison if my bear ever dances but to the very genteelest of tunes. *Water Parted*, or the minuet in *Ariadne*.⁵

Second Fellow. What a pity it is the squire is not come to his own. It would be well for all the publicans within ten miles round of him.

Tony. Ecod, and so it would, Master Slang. I'd then show what it was to keep choice of company.

Second Fellow. Oh, he takes after his own father for that. To be sure old squire Lumpkin was the finest gentleman I ever set my eyes on. For winding the straight horn, or beating a thicket for a hare or a wench he never had his fellow. It was a saying in the place, that he kept the best horses, dogs and girls in the whole county.

Tony. Ecod, and when I'm of age I'll be no bastard, I promise you. I have been thinking of Bett Bouncer and the miller's grey mare to begin with. But come, my boys, drink about and be merry, for you pay no reckoning. Well, Stingo, what's the matter?

Enter LANDLORD.

Landlord. There be two gentlemen in a post-chaise at the door. They have lost their way upo' the forest; and they are talking something about Mr. Hardcastle.

Tony. As sure as can be, one of them must be the gentleman that's coming down to court my sister. Do they seem to be Londoners?

Landlord. I believe they may. They look woundily like Frenchmen.

Tony. Then desire them to step this way, and I'll set them right in a twinkling. (*Exit* LANDLORD.) Gentlemen, as they mayn't be good enough company for you, step down for a moment, and I'll be with you in the squeezing of a lemon.

Exeunt MOB.

TONY, *solus*.

Tony. Father-in-law has been calling me whelp and hound, this half year. Now if I pleased, I could be so revenged upon the old grumbletonian. But then I'm afraid—afraid of what? I shall soon be worth fifteen hundred a year, and let him frighten me out of that if he can.

Enter LANDLORD, *conducting* MARLOW *and* HASTINGS.

Marlow. What a tedious, uncomfortable day have we had of it! We were told it was but forty miles across the country, and we have come above threescore.

Hastings. And all, Marlow, from that unaccountable reserve of yours that would not let us enquire more frequently on the way.

Marlow. I own, Hastings, I am unwilling to lay myself under an obligation to every one I meet; and often, stand the chance of an unmannerly answer.

Hastings. At present, however, we are not likely to receive any answer.

Tony. No offence, gentlemen. But I'm told you have been enquiring for one Mr. Hardcastle in these parts. Do you know what part of the country you are in?

Hastings. Not in the least, sir, but should thank you for information.

Tony. Nor the way you came?

Hastings. No, sir; but if you can inform us—

Tony. Why, gentlemen, if you know neither the road you are going, nor where you are, nor the road you came, the first thing I have to inform you is, that—You have lost your way.

Marlow. We wanted no ghost to tell us that.

Tony. Pray, gentlemen, may I be so bold as to ask the place from whence you came?

Marlow. That's not necessary towards directing us where we are to go.

Tony. No offence; but question for question is all fair, you know. Pray, gentlemen, is not this the same Hardcastle a cross-grained, old-fashioned, whimsical fellow, with an ugly face, a daughter, and a pretty son?

Hastings. We have not seen the gentleman, but he has the family you mention.

Tony. The daughter, a tall, trapesing, trolloping, talkative maypole—The son, a pretty, well-bred, agreeable youth that everybody is fond of.

Marlow. Our information differs in this. The daughter is said to be well-bred and beautiful; the son, an awkward booby, reared up and spoiled at his mother's apron-string.

Tony. He-he-hem—Then, gentlemen, all I have to tell you is, that you won't reach Mr. Hardcastle's house this night, I believe.

Hastings. Unfortunate!

Tony. It's a damn'd long, dark, boggy, dirty, dangerous way. Stingo, tell the gentlemen the way to Mr. Hardcastle's; (*Winking upon the* LANDLORD.) Mr. Hardcastle's, of Quagmire Marsh, you understand me.

Landlord. Master Hardcastle's! Lack-a-daisy, my masters, you're come a deadly deal wrong! When you came to the bottom of the hill, you should have crossed down Squash-lane.

Marlow. Cross down Squash-lane!

Landlord. Then you were to keep straight forward, 'till you came to four roads.

Marlow. Come to where four roads meet!

Tony. Ay; but you must be sure to take only one of them.

Marlow. O sir, you're facetious.

Tony. Then, keeping to the right, you are to go side-ways till you come upon Crack-skull Common. There you must look sharp for the track of the wheel and go forward 'till you come to farmer Murrain's barn. Coming to the farmer's barn, you are to turn to the right, and then to the left, and then to the right about again, till you find out the old mill—

Marlow. Zounds, man! we could as soon find out the longitude!

Hastings. What's to be done, Marlow?

Marlow. This house promises but a poor reception; though perhaps the Landlord can accommodate us.

Landlord. Alack, master, we have but one spare bed in the whole house.

Tony. And to my knowledge, that's taken up by three lodgers already. (*After a pause in which the rest seem disconcerted.*) I have hit it. Don't you think, Stingo, our landlady could accommodate the gentlemen by the fire-side, with—three chairs and a bolster?

Hastings. I hate sleeping by the fire-side.

Marlow. And I detest your three chairs and a bolster.

Tony. You do, do you?—then let me see—what—if you go on a mile further to the Buck's Head; the old Buck's Head on the hill, one of the best inns in the whole county?

Hastings. O ho! so we have escaped an adventure for this night, however.

Landlord. (*Apart to* TONY.) Sure, you ben't sending them to your father's as an inn, be you?

Tony. Mum, you fool you. Let *them* find that out. (*To them.*) You have only to keep on straight forward till you come to a large old house by the road side. You'll see a pair of large horns over the door. That's the sign. Drive up the yard and call stoutly about you.

Hastings. Sir, we are obliged to you. The servants can't miss the way?

Tony. No, no. But I tell you though, the landlord is rich and going to leave off business; so he wants to be thought a gentleman, saving your presence, he! he! he! He'll be for giving you his company, and, ecod, if you mind him, he'll persuade you that his mother was an alderman, and his aunt a justice of peace.

Landlord. A troublesome old blade, to be sure; but a keeps as good wines and beds as any in the whole country.

Marlow. Well, if he supplies us with these, we shall want no further connection. We are to turn to the right, did you say?

Tony. No, no; straight forward. I'll just step myself, and show you a piece of the way. (*To the* LANDLORD.) Mum.

Landlord. Ah, bless your heart, for a sweet, pleasant—damn'd mischievous son of a whore.   *Exeunt.*

ACT II

SCENE I: *An old-fashioned house.*

Enter HARDCASTLE, *followed by three or four awkward* SERVANTS.

Hardcastle. Well, I hope you're perfect in the table exercise I have been teaching you these three days. You all know your posts and your places and can show that you have been used to good company, without ever stirring from home.

Omnes. Ay, ay.

Hardcastle. When company comes, you are not to pop out and stare, and then run in again, like frightened rabbits in a warren.

Omnes. No, no.

Hardcastle. You, Diggory, whom I have taken from the barn, are to make a show at the side-table; and you, Roger, whom I have advanced from the plough, are to place yourself behind *my* chair. But you're not to stand so, with your hands in your pockets. Take your hands from your pockets, Roger; and from your head, you blockhead you. See how Diggory carries his hands. They're a little too stiff indeed, but that's no great matter.

Diggory. Ay, mind how I hold them. I learned to hold my

hands this way when I was upon drill for the militia. And so being upon drill—

Hardcastle. You must not be so talkative, Diggory. You must be all attention to the guests. You must hear us talk and not think of talking; you must see us drink and not think of drinking; you must see us eat and not think of eating.

Diggory. By the laws, your worship, that's perfectly unpossible. Whenever Diggory sees yeating going forward, ecod, he's always wishing for a mouthful himself.

Hardcastle. Blockhead! Is not a belly-full in the kitchen as good as a belly-full in the parlor? Stay your stomach with that reflection.

Diggory. Ecod, I thank your worship, I'll make a shift to stay my stomach with a slice of cold beef in the pantry.

Hardcastle. Diggory, you are too talkative. Then, if I happen to say a good thing, or tell a good story at table, you must not all burst out a-laughing, as if you made part of the company.

Diggory. Then, ecod, your worship must not tell the story of Ould Grouse in the gun-room: I can't help laughing at that—he! he! he!—for the soul of me. We have laughed at that these twenty years—ha! ha! ha!

Hardcastle. Ha! ha! ha! The story is a good one. Well, honest Diggory, you may laugh at that—but still remember to be attentive. Suppose one of the company should call for a glass of wine, how will you behave? A glass of wine, sir, if you please. (*To* DIGGORY.)—Eh, why don't you move?

Diggory. Ecod, your worship, I never have courage till I see the eatables and drinkables brought upo' the table, and then I'm as bauld as a lion.

Hardcastle. What, will nobody move?

First Servant. I'm not to leave this pleace.

Second Servant. I'm sure it's no pleace of mine.

Third Servant. Nor mine, for sartain.

Diggory. Wauns, and I'm sure it canna be mine.

Hardcastle. You numbskulls! and so while, like your betters, you are quarrelling for places, the guests must be starved. O you dunces! I find I must begin all over again.— But don't I hear a coach drive into the yard? To your posts, you blockheads. I'll go in the mean time and give my old friend's son a hearty reception at the gate.   *Exit.*

Diggory. By the elevens, my pleace is gone quite out of my head.

Roger. I know that my pleace is to be everywhere.

First Servant. Where the devil is mine?

Second Servant. My pleace is to be nowhere at all; and so I'ze go about my business.

Exeunt SERVANTS, *running about as if frighted, different ways.*

Enter SERVANT *with candles, showing in* MARLOW *and* HAST-
          INGS.

 Servant. Welcome, gentlemen, very welcome. This way.
 Hastings. After the disappointments of the day, welcome
once more, Charles, to the comforts of a clean room and a
good fire. Upon my word, a very well-looking house; antique, but creditable.
 Marlow. The usual fate of a large mansion. Having first
ruined the master by good housekeeping, it at last comes to
levy contributions as an inn.
 Hastings. As you say, we passengers are to be taxed to pay
all these fineries. I have often seen a good sideboard, or a
marble chimney-piece, though not actually put in the bill, en-
flame a reckoning confoundedly.
 Marlow. Travellers, George, must pay in all places. The
only difference is, that in good inns, you pay dearly for luxuries; in bad inns, you are fleeced and starved.
 Hastings. You have lived pretty much among them. In
truth, I have been often surprised that you who have seen so
much of the world, with your natural good sense, and your
many opportunities, could never yet acquire a requisite share
of assurance.
 Marlow. The Englishman's malady. But tell me, George,
where could I have learned that assurance you talk of? My
life has been chiefly spent in a college or an inn, in seclu-
sion from that lovely part of the creation that chiefly teach
men confidence. I don't know that I was ever familiarly acquainted with a single modest woman—except my mother—
But among females of another class, you know—
 Hastings. Ay, among them you are impudent enough of all
conscience.
 Marlow. They are of *us,* you know.
 Hastings. But in the company of women of reputation I
never saw such an idiot, such a trembler; you look for all
the world as if you wanted an opportunity of stealing out of
the room.
 Marlow. Why, man. that's because I *do* want to steal out of
the room. Faith, I have often formed a resolution to break
the ice, and rattle away at any rate. But I don't know how, a
single glance from a pair of fine eyes has totally overset my
resolution. An impudent fellow may counterfeit modesty, but
I'll be hanged if a modest man can ever counterfeit impudence.
 Hastings. If you could but say half the fine things to them

that I have heard you lavish upon the bar-maid of an inn, or even a college bed maker—

Marlow. Why, George, I can't say fine things to them. They freeze, they petrify me. They may talk of a comet, or a burning mountain, or some such bagatelle. But to me, a modest woman, dressed out in all her finery, is the most tremendous object of the whole creation.

Hastings. Ha! ha! ha! At this rate, man, how can you ever expect to marry!

Marlow. Never, unless, as among kings and princes, my bride were to be courted by proxy. If, indeed, like an Eastern bridegroom, one were to be introduced to a wife he never saw before, it might be endured. But to go through all the terrors of a formal courtship, together with the episode of aunts, grandmothers and cousins, and at last to blurt out the broad staring question of, *Madam, will you marry me?* No, no, that's a strain much above me, I assure you.

Hastings. I pity you. But how do you intend behaving to the lady you are come down to visit at the request of your father?

Marlow. As I behave to all other ladies. Bow very low. Answer yes, or no, to all her demands—But for the rest, I don't think I shall venture to look in her face, till I see my father's again.

Hastings. I'm surprised that one who is so warm a friend can be so cool a lover.

Marlow. To be explicit, my dear Hastings, my chief inducement down was to be instrumental in forwarding your happiness, not my own. Miss Neville loves you, the family don't know you; as my friend you are sure of a reception, and let honor do the rest.

Hastings. My dear Marlow! But I'll suppress the emotion. Were I a wretch, meanly seeking to carry off a fortune, you should be the last man in the world I would apply to for assistance. But Miss Neville's person is all I ask, and that is mine, both from her deceased father's consent and her own inclination.

Marlow. Happy man! You have talents and art to captivate any woman. I'm doomed to adore the sex, and yet to converse with the only part of it I despise. This stammer in my address and this awkward prepossessing visage of mine can never permit me to soar above the reach of a milliner's 'prentice, or one of the duchesses of Drury Lane.[6] Pshaw! this fellow here to interrupt us.

Enter HARDCASTLE.

Hardcastle. Gentlemen, once more you are heartily welcome. Which is Mr. Marlow? Sir, you're heartily welcome. It's not my way, you see, to receive my friends with my back to the fire. I like to give them a hearty reception in the old style, at my gate. I like to see their horses and trunks taken care of.

Marlow. (Aside.) He has got our names from the servants already. *(To him.)* We approve your caution and hospitality, sir. *(To* HASTINGS.*)* I have been thinking, George, of changing our travelling dresses in the morning. I am grown confoundedly ashamed of mine.

Hardcastle. I beg, Mr. Marlow, you'll use no ceremony in this house.

Hastings. I fancy, Charles, you're right: the first blow is half the battle. I intend opening the campaign with the white and gold.

Mr. Hardcastle. Mr. Marlow—Mr. Hastings—gentlemen —pray be under no constraint in this house. This is Liberty-Hall, gentlemen. You may do just as you please here.

Marlow. Yet, George, if we open the campaign too fiercely at first, we may want ammunition before it is over. I think to reserve the embroidery to secure a retreat.

Hardcastle. Your talking of a retreat, Mr. Marlow, puts me in mind of the Duke of Marlborough, when we went to besiege Denain. He first summoned the garrison—

Marlow. Don't you think the *ventre d'or* waistcoat will do with the plain brown?

Hardcastle. He first summoned the garrison, which might consist of about five thousand men—

Hastings. I think not: brown and yellow mix but very poorly.

Hardcastle. I say, gentlemen, as I was telling you, he summoned the garrison, which might consist of about five thousand men—

Marlow. The girls like finery.

Hardcastle. Which might consist of about five thousand men, well appointed with stores, ammunition, and other implements of war. "Now," says the Duke of Marlborough, to George Brooks, that stood next to him—You must have heard of George Brooks—"I'll pawn my Dukedom," says he, "but I take that garrison without spilling a drop of blood." So—

Marlow. What, my good friend, if you gave us a glass of punch in the mean time; it would help us to carry on the siege with vigor.

Hardcastle. Punch, sir! *(Aside.)* This is the most unaccountable kind of modesty I ever met with.

Marlow. Yes, sir, punch. A glass of warm punch, after our journey, will be comfortable. This is Liberty-Hall, you know.

Hardcastle. Here's cup, sir.

Marlow. (Aside.) So this fellow, in his Liberty-Hall, will only let us have just what he pleases.

Hardcastle. (Taking the Cup.) I hope you'll find it to your mind. I have prepared it with my own hands, and I believe you'll own the ingredients are tolerable. Will you be so good as to pledge me, sir? Here, Mr. Marlow, here is to our better acquaintance. *(Drinks.)*

Marlow. (Aside.) A very impudent fellow this! but he's a character and I'll humor him a little. Sir, my service to you. *(Drinks.)*

Hastings. (Aside.) I see this fellow wants to give us his company, and forgets that he's an innkeeper, before he has learned to be a gentleman.

Marlow. From the excellence of your cup, my old friend, I suppose you have a good deal of business in this part of the country. Warm work, now and then, at elections, I suppose?

Hardcastle. No, sir, I have long given that work over. Since our betters have hit upon the expedient of electing each other, there's no business *for us that sell ale.*[7]

Hastings. So, then you have no turn for politics, I find.

Hardcastle. Not in the least. There was a time, indeed, I fretted myself about the mistakes of government, like other people; but finding myself every day grow more angry, and the government growing no better, I left it to mend itself. Since that, I no more trouble my head about Heyder Ally, or Ally Cawn, than about Ally Croaker.[8] Sir, my service to you.

Hastings. So that with eating above stairs, and drinking below, with receiving your friends within, and amusing them without you lead a good, pleasant, bustling life of it.

Hardcastle. I do stir about a great deal, that's certain. Half the differences of the parish are adjusted in this very parlor.

Marlow. (After drinking.) And you have an argument in your cup, old gentleman, better than any in Westminster Hall.

Hardcastle. Ay, young gentleman, that, and a little philosophy.

Marlow. (Aside.) Well, this is the first time I ever heard of an innkeeper's philosophy.

Hastings. So then, like an experienced general, you attack them on every quarter. If you find their reason manageable, you attack it with your philosophy; if you find they have no reason, you attack them with this. Here's your health, my philosopher. *(Drinks.)*

Hardcastle. Good, very good, thank you; ha! ha! Your generalship puts me in mind of Prince Eugene, when he fought the Turks at the battle of Belgrade. You shall hear—

Marlow. Instead of the battle of Belgrade, I believe it's almost time to talk about supper. What has your philosophy got in the house for supper?

Hardcastle. For supper, sir! (*Aside.*) Was ever such a request to a man in his own house!

Marlow. Yes, sir, supper, sir; I begin to feel an appetite. I shall make devilish work tonight in the larder, I promise you.

Hardcastle. (*Aside.*) Such a brazen dog sure never my eyes beheld. (*To him.*) Why really, sir, as for supper I can't well tell. My Dorothy, and the cook-maid, settle these things between them. I leave these kind of things entirely to them.

Marlow. You do, do you?

Hardcastle. Entirely. By-the-bye, I believe they are in actual consultation upon what's for supper this moment in the kitchen.

Marlow. Then I beg they'll admit *me* as one of their privy council. It's a way I have got. When I travel, I always choose to regulate my own supper. Let the cook be called. No offence, I hope, sir.

Hardcastle. O no, sir, none in the least; yet I don't know how: our Bridget, the cook maid, is not very communicative upon these occasions. Should we send for her, she might scold us all out of the house.

Hastings. Let's see your list of the larder then. I ask it as a favor. I always match my appetite to my bill of fare.

Marlow. (*To* HARDCASTLE, *who looks at them with surprise.*) Sir, he's very right, and it's my way too.

Hardcastle. Sir, you have a right to command here. Here, Roger, bring us the bill of fare for tonight's supper. I believe it's drawn out. Your manner, Mr. Hastings, puts me in mind of my uncle, Colonel Wallop. It was a saying of his, that no man was sure of his supper till he had eaten it.

Hastings. (*Aside.*) All upon the high ropes! His uncle a Colonel! We shall soon hear of his mother being a justice of peace. But let's hear the bill of fare.

Marlow. (*Perusing.*) What's here? For the first course; for the second course; for the dessert. The devil, sir, do you think we have brought down the whole Joiners Company, or the Corporation of Bedford, to eat up such a supper? Two or three little things, clean and comfortable, will do.

Hastings. But, let's hear it.

Marlow. (*Reading.*) For the first course, at the top, a pig and prune sauce.

Hastings. Damn your pig, I say.

Marlow. And damn your prune sauce, say I.

Hardcastle. And yet, gentlemen, to men that are hungry, pig with prune sauce is very good eating.

Marlow. At the bottom, a calve's tongue and brains.

Hastings. Let your brains be knocked out, my good sir; I don't like them.

Marlow. Or you may clap them on a plate by themselves. I do.

Hardcastle. (*Aside*.) Their impudence confounds me. (*To them*.) Gentlemen, you are my guests; make what alterations you please. Is there any thing else you wish to retrench or alter, gentlemen?

Marlow. Item: A pork pie, a boiled rabbit and sausages, a florentine, a shaking pudding, and a dish of tiff—taff—taffety cream![9]

Hastings. Confound your made dishes, I shall be as much at a loss in this house as at a green and yellow dinner at the French ambassador's table. I'm for plain eating.

Hardcastle. I'm sorry, gentlemen, that I have nothing you like, but if there be any thing you have a particular fancy to—

Marlow. Why, really, sir, your bill of fare is so exquisite that any one part of it is full as good as another. Send us what you please. So much for supper. And now to see that our beds are aired, and properly taken care of.

Hardcastle. I entreat you'll leave all that to me. You shall not stir a step.

Marlow. Leave that to you! I protest, sir, you must excuse me, I always look to these things myself.

Hardcastle. I must insist, sir, you'll make yourself easy on that head.

Marlow. You see I'm resolved on it. (*Aside*.) A very troublesome fellow this, as ever I met with.

Hardcastle. Well, sir, I'm resolved at least to attend you. (*Aside*.) This may be modern modesty, but I never saw anything look so like old-fashioned impudence.

Exeunt MARLOW *and* HARDCASTLE.

HASTINGS, *solus*.

Hastings. So I find this fellow's civilities begin to grow troublesome. But who can be angry at those assiduities which are meant to please him? Ha! what do I see? Miss Neville, by all that's happy!

Enter MISS NEVILLE.

Miss Neville. My dear Hastings! To what unexpected good fortune, to what accident am I to ascribe this happy meeting?

Hastings. Rather let me ask the same question, as I could never have hoped to meet my dearest Constance at an inn.

Miss Neville. An inn! sure you mistake! my aunt, my guardian, lives here. What could induce you to think this house an inn?

Hastings. My friend, Mr. Marlow, with whom I came down, and I, have been sent here as to an inn, I assure you. A young fellow whom we accidentally met at a house hard by directed us hither.

Miss Neville. Certainly it must be one of my hopeful cousin's tricks, of whom you have heard me talk so often, ha! ha! ha!

Hastings. He whom your aunt intends for you? He of whom I have such just apprehensions?

Miss Neville. You have nothing to fear from him, I assure you. You'd adore him if you knew how heartily he despises me. My aunt knows it too, and has undertaken to court me for him, and actually begins to think she has made a conquest.

Hastings. Thou dear dissembler! You must know, my Constance, I have just seized this happy opportunity of my friend's visit here to get admittance into the family. The horses that carried us down are now fatigued with their journey, but they'll soon be refreshed; and then, if my dearest girl will trust in her faithful Hastings, we shall soon be landed in France, where even among slaves the laws of marriage are respected.

Miss Neville. I have often told you, that though ready to obey you, I yet should leave my little fortune behind with reluctance. The greatest part of it was left me by my uncle, the India Director,[10] and chiefly consists in jewels. I have been for some time persuading my aunt to let me wear them. I fancy I'm very near succeeding. The instant they are put into my possession you shall find me ready to make them and myself yours.

Hastings. Perish the baubles! Your person is all I desire. In the meantime, my friend Marlow must not be let into his mistake. I know the strange reserve of his temper is such that if abruptly informed of it, he would instantly quit the house before our plan was ripe for execution.

Miss Neville. But how shall we keep him in the deception? Miss Hardcastle is just returned from walking; what if we still continue to deceive him?—This, this way—

(They confer.)

Enter Marlow.

Marlow. The assiduities of these good people tease me beyond bearing. My host seems to think it ill manners to leave me alone and so he claps not only himself but his old-fashioned wife on my back. They talk of coming to sup with us too; and then, I suppose, we are to run the gauntlet through all the rest of the family.—What have we got here!—

Hastings. My dear Charles! Let me congratulate you!—The most fortunate accident!—Who do you think is just alighted?

Marlow. Cannot guess.

Hastings. Our mistresses, boy, Miss Hardcastle and Miss Neville. Give me leave to introduce Miss Constance Neville to your acquaintance. Happening to dine in the neighborhood, they called, on their return, to take fresh horses, here. Miss Hardcastle has just stepped into the next room and will be back in an instant. Wasn't it lucky? eh!

Marlow. (Aside.) I have just been mortified enough of all conscience; and here comes something to complete my embarrassment.

Hastings. Well! but wasn't it the most fortunate thing in the world?

Marlow. Oh! yes. Very fortunate—a most joyful encounter —But our dresses, George, you know, are in disorder—What if we should postpone the happiness 'till tomorrow?—tomorrow at her own house—It will be every bit as convenient— And rather more respectful—Tomorrow let it be.

(Offering to go.)

Miss Neville. By no means, sir. Your ceremony will displease her. The disorder of your dress will show the ardor of your impatience. Besides, she knows you are in the house and will permit you to see her.

Marlow. Oh! the devil! how shall I support it? Hem! hem! Hastings, you must not go. You are to assist me, you know. I shall be confoundly ridiculous. Yet, hang it! I'll take courage. Hem!

Hastings. Pshaw, man! it's but the first plunge, and all's over. She's but a woman, you know.

Marlow. And of all women, she that I dread most to encounter!

Enter MISS HARDCASTLE *as returned from walking,
a Bonnet, &c.*

Hastings. (Introducing them.) Miss Hardcastle, Mr. Marlow; I'm proud of bringing two persons of such merit together, that only want to know, to esteem each other.

Miss Hardcastle. (Aside.) Now, for meeting my modest gentleman with a demure face and quite in his own manner.

(After a pause in which he appears very uneasy and discon-certed.) I'm glad of your safe arrival, sir—I'm told you had some accidents by the way.

Marlow. Only a few, madam. Yes, we had some. Yes, madam, a good many accidents, but should be sorry— madam—or rather glad of any accidents—that are so agree-ably concluded. Hem!

Hastings. (To him.) You never spoke better in your whole life. Keep it up, and I'll insure you the victory.

Miss Hardcastle. I'm afraid you flatter, sir. You that have seen so much of the finest company can find little entertain-ment in an obscure corner of the country.

Marlow. (Gathering courage.) I have lived, indeed, in the world, madam; but I have kept very little company. I have been but an observer upon life, madam, while others were enjoying it.

Miss Neville. But that, I am told, is the way to enjoy it at last.

Hastings. (To him.) Cicero never spoke better. Once more, and you are confirmed in assurance for ever.

Marlow. (To him.) Hem! Stand by me then, and when I'm down, throw in a word or two to set me up again.

Miss Hardcastle. An observer, like you, upon life were, I fear, disagreeably employed, since you must have had much more to censure than to approve.

Marlow. Pardon me, madam. I was always willing to be amused. The folly of most people is rather an object of mirth than uneasiness.

Hastings. (To him.) Bravo, bravo! Never spoke so well in your whole life. Well! Miss Hardcastle, I see that you and Mr. Marlow are going to be very good company. I believe our being here will but embarrass the interview.

Marlow. Not in the least, Mr. Hastings. We like your com-pany of all things. *(To him.)* Zounds! George, sure you won't go? How can you leave us?

Hastings. Our presence will but spoil conversation, so we'll retire to the next room. *(To him.)* You don't consider, man, that we are to manage a little *tête-à-tête* of our own. *Exeunt.*

Miss Hardcastle. (After a pause.) But you have not been wholly an observer, I presume, sir: The ladies I should hope have employed some part of your addresses.

Marlow. (Relapsing into timidity.) Pardon me, madam, I— I—I—as yet have studied—only—to—deserve them.

Miss Hardcastle. And that, some say, is the very worst way to obtain them.

Marlow. Perhaps so, madam. But I love to converse only

with the more grave and sensible part of the sex.—But I'm afraid I grow tiresome.

Miss Hardcastle. Not at all, sir; there is nothing I like so much as grave conversation myself; I could hear it for ever. Indeed I have often been surprised how a man of *sentiment* could ever admire those light, airy pleasures, where nothing reaches the heart.

Marlow. It's—a disease—of the mind, Madam. In the variety of tastes there must be some who, wanting a relish—for—um—a—um.

Miss Hardcastle. I understand you, sir. There must be some, who, wanting a relish for refined pleasures, pretend to despise what they are incapable of tasting.

Marlow. My meaning, madam, but infinitely better expressed. And I can't help observing—a—

Miss Hardcastle. (Aside.) Who could ever suppose this fellow impudent upon some occasions. *(To him.)* You were going to observe, sir—

Marlow. I was observing, madam—I protest, madam, I forget what I was going to observe.

Miss Hardcastle. (Aside.) I vow and so do I. *(To him.)* You were observing, sir, that in this age of hypocrisy—something about hypocrisy, sir.

Marlow. Yes, madam. In this age of hypocrisy there are few who upon strict enquiry do not—a—a—a—

Miss Hardcastle. I understand you perfectly, sir.

Marlow. (Aside.) Egad! and that's more than I do myself.

Miss Hardcastle. You mean that in this hypocritical age there are few that do not condemn in public what they practise in private and think they pay every debt to virtue when they praise it.

Marlow. True, madam; those who have most virtue in their mouths, have least of it in their bosoms. But I'm sure I tire you, Madam.

Miss Hardcastle. Not in the least, sir; there's something so agreeable and spirited in your manner, such life and force—pray, sir, go on.

Marlow. Yes, madam. I was saying—that there are some occasions—when a total want of courage, madam, destroys all the—and puts us—upon a—a—a—

Miss Hardcastle. I agree with you entirely: a want of courage upon some occasions assumes the appearance of ignorance and betrays us when we most want to excel. I beg you'll proceed.

Marlow. Yes, madam. Morally speaking, madam—But I see Miss Neville expecting us in the next room. I would not intrude for the world.

Miss Hardcastle. I protest, sir, I never was more agreeably entertained in all my life. Pray go on.

Marlow. Yes, madam. I was—But she beckons us to join her. Madam, shall I do myself the honor to attend you?

Miss Hardcastle. Well then, I'll follow.

Marlow. (*Aside.*) This pretty, smooth dialogue has done for me.   *Exit.*

MISS HARDCASTLE, *sola.*

Miss Hardcastle. Ha! ha! ha! Was there ever such a sober, sentimental interview? I'm certain he scarce looked in my face the whole time. Yet the fellow, but for his unaccountable bashfulness, is pretty well, too. He has good sense, but then so buried in his fears that it fatigues one more than ignorance. If I could teach him a little confidence, it would be doing somebody that I know of a piece of service. But who is that somebody?—that, faith, is a question I can scarce answer.   *Exit.*

Enter TONY *and* MISS NEVILLE, *followed by*
MRS. HARDCASTLE *and* HASTINGS.

Tony. What do you follow me for, cousin Con? I wonder you're not ashamed to be so very engaging.

Miss Neville. I hope, cousin, one may speak to one's own relations and not be to blame.

Tony. Ay, but I know what sort of a relation you want to make me though; but it won't do. I tell you, cousin Con, it won't do; so I beg you'll keep your distance. I want no nearer relationship.

(*She follows coquetting him to the back scene.*)

Mrs. Hardcastle. Well! I vow Mr. Hastings, you are very entertaining. There's nothing in the world I love to talk of so much as London and the fashions, though I was never there myself.

Hastings. Never there! You amaze me! From your air and manner, I concluded you had been bred all your life either at Ranelagh, St. James's, or Tower Wharf.[11]

Mrs. Hardcastle. O! Sir, you're only pleased to say so. We country persons can have no manner at all. I'm in love with the town and that serves to raise me above some of our neighbouring rustics; but who can have a manner that has never seen the Pantheon, the Grotto Gardens, the Borough, and such places where the Nobility chiefly resort? All I can do is to enjoy London at second-hand. I take care to know every *tête-à-tête* from the *Scandalous Magazine,*[12] and have all the fashions, as they come out, in a letter from the two

Miss Rickets of Crooked Lane. Pray how do you like this head, Mr. Hastings?

Hastings. Extremely elegant and *degagée,* upon my word, Madam. Your *friseur i*s a Frenchman, I suppose?

Mrs. Hardcastle. I protest I dressed it myself from a print in the *Ladies Memorandum book* for the last year.

Hastings. Indeed. Such a head in a side-box, at the Playhouse, would draw as many gazers as my Lady May'ress at a City Ball.

Mrs. Hardcastle. I vow, since inoculation[13] began, there is no such thing to be seen as a plain woman; so one must dress a little particular or one may escape in the crowd.

Hastings. But that can never be your case madam, in any dress. *(Bowing.)*

Mrs. Hardcastle. Yet, what signifies *my* dressing when I have such a piece of antiquity by my side as Mr. Hardcastle. All I can say will never argue down a single button from his cloths. I have often wanted him to throw off his great flaxen wig, and where he was bald, to plaster it over like my Lord Pately, with powder.

Hastings. You are right, Madam; for, as among the ladies, there are none ugly, so among the men there are none old.

Mrs. Hardcastle. But what do you think his answer was? Why, with his usual Gothic vivacity, he said I only wanted him to throw off his wig to convert it into a *tête* for my own wearing.

Hastings. Intolerable! At your age you may wear what you please, and it must become you.

Mrs. Hardcastle. Pray, Mr. Hastings, what do you take to be the most fashionable age about town?

Hastings. Some time ago, forty was all the mode; but I'm told the ladies intend to bring up fifty for the ensuing winter.

Mrs. Hardcastle. Seriously? Then I shall be too young for the fashion.

Hastings. No lady begins now to put on jewels 'till she's past forty. For instance, Miss there, in a polite circle, would be considered as a child, as a mere maker of samplers.

Mrs. Hardcastle. And yet Mrs. Niece thinks herself as much a woman and is as fond of jewels as the oldest of us all.

Hastings. Your niece, is she? And that young gentleman, —a brother of yours, I should presume?

Mrs. Hardcastle. My son, sir. They are contracted to each other. Observe their little sports. They fall in and out ten times a day, as if they were man and wife already. *(To them.)* Well, Tony, child, what soft things are you saying to your cousin Constance this evening?

Tony. I have been saying no soft things; but that it's very hard to be followed about so. Ecod! I've not a place in the house now that's left to myself but the stable.

Mrs. Hardcastle. Never mind him, Con, my dear. He's in another story behind your back.

Miss Neville. There's something generous in my cousin's manner. He falls out before faces to be forgiven in private.

Tony. That's a damned confounded—crack.

Mrs. Hardcastle. Ah! he's a sly one. Don't you think they're like each other about the mouth, Mr. Hastings? The Blenkinsop mouth to a T. They're of a size too. Back to back, my pretties, that Mr. Hastings may see you. Come Tony.

Tony. You had as good not make me, I tell you.

(Measuring.)

Miss Neville. O lud! he has almost cracked my head.

Mrs. Hardcastle. O the monster! For shame, Tony. You a man, and behave so!

Tony. If I'm a man, let me have my fortin. Ecod! I'll not be made a fool of no longer.

Mrs. Hardcastle. Is this, ungrateful boy, all that I'm to get for the pains I have taken in your education? I that have rocked you in your cradle, and fed that pretty mouth with a spoon! Did not I work that waistcoat to make you genteel? Did not I prescribe for you every day and weep while the receipt was operating?

Tony. Ecod! you had reason to weep, for you have been dosing me ever since I was born. I have gone through every receipt in the complete huswife ten times over; and you have thoughts of coursing me through *Quincy*[14] next spring. But, ecod! I tell you, I'll not be made a fool of no longer.

Mrs. Hardcastle. Wasn't it all for your good, viper? Wasn't it all for your good?

Tony. I wish you'd let me and my good alone then. Snubbing this way when I'm in spirits. If I'm to have any good, let it come of itself; not to keep dinging it, dinging it into one so.

Mrs. Hardcastle. That's false; I never see you when you're in spirits. No, Tony, you then go to the alehouse or kennel. I'm never to be delighted with your agreeable, wild notes, unfeeling monster!

Tony. Ecod! Mamma, your own notes are the wildest of the two.

Mrs. Hardcastle. Was ever the like? But I see he wants to break my heart, I see he does.

Hastings. Dear Madam, permit me to lecture the young gentleman a little. I'm certain I can persuade him to his duty.

Mrs. Hardcastle. Well! I must retire. Come, Constance, my

love. You see, Mr. Hastings, the wretchedness of my situation: Was ever poor woman so plagued with a dear, sweet,
pretty, provoking, undutiful boy.

                Exeunt MRS. HARDCASTLE *and* MISS NEVILLE.

HASTINGS, TONY.

  Tony. (*Singing.*) *There was a young man riding by, and
fain would have his will. Rang do didlo dee.* Don't mind her.
Let her cry. It's the comfort of her heart. I have seen her and
sister cry over a book for an hour together, and they said,
they liked the book the better the more it made them cry.

  Hastings. Then you're no friend to the ladies, I find, my
pretty young gentleman?

  Tony. That's as I find 'um.

  Hastings. Not to her of your mother's choosing, I dare
answer? And yet she appears to me a pretty, well-tempered
girl.

  Tony. That's because you don't know her as well as I.
Ecod! I know every inch about her; and there's not a more
bitter, cantankerous toad in all Christendom.

  Hastings. (*Aside.*) Pretty encouragement this for a lover!

  Tony. I have seen her since the height of that. She has as
many tricks as a hare in a thicket, or a colt the first day's
breaking.

  Hastings. To me she appears sensible and silent!

  Tony. Ay, before company. But when she's with her play-
mates, she's as loud as a hog in a gate.

  Hastings. But there is a meek modesty about her that
charms me.

  Tony. Yes, but curb her never so little, she kicks up, and
you're flung in a ditch.

  Hastings. Well, but you must allow her a little beauty.—
Yes, you must allow her some beauty.

  Tony. Bandbox! She's all a made up thing, mun. Ah!
could you but see Bet Bouncer of these parts, you might then
talk of beauty. Ecod, she has two eyes as black as sloes, and
cheeks as broad and red as a pulpit cushion. She'd make
two of she.

  Hastings. Well, what say you to a friend that would take
this bitter bargain off your hands?

  Tony. Anon.

  Hastings. Would you thank him that would take Miss
Neville and leave you to happiness and your dear Betsy?

  Tony. Ay; but where is there such a friend, for who would
take *her*?

Hastings. I am he. If you but assist me, I'll engage to whip her off to France and you shall never hear more of her.

Tony. Assist you! Ecod, I will, to the last drop of my blood. I'll clap a pair of horses to your chaise that shall trundle you off in a twinkling, and maybe get you a part of her fortin beside, in jewels, that you little dream of.

Hastings. My dear squire, this looks like a lad of spirit.

Tony. Come along then, and you shall see more of my spirit before you have done with me.   *(Singing.)*

> *We are the boys*
> *That fears no noise*
> *Where the thundering cannons roar.*   *Exeunt.*

ACT III

SCENE I: *The house.*

Enter HARDCASTLE, *solus.*

Hardcastle. What could my old friend Sir Charles mean by recommending his son as the modestest young man in town? To me he appears the most impudent piece of brass that ever spoke with a tongue. He has taken possession of the easy chair by the fire-side already. He took off his boots in the parlor, and desired me to see them taken care of. I'm desirous to know how his impudence affects my daughter.— She will certainly be shocked at it.

Enter MISS HARDCASTLE, *plainly dressed.*

Hardcastle. Well, my Kate, I see you have changed your dress as I bid you; and yet, I believe, there was no great occasion.

Miss Hardcastle. I find such a pleasure, sir, in obeying your commands, that I take care to observe them without ever debating their propriety.

Hardcastle. And yet, Kate, I sometimes give you some cause, particularly when I recommended my *modest* gentleman to you as a lover today.

Miss Hardcastle. You taught me to expect something extraordinary, and I find the original exceeds the description.

Hardcastle. I was never so surprised in my life! He has quite confounded all my faculties!

Miss Hardcastle. I never saw anything like it. And a man of the world too!

Hardcastle. Ay, he learned it all abroad,—what a fool was I, to think a young man could learn modesty by travelling. He might as soon learn wit at a masquerade.

Miss Hardcastle. It seems all natural to him.

Hardcastle. A good deal assisted by bad company and a French dancing-master.

Miss Hardcastle. Sure you mistake, papa! a French dancing-master could never have taught him that timid look,—that awkward address,—that bashful manner—

Hardcastle. Whose look? whose manner? child!

Miss Hardcastle. Mr. Marlow's: his *mauvaise honte*[15], his timidity struck me at the first sight.

Hardcastle. Then your first sight deceived you; for I think him one of the most brazen first sights that ever astonished my senses.

Miss Hardcastle. Sure, sir, you rally! I never saw any one so modest.

Hardcastle. And can you be serious! I never saw such a bouncing, swaggering puppy since I was born. Bully Dawson[16] was but a fool to him.

Miss Hardcastle. Surprising! He met me with a respectful bow, a stammering voice, and a look fixed on the ground.

Hardcastle. He met me with a loud voice, a lordly air, and a familiarity that made my blood freeze again.

Miss Hardcastle. He treated me with diffidence and respect; censured the manners of the age; admired the prudence of girls that never laughed; tired me with apologies for being tiresome; then left the room with a bow, and, "madam, I would not for the world detain you."

Hardcastle. He spoke to me as if he knew me all his life before. Asked twenty questions, and never waited for an answer. Interrupted my best remarks with some silly pun, and when I was in my best story of the Duke of Marlborough and Prince Eugene, he asked if I had not a good hand at making punch. Yes, Kate, he ask'd your father if he was a maker of punch!

Miss Hardcastle. One of us must certainly be mistaken.

Hardcastle. If he be what he has shown himself, I'm determined he shall never have my consent.

Miss Hardcastle. And if he be the sullen thing I take him, he shall never have mine.

Hardcastle. In one thing then we are agreed—to reject him.

Miss Hardcastle. Yes. But upon conditions. For if you should find him less impudent, and I more presuming; if you find him more respectful, and I more importunate—I don't

know—the fellow is well enough for a man—Certainly we
don't meet many such at a horse race in the country.

Hardcastle. If we should find him so—But that's impossible. The first appearance has done my business. I'm seldom
deceived in that.

Miss Hardcastle. And yet there may be many good qualities under that first appearance.

Hardcastle. Ay, when a girl finds a fellow's outside to her
taste, she then sets about guessing the rest of his furniture.
With her, a smooth face stands for good sense, and a genteel figure for every virtue.

Miss Hardcastle. I hope, sir, a conversation begun with a
compliment to my good sense won't end with a sneer at my
understanding?

Hardcastle. Pardon me, Kate. But if young Mr. Brazen
can find the art of reconciling contradictions, he may please
us both, perhaps.

Miss Hardcastle. And as one of us must be mistaken,
what if we go to make further discoveries?

Hardcastle. Agreed. But depend on't I'm in the right.

Miss Hardcastle. And depend on't I'm not much in the
wrong.   *Exeunt.*

Enter TONY, *running in with a casket.*

Tony. Ecod! I have got them. Here they are. My Cousin
Con's necklaces, bobs and all. My mother shan't cheat the
poor souls out of their fortin neither. O! my genius, is that
you?

Enter HASTINGS.

Hastings. My dear friend, how have you managed with
your mother? I hope you have amused her with pretending
love for your cousin, and that you are willing to be reconciled at last? Our horses will be refreshed in a short time,
and we shall soon be ready to set off.

Tony. And here's something to bear your charges by the
way. (*Giving the casket.*) Your sweetheart's jewels. Keep
them, and hang those, I say, that would rob you of one of
them.

Hastings. But how have you procured them from your
mother?

Tony. Ask me no questions, and I'll tell you no fibs. I
procured them by the rule of thumb. If I had not a key to
every drawer in mother's bureau, how could I go to the ale-

house so often as I do? An honest man may rob himself of his own at any time.

Hastings. Thousands do it every day. But to be plain with you; Miss Neville is endeavoring to procure them from her aunt this very instant. If she succeeds, it will be the most delicate way at least of obtaining them.

Tony. Well, keep them, till you know how it will be. But I know how it will be well enough; she'd as soon part with the only sound tooth in her head.

Hastings. But I dread the effects of her resentment, when she finds she has lost them.

Tony. Never you mind her resentment; leave *me* to manage that. I don't value her resentment the bounce of a cracker.[17] Zounds! here they are. Morrice.[18] Prance.

Exit HASTINGS.

TONY, MRS. HARDCASTLE, MISS NEVILLE.

Mrs. Hardcastle. Indeed, Constance, you amaze me. Such a girl as you want jewels? It will be time enough for jewels, my dear, twenty years hence, when your beauty begins to want repairs.

Miss Neville. But what will repair beauty at forty, will certainly improve it at twenty, madam.

Mrs. Hardcastle. Yours, my dear, can admit of none. That natural blush is beyond a thousand ornaments. Besides, child, jewels are quite out at present. Don't you see half the ladies of our acquaintance, my Lady Kill-day-light, and Mrs. Crump, and the rest of them, carry their jewels to town, and bring nothing but Paste and Marcasites[19] back?

Miss Neville. But who knows, madam, but somebody that shall be nameless would like me best with all my little finery about me?

Mrs. Hardcastle. Consult your glass, my dear, and then see if with such a pair of eyes you want any better sparklers. What do you think, Tony, my dear, does your Cousin Con want any jewels, in your eyes, to set off her beauty?

Tony. That's as thereafter may be.

Miss Neville. My dear aunt, if you knew how it would oblige me.

Mrs. Hardcastle. A parcel of old-fashioned rose and table-cut things.[20] They would make you look like the court of King Solomon at a puppet-show. Besides, I believe I can't readily come at them. They may be missing, for aught I know to the contrary.

Tony. (*Apart to* MRS. HARDCASTLE.) Then why don't you

tell her so at once, as she's so longing for them. Tell her they're lost. It's the only way to quiet her. Say they're lost, and call me to bear witness.

Mrs. Hardcastle. (*Apart to Tony.*) You know, my dear, I'm only keeping them for you. So if I say they're gone, you'll bear me witness, will you? He! he! he!

Tony. Never fear me. Ecod! I'll say I saw them taken out with my own eyes.

Miss Neville. I desire them but for a day, madam. Just to be permitted to show them as relics, and then they may be locked up again.

Mrs. Hardcastle. To be plain with you, my dear Constance, if I could find them, you should have them. They're missing, I assure you. Lost, for aught I know; but we must have patience wherever they are.

Miss Neville. I'll not believe it; this is but a shallow pretence to deny me. I know they're too valuable to be so slightly kept, and as you are to answer for the loss.

Mrs. Hardcastle. Don't be alarmed, Constance. If they be lost, I must restore an equivalent. But my son knows they are missing, and not to be found.

Tony. That I can bear witness to. They are missing and not to be found, I'll take my oath on't.

Mrs. Hardcastle. You must learn resignation, my dear; for though we lose our fortune, yet we should not lose our patience. See me, how calm I am.

Miss Neville. Ay, people are generally calm at the misfortunes of others.

Mrs. Hardcastle. Now, I wonder a girl of your good sense should waste a thought upon such trumpery. We shall soon find them; and, in the meantime, you shall make use of my garnets till your jewels be found.

Miss Neville. I detest garnets.

Mrs. Hardcastle. The most becoming things in the world to set off a clear complexion. You have often seen how well they look upon me. You *shall* have them.   *Exit.*

Miss Neville. I dislike them of all things. You shan't stir. —Was ever any thing so provoking—to mislay my own jewels and force me to wear her trumpery.

Tony. Don't be a fool. If she gives you the garnets, take what you can get. The jewels are your own already. I have stolen them out of her bureau and she does not know it. Fly to your spark; he'll tell you more of the matter. Leave me to manage *her*.

Miss Neville. My dear cousin!

Tony. Vanish. She's here and has missed them already.

(*Exit* Miss Neville.) Zounds! how she fidgets and spits about like a Catharine wheel.[21]

Enter Mrs. Hardcastle.

Mrs. Hardcastle. Confusion! thieves! robbers! We are cheated, plundered, broke open, undone.

Tony. What's the matter, what's the matter, mamma? I hope nothing has happened to any of the good family!

Mrs. Hardcastle. We are robbed. My bureau has been broke open, the jewels taken out, and I'm undone.

Tony. Oh, is that all? Ha! ha! ha! By the laws I never saw it better acted in my life. Ecod, I thought you was ruined in earnest, ha, ha, ha!

Mrs. Hardcastle. Why boy, I *am* ruined in earnest. My bureau has been broken open, and all taken away.

Tony. Stick to that; ha, ha, ha! stick to that. I'll bear witness, you know, call me to bear witness.

Mrs. Hardcastle. I tell you, Tony, by all that's precious, the jewels are gone, and I shall be ruined for ever.

Tony. Sure I know they're gone, and I am to say so.

Mrs. Hardcastle. My dearest Tony, but hear me. They're gone, I say.

Tony. By the laws, mamma, you make me for to laugh, ha! ha! I know who took them well enough, ha! ha! ha!

Mrs. Hardcastle. Was there ever such a blockhead, that can't tell the difference between jest and earnest. I tell you I'm not in jest, booby.

Tony. That's right, that's right. You must be in a bitter passion, and then nobody will suspect either of us. I'll bear witness that they are gone.

Mrs. Hardcastle. Was there ever such a cross-grained brute, that won't hear me! Can you bear witness that you're no better than a fool? Was ever poor woman so beset with fools on one hand, and thieves on the other?

Tony. I can bear witness to that.

Mrs. Hardcastle. Bear witness again, you blockhead you, and I'll turn you out of the room directly. My poor niece, what will become of *her!* Do you laugh, you unfeeling brute, as if you enjoyed my distress?

Tony. I can bear witness to that.

Mrs. Hardcastle. Do you insult me, monster? I'll teach you to vex your mother, I will.

Tony. I can bear witness to that.

He runs off, she follows him.

Enter MISS HARDCASTLE *and* MAID.

Miss Hardcastle. What an unaccountable creature is that brother of mine to send them to the house as an inn, ha! ha! I don't wonder at his impudence.

Maid. But what is more, madam, the young gentleman as you passed by in your present dress, asked me if you were the barmaid? He mistook you for the barmaid, Madam.

Miss Hardcastle. Did he? Then as I live, I'm resolved to keep up the delusion. Tell me, Pimple, how do you like my present dress? Don't you think I look something like Cherry in the *Beaux' Stratagem?*[22]

Maid. It's the dress, madam, that every lady wears in the country, but when she visits, or receives company.

Miss Hardcastle. And are you sure he does not remember my face or person?

Maid. Certain of it.

Miss Hardcastle. I vow, I thought so; for though we spoke for some time together, yet his fears were such that he never once looked up during the interview. Indeed, if he had, my bonnet would have kept him from seeing me.

Maid. But what do you hope from keeping him in his mistake?

Miss Hardcastle. In the first place, I shall be *seen*, and that is no small advantage to a girl who brings her face to market. Then I shall perhaps make an acquaintance, and that's no small victory gained over one who never addresses any but the wildest of her sex. But my chief aim is to take my gentleman off his guard, and, like an invisible champion of romance, examine the giant's force before I offer to combat.

Maid. But are you sure you can act your part and disguise your voice, so that he may mistake that, as he has already mistaken your person?

Miss Hardcastle. Never fear me. I think I have got the true bar-cant.—Did your honor call?—Attend the Lion there. —Pipes and tobacco for the Angel.—The Lamb has been outrageous this half hour.[23]

Maid. It will do, madam. But he's here.   *Exit.*

Enter MARLOW.

Marlow. What a bawling in every part of the house. I have scarce a moment's repose. If I go to the best room, there I find my host and his story. If I fly to the gallery there we have my hostess with her curtsy down to the ground.

I have at last got a moment to myself, and now for recollection. *(Walks and muses.)*

Miss Hardcastle. Did you call, sir? Did your honor call?

Marlow. (Musing.) As for Miss Hardcastle, she's too grave
and sentimental for me.

Miss Hardcastle. Did your honor call?

(She still places herself before him, he turning away.)

Marlow. No, child. *(Musing.)* Besides, from the glimpse I
had of her, I think she squints.

Miss Hardcastle. I'm sure, sir, I heard the bell ring.

Marlow. No, no. *(Musing.)* I have pleased my father, however, by coming down, and I'll tomorrow please myself by
returning.

(Taking out his tablets,[24] *and perusing.)*

Miss Hardcastle. Perhaps the other gentleman called, sir?

Marlow. I tell you, no.

Miss Hardcastle. I should be glad to know, sir. We have
such a parcel of servants.

Marlow. No, no, I tell you. *(Looks full in her face.)* Yes,
child, I think I did call. I wanted—I wanted—I vow, child,
you are vastly handsome.

Miss Hardcastle. O la, sir, you'll make one ashamed.

Marlow. Never saw a more sprightly, malicious eye. Yes,
yes, my dear, I did call. Have you got any of your—a—what
d'ye call it in the house?

Miss Hardcastle. No, sir, we have been out of that these
ten days.

Marlow. One may call in this house, I find, to very little
purpose. Suppose I should call for a taste, just by way of
trial, of the nectar of your lips; perhaps I might be disappointed in that too.

Miss Hardcastle. Nectar! nectar! That's a liquor there's no
call for in these parts. French, I suppose. We keep no French
wines here, sir.

Marlow. Of true English growth, I assure you.

Miss Hardcastle. Then it's odd I should not know it. We
brew all sorts of wines in this house, and I have lived here
these eighteen years.

Marlow. Eighteen years! Why one would think, child, you
kept the bar before you were born. How old are you?

Miss Hardcastle. O! Sir, I must not tell my age. They say
women and music should never be dated.

Marlow. To guess at this distance, you can't be much
above forty. *(Approaching.)* Yet nearer, I don't think so
much. *(Approaching.)* By coming close to some women, they
look younger still; but when we come very close indeed—

(Attempting to kiss her.)

Miss Hardcastle. Pray, sir, keep your distance. One would think you wanted to know one's age as they do horses, by mark of mouth.

Marlow. I protest, child, you use me extremely ill. If you keep me at this distance how is it possible you and I can be ever acquainted?

Miss Hardcastle. And who wants to be acquainted with you? I want no such acquaintance, not I. I'm sure you did not treat Miss Hardcastle that was here awhile ago in this obstropalous manner. I'll warrant me, before her you looked dashed, and kept bowing to the ground, and talked for all the world as if you was before a justice of peace.

Marlow. *(Aside.)* Egad! she has hit it, sure enough. *(To her.)* In awe of her, child? Ha! ha! ha! A mere, awkward, squinting thing? no, no! I find you don't know me. I laughed and rallied her a little; but I was unwilling to be too severe. No, I could not be too severe, curse me!

Miss Hardcastle. Oh! then, sir, you are a favorite, I find, among the ladies?

Marlow. Yes, my dear, a great favorite. And yet, hang me, I don't see what they find in me to follow. At the Ladies Club in town, I'm called their agreeable Rattle. Rattle, child, is not my real name, but one I'm known by. My name is Solomons. Mr. Solomons, my dear, at your service.

(Offering to salute her.)

Miss Hardcastle. Hold, sir; you are introducing me to your club, not to yourself. And you're so great a favorite there, you say?

Marlow. Yes, my dear. There's Mrs. Mantrap, Lady Betty Blackleg, the Countess of Sligo, Mrs. Langhorns, old Miss Biddy Buckskin, and your humble servant, keep up the spirit of the place.

Miss Hardcastle. Then it's a very merry place, I suppose?

Marlow. Yes, as merry as cards, suppers, wine, and old women can make us.

Miss Hardcastle. And their agreeable Rattle, ha! ha! ha!

Marlow. *(Aside.)* Egad! I don't quite like this chit. She looks knowing, methinks. You laugh, child!

Miss Hardcastle. I can't but laugh to think what time they all have for minding their work or their family.

Marlow. *(Aside.)* All's well; she don't laugh at me. *(To her.)* Do *you* ever work, child?

Miss Hardcastle. Ay, sure. There's not a screen or a quilt in the whole house but what can bear witness to that.

Marlow. Odso! Then you must show me your embroidery.

I embroider and draw patterns myself a little. If you want a judge of your work you must apply to me.

(Seizing her hand.)

Miss Hardcastle. Ay, but the colors don't look well by candlelight. You shall see all in the morning. *(Struggling.)*

Marlow. And why not now, my angel? Such beauty fires beyond the power of resistance.—Pshaw! the father here! My old luck: I never nicked seven that I did not throw ames ace three times following.[25] *Exit.*

Enter HARDCASTLE, *who stands in surprise.*

Hardcastle. So, madam. So I find *this* is your *modest* lover. This is your humble admirer that kept his eyes fixed on the ground, and only adored at humble distance. Kate, Kate, art thou not ashamed to deceive your father so?

Miss Hardcastle. Never trust me, dear papa, but he's still the modest man I first took him for; you'll be convinced of it as well as I.

Hardcastle. By the hand of my body, I believe his impudence is infectious! Didn't I see him seize your hand? Didn't I see him haul you about like a milkmaid? and now you talk of his respect and his modesty, forsooth!

Miss Hardcastle. But if I shortly convince you of his modesty, that he has only the faults that will pass off with time, and the virtues that will improve with age, I hope you'll forgive him.

Hardcastle. The girl would actually make one run mad! I tell you I'll not be convinced. I am convinced. He has scarcely been three hours in the house, and he has already encroached on all my prerogatives. You may like his impudence, and call it modesty. But my son-in-law, madam, must have very different qualifications.

Miss Hardcastle. Sir, I ask but this night to convince you.

Hardcastle. You shall not have half the time, for I have thoughts of turning him out this very hour.

Miss Hardcastle. Give me that hour then, and I hope to satisfy you.

Hardcastle. Well, an hour let it be then. But I'll have no trifling with your father. All fair and open, do you mind me?

Miss Hardcastle. I hope, sir, you have ever found that I considered your commands as my pride; for your kindness is such that my duty as yet has been inclination. *Exeunt.*

ACT IV

SCENE I: *The house.*

Enter HASTINGS *and* MISS NEVILLE.

Hastings. You surprise me! Sir Charles Marlow expected here this night? Where have you had your information?

Miss Neville. You may depend upon it. I just saw his letter to Mr. Hardcastle, in which he tells him he intends setting out a few hours after his son.

Hastings. Then, my Constance, all must be completed before he arrives. He knows me; and should he find me here, would discover my name and perhaps my designs to the rest of the family.

Miss Neville. The jewels, I hope, are safe.

Hastings. Yes, yes. I have sent them to Marlow, who keeps the keys of our baggage. In the meantime, I'll go to prepare matters for our elopement. I have had the squire's promise of a fresh pair of horses; and, if I should not see him again will write him further directions.   *Exit.*

Miss Neville. Well! success attend you. In the meantime, I'll go amuse my aunt with the old pretence of a violent passion for my cousin.   *Exit.*

Enter MARLOW, *followed by a* SERVANT.

Marlow. I wonder what Hastings could mean by sending me so valuable a thing as a casket to keep for him, when he knows the only place I have is the seat of a post-coach at an inn door. Have you deposited the casket with the landlady, as I ordered you? Have you put it into her own hands?

Servant. Yes, your honor.

Marlow. She said she'd keep it safe, did she?

Servant. Yes, she said she'd keep it safe enough; she asked me how I came by it? and she said she had a great mind to make me give an account of myself.   *Exit.*

Marlow. Ha! ha! ha! They're safe, however. What an unaccountable set of beings have we got amongst! This little barmaid, though, runs in my head most strangely and drives out the absurdities of all the rest of the family. She's mine, she must be mine, or I'm greatly mistaken.

Enter HASTINGS.

Hastings. Bless me! I quite forgot to tell her that I intended to prepare at the bottom of the garden. Marlow here, and in spirits too!

Marlow. Give me joy, George! Crown me, shadow me with laurels! Well, George, after all, we modest fellows don't want for success among the women.

Hastings. Some women, you mean. But what success has your honor's modesty been crowned with now, that it grows so insolent upon us?

Marlow. Didn't you see the tempting, brisk, lovely, little thing that runs about the house with a bunch of keys to its girdle?

Hastings. Well! and what then?

Marlow. She's mine, you rogue you. Such fire, such motion, such eyes, such lips—but, egad! she would not let me kiss them, though.

Hastings. But are you so sure, so very sure of her?

Marlow. Why man, she talked of showing me her work above-stairs, and I am to improve the pattern.

Hastings. But how can *you,* Charles, go about to rob a woman of her honor?

Marlow. Pshaw! pshaw! we all know the honor of the barmaid of an inn. I don't intend to *rob* her, take my word for it; there's nothing in this house I shan't honestly *pay* for.

Hastings. I believe the girl has virtue.

Marlow. And if she has, I should be the last man in the world that would attempt to corrupt it.

Hastings. You have taken care, I hope, of the casket I sent you to lock up? It's in safety?

Marlow. Yes, yes. It's safe enough. I have taken care of it. But how could you think the seat of a post-coach at an inn door a place of safety? Ah! numbskull! I have taken better precautions for you than you did for yourself.—I have—

Hastings. What!

Marlow. I have sent it to the landlady to keep for you.

Hastings. To the landlady!

Marlow. The landlady.

Hastings. You did!

Marlow. I did. She's to be answerable for its forthcoming, you know.

Hastings. Yes, she'll bring it forth, with a witness.

Marlow. Wasn't I right? I believe you'll allow that I acted prudently upon this occasion?

Hastings. (*Aside.*) He must not see my uneasiness.

Marlow. You seem a little disconcerted though, methinks. Sure nothing has happened?

Hastings. No, nothing. Never was in better spirits in all my life. And so you left it with the landlady, who, no doubt, very readily undertook the charge?

Marlow. Rather too readily. For she not only kept the casket; but, through her great precaution, was going to keep the messenger too. Ha! ha! ha!

Hastings. He! he! he! They're safe, however.

Marlow. As a guinea in a miser's purse.

Hastings. (*Aside.*) So now all hopes of fortune are at an end, and we must set off without it. (*To him.*) Well, Charles, I'll leave you to your meditations on the pretty barmaid, and, he! he! he! may you be as successful for yourself as you have been for me.   *Exit.*

Marlow. Thank ye, George! I ask no more! Ha! ha! ha!

Enter HARDCASTLE.

Hardcastle. I no longer know my own house. It's turned all topsey-turvey. His servants have got drunk already. I'll bear it no longer, and yet, from my respect for his father, I'll be calm. (*To him.*) Mr. Marlow, your servant. I'm your very humble servant.   (*Bowing low.*)

Marlow. Sir, your humble servant. (*Aside.*) What's to be the wonder now?

Hardcastle. I believe, sir, you must be sensible, sir, that no man alive ought to be more welcome than your father's son, sir. I hope you think so?

Marlow. I do from my soul, sir. I don't want much intreaty. I generally make my father's son welcome wherever he goes.

Hardcastle. I believe you do, from my soul, sir. But though I say nothing to your own conduct, that of your servants is insufferable. Their manner of drinking is setting a very bad example in this house, I assure you.

Marlow. I protest, my very good sir, that's no fault of mine. If they don't drink as they ought, *they* are to blame. I ordered them not to spare the cellar. I did, I assure you. (*To the side scene.*) Here, let one of my servants come up. (*To him.*) My positive directions were, that as I did not drink myself, they should make up for my deficiencies below.

Hardcastle. Then they had your orders for what they do! I'm satisfied!

Marlow. They had, I assure you. You shall hear from one of themselves.

Enter SERVANT *drunk.*

Marlow. You, Jeremy! Come forward, sirrah! What were my orders? Were you not told to drink freely, and call for what you thought fit, for the good of the house?

Hardcastle. *(Aside.)* I begin to lose my patience.

Jeremy. Please your honor, liberty and Fleet Street for ever! Though I'm but a servant, I'm as good as another man. I'll drink for no man before supper, sir, dammy! Good liquor will sit upon a good supper, but a good supper will not sit upon—*hiccup*—upon my conscience, sir.   *Exit.*

Marlow. You see, my old friend, the fellow is as drunk as he can possibly be. I don't know what you'd have more, unless you'd have the poor devil soused in a beer-barrel.

Hardcastle. Zounds! He'll drive me distracted if I contain myself any longer.—Mr. Marlow, sir; I have submitted to your insolence for more than four hours, and I see no likelihood of its coming to an end. I'm now resolved to be master here, sir, and I desire that you and your drunken pack may leave my house directly.

Marlow. Leave your house!—Sure you jest, my good friend! What, when I'm doing what I can to please you!

Hardcastle. I tell you, sir, you don't please me; so I desire you'll leave my house.

Marlow. Sure you cannot be serious? At this time o'night, and such a night? You only mean to banter me?

Hardcastle. I tell you, sir, I'm serious; and, now that my passions are roused, I say this house is mine, sir; this house is mine, and I command you to leave it directly.

Marlow. Ha! ha! ha! A puddle in a storm. I shan't stir a step, I assure you. *(In a serious tone.)* This, your house, fellow! It's my house. This is my house. Mine, while I choose to stay. What right have you to bid me leave this house, sir? I never met with such impudence, curse me, never in my whole life before.

Hardcastle. Nor I, confound me if ever I did. To come to my house, to call for what he likes, to turn me out of my own chair, to insult the family, to order his servants to get drunk, and then to tell me *This house is mine, sir.* By all that's impudent, it makes me laugh. Ha! ha! ha! Pray, sir, *(bantering)* as you take the house, what think you of taking the rest of the furniture? There's a pair of silver candlesticks, and there's a fire-screen, and here's a pair of brazen-nosed bellows, perhaps you may take a fancy to them?

Marlow. Bring me your bill, sir, bring me your bill, and let's make no more words about it.

Hardcastle. There are a set of prints too. What think you of *The Rake's Progress*²⁶ for your own apartment?

Marlow. Bring me your bill, I say; and I'll leave you and your infernal house directly.

Hardcastle. Then there's a mahogany table, that you may see your own face in.

Marlow. My bill, I say.

Hardcastle. I had forgot the great chair, for your own particular slumbers after a hearty meal.

Marlow. Zounds! bring me my bill, I say, and let's hear no more on't.

Hardcastle. Young man, young man, from your father's letter to me, I was taught to expect a well-bred, modest man, as a visitor here, but now I find him no better than a coxcomb and a bully; but he will be down here presently, and shall hear more of it.   *Exit.*

Marlow. How's this! Sure I have not mistaken the house? Everything looks like an inn. The servants cry, *Coming.* The attendance is awkward; the barmaid, too, to attend us. But she's here, and will further inform me. Whither so fast, child? A word with you.

Enter MISS HARDCASTLE.

Miss Hardcastle. Let it be short then. I'm in a hurry. (*Aside.*) I believe he begins to find out his mistake, but it's too soon quite to undeceive him.

Marlow. Pray, child, answer me one question. What are you, and what may your business in this house be?

Miss Hardcastle. A relation of the family, sir.

Marlow. What! A poor relation?

Miss Hardcastle. Yes, sir. A poor relation appointed to keep the keys, and to see that the guests want nothing in my power to give them.

Marlow. That is, you act as the barmaid of this inn.

Miss Hardcastle. Inn! O law—what brought that in your head? One of the best families in the county keep an inn! Ha, ha, ha, old Mr. Hardcastle's house an inn?

Marlow. Mr. Hardcastle's house? Is this house Mr. Hardcastle's house, child?

Miss Hardcastle. Ay, sure. Whose else should it be?

Marlow. So then all's out, and I have been damnably imposed on. Oh, confound my stupid head, I shall be laughed at over the whole town. I shall be stuck up in *caricatura* in all the printshops. The Dullissimo Maccaroni.²⁷ To mistake this house of all others for an inn, and my father's old friend for an inn-keeper. What a swaggering puppy must he take me for. What a silly puppy do I find myself. There again, may I be hanged, my dear, but I mistook you for the barmaid.

Miss Hardcastle. Dear me! dear me! I'm sure there's nothing in my *behavior* to put me upon a level with one of that stamp.

Marlow. Nothing, my dear, nothing. But I was in for a list of blunders, and could not help making you a subscriber. My stupidity saw everything the wrong way. I mistook your assiduity for assurance and your simplicity for allurement. But it's over—This house I no more show *my* face in.

Miss Hardcastle. I hope, sir, I have done nothing to disoblige you. I'm sure I should be sorry to affront any gentleman who has been so polite, and said so many civil things to me. I'm sure I should be sorry *(pretending to cry)* if he left the family upon my account. I'm sure I should be sorry, people said anything amiss, since I have no fortune but my character.

Marlow. (*Aside.*) By heaven, she weeps. This is the first mark of tenderness I ever had from a modest woman, and it touches me. *(To her.)* Excuse me, my lovely girl, you are the only part of the family I leave with reluctance. But to be plain with you, the difference of our birth, fortune, and education make an honorable connection impossible; and I can never harbor a thought of seducing simplicity that trusted in my honor, or bringing ruin upon one, whose only fault was being too lovely.

Miss Hardcastle. (*Aside.*) Generous man! I now begin to admire him. *(To him.)* But I'm sure my family is as good as Miss Hardcastle's, and though I'm poor, that's no great misfortune to a contented mind, and, until this moment, I never thought that it was bad to want fortune.

Marlow. And why now, my pretty simplicity?

Miss Hardcastle. Because it puts me at a distance from one that if I had a thousand pound I would give it all to.

Marlow. (*Aside.*) This simplicity bewitches me, so that if I stay I'm undone. I must make one bold effort, and leave her. *(To her.)* Your partiality in my favor, my dear, touches me most sensibly, and were I to live for myself alone, I could easily fix my choice. But I owe too much to the opinion of the world, too much to the authority of a father, so that—I can scarcely speak it—it affects me. Farewell.   *Exit*.

Miss Hardcastle. I never knew half his merit till now. He shall not go, if I have power or art to detain him. I'll still preserve the character in which I stooped to conquer, but will undeceive my papa, who, perhaps, may laugh him out of his resolution.   *Exit*.

Enter Tony, Miss Neville.

Tony. Ay, you may steal for yourselves the next time. I have done my duty. She has got the jewels again, that's a sure thing; but she believes it was all a mistake of the servants.

Miss Neville. But, my dear cousin, sure you won't forsake us in this distress. If she in the least suspects that I am going off, I shall certainly be locked up or sent to my Aunt Pedigree's, which is ten times worse.

Tony. To be sure, aunts of all kinds are damned bad things. But what can I do? I have got you a pair of horses that will fly like Whistlejacket, and I'm sure you can't say but I have courted you nicely before her face. Here she comes; we must court a bit or two more, for fear she should suspect us.

(They retire, and seem to fondle.)

Enter Mrs. Hardcastle.

Mrs. Hardcastle. Well, I was greatly fluttered, to be sure. But my son tells me it was all a mistake of the servants. I shan't be easy, however, until they are fairly married, and then let her keep her own fortune. But what do I see! Fondling together, as I'm alive. I never saw Tony so sprightly before. Ah! have I caught you, my pretty doves? What, billing, exchanging stolen glances, and broken murmurs. Ah!

Tony. As for murmurs, mother, we grumble a little now and then, to be sure. But there's no love lost between us.

Mrs. Hardcastle. A mere sprinkling, Tony, upon the flame, only to make it burn brighter.

Miss Neville. Cousin Tony promises to give us more of his company at home. Indeed, he shan't leave us any more. It won't leave us, cousin Tony, will it?

Tony. Oh! it's a pretty creature. No, I'd sooner leave my horse in a pound, than leave you when you smile upon one so. Your laugh makes you so becoming.

Miss Neville. Agreeable cousin! Who can help admiring that natural humor, that pleasant, broad, red, thoughtless *(patting his cheek)* ah! it's a bold face.

Mrs. Hardcastle. Pretty innocence!

Tony. I'm sure I always loved cousin Con's hazel eyes, and her pretty long fingers, that she twists this way and that over the haspicholls,[28] like a parcel of bobbins.

Mrs. Hardcastle. Ah, he would charm the bird from the tree. I was never so happy before. My boy takes after his father, poor Mr. Lumpkin, exactly. The jewels, my dear Con, shall be yours incontinently. You shall have them. Isn't he a sweet boy, my dear? You shall be married tomorrow, and we'll put off the rest of his education, like Dr. Drowsy's sermons, to a fitter opportunity.

Enter DIGGORY.

Diggory. Where's the squire? I have got a letter for your worship.

Tony. Give it to my mamma. She reads all my letters first.

Diggory. I had orders to deliver it into your own hands.

Tony. Who does it come from?

Diggory. Your worship mun ask that o' the letter itself.

Exit.

Tony. I could wish to know, though.

(Turning the letter, and gazing on it.)

Miss Neville. (Aside.) Undone, undone. A letter to him from Hastings. I know the hand. If my aunt sees it, we are ruined for ever. I'll keep her employed a little if I can. (*To* MRS. HARDCASTLE.) But I have not told you, Madam, of my cousin's smart answer just now to Mr. Marlow. We so laughed—You must know, Madam—this way a little, for he must not hear us. *(They confer.)*

Tony. (Still gazing.) A damned cramp piece of penmanship, as ever I saw in my life. I can read your print-hand very well. But here there are such handles, and shanks, and dashes, that one can scarce tell the head from the tail. *To Anthony Lumpkin, Esquire.* It's very odd, I can read the outside of my letters, where my own name is, well enough. But when I come to open it, it's all—buzz. That's hard, very hard; for the inside of the letter is always the cream of the correspondence.

Mrs. Hardcastle. Ha! ha! ha! Very well, very well! And so my son was too hard for the philosopher.

Miss Neville. Yes, madam; but you must hear the rest, madam. A little more this way, or he may hear us. You'll hear how he puzzled him again.

Mrs. Hardcastle. He seems strangely puzzled now himself, methinks.

Tony. (Still gazing.) A damned up-and-down hand, as if it was disguised in liquor. *(Reading.) Dear Sir.* Ay, that's that. Then there's an *M,* and a *T,* and an *S,* but whether the next be an *izzard* or an *R,* confound me, I cannot tell.

Mrs. Hardcastle. What's that, my dear? Can I give you any assistance?

Miss Neville. Pray, aunt, let me read it. Nobody reads a cramp hand better than I. *(Twitching the letter from her.)* Do you know who it is from?

Tony. Can't tell, except from Dick Ginger the feeder.

Miss Neville. Ay, so it is. *(Pretending to read.)* Dear Squire, Hoping that you're in health, as I am at this present. The gentlemen of the Shake-bag club has cut the gentlemen of Goose-green quite out of feather. The odds—um—odd battle —um—long fighting—um, here, here, it's all about cocks, and fighting; it's of no consquence; here, put it up, put it up.

(Thrusting the crumpled letter upon him.)

Tony. But I tell you, miss, it's of all the consequence in the world. I would not lose the rest of it for a guinea. Here, mother, do you make it out. Of no consequence!

(Giving Mrs. Hardcastle *the letter.)*

Mrs. Hardcastle. How's this! *(Reads.)* "Dear Squire, I'm now waiting for Miss Neville with a post-chaise and pair at the bottom of the garden, but I find my horses yet unable to perform the journey. I expect you'll assist us with a pair of fresh horses, as you promised. Dispatch is necessary, as the *hag,* (ay, the hag) your mother, will otherwise suspect us. Yours, Hastings." Grant me patience. I shall run distracted! My rage chokes me!

Miss Neville. I hope, madam, you'll suspend your resentment for a few miments, and not impute to me any impertinence, or sinister design that belongs to another.

Mrs. Hardcastle. (Curtsying very low.) Fine spoken, madam; you are most miraculously polite and engaging and quite the very pink of courtesy and circumspection, madam. *(Changing her tone.)* And you, you great ill-fashioned oaf, with scarce sense enough to keep your mouth shut. Were you too joined against me? But I'll defeat all your plots in a moment. As for you, madam, since you have got a pair of fresh horses ready, it would be cruel to disappoint them. So, if you please, instead of running away with your spark, prepare, this very moment, to run off with *me.* Your old Aunt Pedigree will keep you secure, I'll warrant me. You too, sir, may mount your horse, and guard us upon the way. Here, Thomas, Roger, Diggory! I'll show you, that I wish you better than you do yourselves.   *Exit.*

Miss Neville. So now I'm completely ruined.

Tony. Ay, that's a sure thing.

Miss Neville. What better could be expected from being connected with such a stupid fool, and after all the nods and signs I made him.

Tony. By the laws, miss, it was your own cleverness and not my stupidity that did your business. You were so nice and so busy with your Shake-bags and Goose-greens, that I thought you could never be making believe.

Enter HASTINGS.

Hastings. So, sir, I find by my servant, that you have shown my letter, and betrayed us. Was this well done, young gentleman?

Tony. Here's another. Ask miss there who betrayed you. Ecod, it was her doing, not mine.

Enter MARLOW.

Marlow. So I have been finely used here among you. Rendered contemptible, driven into ill manners, despised, insulted, laughed at.

Tony. Here's another. We shall have old Bedlam broke loose presently.

Miss Neville. And there, sir, is the gentlemen to whom we all owe every obligation.

Marlow. What can I say to him, a mere boy, an idiot, whose ignorance and age are a protection.

Hastings. A poor contemptible booby that would but disgrace correction.

Miss Neville. Yet with cunning and malice enough to make himself merry with all our embarrassments.

Hastings. An insensible cub.

Marlow. Replete with tricks and mischief.

Tony. Baw! damme, but I'll fight you both one after the other,—with baskets.[29]

Marlow. As for him, he's below resentment. But your conduct, Mr. Hastings, requires an explanation. You knew of my mistakes, yet would not undeceive me.

Hastings. Tortured as I am with my own disappointments, is this a time for explanations? It is not friendly, Mr. Marlow.

Marlow. But, sir—

Miss Neville. Mr. Marlow, we never kept on your mistake, till it was too late to undeceive you. Be pacified.

Enter SERVANT.

Servant. My mistress desires you'll get ready immediately, madam. The horses are putting to. Your hat and things are in the next room. We are to go thirty miles before morning.
Exit.

Miss Neville. Well, well; I'll come presently.

Marlow. (*To* HASTINGS.) Was it well done, sir, to assist in rendering me ridiculous? To hang me out for the scorn of all my acquaintance? Depend upon it, sir, I shall expect an explanation.

Hastings. Was it well done, sir, if you're upon that subject to deliver what I entrusted to yourself to the care of another, sir?

Miss Neville. Mr. Hastings! Mr. Marlow! Why will you increase my distress by this groundless dispute? I implore, I intreat you—

Enter SERVANT.

Servant. Your cloak, madam. My mistress is impatient.

Miss Neville. I come. (*Exit* SERVANT.) Pray be pacified. If I leave you thus, I shall die with apprehension.

Enter SERVANT.

Servant. Your fan, muff, and gloves, madam. The horses are waiting.

Miss Neville. Oh, Mr. Marlow! if you knew what a scene of constraint and ill-nature lies before me, I'm sure it would convert your resentment into pity.

Marlow. I'm so distracted with a variety of passions that I don't know what I do. Forgive me, madam. George, forgive me. You know my hasty temper, and should not exasperate it.

Hastings. The torture of my situation is my only excuse.

Miss Neville. Well, my dear Hastings, if you have that esteem for me that I think, that I am sure you have, your constancy for three years will but increase the happiness of our future connection. If—

Mrs. Hardcastle. (*Within.*) Miss Neville! Constance, why Constance, I say!

Miss Neville. I'm coming. Well, constancy. Remember, constancy is the word.   *Exit.*

Hastings. My heart! How can I support this. To be so near happiness, and such happiness.

Marlow. (*To* TONY.) You see now, young gentleman, the effects of your folly. What might be amusement to you, is here disappointment, and even distress.

Tony. (*From a reverie.*) Ecod, I have hit it. It's here. Your hands. Yours and yours, my poor Sulky. My boots there, ho! Meet me two hours hence at the bottom of the garden; and if you don't find Tony Lumpkin a more good-natured fellow than you thought for, I'll give you leave to take my best horse and Bet Bouncer into the bargain. Come along. My boots, ho!   *Exeunt.*

ACT V

SCENE I: *The house.*

Enter HASTINGS *and* SERVANT.

Hastings. You saw the old lady and Miss Neville drive off, you say?

Servant. Yes, your honor. They went off in a post coach, and the young 'Squire went on horseback. They're thirty miles off by this time.

Hastings. Then all my hopes are over.

Servant. Yes, sir. Old Sir Charles is arrived. He and the old gentleman of the house have been laughing at Mr. Marlow's mistake this half hour. They are coming this way.

Hastings. Then I must not be seen. So now to my fruitless appointment at the bottom of the garden. This is about the time.   *Exit.*

Enter SIR CHARLES *and* HARDCASTLE.

Hardcastle. Ha! ha! ha! The peremptory tone in which he sent forth his sublime commands.

Sir Charles. And the reserve with which I suppose he treated all your advances.

Hardcastle. And yet he might have seen something in me above a common inn-keeper, too.

Sir Charles. Yes, Dick, but he mistook you for an uncommon inn-keeper, ha! ha! ha!

Hardcastle. Well, I'm in too good spirits to think of any thing but joy. Yes, my dear friend, this union of our families will make our personal friendships hereditary; and though my daughter's fortune is but small—

Sir Charles. Why, Dick, will you talk of fortune to *me*. My son is possessed of more than a competence already, and can want nothing but a good and virtuous girl to share his happiness and increase it. If they like each other as you say they do—

Hardcastle. If, man! I tell you they *do* like each other. My daughter as good as told me so.

217

Sir Charles. But girls are apt to flatter themselves, you know.

Hardcastle. I saw him grasp her hand in the warmest manner myself; and here he comes to put you out of your *ifs*, I warrant him.

Enter MARLOW.

Marlow. I come, sir, once more, to ask your pardon for my strange conduct. I can scarce reflect on my insolence without confusion.

Hardcastle. Tut, boy, a trifle. You take it too gravely. An hour or two's laughing with my daughter will set all to rights again. She'll never like you the worse for it.

Marlow. Sir, I shall be always proud of her approbation.

Hardcastle. Approbation is but a cold word, Mr. Marlow; if I am not deceived, you have something more than approbation thereabouts. You take me.

Marlow. Really, sir, I have not that happiness.

Hardcastle. Come, boy, I'm an old fellow, and know what's what, as well as you that are younger. I know what has past between you; but mum.

Marlow. Sure, sir, nothing has past between us but the most profound respect on my side, and the most distant reserve on hers. You don't think, sir, that my impudence has been past upon all the rest of the family?

Hardcastle. Impudence! No, I don't say that—Not quite impudence—Though girls like to be played with, and rumpled a little, too, sometimes. But she has told no tales, I assure you.

Marlow. I never gave her the slightest cause.

Hardcastle. Well, well, I like modesty in its place well enough. But this is over-acting, young gentleman. You may be open. Your father and I will like you the better for it.

Marlow. May I die, sir, if I ever—

Hardcastle. I tell you, she don't dislike you; and as I'm sure you like her—

Marlow. Dear sir—I protest, sir,—

Hardcastle. I see no reason why you should not be joined as fast as the parson can tie you.

Marlow. But hear me, sir—

Hardcastle. Your father approves the match, I admire it, every moment's delay will be doing mischief, so—

Marlow. But why won't you hear me? By all that's just and true, I never gave Miss Hardcastle the slightest mark of my attachment, or even the most distant hint to suspect me of a affection. We had but one interview, and that was formal, modest and uninteresting.

Hardcastle. (Aside.) This fellow's formal, modest impudence is beyond bearing.

Sir Charles. And you never grasped her hand, or made any protestations!

Marlow. As heaven is my witness, I came down in obedience to your commands. I saw the lady without emotion, and parted without reluctance. I hope you'll exact no further proofs of my duty, nor prevent me from leaving a house in which I suffer so many mortifications.   *Exit.*

Sir Charles. I'm astonished at the air of sincerity with which he parted.

Hardcastle. And I'm astonished at the deliberate intrepidity of his assurance.

Sir Charles. I dare pledge my life and honor upon his truth.

Hardcastle. Here comes my daughter, and I would stake my happiness upon her veracity.

Enter MISS HARDCASTLE.

Hardcastle. Kate, come hither, child. Answer us sincerely, and without reserve; has Mr. Marlow made you any professions of love and affection?

Miss Hardcastle. The question is very abrupt, sir! But since you require unreserved sincerity, I think he has.

Hardcastle. (To SIR CHARLES.*)* You see.

Sir Charles. And pray, madam, have you and my son had more than one interview?

Miss Hardcastle. Yes, sir, several.

Hardcastle. (To SIR CHARLES.*)* You see.

Sir Charles. But did he profess any attachment?

Miss Hardcastle. A lasting one.

Sir Charles. Did he talk of love?

Miss Hardcastle. Much, sir.

Sir Charles. Amazing! And all this formally?

Miss Hardcastle. Formally.

Hardcastle. Now, my friend, I hope you are satisfied.

Sir Charles. And how did he behave, Madam?

Miss Hardcastle. As most professed admirers do. Said some civil things of my face, talked much of his want of merit, and the greatness of mine; mentioned his heart, and gave a short tragedy speech, and ended with pretended rapture.

Sir Charles. Now I'm perfectly convinced, indeed. I know his conversation among women to be modest and submissive. This forward, canting, ranting manner by no means describes him, and I am confident, he never sat for the picture.

Miss Hardcastle. Then what, sir, if I should convince you to your face of my sincerity? If you and my papa, in about half an hour, will place yourselves behind that screen, you shall hear him declare his passion to me in person.

Sir Charles. Agreed. And if I find him what you describe, all my happiness in him must have an end.   *Exit.*

Miss Hardcastle. And if you don't find him what I describe —I fear my happiness must never have a beginning. *Exeunt.*

SCENE II: *Scene changes to the back of the garden.*

Enter HASTINGS.

Hastings. What an idiot am I, to wait here for a fellow, who probably takes delight in mortifying me. He never intended to be punctual, and I'll wait no longer. What do I see! It is he, and perhaps with news of my Constance.

Enter TONY, *booted and spattered.*

Hastings. My honest squire! I now find you a man of your word. This looks like friendship.

Tony. Ay, I'm your friend, and the best friend you have in the world, if you knew but all. This riding by night, by the bye, is cursedly tiresome. It has shook me worse than the basket of a stage-coach.

Hastings. But how? Where did you leave your fellow travellers? Are they in safety? Are they housed?

Tony. Five and twenty miles in two hours and a half is no such bad driving. The poor beasts have smoked for it: Rabbit me, but I'd rather ride forty miles after a fox, than ten with such *varment*.

Hastings. Well, but where have you left the ladies? I die with impatience.

Tony. Left them? Why, where should I leave them, but where I found them?

Hastings. This is a riddle.

Tony. Riddle me this then. What's that goes round the house, and round the house, and never touches the house?

Hastings. I'm still astray.

Tony. Why that's it, mon. I have led them astray. By jingo, there's not a pond or slough within five miles of the place but they can tell the taste of.

Hastings. Ha, ha, ha, I understand; you took them in a round, while they supposed themselves going forward. And so you have at last brought them home again.

Tony. You shall hear. I first took them down Feather-bed-lane, where we stuck fast in the mud. I then rattled them crack over the stones of Up-and-down Hill—I then introduced them to the gibbet on Heavy-tree Heath, and from that, with a circumbendibus, I fairly lodged them in the horse-pond at the bottom of the garden.

Hastings. But no accident, I hope.

Tony. No, no! Only mother is confoundedly frightened. She thinks herself forty miles off. She's sick of the journey, and the cattle can scarce crawl. So if your own horses be ready, you may whip off with cousin, and I'll be bound that no soul here can budge a foot to follow you.

Hastings. My dear friend, how can I be grateful?

Tony. Ay, now it's "dear friend," "noble squire." Just now, it was all "idiot," "cub," and "run me through the guts." Damn *your* way of fighting, I say. After we take a knock in this part of the country, we kiss and be friends. But if you had run me through the guts, then I should be dead, and you might go kiss the hangman.

Hastings. The rebuke is just. But I must hasten to relieve Miss Neville; if you keep the old lady employed, I promise to take care of the young one. *Exit.*

Tony. Never fear me. Here she comes. Vanish. She's got from the pond, and draggled up to the waist like a mermaid.

Enter MRS. HARDCASTLE.

Mrs. Hardcastle. Oh, Tony, I'm killed! Shook! Battered to death! I shall never survive it. That last jolt that laid us against the quickset hedge has done my business.

Tony. Alack, mama, it was all your own fault. You would be for running away by night, without knowing one inch of the way.

Mrs. Hardcastle. I wish we were at home again. I never met so many accidents in so short a journey. Drenched in the mud, overturned in a ditch, stuck fast in a slough, jolted to a jelly, and at last to lose our way. Whereabouts do you think we are, Tony?

Tony. By my guess we should be upon Crackskull common, about forty miles from home.

Mrs. Hardcastle. O lud! O lud! the most notorious spot in all the country. We only want a robbery to make a complete night on't.

Tony. Don't be afraid, mama, don't be afraid. Two of the five that kept here are hanged, and the other three may not find us. Don't be afraid. Is that a man that's galloping behind us? No; it's only a tree. Don't be afraid.

Mrs. Hardcastle. The fright will certainly kill me.

Tony. Do you see anything like a black hat moving behind the thicket?

Mrs. Hardcastle. O death!

Tony. No, it's only a cow. Don't be afraid, mama; don't be afraid!

Mrs. Hardcastle. As I'm alive, Tony, I see a man coming towards us. Ah! I'm sure on't. If he perceives us, we are undone.

Tony. (*Aside.*) Father-in-law, by all that's unlucky, come to take one of his night walks. (*To her.*) Ah, it's a highwayman, with pistols as long as my arm. A damned ill-looking fellow.

Mrs. Hardcastle. Good heaven defend us! He approaches!

Tony. Do you hide yourself in that thicket, and leave me to manage him. If there be danger, I'll cough, and cry hem. When I cough be sure to keep close.

(MRS. HARDCASTLE *hides behind a tree in the back scene.*)

Enter HARDCASTLE.

Hardcastle. I'm mistaken, or I heard voices of people in want of help. Oh, Tony, is that you? I did not expect you so soon back. Are your mother and her charge in safety?

Tony. Very safe, sir, at my Aunt Pedigree's. Hem.

Mrs. Hardcastle. (*From behind.*) Ah death! I find there's danger.

Hardcastle. Forty miles in three hours; sure, that's too much, my youngster.

Tony. Stout horses and willing minds make short journies, as they say. Hem.

Mrs. Hardcastle. (*From behind.*) Sure he'll do the dear boy no harm.

Hardcastle. But I heard a voice here; I should be glad to know from whence it came?

Tony. It was I, sir, talking to myself, sir. I was saying that forty miles in four hours was very good going. Hem! As to be sure it was. Hem! I have got a sort of cold by being out in the air. We'll go in, if you please. Hem!

Hardcastle. But if you talk'd to yourself, you did not answer yourself. I am certain I heard two voices, and am resolved (*raising his voice*) to find the other out.

Mrs. Hardcastle. (*From behind.*) Oh! he's coming to find me out. Oh!

Tony. What need you go, sir, if I tell you? Hem. I'll lay down my life for the truth—hem—I'll tell you all, sir.

(*Detaining him.*)

Hardcastle. I tell you, I will not be detained. I insist on seeing. It's in vain to expect I'll believe you.

Mrs. Hardcastle. (Running forward from behind.) O lud, he'll murder my poor boy, my darling. Here, good gentlemen, whet your rage upon me. Take my money, my life, but spare that young gentleman, spare my child, if you have any mercy!

Hardcastle. My wife! as I'm a Christian. From whence can she come, or what does she mean?

Mrs. Hardcastle. (Kneeling.) Take compassion on us, good Mr. Highwayman. Take our money, our watches, all we have, but spare our lives. We will never bring you to justice, indeed we won't, good Mr. Highwayman.

Hardcastle. I believe the woman's out of her senses. What, Dorothy, don't you know *me?*

Mrs. Hardcastle. Mr. Hardcastle, as I'm alive! My fears blinded me. But who, my dear, could have expected to meet you here, in this frightful place, so far from home? What has brought you to follow us?

Hardcastle. Sure, Dorothy, you have not lost your wits. So far from home, when you are within forty yards of your own door. *(To him.)* This is one of your old tricks, you graceless rogue you. *(To her.)* Don't you know the gate, and the mulberry-tree; and don't you remember the horse-pond, my dear?

Mrs. Hardcastle. Yes, I shall remember the horse-pond as long as I live; I have caught my death in it. *(To* Tony.*)* And is it to you, you graceless varlet, I owe all this? I'll teach you to abuse your mother, I will.

Tony. Ecod, mother, all the parish says you have spoiled me, and so you may take the fruits on't.

Mrs. Hardcastle. I'll spoil you, I will.

Follows him off stage. Exit.

Hardcastle. There's morality, however, in his reply. *Exit.*

Enter HASTINGS *and* MISS NEVILLE.

Hastings. My dear Constance, why will you deliberate thus? If we delay a moment, all is lost for ever. Pluck up a little resolution, and we shall soon be out of reach of her malignity.

Miss Neville. I find it impossible. My spirits are so sunk with the agitations I have suffered, that I am unable to face any new danger. Two or three years patience will at last crown us with happiness.

Hastings. Such a tedious delay is worse than inconstancy. Let us fly, my charmer. Let us date our happiness from this very moment. Perish fortune. Love and content will increase what we possess beyond a monarch's revenue. Let me prevail.

Miss Neville. No, Mr. Hastings; no. Prudence once more comes to my relief, and I will obey its dictates. In the moment of passion, fortune may be despised, but it produces a lasting repentance. I'm resolved to apply to Mr. Hardcastle's compassion and justice for redress.

Hastings. But though he has the will, he has not the power to relieve you.

Miss Neville. But he has influence, and upon that I am resolved to rely.

Hastings. I have no hopes. But since you persist, I must reluctantly obey you.   *Exeunt.*

SCENE III: *Scene changes to the parlor.*

Enter SIR CHARLES *and* MISS HARDCASTLE.

Sir Charles. What a situation am I in. If what you say appears, I shall then find a guilty son. If what he says be true, I shall then lose one that, of all others, I most wished for a daughter.

Miss Hardcastle. I am proud of your approbation, and to show I merit it, if you place yourselves as I directed, you shall hear his explicit declaration. But he comes.

Sir Charles. I'll to your father, and keep him to the appointment.   *Exit.*

Enter MARLOW.

Marlow. Though prepared for setting out, I come once more to take leave, nor did I, till this moment, know the pain I feel in the separation.

Miss Hardcastle. (In her own natural manner.) I believe these sufferings cannot be very great, sir, which you can so easily remove. A day or two longer, perhaps, might lessen your uneasiness, by showing the little value of what you now think proper to regret.

Marlow. (Aside.) This girl every moment improves upon me. *(To her.)* It must not be, madam. I have already trifled too long with my heart. My very pride begins to submit to my passion. The disparity of education and fortune, the anger of a parent, and the contempt of my equals, begin to lose their weight; and nothing can restore me to myself but this painful effort of resolution.

Miss Hardcastle. Then go, sir. I'll urge nothing more to detain you. Though my family be as good as hers you came down to visit, and my education, I hope, not inferior, what are these advantages without equal affluence? I must remain contented with the slight approbation of imputed merit; I must have only the mockery of your addresses, while all your serious aims are fixed on fortune.

Enter HARDCASTLE *and* SIR CHARLES *from behind.*

Sir Charles. Here, behind this screen.

Hardcastle. Ay, ay, make no noise. I'll engage my Kate covers him with confusion at last.

Marlow. By heavens, madam, fortune was ever my smallest consideration. Your beauty at first caught my eye; for who could see that without emotion? But every moment that I converse with you steals in some new grace, heightens the picture and gives it stronger expression. What at first seemed rustic plainness, now appears refined simplicity. What seemed forward assurance, now strikes me as the result of courageous innocence, and conscious virtue.

Sir Charles. What can it mean! He amazes me!

Hardcastle. I told you how it would be. Hush!

Marlow. I am now determined to stay, madam, and I have too good an opinion of my father's discernment, when he sees you, to doubt his approbation.

Miss Hardcastle. No, Mr. Marlow, I will not, cannot detain you. Do you think I could suffer a connection, in which there is the smallest room for repentance? Do you think I would take the mean advantage of a transient passion, to load you with confusion? Do you think I could ever relish that happiness, which was acquired by lessening yours?

Marlow. By all that's good, I can have no happiness but what's in your power to grant me. Nor shall I ever feel repentance, but in not having seen your merits before. I will stay, even contrary to your wishes; and though you should persist to shun me, I will make my respectful assiduities atone for the levity of my past conduct.

Miss Hardcastle. Sir, I must entreat you'll desist. As our acquaintance began, so let it end, in indifference. I might have given an hour or two to levity; but seriously, Mr. Marlow, do you think I could ever submit to a connection, where *I* must appear mercenary, and *you* imprudent? Do you think I could ever catch at the confident addresses of a secure admirer?

Marlow. (*Kneeling.*) Does this look like security? Does this look like confidence? No, madam, every moment that shows me your merit, only serves to increase my diffidence and confusion. Here let me continue—

Sir Charles. I can hold it no longer! Charles, Charles, how hast thou deceived me! Is this your indifference, your uninteresting conversation?

Hardcastle. Your cold contempt; your formal interview! What have you to say now?

Marlow. That I'm all amazement. What can it mean!

Hardcastle. It means that you can say and unsay things at pleasure. That you can address a lady in private, and deny it in public; that you have one story for us, and another for my daughter.

Marlow. Daughter!—this lady your daughter!

Hardcastle. Yes, sir, my only daughter. My Kate, whose else should she be?

Marlow. Oh, the devil!

Miss Hardcastle. Yes, sir, that very identical tall, squinting lady you were pleased to take me for. *(Curtsying.)* She that you addressed as the mild, modest, sentimental man of gravity, and the bold, forward, agreeable Rattle of the Ladies Club; ha, ha, ha.

Marlow. Zounds, there's no bearing this; it's worse than death.

Miss Hardcastle. In which of your characters, Sir, will you give us leave to address you? As the faltering gentleman, with looks on the ground, that speaks just to be heard, and hates hypocrisy; or the loud, confident creature, that keeps it up with Mrs. Mantrap, and old Miss Biddy Buckskin, till three in the morning; ha, ha, ha!

Marlow. Oh, curse on my noisy head. I never attempted to be impudent yet, that I was not taken down. I must be gone.

Hardcastle. By the hand of my body, but you shall not. I see it was all a mistake, and I am rejoiced to find it. You shall not, sir, I tell you. I know she'll forgive you. Won't you forgive him, Kate? We'll all forgive you. Take courage, man.

They retire, she tormenting him, to the back scene.

Enter MRS. HARDCASTLE, TONY.

Mrs. Hardcastle. So, so they're gone off. Let them go, I care not.

Hardcastle. Who gone?

Mrs. Hardcastle. My dutiful niece and her gentleman, Mr. Hastings, from town. He who came down with our modest visitor here.

Sir Charles. Who, my honest George Hastings? As worthy a fellow as lives, and the girl could not have made a more prudent choice.

Hardcastle. Then, by the hand of my body, I'm proud of the connection.

Mrs. Hardcastle. Well, if he has taken away the lady, he has not taken her fortune; that remains in this family to console us for her loss.

Hardcastle. Sure, Dorothy, you would not be so mercenary?

Mrs. Hardcastle. Ay, that's my affair, not yours.

Hardcastle.[30] But you know if your son, when of age, refuses to marry his cousin, her whole fortune is then at her own disposal.

Mrs. Hardcastle. Ay, but he's not of age, and she has not thought proper to wait for his refusal.

Enter HASTINGS *and* MISS NEVILLE.

Mrs. Hardcastle. (*Aside.*) What! returned so soon? I begin not to like it.

Hastings. (*To* HARDCASTLE.) For my late attempt to fly off with your niece, let my present confusion be my punishment. We are now come back, to appeal from your justice to your humanity. By her father's consent, I first paid her my addresses, and our passions were first founded in duty.

Miss Neville. Since his death, I have been obliged to stoop to dissimulation to avoid oppression. In an hour of levity, I was ready even to give up my fortune to secure my choice. But I'm now recovered from the delusion, and hope from your tenderness what is denied me from a nearer connection.

Mrs. Hardcastle. Pshaw, pshaw, this is all but the whining end of a modern novel.

Hardcastle. Be it what it will, I'm glad they're come back to reclaim their due. Come hither, Tony boy. Do you refuse this lady's hand whom I now offer you?

Tony. What signifies my refusing? You know I can't refuse her till I'm of age, father.

Hardcastle. While I thought concealing your age, boy, was likely to conduce to your improvement, I concurred with your mother's desire to keep it secret. But since I find she turns it to a wrong use, I must now declare, you have been of age these three months.

Tony. Of age! Am I of age, father?

Hardcastle. Above three months.

Tony. Then you'll see the first use I'll make of my liberty. (*Taking* MISS NEVILLE'S *hand.*) Witness all men by these presents, that I, Anthony Lumpkin, Esquire, of Blank place, refuse you, Constantia Neville, spinster, of no place at all, for my true and lawful wife. So Constance Neville may marry whom she pleases, and Tony Lumpkin is his own man again!

Sir Charles. O brave squire!

Hastings. My worthy friend!

Mrs. Hardcastle. My undutiful offspring!

Marlow. Joy, my dear George, I give you joy sincerely. And could I prevail upon my little tyrant here to be less arbitrary, I should be the happiest man alive, if you would return me the favor.

Hastings. (To Miss Hardcastle.) Come, madam, you are now driven to the very last scene of all your contrivances. I know you like him, I'm sure he loves you, and you must and shall have him.

Hardcastle. (Joining their hands.) And I say so too. And Mr. Marlow, if she makes as good a wife as she has a daughter, I don't believe you'll ever repent your bargain. So now to supper; tomorrow we shall gather all the poor of the parish about us, and the Mistakes of the Night shall be crowned with a merry morning; so boy, take her; and as you have been mistaken in the mistress, my wish is, that you may never be mistaken in the wife.

EPILOGUE

BY DR. GOLDSMITH

Spoken by MISS HARDCASTLE.

Well, having stooped to conquer with success,
And gained a husband without aid from dress,
Still as a Barmaid, I could wish it too,
As I have conquered him to conquer you:
And let me say, for all your resolution,
That pretty Barmaids have done execution.
Our life is all a play, composed to please,
"We have our exits and our entrances."
The first act shows the simple country maid,
Harmless and young, of everything afraid;
Blushes when hired, and with unmeaning action,
'I hopes as how to give you satisfaction.'
Her second act displays a livelier scene,—
The unblushing Barmaid of a country inn,
Who whisks about the house, at market caters,
Talks loud, coquets the guests, and scolds the waiters.
Next the scene shifts to town, and there she soars,
The chop-house toast of ogling connoisseurs.
On 'squires and cits she there displays her arts,
And on the gridiron broils her lovers' hearts—
And as she smiles, her triumphs to complete,
Even Common Councilmen forget to eat.
The fourth act shows her wedded to the 'Squire,
And madam now begins to hold it higher;
Pretends to taste, at Operas cries 'Caro,'
And quits her Nancy Dawson,[31] for '*Che Faro*.'[32]
Doats upon dancing, and in all her pride,
Swims round the room, the Heinel[33] of Cheapside:
Ogles and leers with artificial skill,
Till having lost in age the power to kill,
She sits all night at cards, and ogles at spadille.[34]
Such, through our lives, the eventful history—
The fifth and last act still remains for me.
The Barmaid now for your protection prays,
Turns female barrister, and pleads for Bayes.[35]

EPILOGUE

By J. Craddock, Esq.

Spoken by Tony Lumpkin.

Well—now all's ended—and my comrades gone,
Pray what becomes of mother's nonly son?
A hopeful blade!—in town I'll fix my station,
And try to make a bluster in the nation.
As for my cousin Neville, I renounce her,
Off—in a crack—I'll carry big Bet Bouncer.
Why should not I in the great world appear?
I soon shall have a thousand pounds a year;
No matter what a man may here inherit,
In London—'gad, they've some regard to spirit.
I see the horses prancing up the streets,
And big Bet Bouncer bobs to all she meets;
Then hoikes to jiggs and pastimes every night—
Not to the plays—they say it a'n't polite,
To Sadler's Wells perhaps, or operas go,
And once, by chance, to the roratorio.
Thus here and there, for ever up and down,
We'll set the fashions, too, to half the town;
And then at auctions—money ne'er regard,
Buy pictures like the great, ten pounds a yard;
Zounds, we shall make these London gentry say,
We know what's damn'd genteel, as well as they.

The School for Scandal

by
Richard Brinsley Sheridan

PROLOGUE

By Mr. Garrick

Spoken by Sir Peter Teazle.

A School for Scandal! tell me, I beseech you,
Needs there a school this modish art to teach you?
No need of lessons now, the knowing think;
We might as well be taught to eat and drink.
Caused by a dearth of scandal, should the vapors
Distress our fair ones—let them read the papers;
Their powerful mixtures such disorders hit;
Crave what you will—there's *quantum suffícit*.[1]
"Lord!" cries my Lady Wormwood (who loves tattle,
And puts much salt and pepper in her prattle),
Just risen at noon, all night at cards when threshing
Strong tea and scandal—"Bless me, how refreshing!
Give me the papers, Lisp—how bold and free!   *(Sips.)*
Last night Lord L.—(Sips.) was caught with Lady D.
For aching heads what charming sal volatile!   *(Sips.)*
If Mrs. B. will still continue flirting,
We hope she'll draw, *or we'll* undraw *the curtain.*
Fine satire, poz[2]—in public all abuse it,
But, by ourselves—*(Sips.)*, our praise we can't refuse it.
Now, Lisp, read you—there at that dash and star."
"Yes, ma'am—*A certain Lord had best beware,*
Who lives not twenty miles from Grosvenor Square;
For should he Lady W. find willing,
Wormwood is bitter"——"Oh! that's me! the villain!
Throw it behind the fire, and never more
Let that vile paper come within my door."
Thus at our friends we laugh, who feel the dart;
To reach our feelings, we ourselves must smart.
Is our young bard so young, to think that he
Can stop the full spring-tide of calumny?
Knows he the world so little, and its trade?
Alas! the devil's sooner raised than laid.
So strong, so swift, the monster there's no gagging:
Cut Scandal's head off, still the tongue is wagging.
Proud of your smiles once lavishly bestowed,

Again our young Don Quixote takes the road;
To show his gratitude he draws his pen,
And seeks his hydra, Scandal, in his den.
For your applause all perils he would through—
He'll fight—that's *write*—a cavalliero true,
Till every drop of blood—that's *ink*—is spilt for you.

DRAMATIS PERSONÆ

SIR PETER TEAZLE
SIR OLIVER SURFACE
JOSEPH SURFACE
CHARLES SURFACE
CARELESS
SNAKE
SIR BENJAMIN BACKBITE
CRABTREE
ROWLEY
MOSES
TRIP
SIR TOBY BUMPER[3]

LADY TEAZLE
MARIA
LADY SNEERWELL
MRS. CANDOUR

Gentlemen, Maid, *and* Servants.

Scene—LONDON.

ACT I

SCENE I: LADY SNEERWELL'S *Dressing-room*.

LADY SNEERWELL *at her toilet;* SNAKE *drinking chocolate.*

Lady Sneerwell. The paragraphs, you say, Mr. Snake, were all inserted?

Snake. They were, madam; and, as I copied them myself in a feigned hand, there can be no suspicion whence they came.

Lady Sneerwell. Did you circulate the report of Lady Brittle's intrigue with Captain Boastall?

Snake. That's in as fine a train as your ladyship could wish. In the common course of things, I think it must reach Mrs. Clackitt's ears within four-and-twenty hours; and then, you know, the business is as good as done.

Lady Sneerwell. Why, truly, Mrs. Clackitt has a very pretty talent, and a great deal of industry.

Snake. True, madam, and has been tolerably successful in her day. To my knowledge, she has been the cause of six matches being broken off, and three sons being disinherited; of four forced elopments, and as many close confinements; nine separate maintenances, and two divorces. Nay, I have more than once traced her causing a *tête-à-tête* in the *Town and Country Magazine*,[4] when the parties, perhaps, had never seen each other's face before in the course of their lives.

Lady Sneerwell. She certainly has talents, but her manner is gross.

Snake. 'Tis very true. She generally designs well, has a free tongue and a bold invention; but her coloring is too dark, and her outlines often extravagant. She wants that delicacy of tint, and mellowness of sneer, which distinguish your ladyship's scandal.

Lady Sneerwell. You are partial, Snake.

Snake. Not in the least; everybody allows that Lady Sneerwell can do more with a word or look than many can with the most labored detail, even when they happen to have a little truth on their side to support it.

Lady Sneerwell. Yes, my dear Snake; and I am no hypocrite to deny the satisfaction I reap from the success of my efforts. Wounded myself in the early part of my life, by the envenomed tongue of slander, I confess I have since known no pleasure equal to the reducing others to the level of my own injured reputation.

Snake. Nothing can be more natural. But, Lady Sneerwell, there is one affair in which you have lately employed me, wherein, I confess, I am at a loss to guess your motives.

Lady Sneerwell. I conceive you mean with respect to my neighbor, Sir Peter Teazle, and his family?

Snake. I do. Here are two young men, to whom Sir Peter has acted as a kind of guardian since their father's death; the eldest possessing the most amiable character, and universally well spoken of—the youngest, the most dissipated and extravagant young fellow in the kingdom, without friends or character: the former an avowed admirer of your ladyship, and apparently your favorite; the latter attached to Maria, Sir Peter's ward, and confessedly beloved by her. Now, on the face of these circumstances, it is utterly unaccountable to me why you, the widow of a city knight,[5] with a good jointure, should not close with the passion of a man of such character and expectations as Mr. Surface; and more so, why you should be so uncommonly earnest to destroy the mutual attachment subsisting between his brother Charles and Maria.

Lady Sneerwell. Then, at once to unravel this mystery, I must inform you that love has no share whatever in the intercourse between Mr. Surface and me.

Snake. No!

Lady Sneerwell. His real attachment is to Maria or her fortune; but, finding in his brother a favorite rival, he has been obliged to mask his pretensions and profit by my assistance.

Snake. Yet still I am more puzzled why you should interest yourself in his success.

Lady Sneerwell. Heavens! how dull you are! Cannot you surmise the weakness which I hitherto, through shame, have concealed even from you? Must I confess that Charles—that libertine, that extravagant, that bankrupt in fortune and reputation—that he it is for whom I am thus anxious and malicious, and to gain whom I would sacrifice everything?

Snake. Now, indeed, your conduct appears consistent; but how came you and Mr. Surface so confidential?

Lady Sneerwell. For our mutual interest. I have found him out a long time since. I know him to be artful, selfish, and malicious—in short, a sentimental knave; while with Sir Peter, and indeed with all his acquaintance, he passes for a youthful miracle of prudence, good sense, and benevolence.

Snake. Yes! yet Sir Peter vows he has not his equal in

England; and, above all, he praises him as a man of sentiment.

Lady Sneerwell. True; and with the assistance of his sentiment and hypocrisy he has brought Sir Peter entirely into his interest with regard to Maria; while poor Charles has no friend in the house—though, I fear, he has a powerful one in Maria's heart, against whom we must direct our schemes.

Enter SERVANT.

Servant. Mr. Surface.

Lady Sneerwell. Show him up. (*Exit* SERVANT.) He generally calls about this time. I don't wonder at people giving him to me for a lover.

Enter JOSEPH SURFACE.

Joseph Surface. My dear Lady Sneerwell, how do you do today? Mr. Snake, your most obedient.

Lady Sneerwell. Snake has just been rallying me on our mutual attachment; but I have informed him of our real views. You know how useful he has been to us; and, believe me, the confidence is not ill placed.

Joseph Surface. Madam, it is impossible for me to suspect a man of Mr. Snake's sensibility and discernment.

Lady Sneerwell. Well, well, no compliments now; but tell me when you saw your mistress, Maria—or, what is more material to me, your brother.

Joseph Surface. I have not seen either since I left you; but I can inform you that they never meet. Some of your stories have taken a good effect on Maria.

Lady Sneerwell. Ah, my dear Snake! the merit of this belongs to you. But do your brother's distresses increase?

Joseph Surface. Every hour. I am told he has had another execution in the house yesterday. In short, his dissipation and extravagance exceed anything I have ever heard of.

Lady Sneerwell. Poor Charles!

Joseph Surface. True, madam; notwithstanding his vices, one can't help feeling for him. Poor Charles! I'm sure I wish it were in my power to be of any essential service to him; for the man who does not share in the distresses of a brother, even though merited by his own misconduct, deserves——

Lady Sneerwell. O Lud! you are going to be moral and forget that you are among friends.

Joseph Surface. Egad, that's true! I'll keep that sentiment till I see Sir Peter. However, it is certainly a charity to rescue Maria from such a libertine, who, if he is to be reclaimed,

can be so only by a person of your ladyship's superior accomplishments and understanding.

Snake. I believe, Lady Sneerwell, here's company coming.
I'll go and copy the letter I mentioned to you. Mr. Surface,
your most obedient.

Joseph Surface. Sir, your very devoted. *(Exit* SNAKE.*)* Lady
Sneerwell, I am very sorry you have put any further confidence in that fellow.

Lady Sneerwell. Why so?

Joseph Surface. I have lately detected him in frequent conference with old Rowley, who was formerly my father's
steward and has never, you know, been a friend of mine.

Lady Sneerwell. And do you think he would betray us?

Joseph Surface. Nothing more likely: take my word for't,
Lady Sneerwell, that fellow hasn't virtue enough to be faithful even to his own villainy. Ah, Maria!

Enter MARIA.

Lady Sneerwell. Maria, my dear, how do you do? What's
the matter?

Maria. Oh! there's that disagreeable lover of mine, Sir
Benjamin Backbite, has just called at my guardian's with his
odious uncle, Crabtree; so I slipped out and ran hither to
avoid them.

Lady Sneerwell. Is that all?

Joseph Surface. If my brother Charles had been of the
party, madam, perhaps you would not have been so much
alarmed.

Lady Sneerwell. Nay, now you are severe; for I dare swear
the truth of the matter is, Maria heard you were here. But,
my dear, what has Sir Benjamin done that you should avoid
him so?

Maria. Oh, he has done nothing—but 'tis for what he has
said. His conversation is a perpetual libel on all his acquaintance.

Joseph Surface. Ay, and the worst of it is, there is no advantage in not knowing him, for he'll abuse a stranger just as
soon as his best friend; and his uncle's as bad.

Lady Sneerwell. Nay, but we should make allowance; Sir
Benjamin is a wit and a poet.

Maria. For my part, I own, madam, wit loses its respect
with me when I see it in company with malice. What do you
think, Mr. Surface?

Joseph Surface. Certainly, madam. To smile at the jest
which plants a thorn in another's breast is to become a principal in the mischief.

Lady Sneerwell. Psha! there's no possibility of being witty without a little ill nature. The malice of a good thing is the barb that makes it stick. What's your opinion, Mr. Surface?

Joseph Surface. To be sure, madam; that conversation, where the spirit of raillery is suppressed, will ever appear tedious and insipid.

Maria. Well, I'll not debate how far scandal may be allowable; but in a man, I am sure, it is always contemptible. We have pride, envy, rivalship, and a thousand motives to depreciate each other; but the male slanderer must have the cowardice of a woman before he can traduce one.

Enter SERVANT.

Servant. Madam, Mrs. Candour is below, and, if your ladyship's at leisure, will leave her carriage.

Lady Sneerwell. Beg her to walk in. (*Exit* SERVANT.) Now, Maria, here is a character to your taste; for, though Mrs. Candour is a little talkative, everybody knows her to be the best natured and best sort of woman.

Maria. Yes, with a very gross affection of good nature and benevolence, she does more mischief than the direct malice of old Crabtree.

Joseph Surface. I'faith that's true, Lady Sneerwell: whenever I hear the current running against the characters of my friends, I never think them in such danger as when Candour undertakes their defence.

Lady Sneerwell. Hush!—here she is!

Enter MRS. CANDOUR.

Mrs. Candour. My dear Lady Sneerwell, how have you been this century?—Mr. Surface, what news do you hear?—though indeed it is no matter, for I think one hears nothing else but scandal.

Joseph Surface. Just so, indeed, ma'am.

Mrs. Candour. Oh, Maria! child—what, is the whole affair off between you and Charles? His extravagance, I presume—the town talks of nothing else.

Maria. I am very sorry, ma'am, the town has so little to do.

Mrs. Candour. True, true, child: but there's no stopping people's tongues. I own I was hurt to hear it, as I indeed was to learn, from the same quarter, that your guardian, Sir Peter, and Lady Teazle have not agreed lately as well as could be wished.

Maria. 'Tis strangely impertinent for people to busy themselves so.

Mrs. Candour. Very true, child; but what's to be done? People will talk—there's no preventing it. Why, it was but yesterday I was told that Miss Gadabout had eloped with Sir Filagree Flirt. But, Lord! there's no minding what one hears; though, to be sure, I had this from very good authority.

Maria. Such reports are highly scandalous.

Mrs. Candour. So they are, child—shameful, shameful! But the world is so censorious, no character escapes. Lord, now who would have suspected your friend, Miss Prim, of an indiscretion? Yet such is the ill nature of people that they say her uncle stopped her last week just as she was stepping into the York diligence[6] with her dancing-master.

Maria. I'll answer for't there are no grounds for that report.

Mrs. Candour. Ah, no foundation in the world, I dare swear: no more, probably, than for the story circulated last month, of Mrs. Festino's affair with Colonel Cassino— though, to be sure, that matter was never rightly cleared up.

Joseph Surface. The license of invention some people take is monstrous indeed.

Maria. 'Tis so; but, in my opinion, those who report such things are equally culpable.

Mrs. Candour. To be sure they are; tale bearers are as bad as the tale makers—'tis an old observation and a very true one: but what's to be done, as I said before? how will you prevent people from talking? Today, Mrs. Clackitt assured me Mr. and Mrs. Honeymoon were at last become mere man and wife like the rest of their acquaintance. She likewise hinted that a certain widow in the next street had got rid of her dropsy and recovered her shape in a most surprising manner. And at the same time Miss Tattle, who was by, affirmed that Lord Buffalo had discovered his lady at a house of no extraordinary fame; and that Sir Harry Bouquet and Tom Saunter were to measure swords on a similar provocation. But, Lord, do you think I would report these things! No, no! tale bearers, as I said before, are just as bad as the tale makers.

Joseph Surface. Ah! Mrs. Candour, if everybody had your forbearance and good nature!

Mrs. Candour. I confess, Mr. Surface, I cannot bear to hear people attacked behind their backs; and when ugly circumstances come out against our acquaintance, I own I always love to think the best. By-the-bye, I hope 'tis not true that your brother is absolutely ruined?

Joseph Surface. I am afraid his circumstances are very bad indeed, ma'am.

Mrs. Candour. Ah!—I heard so—but you must tell him to keep up his spirits; everybody almost is in the same way: Lord Spindle, Sir Thomas Splint, Captain Quinze, and Mr. Nickit—all up, I hear, within this week; so, if Charles is undone, he'll find half his acquaintance ruined too; and that, you know, is a consolation.

Joseph Surface. Doubtless, ma'am—a very great one.

Enter SERVANT.

Servant. Mr. Crabtree and Sir Benjamin Backbite. *(Exit.)*

Lady Sneerwell. So, Maria, you see your lover pursues you; positively you shan't escape.

Enter CRABTREE *and* SIR BENJAMIN BACKBITE.

Crabtree. Lady Sneerwell, I kiss your hand. Mrs. Candour, I don't believe you are acquainted with my nephew, Sir Benjamin Backbite? Egad, ma'am, he has a pretty wit and is a pretty poet too. Isn't he, Lady Sneerwell?

Sir Benjamin. Oh, fie, uncle!

Crabtree. Nay, egad it's true: I back him at a rebus or a charade against the best rhymer in the kingdom. Has your ladyship heard the epigram he wrote last week on Lady Frizzle's feather catching fire?—Do, Benjamin, repeat it, or the charade you made last night extempore at Mrs. Drowzie's *conversazione*. Come now; your first is the name of a fish, your second a great naval commander, and——

Sir Benjamin. Uncle, now——prithee——

Crabtree. I'faith, ma'am, 'twould surprise you to hear how ready he is at all these sort of things.

Lady Sneerwell. I wonder, Sir Benjamin, you never publish anything.

Sir Benjamin. To say truth, ma'am, 'tis very vulgar to print; and, as my little productions are mostly satires and lampoons on particular people, I find they circulate more by giving copies in confidence to the friends of the parties. However, I have some love elegies, which, when favored with this lady's smiles, I mean to give the public.

Crabtree (To MARIA.*)* 'Fore heaven, ma'am, they'll immortalize you—you will be handed down to posterity like Petrarch's Laura,[7] or Waller's Sacharissa.

Sir Benjamin. (To MARIA.*)* Yes, madam, I think you will like them when you shall see them on a beautiful quarto page, where a neat rivulet of text shall meander through a meadow of margin. 'Fore gad, they will be the most elegant things of their kind!

Crabtree. But, ladies, that's true—have you heard the news?

Mrs. Candour. What, sir, do you mean the report of—

Crabtree. No, ma'am, that's not it. Miss Nicely is going to be married to her own footman.

Mrs. Candour. Impossible!

Crabtree. Ask Sir Benjamin.

Sir Benjamin. 'Tis very true, ma'am: everything is fixed and the wedding liveries bespoke.

Crabtree. Yes—and they do say there were pressing reasons for it.

Lady Sneerwell. Why, I have heard something of this before.

Mrs. Candour. It can't be—and I wonder any one should believe such a story of so prudent a lady as Miss Nicely.

Sir Benjamin. O lud! ma'am, that's the very reason 'twas believed at once. She has always been so cautious and so reserved, that everybody was sure there was some reason for it at bottom.

Mrs. Candour. Why, to be sure, a tale of scandal is as fatal to the credit of a prudent lady of her stamp as a fever is generally to those of the strongest constitution. But there is a sort of puny, sickly reputation, that is always ailing, yet will outlive the robuster characters of a hundred prudes.

Sir Benjamin. True, madam, there are valetudinarians in reputation as well as constitution, who, being conscious of their weak part, avoid the least breath of air and supply their want of stamina by care and circumspection.

Mrs. Candour. Well, but this may be all a mistake. You know, Sir Benjamin, very trifling circumstances often give rise to the most injurious tales.

Crabtree. That they do, I'll be sworn, ma'am. Did you ever hear how Miss Piper came to lose her lover and her character last summer at Tunbridge? Sir Benjamin, you remember it?

Sir Benjamin. Oh, to be sure!—the most whimsical circumstance.

Lady Sneerwell. How was it, pray?

Crabtree. Why, one evening at Mrs. Ponto's assembly, the conversation happened to turn on the breeding Nova Scotia sheep in this country. Says a young lady in company, "I have known instances of it; for Miss Letitia Piper, a first cousin of mine, had a Nova Scotia sheep that produced her twins." "What!" cries the Lady Dowager Dundizzy (who you know is as deaf as a post), "has Miss Piper had twins?" This mistake, as you may imagine, threw the whole company into a fit of laughter. However, 'twas the next morning everywhere reported, and in a few days believed by the whole town, that

Miss Letitia Piper had actually been brought to bed of a fine boy and a girl: and in less than a week there were some people who could name the father, and the farm-house where the babies were put to nurse.

Lady Sneerwell. Strange, indeed!

Crabtree. Matter of fact, I assure you. O lud! Mr. Surface, pray is it true that your uncle, Sir Oliver, is coming home?

Joseph Surface. Not that I know of, indeed, sir.

Crabtree. He has been in the East Indies a long time. You can scarcely remember him, I believe? Sad comfort, whenever he returns, to hear how your brother has gone on!

Joseph Surface! Charles has been imprudent, sir, to be sure; but I hope no busy people have already prejudiced Sir Oliver against him. He may reform.

Sir Benjamin. To be sure he may. For my part I never believed him to be so utterly void of principle as people say; and though he has lost all his friends, I am told nobody is better spoken of by the Jews.

Crabtree. That's true, egad, nephew. If the old Jewry was a ward, I believe Charles would be an alderman: no man more popular there, 'fore gad! I hear he pays as many annuities as the Irish tontine;[8] and that whenever he is sick they have prayers for the recovery of his health in all the synagogues.

Sir Benjamin. Yet no man lives in greater splendor. They tell me, when he entertains his friends he will sit down to dinner with a dozen of his own securities, have a score of tradesmen in the ante-chamber, and an officer behind every guest's chair.

Joseph Surface. This may be entertainment to you, gentlemen, but you pay very little regard to the feelings of a brother.

Maria. (Aside.) Their malice is intolerable!—(Aloud.) Lady Sneerwell, I must wish you a good morning: I'm not very well.   *Exit.*

Mrs. Candour. O dear! she changes color very much.

Lady Sneerwell. Do, Mrs. Candour, follow her; she may want assistance.

Mrs. Candour. That I will, with all my soul, ma'am. Poor dear girl, who knows what her situation may be!   *Exit.*

Lady Sneerwell. 'Twas nothing but that she could not bear to hear Charles reflected on, notwithstanding their difference.

Sir Benjamin. The young lady's *penchant* is obvious.

Crabtree. But, Benjamin, you must not give up the pursuit for that: follow her and put her into good humor. Repeat her some of your own verses. Come, I'll assist you.

Sir Benjamin. Mr. Surface, I did not mean to hurt you; but depend on't your brother is utterly undone.

Crabtree. O lud, ay! undone as ever man was—can't raise a guinea!

Sir Benjamin. And everything sold, I'm told, that was movable.

Crabtree. I have seen one that was at his house. Not a thing left but some empty bottles that were overlooked and the family pictures which I believe are framed in the wainscots.

Sir Benjamin. And I'm very sorry also to hear some bad stories against him. *(Going.)*

Crabtree. Oh, he has done many mean things, that's certain.

Sir Benjamin. But, however, as he's your brother—— *(Going.)*

Crabtree. We'll tell you all another opportunity.

Exeunt CRABTREE *and* SIR BENJAMIN.

Lady Sneerwell. Ha, ha! 'tis very hard for them to leave a subject they have not quite run down.

Joseph Surface. And I believe the abuse was no more acceptable to your ladyship than to Maria.

Lady Sneerwell. I doubt[9] her affections are further engaged than we imagine. But the family are to be here this evening, so you may as well dine where you are and we shall have an opportunity of observing further. In the meantime, I'll go and plot mischief and you shall study sentiment. *Exeunt.*

SCENE II: SIR PETER TEAZLE'S *House.*

Enter SIR PETER.

Sir Peter. When an old bachelor marries a young wife, what is he to expect? 'Tis now six months since Lady Teazle made me the happiest of men—and I have been the most miserable dog ever since! We tift a little going to church and fairly quarrelled before the bells had done ringing. I was more than once nearly choked with gall during the honeymoon, and had lost all comfort in life before my friends had done wishing me joy. Yet I chose with caution—a girl bred wholly in the country, who never knew luxury beyond one silk gown, nor dissipation above the annual gala of a race ball. Yet she now plays her part in all the extravagant fopperies of fashion and the town, with as ready a grace as if she never had seen a bush or a grass-plot out of Grosvenor Square! I am sneered at by all my acquaintance and paragraphed in the newspapers. She dissipates my fortune, and contradicts all my humors; yet the worst of it is, I doubt I love her, or I should never bear all this. However, I'll never be weak enough to own it.

Enter ROWLEY.

Rowley. Oh! Sir Peter, your servant: how is it with you, sir?

Sir Peter. Very bad, Master Rowley, very bad. I meet with nothing but crosses and vexations.

Rowley. What can have happened to trouble you since yesterday?

Sir Peter. A good question to a married man!

Rowley. Nay, I'm sure, Sir Peter, your lady can't be the cause of your uneasiness.

Sir Peter. Why, has anybody told you she was dead?

Rowley. Come, come, Sir Peter, you love her, notwithstanding your tempers don't exactly agree.

Sir Peter. But the fault is entirely hers, Master Rowley. I am myself the sweetest tempered man alive, and hate a teasing temper; and so I tell her a hundred times a day.

Rowley. Indeed!

Sir Peter. Ay; and what is very extraordinary, in all our disputes she is always in the wrong! But Lady Sneerwell and the set she meets at her house encourage the perverseness of her disposition. Then, to complete my vexation, Maria, my ward, whom I ought to have the power of a father over, is determined to turn rebel too and absolutely refuses the man whom I have long resolved on for her husband; meaning, I suppose, to bestow herself on his profligate brother.

Rowley. You know, Sir Peter, I have always taken the liberty to differ with you on the subject of these two young gentlemen. I only wish you may not be deceived in your opinion of the elder. For Charles, my life on't! he will retrieve his errors yet. Their worthy father, once my honored master, was, at his years, nearly as wild a spark; yet, when he died, he did not leave a more benevolent heart to lament his loss.

Sir Peter. You are wrong, Master Rowley. On their father's death, you know, I acted as a kind of guardian to them both till their uncle Sir Oliver's liberality gave them an early independence. Of course no person could have more opportunities of judging of their hearts, and I was never mistaken in my life. Joseph is indeed a model for the young men of the age. He is a man of sentiment and acts up to the sentiments he professes; but, for the other, take my word for't, if he had any grain of virtue by descent, he has dissipated it with the rest of his inheritance. Ah! my old friend Sir Oliver will be deeply mortified when he finds how part of his bounty has been misapplied.

Rowley. I am sorry to find you so violent against the young man, because this may be the most critical period of his fortune. I came hither with news that will surprise you.

Sir Peter. What! let me hear.

Rowley. Sir Oliver is arrived, and at this moment in town.

Sir Peter. How! you astonish me! I thought you did not expect him this month.

Rowley. I did not: but his passage has been remarkably quick.

Sir Peter. Egad, I shall rejoice to see my old friend. 'Tis sixteen years since we met. We have had many a day together: but does he still enjoin us not to inform his nephews of his arrival?

Rowley. Most strictly. He means, before it is known, to make some trial of their dispositions.

Sir Peter. Ah! There needs no art to discover their merits —however, he shall have his way; but, pray, does he know I am married?

Rowley. Yes, and will soon wish you joy.

Sir Peter. What, as we drink health to a friend in consumption! Ah, Oliver will laugh at me. We used to rail at matrimony together, but he has been steady to his text. Well, he must be soon at my house, though—I'll instantly give orders for his reception. But, Master Rowley, don't drop a word that Lady Teazle and I ever disagree.

Rowley. By no means.

Sir Peter. For I should never be able to stand Noll's jokes; so I'll have him think, Lord forgive me! that we are a very happy couple.

Rowley. I understand you: but then you must be very careful not to differ while he is in the house with you.

Sir Peter. Egad, and so we must—and that's impossible. Ah! Master Rowley, when an old bachelor marries a young wife, he deserves—no—the crime carries its punishment along with it. *Exeunt.*

ACT II

SCENE I: SIR PETER TEAZLE'S *House.*

Enter SIR PETER *and* LADY TEAZLE.

Sir Peter. Lady Teazle, Lady Teazle, I'll not bear it!

Lady Teazle. Sir Peter, Sir Peter, you may bear it or not as you please; but I ought to have my own way in everything, and what's more, I will too. What though I was educated in the country, I know very well that women of fashion in London are accountable to nobody after they are married.

Sir Peter. Very well, ma'am, very well; so a husband is to have no influence, no authority?

Lady Teazle. Authority! No, to be sure. If you wanted authority over me, you should have adopted me and not married me: I am sure you were old enough.

Sir Peter. Old enough! ay, there it is! Well, well, Lady Teazle, though my life may be made unhappy by your temper, I'll not be ruined by your extravagance!

Lady Teazle. My extravagance! I'm sure I'm not more extravagant than a woman of fashion ought to be.

Sir Peter. No, no, madam, you shall throw away no more sums on such unmeaning luxury. 'Slife! to spend as much to furnish your dressing-room with flowers in winter as would suffice to turn the Pantheon[10] into a greenhouse, and give a *fête champêtre*[11] at Christmas.

Lady Teazle. And am I to blame, Sir Peter, because flowers are dear in cold weather? You should find fault with the climate, and not with me. For my part, I'm sure I wish it was spring all the year round and that roses grew under our feet!

Sir Peter. Oons! madam—if you had been born to this, I shouldn't wonder at your talking thus; but you forget what your situation was when I married you.

Lady Teazle. No, no, I don't; 'twas a very disagreeable one, or I should never have married you.

Sir Peter. Yes, yes, madam, you were then in somewhat a humbler style—the daughter of a plain country squire. Recollect, Lady Teazle, when I saw you first sitting at your tambour[12] in a pretty figured linen gown with a bunch of keys at your side, your hair combed smooth over a roll and your apartment hung round with fruits in worsted of your own working.

Lady Teazle. Oh, yes! I remember it very well, and a curious life I led. My daily occupation to inspect the dairy, superintend the poultry, make extracts from the family receipt-book, and comb my aunt Deborah's lapdog.

Sir Peter. Yes, yes, ma'am, 'twas so indeed.

Lady Teazle. And then, you know, my evening amusements! To draw patterns for ruffles, which I had not the materials to make up; to play Pope Joan[13] with the Curate; to read a sermon to my aunt; or to be stuck down to an old spinet to strum my father to sleep after a fox-chase.

Sir Peter. I am glad you have so good a memory. Yes, madam, these were the recreations I took you from; but now you must have your coach—*vis-à-vis*[14]—and three powdered footmen before your chair; and, in the summer, a pair of white cats[15] to draw you to Kensington Gardens. No recollection, I suppose, when you were content to ride double, behind the butler, on a docked coach-horse?

Lady Teazle. No—I swear I never did that; I deny the butler and the coach-horse.

Sir Peter. This, madam, was your situation; and what have I done for you? I have made you a woman of fashion, of fortune, of rank—in short, I have made you my wife.

Lady Teazle. Well, then, and there is but one thing more you can make me to add to the obligation, that is——

Sir Peter. My widow, I suppose?

Lady Teazle. Hem! hem!

Sir Peter. I thank you, madam—but don't flatter yourself; for, though your ill-conduct may disturb my peace it shall never break my heart, I promise you. However, I am equally obliged to you for the hint.

Lady Teazle. Then why will you endeavor to make yourself so disagreeable to me and thwart me in every little elegant expense?

Sir Peter. 'Slife, madam, I say; had you any of these little elegant expenses when you married me?

Lady Teazle. Lud, Sir Peter! would you have me be out of the fashion?

Sir Peter. The fashion, indeed! what had you to do with the fashion before you married me?

Lady Teazle. For my part, I should think you would like to have your wife thought a woman of taste.

Sir Peter. Ay—there again—taste! Zounds! madam, you had no taste when you married me!

Lady Teazle. That's very true, indeed, Sir Peter! and, after having married you, I should never pretend to taste again, I allow. But now, Sir Peter, since we have finished our daily jangle, I presume I may go to my engagement at Lady Sneerwell's?

Sir Peter. Ay, there's another precious circumstance—a charming set of acquaintance you have made there!

Lady Teazle. Nay, Sir Peter, they are all people of rank and fortune and remarkably tenacious of reputation.

Sir Peter. Yes, egad, they are tenacious of reputation with a vengeance; for they don't choose anybody should have a character but themselves! Such a crew! Ah! many a wretch has rid on a hurdle who has done less mischief than these utterers of forged tales, coiners of scandal, and clippers of reputation.

Lady Teazle. What, would you restrain the freedom of speech?

Sir Peter. Ah! they have made you just as bad as any one of the society.

Lady Teazle. Why, I believe I do bear a part with a tolerable grace. But I vow I bear no malice against the people I abuse: when I say an ill natured thing, 'tis out of pure good humor; and I take it for granted they deal exactly in the same manner with me. But, Sir Peter, you know you promised to come to Lady Sneerwell's too.

Sir Peter. Well, well, I'll call in just to look after my own character.

Lady Teazle. Then, indeed, you must make haste after me or you'll be too late. So goodbye to ye.   *Exit.*

Sir Peter. So—I have gained much by my intended expostulation! Yet with what a charming air she contradicts everything I say, and how pleasantly she shows her contempt for my authority! Well, though I can't make her love me, there is great satisfaction in quarrelling with her; and I think she never appears to such advantage as when she is doing everything in her power to plague me.   *Exit.*

SCENE II: LADY SNEERWELL'S *House.*

LADY SNEERWELL, MRS. CANDOUR, CRABTREE, SIR BENJAMIN BACKBITE, *and* JOSEPH SURFACE.

Lady Sneerwell. Nay, positively, we will hear it.

Joseph Surface. Yes, yes, the epigram, by all means.

Sir Benjamin. O plague on't, uncle! 'tis mere nonsense.

Crabtree. No, no; 'fore gad, very clever for an extempore!

Sir Benjamin. But, ladies, you should be acquainted with the circumstance. You must know, that one day last week as Lady Betty Curricle was taking the dust in Hyde Park, in a sort of duodecimo phaeton, she desired me to write some verses on her ponies; upon which, I took out my pocketbook, and in one moment produced the following:——

Sure never were seen two such beautiful ponies;

Other horses are clowns, but these macaronies:[16]

To give them this title I am sure can't be wrong.

Their legs are so slim, and their tails are so long.

Crabtree. There, ladies, done in the smack of a whip, and on horseback too.

Joseph Surface. A very Phœbus mounted—indeed, Sir Benjamin!

Sir Benjamin. Oh dear, sir!—trifles—trifles.

Enter LADY TEAZLE *and* MARIA.

Mrs. Candour. I must have a copy.

Lady Sneerwell. Lady Teazle, I hope we shall see Sir Peter?

Lady Teazle. I believe he'll wait on your ladyship presently.

Lady Sneerwell. Maria, my love, you look grave. Come, you shall sit down to piquet with Mr. Surface.

Maria. I take very little pleasure in cards—however, I'll do as your ladyship pleases.

Lady Teazle. (*Aside.*) I am surprised Mr. Surface should sit down with her; I thought he would have embraced this opportunity of speaking to me before Sir Peter came.

Mrs. Candour. Now, I'll die; but you are so scandalous, I'll forswear your society.

Lady Teazle. What's the matter, Mrs. Candour?

Mrs. Candour. They'll not allow our friend Miss Vermillion to be handsome.

Lady Sneerwell. Oh, surely she is a pretty woman.

Crabtree. I am very glad you think so, ma'am.

Mrs. Candour. She has a charming fresh color.

Lady Teazle. Yes, when it is fresh put on.

Mrs. Candour. Oh, fie! I'll swear her color is natural: I have seen it come and go!

Lady Teazle. I dare swear you have, ma'am: it goes off at night and comes again in the morning.

Sir Benjamin. True, ma'am, it not only comes and goes; but, what's more, egad, her maid can fetch and carry it!

Mrs. Candour. Ha! ha! ha! how I hate to hear you talk so! But surely, now, her sister is, or was, very handsome.

Crabtree. Who? Mrs. Evergreen? O Lord! she's six-and-fifty if she's an hour!

Mrs. Candour. Now positively you wrong her; fifty-two or fifty-three is the utmost—and I don't think she looks more.

Sir Benjamin. Ah! there's no judging by her looks, unless one could see her face.

Lady Sneerwell. Well, well, if Mrs. Evergreen does take some pains to repair the ravages of time, you must allow she effects it with great ingenuity; and surely that's better than the careless manner in which the widow Ochre caulks her wrinkles.

Sir Benjamin. Nay, now, Lady Sneerwell, you are severe upon the widow. Come, come, 'tis not that she paints so ill —but, when she has finished her face, she joins it on so badly to her neck, that she looks like a mended statue, in which the connoisseur may see at once that the head's modern, though the trunk's antique!

Crabtree. Ha! ha! ha! Well said, nephew!

Mrs. Candour. Ha! ha! ha! Well, you make me laugh; but I vow I hate you for it. What do you think of Miss Simper?

Sir Benjamin. Why, she has very pretty teeth.

Lady Teazle. Yes; and on that account, when she is neither speaking nor laughing (which very seldom happens), she never absolutely shuts her mouth, but leaves it always on ajar, as it were—thus. *(Shows her teeth.)*

Mrs. Candour. How can you be so ill natured?

Lady Teazle. Nay, I allow even that's better than the pains Mrs. Prim takes to conceal her losses in front. She draws her mouth till it positively resembles the aperture of a poor's-box, and all her words appear to slide out edgewise, as it were—thus: *How do you do, madam? Yes, madam.*

Lady Sneerwell. Very well, Lady Teazle; I see you can be a little severe.

Lady Teazle. In defence of a friend it is but justice. But here comes Sir Peter to spoil our pleasantry.

Enter SIR PETER.

Sir Peter. Ladies, your most obedient—*(Aside.)* Mercy on me, here is the whole set! a character dead at every word, I suppose.

Mrs. Candour. I am rejoiced you are come, Sir Peter. They have been so censorious—and Lady Teazle as bad as any one.

Sir Peter. That must be very distressing to you, Mrs. Candour, I dare swear.

Mrs. Candour. Oh, they will allow good qualities to nobody; not even good nature to our friend Mrs. Pursy.

Lady Teazle. What, the fat dowager who was at Mrs. Quadrille's last night.

Mrs. Candour. Nay, her bulk is her misfortune; and, when she takes so much pains to get rid of it, you ought not to reflect on her.

Lady Sneerwell. That's very true, indeed.

Lady Teazle. Yes, I know she almost lives on acids and small whey; laces herself by pulleys; and often, in the hottest noon in summer, you may see her on a little squat pony, with her hair plaited up behind like a drummer's and puffing round the Ring[17] on a full trot.

Mrs. Candour. I thank you, Lady Teazle, for defending her.

Sir Peter. Yes, a good defence, truly.

Mrs. Candour. Truly, Lady Teazle is as censorious as Miss Sallow.

Crabtree. Yes, and she is a curious being to pretend to be censorious—an awkward gawky, without any one good point under heaven.

Mrs. Candour. Positively you shall not be so very severe. Miss Sallow is a near relation of mine by marriage, and, as for her person, great allowance is to be made; for, let me tell you, a woman labors under many disadvantages who tries to pass for a girl of six-and-thirty.

Lady Sneerwell. Though, surely, she is handsome still—and for the weakness in her eyes, considering how much she reads by candlelight, it is not to be wondered at.

Mrs. Candour. True; and then as to her manner, upon my word, I think it is particularly graceful, considering she never had the least education; for you know her mother was a Welsh milliner, and her father a sugar-baker at Bristol.

Sir Benjamin. Ah! you are both of you too good natured!

Sir Peter. (*Aside.*) Yes, damned good natured! This their own relation! mercy on me!

Mrs. Candour. For my part, I own I cannot bear to hear a friend ill spoken of.

Sir Peter. No, to be sure.

Sir Benjamin. Oh! you are of a moral turn. Mrs. Candour and I can sit for an hour and hear Lady Stucco talk sentiment.

Lady Teazle. Nay, I vow Lady Stucco is very well with the dessert after dinner; for she's just like the French fruit[18] one cracks for mottoes—made up of paint and proverb.

Mrs. Candour. Well, I will never join in ridiculing a friend; and so I constantly tell my cousin Ogle, and you all know what pretensions she has to be critical on beauty.

Crabtree. Oh, to be sure! she has herself the oddest countenance that ever was seen; 'tis a collection of features from all the different countries of the globe.

Sir Benjamin. So she has, indeed—an Irish front——

Crabtree. Caledonian locks——

Sir Benjamin. Dutch nose——

Crabtree. Austrian lips——

Sir Benjamin. Complexion of a Spaniard——

Crabtree. And teeth *à la Chinoise*——

Sir Benjamin. In short, her face resembles a *table d'hôte* at Spa—where no two guests are of a nation——

Crabtree. Or a congress at the close of a general war—wherein all the members, even to her eyes, appear to have a different interest, and her nose and chin are the only parties likely to join issue.

Mrs. Candour. Ha! ha! ha!

Sir Peter. (*Aside.*) Mercy on my life!—a person they dine with twice a week!

Lady Sneerwell. Go—go—you are a couple of provoking toads.

Mrs. Candour. Nay, but I vow you shall not carry the laugh off so—for give me leave to say, that Mrs. Ogle——

Sir Peter. Madam, madam, I beg your pardon—there's no stopping these good gentlemen's tongues. But when I tell you, Mrs. Candour, that the lady they are abusing is a particular friend of mine, I hope you'll not take her part.

Lady Sneerwell. Ha! ha! ha! well said, Sir Peter! but you are a cruel creature—too phlegmatic yourself for a jest, and too peevish to allow wit in others.

Sir Peter. Ah, madam, true wit is more nearly allied to good nature than your ladyship is aware of.

Lady Teazle. True, Sir Peter: I believe they are so near akin that they can never be united.

Sir Benjamin. Or rather, madam, I suppose them man and wife because one seldom sees them together.

Lady Teazle. But Sir Peter is such an enemy to scandal, I believe he would have it put down by Parliament.

Sir Peter. 'Fore heaven, madam, if they were to consider the sporting with reputation of as much importance as poaching on manors, and pass an act for the preservation of fame, I believe many would thank them for the bill.

Lady Sneerwell. O Lud! Sir Peter; would you deprive us of our privileges?

Sir Peter. Ay, madam; and then no person should be permitted to kill characters and run down reputations, but qualified old maids and disappointed widows.

Lady Sneerwell. Go, you monster!

Mrs. Candour. But, surely, you would not be quite so severe on those who only report what they hear?

Sir Peter. Yes, madam, I would have law merchant[19] for them too; and in all cases of slander currency, whenever the drawer of the lie was not to be found, the injured parties should have a right to come on any of the indorsers.

Crabtree. Well, for my part, I believe there never was a scandalous tale without some foundation.

Lady Sneerwell. Come, ladies, shall we sit down to cards in the next room?

Enter SERVANT, *who whispers* SIR PETER.

Sir Peter. I'll be with them directly.—(*Exit* SERVANT.) (*Aside.*) I'll get away unperceived.

Lady Sneerwell. Sir Peter, you are not going to leave us?

Sir Peter. Your ladyships must excuse me: I'm called away

by particular business. But I leave my character behind me.

Exit.

Sir Benjamin. Well—certainly, Lady Teazle, that lord of yours is a strange being. I could tell you some stories of him would make you laugh heartily if he were not your husband.

Lady Teazle. Oh, pray don't mind that; come, do let's hear them. *(Exeunt all but* JOSEPH SURFACE *and* MARIA.)

Joseph Surface. Maria, I see you have no satisfaction in this society.

Maria. How is it possible I should? If to raise malicious smiles at the infirmities or misfortunes of those who have never injured us be the province of wit or humor, Heaven grant me a double portion of dullness!

Joseph Surface. Yet they appear more ill natured than they are; they have no malice at heart.

Maria. Then is their conduct still more contemptible; for, in my opinion, nothing could excuse the intemperance of their tongues but a natural and uncontrollable bitterness of mind.

Joseph Surface. Undoubtedly, madam; and it has always been a sentiment of mine that to propagate a malicious truth wantonly is more despicable than to falsify from revenge. But can you, Maria, feel thus for others, and be unkind to me alone? Is hope to be denied the tenderest passion?

Maria. Why will you distress me by renewing this subject?

Joseph Surface. Ah, Maria! you would not treat me thus, and oppose your guardian, Sir Peter's will, but that I see that profligate Charles is still a favored rival.

Maria. Ungenerously urged! But whatever my sentiments are for that unfortunate young man, be assured I shall not feel more bound to give him up, because his distresses have lost him the regard even of a brother.

Joseph Surface. Nay, but, Maria, do not leave me with a frown: by all that's honest, I swear—— *(Kneels.)*

Enter LADY TEAZLE.

(Aside.) Gad's life, here's Lady Teazle.—*(Aloud to* MARIA.) You must not—no, you shall not—for, though I have the greatest regard for Lady Teazle——

Maria. Lady Teazle!

Joseph Surface. Yet were Sir Peter to suspect——

Lady Teazle. (Coming forward.) What is this, pray? Do you take her for me?—Child, you are wanted in the next room.—*(Exit* MARIA.*)* What is all this, pray?

Joseph Surface. Oh, the most unlucky circumstance in nature! Maria has somehow suspected the tender concern I have for your happiness, and threatened to acquaint Sir Peter with her suspicions, and I was just endeavoring to reason with her when you came in.

Lady Teazle. Indeed! but you seemed to adopt a very tender mode of reasoning—do you usually argue on your knees?

Joseph Surface. Oh, she's a child and I thought a little bombast——but, Lady Teazle, when are you to give me your judgment on my library, as you promised?

Lady Teazle. No, no; I begin to think it would be imprudent, and you know I admit you as a lover no farther than fashion requires.

Joseph Surface.—True—a mere Platonic *cicisbeo*,[20] what every wife is entitled to.

Lady Teazle. Certainly, one must not be out of the fashion. However, I have so many of my country prejudices left that, though Sir Peter's ill humor may vex me ever so, it never shall provoke me to——

Joseph Surface. The only revenge in your power. Well, I applaud your moderation.

Lady Teazle. Go—you are an insinuating wretch! But we shall be missed—let us join the company.

Joseph Surface. But we had best not return together.

Lady Teazle. Well, don't stay; for Maria shan't come to hear any more of your reasoning, I promise you.   *Exit.*

Joseph Surface. A curious dilemma, truly, my politics have run me into! I wanted, at first, only to ingratiate myself with Lady Teazle, that she might not be my enemy with Maria; and I have, I don't know how, become her serious lover. Sincerely I begin to wish I had never made such a point of gaining so very good a character; for it has led me into so many cursed rogueries that I doubt I shall be exposed at last.
Exit.

SCENE III: SIR PETER TEAZLE'S *House.*

Enter SIR OLIVER SURFACE *and* ROWLEY.

Sir Oliver. Ha! ha! ha! so my old friend is married, hey?— a young wife out of the country. Ha! ha! ha! that he should have stood bluff[21] to old bachelor so long and sink into a husband at last!

Rowley. But you must not rally him on the subject, Sir Oliver; 'tis a tender point, I assure you, though he has been married only seven months.

Sir Oliver. Then he has been just half a year on the stool of repentance!—Poor Peter! But you say he has entirely given up Charles—never sees him, hey?

Rowley. His prejudice against him is astonishing, and I am sure greatly increased by a jealousy of him with Lady Teazle, which he has industriously been led into by a scandalous society in the neighborhood, who have contributed not a little to Charles's ill name. Whereas the truth is, I believe, if the lady is partial to either of them, his brother is the favorite.

Sir Oliver. Ay, I know there are a set of malicious, prating, prudent gossips, both male and female, who murder characters to kill time, and will rob a young fellow of his good name before he has years to know the value of it. But I am not to be prejudiced against my nephew by such, I promise you! No, no; if Charles has done nothing false or mean, I shall compound for his extravagance.

Rowley. Then, my life on't, you will reclaim him. Ah, sir, it gives me new life to find that your heart is not turned against him, and that the son of my good old master has one friend, however, left.

Sir Oliver. What! shall I forget, Master Rowley, when I was at his years myself? Egad, my brother and I were neither of us very prudent youths; and yet, I believe, you have not seen many better men than your old master was?

Rowley. Sir, 'tis this reflection gives me assurance that Charles may yet be a credit to his family. But here comes Sir Peter.

Sir Oliver. Egad, so he does! Mercy on me, he's greatly altered, and seems to have a settled married look! One may read *husband* in his face at this distance!

Enter SIR PETER.

Sir Peter. Ha! Sir Oliver—my old friend! Welcome to England a thousand times!

Sir Oliver. Thank you, thank you, Sir Peter! and i'faith I am glad to find you well, believe me!

Sir Peter. Oh! 'tis a long time since we met—fifteen years, I doubt, Sir Oliver, and many a cross accident in the time.

Sir Oliver. Ay, I have had my share. But, what! I find you are married, hey, my old boy? Well, well, it can't be helped; and so—I wish you joy with all my heart!

Sir Peter. Thank you, thank you, Sir Oliver.—Yes, I have entered into—the happy state; but we'll not talk of that now.

Sir Oliver. True, true, Sir Peter; old friends should not begin on grievances at first meeting. No, no, no.

Rowley. (*Aside to* SIR OLIVER.) Take care, pray, sir.

Sir Oliver. Well, so one of my nephews is a wild rogue, hey?

Sir Peter. Wild! Ah! my old friend, I grieve for your disappointment there; he's a lost young man, indeed. However, his brother will make you amends; Joseph is, indeed, what a youth should be—everybody in the world speaks well of him.

Sir Oliver. I am sorry to hear it; he has too good a character to be an honest fellow. Everybody speaks well of him! Psha! then he has bowed as low to knaves and fools as to the honest dignity of genius and virtue.

Sir Peter. What, Sir Oliver! do you blame him for not making enemies?

Sir Oliver. Yes, if he has merit enough to deserve them.

Sir Peter. Well, well—you'll be convinced when you know him. 'Tis edification to hear him converse; he professes the noblest sentiments.

Sir Oliver. Oh, plague of his sentiments! If he salutes me with a scrap of morality in his mouth, I shall be sick directly. But, however, don't mistake me, Sir Peter; I don't mean to defend Charles's errors: but, before I form my judgment of either of them, I intend to make a trial of their hearts; and my friend Rowley and I have planned something for the purpose.

Rowley. And Sir Peter shall own for once he has been mistaken.

Sir Peter. Oh, my life on Joseph's honor!

Sir Oliver. Well—come, give us a bottle of good wine, and we'll drink the lads' health and tell you our scheme.

Sir Peter. Allons, then!

Sir Oliver. And don't, Sir Peter, be so severe against your old friend's son. Odds my life! I am not sorry that he has run out of the course a little. For my part, I hate to see prudence clinging to the green suckers of youth; 'tis like ivy round a sapling, and spoils the growth of the tree.   *Exeunt.*

ACT III

Scene I: Sir Peter Teazle's *House.*

Enter Sir Peter Teazle, Sir Oliver Surface, *and* Rowley.

Sir Peter. Well, then, we will see this fellow first and have our wine afterwards. But how is this, Master Rowley? I don't see the jet of your scheme.

Rowley. Why, sir, this Mr. Stanley, whom I was speaking of, is nearly related to them by their mother. He was once a merchant in Dublin, but has been ruined by a series of undeserved misfortunes. He has applied, by letter, since his confinement, both to Mr. Surface and Charles. From the former he has received nothing but evasive promises of future service, while Charles has done all that his extravagance has left him power to do; and he is, at this time, endeavoring to raise a sum of money, part of which, in the midst of his own distresses, I know he intends for the service of poor Stanley.

Sir Oliver. Ah, he is my brother's son.

Sir Peter. Well, but how is Sir Oliver personally to——

Rowley. Why, sir, I will inform Charles and his brother that Stanley has obtained permission to apply personally to his friends; and, as they have neither of them ever seen him, let Sir Oliver assume his character, and he will have a fair opportunity of judging, at least, of the benevolence of their dispositions; and believe me, sir, you will find in the youngest brother one who, in the midst of folly and dissipation, has still, as our immortal bard expresses it,—

> a tear for pity, and a hand
> Open as day, for melting charity.[22]

Sir Peter. Psha! What signifies his having an open hand or purse either, when he has nothing left to give? Well, well, make the trial, if you please. But where is the fellow whom you brought for Sir Oliver to examine relative to Charles's affairs?

Rowley. Below, waiting his commands, and no one can give him better intelligence.—This, Sir Oliver, is a friendly Jew, who, to do him justice, has done everything in his power to bring your nephew to a proper sense of his extravagance.

Sir Peter. Pray let us have him in.

Rowley. *(Calls to* SERVANT.*)* Desire Mr. Moses to walk upstairs.

Sir Peter. But, pray, why should you suppose he will speak the truth?

Rowley. Oh, I have convinced him that he has no chance of recovering certain sums advanced to Charles but through the bounty of Sir Oliver, who he knows is arrived; so that you may depend on his fidelity to his own interests. I have also another evidence in my power, one Snake, whom I have detected in a matter little short of forgery and shall shortly produce to remove some of your prejudices, Sir Peter, relative to Charles and Lady Teazle.

Sir Peter. I have heard too much on that subject.

Rowley. Here comes the honest Israelite.

Enter MOSES.

—This is Sir Oliver.

Sir Oliver. Sir, I understand you have lately had great dealings with my nephew Charles.

Moses. Yes, Sir Oliver, I have done all I could for him; but he was ruined before he came to me for assistance.

Sir Oliver. That was unlucky, truly; for you have had no opportunity of showing your talents.

Moses. None at all; I hadn't the pleasure of knowing his distresses till he was some thousands worse than nothing.

Sir Oliver. Unfortunate, indeed! But I suppose you have done all in your power for him, honest Moses?

Moses. Yes, he knows that. This very evening I was to have brought him a gentleman from the city, who does not know him, and will, I believe, advance him some money.

Sir Peter. What, one Charles has never had money from before?

Moses. Yes, Mr. Premium, of Crutched Friars, formerly a broker.

Sir Peter. Egad, Sir Oliver, a thought strikes me!—Charles, you say, does not know Mr. Premium?

Moses. Not at all.

Sir Peter. Now then, Sir Oliver, you may have a better opportunity of satisfying yourself than by an old romancing tale of a poor relation. Go with my friend Moses and represent Premium, and then, I'll answer for it, you'll see your nephew in all his glory.

Sir Oliver. Egad, I like this idea better than the other and I may visit Joseph afterwards as old Stanley.

Sir Peter. True—so you may.

Rowley. Well, this is taking Charles rather at a disadvantage, to be sure. However, Moses, you understand Sir Peter, and will be faithful.

Moses. You may depend upon me.—This is near the time I was to have gone.

Sir Oliver. I'll accompany you as soon as you please, Moses——But hold! I have forgot one thing—how the plague shall I be able to pass for a Jew?

Moses. There's no need—the principal is Christian.

Sir Oliver. Is he? I'm very sorry to hear it. But, then again, an't I rather too smartly dressed to look like a money-lender?

Sir Peter. Not at all; 'twould not be out of character, if you went in your carriage—would it, Moses?

Moses. Not in the least.

Sir Oliver. Well, but how must I talk? there's certainly some cant of usury and mode of treating that I ought to know.

Sir Peter. Oh, there's not much to learn. The great point, as I take it, is to be exorbitant enough in your demands. Hey, Moses?

Moses. Yes, that's a very great point.

Sir Oliver. I'll answer for't I'll not be wanting in that. I'll ask him eight or ten per cent. on the loan, at least.

Moses. If you ask him no more than that, you'll be discovered immediately.

Sir Oliver. Hey! what, the plague! how much then?

Moses. That depends upon the circumstances. If he appears not very anxious for the supply, you should require only forty or fifty per cent.; but if you find him in great distress, and want the moneys very bad, you may ask double.

Sir Peter. A good honest trade you're learning, Sir Oliver!

Sir Oliver. Truly I think so—and not unprofitable.

Moses. Then, you know, you haven't the moneys yourself, but are forced to borrow them for him of a friend.

Sir Oliver. Oh! I borrow it of a friend, do I?

Moses. And your friend is an unconscionable dog: but you can't help that.

Sir Oliver. My friend an unconscionable dog, is he?

Moses. Yes, and he himself has not the moneys by him, but is forced to sell stocks at a great loss.

Sir Oliver. He is forced to sell stocks at a great loss, is he? Well, that's very kind of him.

Sir Peter. I'faith, Sir Oliver—Mr. Premium, I mean—you'll soon be master of the trade. But, Moses! would not you have him run out a little against the Annuity Bill?[23] That would be in character, I should think.

Moses. Very much.

Rowley. And lament that a young man now must be at years of discretion before he is suffered to ruin himself?

Moses. Ay, great pity!

Sir Peter. And abuse the public for allowing merit to an act whose only object is to snatch misfortune and imprudence from the rapacious grip of usury, and give the minor a chance of inheriting his estate without being undone by coming into possession.

Sir Oliver. So, so—Moses shall give me further instructions as we go together.

Sir Peter. You will not have much time, for your nephew lives hard by.

Sir Oliver. Oh, never fear! my tutor appears so able, that though Charles lived in the next street, it must be my own fault if I am not a complete rogue before I turn the corner.

(Exit with Moses.)

Sir Peter. So, now, I think Sir Oliver will be convinced;

you are partial, Rowley, and would have prepared Charles for the other plot.

Rowley. No, upon my word, Sir Peter.

Sir Peter. Well, go bring me this Snake, and I'll hear what he has to say presently. I see Maria and want to speak with her.—*(Exit* ROWLEY.*)* I should be glad to be convinced my suspicions of Lady Teazle and Charles were unjust. I have never yet opened my mind on this subject to my friend Joseph—I am determined I will do it—he will give me his opinion sincerely.

Enter MARIA.

So, child, has Mr. Surface returned with you?

Maria. No, sir; he was engaged.

Sir Peter. Well, Maria, do you not reflect, the more you converse with that amiable young man, what return his partiality for you deserves?

Maria. Indeed, Sir Peter, your frequent importunity on this subject distresses me extremely—you compel me to declare, that I know no man who has ever paid me a particular attention whom I would not prefer to Mr. Surface.

Sir Peter. So—here's perverseness! No, no, Maria, 'tis Charles only whom you would prefer. 'Tis evident his vices and follies have won your heart.

Maria. This is unkind, sir. You know I have obeyed you in neither seeing nor corresponding with him: I have heard enough to convince me that he is unworthy my regard. Yet I cannot think it culpable, if, while my understanding severely condemns his vices, my heart suggests some pity for his distresses.

Sir Peter. Well, well, pity him as much as you please; but give your heart and hand to a worthier object.

Maria. Never to his brother!

Sir Peter. Go, perverse and obstinate! But take care, madam; you have never yet known what the authority of a guardian is. Don't compel me to inform you of it.

Maria. I can only say, you shall not have just reason. 'Tis true, by my father's will, I am for a short period bound to regard you as his substitute; but must cease to think you so, when you would compel me to be miserable. *Exit.*

Sir Peter. Was ever man so crossed as I am, everything conspiring to fret me! I had not been involved in matrimony a fortnight, before her father, a hale and hearty man, died, on purpose, I believe, for the pleasure of plaguing me with the care of his daughter.—(LADY TEAZLE *sings without.*)

But here comes my helpmate! She appears in great good humor. How happy I should be if I could tease her into loving me, though but a little!

Enter LADY TEAZLE.

Lady Teazle. Lud! Sir Peter, I hope you haven't been quarrelling with Maria? It is not using me well to be ill humored when I am not by.

Sir Peter. Ah, Lady Teazle, you might have the power to make me good humored at all times.

Lady Teazle. I am sure I wish I had; for I want you to be in a charming sweet temper at this moment. Do be good humored now, and let me have two hundred pounds, will you?

Sir Peter. Two hundred pounds; what, an't I to be in a good humor without paying for it! But speak to me thus, and i'faith there's nothing I could refuse you. You shall have it; but seal me a bond for the repayment.

Lady Teazle. Oh, no—there—my note of hand will do as well.   *(Offering her hand.)*

Sir Peter. And you shall no longer reproach me with not giving you an independent settlement. I mean shortly to surprise you; but shall we always live thus, hey?

Lady Teazle. If you please; I'm sure I don't care how soon we leave off quarrelling, provided you'll own you were tired first.

Sir Peter. Well—then let our future contest be, who shall be most obliging.

Lady Teazle. I assure you, Sir Peter, good nature becomes you. You look now as you did before we were married, when you used to walk with me under the elms, and tell me stories of what a gallant you were in your youth, and chuck me under the chin, you would; and ask me if I thought I could love an old fellow who would deny me nothing—didn't you?

Sir Peter. Yes, yes, and you were as kind and attentive——

Lady Teazle. Ay, so I was, and would always take your part, when my acquaintance used to abuse you, and turn you into ridicule.

Sir Peter. Indeed!

Lady Teazle. Ay, and when my cousin Sophy has called you a stiff, peevish old bachelor, and laughed at me for thinking of marrying one who might be my father, I have always defended you, and said, I didn't think you so ugly by any means, and that I dared say you'd make a very good sort of a husband.

Sir Peter. And you prophesied right; and we shall now be the happiest couple——

Lady Teazle. And never differ again?

Sir Peter. No, never—though at the same time, indeed, my dear Lady Teazle, you must watch your temper very seriously; for in all our little quarrels, my dear, if you recollect, my love, you always began first.

Lady Teazle. I beg your pardon, my dear Sir Peter: indeed, you always gave the provocation.

Sir Peter. Now, see, my angel! take care—contradicting isn't the way to keep friends.

Lady Teazle. Then, don't you begin it, my love!

Sir Peter. There, now! you—you are going on. You don't perceive, my life, that you are just doing the very thing which you know always makes me angry.

Lady Teazle. Nay, you know if you will be angry without any reason, my dear——

Sir Peter. There! now you want to quarrel again.

Lady Teazle. No, I'm sure I don't; but, if you will be so peevish——

Sir Peter. There now! who begins first?

Lady Teazle. Why, you, to be sure. I said nothing—but there's no bearing your temper.

Sir Peter. No, no, madam: the fault's in your own temper.

Lady Teazle. Ay, you are just what my cousin Sophy said you would be.

Sir Peter. Your cousin Sophy is a forward, impertinent gipsy.

Lady Teazle. You are a great bear, I am sure, to abuse my relations.

Sir Peter. Now may all the plagues of marriage be doubled on me if ever I try to be friends with you any more!

Lady Teazle. So much the better.

Sir Peter. No, no, madam. 'Tis evident you never cared a pin for me, and I was a madman to marry you—a pert, rural coquette, that had refused half the honest 'squires in the neighborhood!

Lady Teazle. And I am sure I was a fool to marry you— an old dangling bachelor, who was single at fifty, only because he never could meet with any one who would have him.

Sir Peter. Ay, ay, madam; but you were pleased enough to listen to me: you never had such an offer before.

Lady Teazle. No! didn't I refuse Sir Tivy Terrier, who everybody said would have been a better match? for his estate is just as good as yours, and he has broke his neck since we have been married.

Sir Peter. I have done with you, madam! You are an un-feeling, ungrateful—but there's an end of everything. I believe you capable of everything that is bad. Yes, madam, I now believe the reports relative to you and Charles, madam. Yes, madam, you and Charles are, not without grounds——

Lady Teazle. Take care, Sir Peter! you had better not insinuate any such thing! I'll not be suspected without cause, I promise you.

Sir Peter. Very well, madam! very well! a separate maintenance as soon as you please. Yes, madam, or a divorce! I'll make an example of myself for the benefit of all old bachelors. Let us separate, madam.

Lady Teazle. Agreed! agreed! And now, my dear Sir Peter, we are of a mind once more, we may be the happiest couple, and never differ again, you know: ha! ha! ha! Well, you are going to be in a passion, I see, and I shall only interrupt you—so, bye! bye!   *Exit.*

Sir Peter. Plagues and tortures! can't I make her angry either! Oh, I am the most miserable fellow! But I'll not bear her presuming to keep her temper: no! she may break my heart, but she shan't keep her temper.   *Exit.*

SCENE II: CHARLES SURFACE'S *House.*

Enter TRIP, MOSES, *and* SIR OLIVER SURFACE.

Trip. Here, Master Moses! if you'll stay a moment; I'll try whether—what's the gentleman's name?

Sir Oliver. (*Aside to* MOSES.) Mr. Moses, what is my name?

Moses. Mr. Premium.

Trip. Premium—very well.   *Exit, taking snuff.*

Sir Oliver. To judge by the servants, one wouldn't believe the master was ruined. But what!—sure, this was my brother's house?

Moses. Yes, sir; Mr. Charles bought it of Mr. Joseph, with the furniture, pictures, &c., just as the old gentleman left it. Sir Peter thought it a piece of extravagance in him.

Sir Oliver. In my mind, the other's economy in selling it to him was more reprehensible by half.

Re-enter TRIP.

Trip. My master says you must wait, gentlemen: he has company, and can't speak with you yet.

Sir Oliver. If he knew who it was wanted to see him, perhaps he would not send such a message?

Trip. Yes, yes, sir; he knows you are here—I did not forget little Premium: no, no, no.

Sir Oliver. Very well; and I pray, sir, what may be your name?

Trip. Trip, sir; my name is Trip, at your service.

Sir Oliver. Well, then, Mr. Trip, you have a pleasant sort of place here, I guess?

Trip. Why, yes—here are three or four of us to pass our time agreeably enough; but then our wages are sometimes a little in arrear—and not very great either—but fifty pounds a year, and find our own bags and bouquets.[24]

Sir Oliver. (*Aside.*) Bags and bouquets! halters and bastinadoes!

Trip. And *à propos*, Moses, have you been able to get me that little bill discounted?

Sir Oliver. (*Aside.*) Wants to raise money, too!—mercy on me! Has his distresses too, I warrant, like a lord, and affects creditors and duns.

Moses. 'Twas not to be done, indeed, Mr. Trip.

Trip. Good lack, you surprise me! My friend Brush has indorsed it, and I thought when he put his name at the back of a bill 'twas the same as cash.

Moses. No, 'twouldn't do.

Trip. A small sum—but twenty pounds. Hark'ee, Moses, do you think you couldn't get it me by way of annuity?

Sir Oliver. (*Aside.*) An annuity! ha! ha! a footman raise money by way of annuity. Well done, luxury, egad!

Moses. Well, but you must insure your place.

Trip. Oh, with all my heart! I'll insure my place and my life too, if you please.

Sir Oliver. (*Aside.*) It's more than I would your neck.

Moses. But is there nothing you could deposit?

Trip. Why, nothing capital of my master's wardrobe has dropped lately; but I could give you a mortgage on some of his winter clothes, with equity of redemption before November—or you shall have the reversion of the French velvet, or a post-obit[25] on the blue and silver. These, I should think, Moses, with a few pair of point ruffles, as a collateral security—hey, my little fellow?

Moses. Well, well.   (*Bell rings.*)

Trip. Egad. I heard the bell! I believe, gentlemen, I can now introduce you. Don't forget the annuity, little Moses! This way, gentlemen, I'll insure my place, you know.

Sir Oliver. (*Aside.*) If the man be a shadow of the master, this is the temple of dissipation indeed!   *Exeunt.*

SCENE III: *Another Room.*

CHARLES SURFACE, CARELESS, &c., &c.,
at a table with wine, &c.

Charles Surface. 'Fore heaven, 'tis true! there's the great degeneracy of the age. Many of our acquaintance have taste, spirit, and politeness; but plague on't they won't drink.

Careless. It is so, indeed, Charles! they give in to all the substantial luxuries of the table, and abstain from nothing but wine and wit. Oh, certainly society suffers by it intolerably! for now, instead of the social spirit of raillery that used to mantle over a glass of bright Burgundy, their conversation is become just like the Spa-water they drink, which has all the pertness and flatulency of champagne, without its spirit or flavor.

1 Gent. But what are they to do who love play better than wine?

Careless. True! there's Sir Harry diets himself for gaming, and is now under a hazard regimen.

Charles Surface. Then he'll have the worst of it. What! you wouldn't train a horse for the course by keeping him from corn? For my part, egad, I'm never so successful as when I am a little merry. Let me throw on a bottle of champagne and I never lose—at least I never feel my losses, which is exactly the same thing.

2 Gent. Ay, that I believe.

Charles Surface. And then, what man can pretend to be a believer in love who is an abjurer of wine? 'Tis the test by which the lover knows his own heart. Fill a dozen bumpers to a dozen beauties, and she that floats at the top is the maid that has bewitched you.

Careless. Now then, Charles, be honest, and give us your real favorite.

Charles Surface. Why, I have withheld her only in compassion to you. If I toast her, you must give her a round of her peers, which is impossible—on earth.

Careless. Oh, then we'll find some canonized vestals or heathen goddesses that will do, I warrant!

Charles Surface. Here then, bumpers, you rogues! bumpers! Maria! Maria—

Sir Toby. Maria who?

Charles Surface. Oh, damn the surname!—'tis too formal to be registered in Love's calendar—but now, Sir Toby, beware, we must have beauty superlative.

266

Careless. Nay, never study, Sir Toby: we'll stand to the toast, though your mistress should want an eye, and you know you have a song will excuse you.

Sir Toby. Egad, so I have! and I'll give him the song instead of the lady. *(Sings.)*

> Here's to the maiden of bashful fifteen;
>   Here's to the widow of fifty;
> Here's to the flaunting extravagant quean,[26]
>   And here's to the housewife that's thrifty.
>
> *Chorus.*   Let the toast pass,
>   Drink to the lass,
> I'll warrant she'll prove an excuse for a glass!
>
> Here's to the charmer whose dimples we prize;
>   Now to the maid who has none, sir;
> Here's to the girl with a pair of blue eyes,
>   And here's to the nymph with but one, sir.
>
> *Chorus.*   Let the toast pass,
>   Drink to the lass,
> I'll warrant she'll prove an excuse for a glass.
>
> Here's to the maid with a bosom of snow;
>   Now to her that's as brown as a berry;
> Here's to the wife with a face full of woe,
>   And now to the damsel that's merry.
>
> *Chorus.*   Let the toast pass,
>   Drink to the lass,
> I'll warrant she'll prove an excuse for a glass.
>
> For let 'em be clumsy, or let 'em be slim,
>   Young or ancient, I care not a feather;
> So fill a pint bumper quite up to the brim,
>   And let us e'en toast them together.
>
> *Chorus.*   Let the toast pass,
>   Drink to the lass,
> I'll warrant she'll prove an excuse for a glass.

All. Bravo! Bravo!

Enter TRIP, *and whispers* CHARLES SURFACE.

Charles Surface. Gentlemen, you must excuse me a little. Careless, take the chair, will you?

Careless. Nay, prithee, Charles, what now? This is one of

your peerless beauties, I suppose, has dropped in by chance?

Charles Surface. No, faith! To tell you the truth, 'tis a Jew and a broker, who are come by appointment.

Careless. Oh, damn it! let's have the Jew in.

1 Gent. Ay, and the broker too, by all means.

2 Gent. Yes, yes, the Jew and the broker!

Charles Surface. Egad, with all my heart!—Trip, bid the gentlemen walk in. (*Exit* TRIP.) Though there's one of them a stranger I can tell you.

Careless. Charles, let us give them some generous Burgundy and perhaps they'll grow conscientious.

Charles Surface. Oh, hang 'em, no! wine does but draw forth a man's natural qualities; and to make them drink would only be to whet their knavery.

Enter TRIP, *with* SIR OLIVER SURFACE *and* MOSES.

Charles Surface. So, honest Moses; walk in, pray, Mr. Premium—that's the gentleman's name, isn't it, Moses?

Moses. Yes, sir.

Charles Surface. Set chairs, Trip.—Sit down, Mr. Premium. Glasses, Trip.—Sit down, Moses.—Come, Mr. Premium, I'll give you a sentiment; here's *Success to usury!*—Moses, fill the gentleman a bumper.

Moses. Success to usury!   (*Drinks.*)

Careless. Right, Moses—usury is prudence and industry, and deserves to succeed.

Sir Oliver. Then here's—All the success it deserves!
                                                      (*Drinks.*)

Careless. No, no, that won't do! Mr. Premium, you have demurred at the toast, and must drink it in a pint bumper.

1 Gent. A pint bumper, at least!

Moses. Oh, pray, sir, consider—Mr. Premium's a gentleman.

Careless. And therefore loves good wine.

2 Gent. Give Moses a quart glass—this is mutiny, and a high contempt for the chair.

Careless. Here, now for't! I'll see justice done, to the last drop of my bottle.

Sir Oliver. Nay, pray, gentlemen—I did not expect this usage.

Charles Surface. No, hang it, you shan't; Mr. Premium's a stranger.

Sir Oliver. (*Aside.*) Odd! I wish I was well out of their company.

Careless. Plague on 'em then! if they won't drink, we'll not sit down with them. Come, Toby, the dice are in the next room.—Charles, you'll join us when you have finished your business with the gentlemen?

Charles Surface. I will! I will!—(*Exeunt* GENTLEMEN.) Careless!

Careless. (*Returning.*) Well?

Charles Surface. Perhaps I may want you.

Careless. Oh, you know I am always ready: word, note, or bond, 'tis all the same to me. *Exit.*

Moses. Sir, this is Mr. Premium, a gentleman of the strictest honor and secrecy; and always performs what he undertakes. Mr. Premium, this is——

Charles Surface. Psha! have done. Sir, my friend Moses is a very honest fellow, but a little slow at expression: he'll be an hour giving us our titles. Mr. Premium, the plain state of the matter is this: I am an extravagant young fellow who wants to borrow money; you I take to be a prudent old fellow, who has got money to lend. I am blockhead enough to give fifty per cent sooner than not have it! and you, I presume, are rogue enough to take a hundred if you can get it. Now, sir, you see we are acquainted at once, and may proceed to business without further ceremony.

Sir Oliver. Exceeding frank, upon my word. I see, sir, you are not a man of many compliments.

Charles Surface. Oh, no, sir! plain dealing in business I always think best.

Sir Oliver. Sir, I like you the better for it. However, you are mistaken in one thing. I have no money to lend, but I believe I could procure some of a friend; but then he's an unconscionable dog. Isn't he, Moses? And must sell stock to accommodate you. Mustn't he, Moses?

Moses. Yes, indeed! You know I always speak the truth, and scorn to tell a lie!

Charles Surface. Right. People that speak truth generally do. But these are trifles, Mr. Premium. What! I know money isn't to be bought without paying for't!

Sir Oliver. Well, but what security could you give? You have no land, I suppose?

Charles Surface. Not a mole-hill, nor a twig, but what's in the bough-pots²⁷ out of the window!

Sir Oliver. Nor any stock, I presume?

Charles Surface. Nothing but live stock—and that's only a few pointers and ponies. But pray, Mr. Premium, are you acquainted at all with any of my connections?

Sir Oliver. Why, to say the truth, I am.

Charles Surface. Then you must know that I have a devilish rich uncle in the East Indies, Sir Oliver Surface, from whom I have the greatest expectations?

Sir Oliver. That you have a wealthy uncle, I have heard; but how your expectations will turn out is more, I believe, than you can tell.

Charles Surface. Oh, no!—there can be no doubt. They tell me I'm a prodigious favorite, and that he talks of leaving me everything.

Sir Oliver. Indeed! this is the first I've heard of it.

Charles Surface. Yes, yes, 'tis just so. Moses knows 'tis true; don't you, Moses?

Moses. Oh, yes! I'll swear to't.

Sir Oliver. (*Aside*.) Egad, they'll persuade me presently I'm at Bengal.

Charles Surface. Now I propose, Mr. Premium, if it's agreeable to you, a post-obit on Sir Oliver's life: though at the same time the old fellow has been so liberal with me, that I give you my word, I should be very sorry to hear that anything had happened to him.

Sir Oliver. Not more than I should, I assure you. But the bond you mention happens to be just the worst security you could offer me—for I might live to be a hundred and never see the principal.

Charles Surface. Oh, yes, you would! the moment Sir Oliver dies, you know, you would come on me for the money.

Sir Oliver. Then I believe I should be the most unwelcome dun you ever had in your life.

Charles Surface. What! I suppose you're afraid that Sir Oliver is too good a life?

Sir Oliver. No, indeed I am not; though I have heard he is as hale and healthy as any man of his years in Christendom.

Charles Surface. There again, now, you are misinformed. No, no, the climate has hurt him considerably, poor uncle Oliver. Yes, yes, he breaks apace, I'm told—and is so much altered lately that his nearest relations would not know him.

Sir Oliver. No! Ha! ha! ha! so much altered lately that his nearest relation would not know him! Ha! ha! ha! egad—ha! ha! ha!

Charles Surface. Ha! ha!—you're glad to hear that, little Premium.

Sir Oliver. No, no, I'm not.

Charles Surface. Yes, yes, you are—ha! ha! ha!—you know that mends your chance.

Sir Oliver. But I'm told Sir Oliver is coming over; nay, some say he has actually arrived.

Charles Surface. Psha! sure I must know better than you

whether he's come or not. No, no, rely on't he's at this moment at Calcutta. Isn't he, Moses?

Moses. Oh, yes, certainly.

Sir Oliver. Very true, as you say, you must know better than I, though I have it from a pretty good authority. Haven't I, Moses?

Moses. Yes, most undoubted!

Sir Oliver. But, sir, as I understand you want a few hundreds immediately, is there nothing you could dispose of?

Charles Surface. How do you mean?

Sir Oliver. For instance, now, I have heard that your father left behind him a great quantity of massy old plate.

Charles Surface. O lud, that's gone long ago. Moses can tell you how better than I can.

Sir Oliver. (*Aside.*) Good lack! all the family race-cups and corporation-bowls![28]—(*Aloud.*) Then it was also supposed that his library was one of the most valuable and compact.

Charles Surface. Yes, yes, so it was—vastly too much for a private gentleman. For my part, I was always of a communicative disposition, so I thought it a shame to keep so much knowledge to myself.

Sir Oliver. (*Aside.*) Mercy upon me! learning that had run in the family like an heirloom!—(*Aloud.*) Pray, what has become of the books?

Charles Surface. You must inquire of the auctioneer, Master Premium, for I don't believe even Moses can direct you.

Moses. I know nothing of books.

Sir Oliver. So, so, nothing of the family property left, I suppose?

Charles Surface. Not much, indeed; unless you have a mind to the family pictures. I have got a room full of ancestors above; and if you have a taste for old paintings, egad, you shall have 'em a bargain!

Sir Oliver. Hey! what the devil! sure, you wouldn't sell your forefathers, would you?

Charles Surface. Every man of them, to the best bidder.

Sir Oliver. What! your great-uncles and aunts?

Charles Surface. Ay, and my great-grandfathers and grandmothers too.

Sir Oliver. (*Aside.*) Now I give him up!—(*Aloud.*) What the plague, have you no bowels for your own kindred? Odd's life! do you take me for Shylock in the play, that you would raise money of me on your own flesh and blood?

Charles Surface. Nay, my little broker, don't be angry. What need you care, if you have your money's worth?

Sir Oliver. Well, I'll be the purchaser. I think I can dispose of the family canvas.—(*Aside.*) Oh, I'll never forgive him this! never!

Enter CARELESS.

Careless. Come, Charles, what keeps you?

Charles Surface. I can't come yet. I'faith, we are going to have a sale above stairs; here's little Premium will buy all my ancestors!

Careless. Oh, burn your ancestors!

Charles Surface. No, he may do that afterwards, if he pleases. Stay, Careless, we want you: egad, you shall be auctioneer—so come along with us.

Careless. Oh, have with you, if that's the case. I can handle a hammer as well as a dice box!

Sir Oliver. (*Aside.*) Oh, the profligates!

Charles Surface. Come, Moses, you shall be appraiser, if we want one. Gad's life, little Premium, you don't seem to like the business?

Sir Oliver. Oh, yes, I do, vastly! Ha! ha! ha! yes, yes, I think it a rare joke to sell one's family by auction—ha! ha!—(*Aside.*) Oh, the prodigal!

Charles Surface. To be sure! when a man wants money, where the plague should he get assistance if he can't make free with his own relations?   *Exeunt.*

ACT IV

SCENE I: *Picture Room at* CHARLES'S.

Enter CHARLES SURFACE, SIR OLIVER SURFACE, MOSES, *and* CARELESS.

Charles Surface. Walk in, gentlemen, pray walk in;—here they are, the family of the Surfaces up to the Conquest.

Sir Oliver. And, in my opinion, a goodly collection.

Charles Surface. Ay, ay, these are done in the true spirit of portrait-painting; no *volontière grace* or expression. Not like the works of your modern Raphaels, who give you the strongest resemblance, yet contrive to make your portrait independent of you; so that you may sink the original and not hurt the picture. No, no; the merit of these is the inveterate likeness—all stiff and awkward as the originals, and like nothing in human nature besides.

Sir Oliver. Ah! we shall never see such figures of men again.

Charles Surface. I hope not. Well, you see, Master Premium, what a domestic character I am; here I sit of an evening surrounded by my family. But come, get to your pulpit, Mr. Auctioneer; here's an old gouty chair of my grandfather's will answer the purpose.

Careless. Ay, ay, this will do. But, Charles, I haven't a hammer; and what's an auctioneer without his hammer?

Charles Surface. Egad, that's true. What parchment have we here? Oh, our genealogy in full. Here, Careless, you shall have no common bit of mahogany, here's the family tree for you, you rogue! This shall be your hammer, and now you may knock down my ancestors with their own pedigree.

Sir Oliver. (Aside.) What an unnatural rogue!—an *ex post facto* parricide!

Careless. Yes, yes, here's a list of your generation indeed; —faith, Charles, this is the most convenient thing you could have found for the business, for 'twill not only serve as a hammer, but a catalogue into the bargain. Come, begin— A-going, a-going, a-going!

Charles Surface. Bravo, Careless! Well, here's my great uncle, Sir Richard Raveline, a marvellous good general in his day, I assure you. He served in all the Duke of Marlborough's wars, and got that cut over his eye at the battle of Malplaquet.[29] What say you, Mr. Premium? look at him—there's a hero! not cut out of his feathers, as your modern clipped captains are, but enveloped in wig and regimentals as a general should be. What do you bid?

Moses. Mr. Premium would have you speak.

Charles Surface. Why, then, he shall have him for ten pounds, and I'm sure that's not dear for a staff-officer.

Sir Oliver. (Aside.) Heaven deliver me! his famous uncle Richard for ten pounds!—*(Aloud.)* Very well, sir, I take him at that.

Charles Surface. Careless, knock down my uncle Richard. —Here, now, is a maiden sister of his, my great-aunt Deborah, done by Kneller,[30] in his best manner, and a very formidable likeness. There she is, you see, a shepherdess feeding her flock. You shall have her for five pounds ten—the sheep are worth the money.

Sir Oliver. (Aside.) Ah! poor Deborah! a woman who set such a value on herself!—*(Aloud.)* Five pounds ten—she's mine.

Charles Surface. Knock down my aunt Deborah! Here, now, are two that were a sort of cousins of theirs.—You see, Moses, these pictures were done some time ago, when beaux wore wigs, and the ladies their own hair.

Sir Oliver. Yes, truly, head-dresses appear to have been a little lower in those days.

Charles Surface. Well, take that couple for the same.

Moses. 'Tis a good bargain.

Charles Surface. Careless!—This, now, is a grandfather of my mother's, a learned judge, well known on the western circuit.—What do you rate him at, Moses?

Moses. Four guineas.

Charles Surface. Four guineas! Gad's life, you don't bid me the price of his wig.—Mr. Premium, you have more respect for the wool-sack;[31] do let us knock his Lordship down at fifteen.

Sir Oliver. By all means.

Careless. Gone!

Charles Surface. And there are two brothers of his, William and Walter Blunt, Esquires, both members of Parliament, and noted speakers; and, what's very extraordinary, I believe, this is the first time they were ever bought or sold.

Sir Oliver. That is very extraordinary, indeed! I'll take them at your own price, for the honor of Parliament.

Careless. Well said, little Premium! I'll knock them down at forty.

Charles Surface. Here's a jolly fellow—I don't know what relation, but he was mayor of Manchester: take him at eight pounds.

Sir Oliver. No, no; six will do for the mayor.

Charles Surface. Come, make it guineas, and I'll throw you the two aldermen there into the bargain.

Sir Oliver. They're mine.

Charles Surface. Careless, knock down the mayor and aldermen. But, plague on't! we shall be all day retailing in this manner; do let us deal wholesale: what say you, little Premium? Give me three hundred pounds for the rest of the family in the lump.

Careless. Ay ay, that will be the best way.

Sir Oliver. Well, well, anything to accommodate you; they are mine. But there is one portrait which you have always passed over.

Careless. What, that ill-looking little fellow over the settee?

Sir Oliver. Yes, sir, I mean that; though I don't think him so ill-looking a little fellow, by any means.

Charles Surface. What, that? Oh; that's my uncle Oliver! 'Twas done before he went to India.

Careless. Your uncle Oliver! Gad, then you'll never be

friends, Charles. That, now, to me, is as stern a looking rogue as ever I saw; an unforgiving eye, and a damned disinheriting countenance! an inveterate knave, depend on't. Don't you think so, little Premium?

Sir Oliver. Upon my soul, sir, I do not; I think it is as honest a looking face as any in the room, dead or alive. But I suppose uncle Oliver goes with the rest of the lumber?

Charles Surface. No, hang it! I'll not part with poor Noll. The old fellow has been very good to me, and, egad, I'll keep his picture while I've a room to put it in.

Sir Oliver. (*Aside.*) The rogue's my nephew after all!—(*Aloud.*) But, sir, I have somehow taken a fancy to that picture.

Charles Surface. I'm sorry for't, for you certainly will not have it. Oons, haven't you got enough of them?

Sir Oliver. (*Aside.*) I forgive him everything!—(*Aloud.*) But, sir, when I take a whim in my head, I don't value money. I'll give you as much for that as for all the rest.

Charles Surface. Don't tease me, master broker; I tell you I'll not part with it, and there's an end of it.

Sir Oliver. (*Aside.*) How like his father the dog is!—(*Aloud.*) Well, well, I have done.—(*Aside.*) I did not perceive it before, but I think I never saw such a striking resemblance. —(*Aloud.*) Here is a draught for your sum.

Charles Surface. Why, 'tis for eight hundred pounds!

Sir Oliver. You will not let Sir Oliver go?

Charles Surface. Zounds! no! I tell you, once more.

Sir Oliver. Then never mind the difference, we'll balance that another time. But give me your hand on the bargain; you are an honest fellow, Charles—I beg pardon, sir, for being so free.—Come, Moses.

Charles Surface. Egad, this is a whimsical old fellow!—But hark'ee, Premium, you'll prepare lodgings for these gentlemen.

Sir Oliver. Yes, yes, I'll send for them in a day or two.

Charles Surface. But hold; do now send a genteel conveyance for them, for, I assure you, they were most of them used to ride in their own carriages.

Sir Oliver. I will, I will—for all but Oliver.

Charles Surface. Ay, all but the little nabob.

Sir Oliver. You're fixed on that?

Charles Surface. Peremptorily.

Sir Oliver. (*Aside.*) A dear extravagant rogue!—(*Aloud.*) Good day!—Come, Moses.—(*Aside.*) Let me hear now who dares call him profligate! *Exeunt* SIR OLIVER *and* MOSES.

Careless. Why, this is the oddest genius of the sort I ever met with!

Charles Surface. Egad, he's the prince of brokers, I think.

I wonder how the devil Moses got acquainted with so honest a fellow.—Ha! here's Rowley.—Do, Careless, say I'll join the company in a few moments.

Careless. I will—but don't let that old blockhead persuade you to squander any of that money on old musty debts, or any such nonsense; for tradesmen, Charles, are the most exorbitant fellows.

Charles Surface. Very true, and paying them is only encouraging them.

Careless. Nothing else.

Charles Surface. Ay, ay, never fear.—(*Exit* CARELESS.) So! this was an odd old fellow, indeed. Let me see, two-thirds of this is mine by right: five hundred and thirty odd pounds. 'Fore heaven! I find one's ancestors are more valuable relations than I took them for!—Ladies and gentlemen, your most obedient and very grateful servant.   (*Bows to the pictures.*)

Enter ROWLEY.

Ha! old Rowley! egad, you are just come in time to take leave of your old acquaintance.

Rowley. Yes, I heard they were a-going. But I wonder you can have such spirits under so many distresses.

Charles Surface. Why, there's the point! my distresses are so many that I can't afford to part with my spirits; but I shall be rich and splenetic, all in good time. However, I suppose you are surprised that I am not more sorrowful at parting with so many near relations; to be sure, 'tis very affecting; but you see they never move a muscle, so why should I?

Rowley. There's no making you serious a moment.

Charles Surface. Yes, faith, I am so now. Here, my honest Rowley, here, get me this changed directly and take a hundred pounds of it immediately to old Stanley.

Rowley. A hundred pounds! Consider only——

Charles Surface. Gad's life, don't talk about it! poor Stanley's wants are pressing, and, if you don't make haste, we shall have some one call that has a better right to the money.

Rowley. Ah! there's the point! I never will cease dunning you with the old proverb——

Charles Surface. "Be just before you're generous."—Why, so I would if I could; but Justice is an old lame, hobbling beldame, and I can't get her to keep pace with Generosity, for the soul of me.

Rowley. Yet, Charles, believe me, one hour's reflection——

Charles Surface. Ay, ay, it's very true; but, hark'ee, Rowley, while I have, by Heaven I'll give; so, damn your economy! and now for hazard.   *Exeunt.*

Scene II: *The parlor.*

Enter Sir Oliver Surface *and* Moses.

Moses. Well, sir, I think, as Sir Peter said, you have seen Mr. Charles in high glory; 'tis great pity he's so extravagant.

Sir Oliver. True, but he would not sell my picture.

Moses. And loves wine and women so much.

Sir Oliver. But he would not sell my picture.

Moses. And games so deep.

Sir Oliver. But he would not sell my picture. Oh, here's Rowley.

Enter Rowley.

Rowley. So, Sir Oliver, I find you have made a purchase——

Sir Oliver. Yes, yes, our young rake has parted with his ancestors like old tapestry.

Rowley. And here has he commissioned me to re-deliver you part of the purchase-money——I mean, though, in your necessitous character of old Stanley.

Moses. Ah! there is the pity of all: he is so damned charitable.

Rowley. And I left a hosier and two tailors in the hall, who, I'm sure, won't be paid, and this hundred would satisfy them.

Sir Oliver. Well, well, I'll pay his debts, and his benevolence too. But now I am no more a broker, and you shall introduce me to the elder brother as old Stanley.

Rowley. Not yet awhile; Sir Peter, I know, means to call there about this time.

Enter Trip.

Trip. Oh, gentlemen, I beg pardon for not showing you out; this way——Moses, a word.   *(Exit with* Moses.)

Sir Oliver. There's a fellow for you! Would you believe it, that puppy intercepted the Jew on our coming, and wanted to raise money before he got to his master!

Rowley. Indeed.

Sir Oliver. Yes, they are now planning an annuity business. Ah, Master Rowley, in my days servants were content with the follies of their masters when they were worn a little threadbare; but now they have their vices, like their birthday clothes,[32] with the gloss on.   *Exeunt.*

SCENE III: *A Library in* JOSEPH SURFACE'S *House.*

Enter JOSEPH SURFACE *and* SERVANT.

Joseph Surface. No letter from Lady Teazle?
Servant. No, sir.
Joseph Surface. (*Aside.*) I am surprised she has not sent, if she is prevented from coming. Sir Peter certainly does not suspect me. Yet I wish I may not lose the heiress through the scrape I have drawn myself into with the wife. However, Charles's imprudence and bad character are great points in my favour.   (*Knocking.*)
Servant. Sir, I believe that must be Lady Teazle.
Joseph Surface. Hold! See whether it is or not before you go to the door. I have a particular message for you if it should be my brother.
Servant. 'Tis her ladyship, sir; she always leaves the chair at the milliner's in the next street.
Joseph Surface. Stay, stay! Draw that screen before the window—that will do;—my opposite neighbour is a maiden lady of so curious a temper.—(SERVANT *draws the screen, and exit.*) I have a difficult hand to play in this affair. Lady Teazle has lately suspected my views on Maria; but she must by no means be let into that secret—at least, till I have her more in my power.

Enter LADY TEAZLE.

Lady Teazle. What, sentiment in soliloquy now? Have you been very impatient? O lud! don't pretend to look grave. I vow I couldn't come before.
Joseph Surface. O madam, punctuality is a species of constancy very unfashionable in a lady of quality.
Lady Teazle. Upon my word, you ought to pity me. Do you know Sir Peter is grown so illnatured to me of late, and so jealous of Charles too—that's the best of the story, isn't it?
Joseph Surface. (*Aside.*) I am glad my scandalous friends keep that up.
Lady Teazle. I am sure I wish he would let Maria marry him, and then perhaps he would be convinced; don't you, Mr. Surface?
Joseph Surface. (*Aside.*) Indeed I do not.—(*Aloud.*) Oh, certainly I do! for then my dear Lady Teazle would also be

convinced how wrong her suspicions were of my having any design on the silly girl.

Lady Teazle. Well, well, I'm inclined to believe you. But isn't it provoking to have the most illnatured things said at one? And there's my friend Lady Sneerwell has circulated I don't know how many scandalous tales of me, and all without any foundation, too; that's what vexes me.

Joseph Surface. Ay, madam, to be sure, that is the provoking circumstance—without foundation; yes, yes, there's the mortification, indeed; for, when a scandalous story is believed against one, there certainly is no comfort like the consciousness of having deserved it.

Lady Teazle. No, to be sure, then I'd forgive their malice; but to attack me, who am really so innocent, and who never say an illnatured thing of anybody—that is, of any friend; and then Sir Peter, too, to have him so peevish, and so suspicious, when I know the integrity of my own heart—indeed 'tis monstrous!

Joseph Surface. But, my dear Lady Teazle, 'tis your own fault if you suffer it. When a husband entertains a groundless suspicion of his wife, and withdraws his confidence from her, the original compact is broken, and she owes it to the honor of her sex to endeavor to outwit him.

Lady Teazle. Indeed! So that, if he suspects me without cause, it follows, that the best way of curing his jealousy is to give him reason for't?

Joseph Surface. Undoubtedly—for your husband should never be deceived in you: and in that case it becomes you to be frail in compliment to his discernment.

Lady Teazle. To be sure, what you say is very reasonable, and when the consciousness of my innocence——

Joseph Surface. Ah, my dear madam, there is the great mistake; 'tis this very conscious innocence that is of the greatest prejudice to you. What is it makes you negligent of forms, and careless of the world's opinion? why, the consciousness of your own innocence. What makes you thoughtless in your conduct and apt to run into a thousand little imprudences? why, the consciousness of your own innocence. What makes you impatient of Sir Peter's temper, and outrageous at his suspicions? why, the consciousness of your innocence.

Lady Teazle. 'Tis very true!

Joseph Surface. Now, my dear Lady Teazle, if you would but once make a trifling *faux pas,* you can't conceive how cautious you would grow, and how ready to humor and agree with your husband.

Lady Teazle. Do you think so?

Joseph Surface. Oh, I'm sure on't! and then you would find all scandal would cease at once, for—in short, your character at present is like a person in a plethora, absolutely dying from too much health.

Lady Teazle. So, so; then I perceive your prescription is that I must sin in my own defence, and part with my virtue to preserve my reputation?

Joseph Surface. Exactly so, upon my credit, ma'am.

Lady Teazle. Well, certainly this is the oddest doctrine, and the newest receipt for avoiding calumny?

Joseph Surface. An infallible one, believe me. Prudence, like experience, must be paid for.

Lady Teazle. Why, if my understanding were once convinced——

Joseph Surface. Oh, certainly, madam, your understanding should be convinced. Yes, yes—Heaven forbid I should persuade you to do anything you thought wrong. No, no, I have too much honor to desire it.

Lady Teazle. Don't you think we may as well leave honor out of the argument?   *(Rises.)*

Joseph Surface. Ah, the ill effects of your country education, I see, still remain with you.

Lady Teazle. I doubt they do, indeed; and I will fairly own to you, that if I could be persuaded to do wrong, it would be by Sir Peter's ill usage sooner than your honorable logic, after all.

Joseph Surface. Then, by this hand, which he is unworthy of——   *(Taking her hand.)*

Enter SERVANT.

'Sdeath, you blockhead—what do you want?

Servant. I beg your pardon, sir, but I thought you would not choose Sir Peter to come up without announcing him.

Joseph Surface. Sir Peter!—Oons—the devil!

Lady Teazle. Sir Peter! O lud! I'm ruined! I'm ruined!

Servant. Sir, 'twasn't I let him in.

Lady Teazle. Oh! I'm quite undone! What will become of me now, Mr. Logic?—Oh! mercy, he's on the stairs—I'll get behind here—and if ever I'm so imprudent again——

                                       (Goes behind the screen.)

Joseph Surface. Give me that book.

          (Sits down. SERVANT *pretends to adjust his chair.)*

Enter SIR PETER TEAZLE.

Sir Peter. Ay, ever improving himself. Mr. Surface, Mr. Surface——

Joseph Surface. Oh, my dear Sir Peter, I beg your pardon.

(Gaping, throws away the book.) I have been dozing over a stupid book. Well, I am much obliged to you for this call. You haven't been here, I believe, since I fitted up this room. Books, you know, are the only things I am a coxcomb in.

Sir Peter. 'Tis very neat indeed. Well, well, that's proper; and you can make even your screen a source of knowledge— hung, I perceive, with maps.

Joseph Surface. Oh, yes, I find great use in that screen.

Sir Peter. I dare say you must, certainly, when you want to find anything in a hurry.

Joseph Surface. (Aside.) Ay, or to hide anything in a hurry either.

Sir Peter. Well, I have a little private business——

Joseph Surface. (To SERVANT.*)* You need not stay.

Servant. No, sir.   *Exit.*

Joseph Surface. Here's a chair, Sir Peter—I beg——

Sir Peter. Well, now we are alone, there is a subject, my dear friend, on which I wish to unburden my mind to you— a point of the greatest moment to my peace; in short, my good friend, Lady Teazle's conduct of late has made me very unhappy.

Joseph Surface. Indeed! I am very sorry to hear it.

Sir Peter. Yes, 'tis but too plain she has not the least regard for me; but, what's worse, I have pretty good authority to suppose she has formed an attachment to another.

Joseph Surface. Indeed! you astonish me!

Sir Peter. Yes! and, between ourselves, I think I've discovered the person.

Joseph Surface. How! you alarm me exceedingly.

Sir Peter. Ay, my dear friend, I knew you would sympathize with me!

Joseph Surface. Yes, believe me, Sir Peter, such a discovery would hurt me just as much as it would you.

Sir Peter. I am convinced of it. Ah! it is a happiness to have a friend whom we can trust even with one's family secrets. But have you no guess who I mean?

Joseph Surface. I haven't the most distant idea. It can't be Sir Benjamin Backbite!

Sir Peter. Oh, no! what say you to Charles?

Joseph Surface. My brother! impossible!

Sir Peter. Oh, my dear friend, the goodness of your own heart misleads you. You judge of others by yourself.

Joseph Surface. Certainly, Sir Peter, the heart that is conscious of its own integrity is ever slow to credit another's treachery.

Sir Peter. True; but your brother has no sentiment—you never hear him talk so.

Joseph Surface. Yet I can't but think Lady Teazle herself has too much principle.

Sir Peter. Ay; but what is principle against the flattery of a handsome, lively young fellow?

Joseph Surface. That's very true.

Sir Peter. And then, you know, the difference of our ages makes it very improbable that she should have any great affection for me; and if she were to be frail, and I were to make it public, why the town would only laugh at me, the foolish old bachelor who had married a girl.

Joseph Surface. That's true, to be sure—they would laugh.

Sir Peter. Laugh! ay, and make ballads, and paragraphs, and the devil knows what of me.

Joseph Surface. No, you must never make it public.

Sir Peter. But then again—that the nephew of my old friend, Sir Oliver, should be the person to attempt such a wrong, hurts me more nearly.

Joseph Surface. Ay, there's the point. When ingratitude barbs the dart of injury, the wound has double danger in it.

Sir Peter. Ay—I that was, in a manner, left his guardian, in whose house he had been so often entertained, who never in my life denied him—my advice!

Joseph Surface. Oh, 'tis not to be credited! There may be a man capable of such baseness, to be sure; but, for my part, till you can give me positive proofs, I cannot but doubt it. However, if it should be proved on him, he is no longer a brother of mine—I disclaim kindred with him: for the man who can break the laws of hospitality and tempt the wife of his friend, deserves to be branded as the pest of society.

Sir Peter. What a difference there is between you! What noble sentiments!

Joseph Surface. Yet I cannot suspect Lady Teazle's honor.

Sir Peter. I am sure I wish to think well of her, and to remove all ground of quarrel between us. She has lately reproached me more than once with having made no settlement on her; and, in our last quarrel, she almost hinted that she should not break her heart if I was dead. Now, as we seem to differ in our ideas of expense, I have resolved she shall have her own way and be her own mistress in that respect for the future; and, if I were to die, she will find I have not been inattentive to her interest while living. Here, my friend, are the drafts of two deeds, which I wish to have your opinion on. By one, she will enjoy eight hundred a year independent while I live; and, by the other, the bulk of my fortune at my death.

Joseph Surface. This conduct, Sir Peter, is indeed truly generous.—(*Aside.*) I wish it may not corrupt my pupil.

Sir Peter. Yes, I am determined she shall have no cause to complain, though I would not have her acquainted with the latter instance of my affection yet awhile.

Joseph Surface. (Aside.) Nor I, if I could help it.

Sir Peter. And now, my dear friend, if you please, we will talk over the situation of your hopes with Maria.

Joseph Surface. (Softly.) Oh, no, Sir Peter; another time, if you please.

Sir Peter. I am sensibly chagrined at the little progress you seem to make in her affections.

Joseph Surface. (Softly.) I beg you will not mention it. What are my disappointments when your happiness is in debate!—— *(Aside.)* 'Sdeath, I shall be ruined every way!

Sir Peter. And though you are averse to my acquainting Lady Teazle with your passion, I'm sure she's not your enemy in the affair.

Joseph Surface. Pray, Sir Peter, now oblige me. I am really too much affected by the subject we have been speaking of to bestow a thought on my own concerns. The man who is entrusted with his friend's distresses can never——

Enter SERVANT.

Well, sir?

Servant. Your brother, sir, is speaking to a gentleman in the street, and says he knows you are within.

Joseph Surface. 'Sdeath, blockhead, I'm not within—I'm out for the day.

Sir Peter. Stay—hold—a thought has struck me: you shall be at home.

Joseph Surface. Well, well, let him up.—*(Exit* SERVANT.) *(Aside.)* He'll interrupt Sir Peter, however.

Sir Peter. Now, my good friend, oblige me, I entreat you. Before Charles comes, let me conceal myself somewhere, then do you tax him on the point we have been talking, and his answer may satisfy me at once.

Joseph Surface. Oh, fie, Sir Peter! would you have me join in so mean a trick?—to trepan my brother too?

Sir Peter. Nay, you tell me you are sure he is innocent; if so, you do him the greatest service by giving him an opportunity to clear himself, and you will set my heart at rest. Come, you shall not refuse me: here, behind the screen will be—Hey! what the devil! there seems to be one listener here already—I'll swear I saw a petticoat!

Joseph Surface. Ha! ha! ha! Well, this is ridiculous enough. I'll tell you, Sir Peter, though I hold a man of intrigue to be a most despicable character, yet you know, it does not follow that one is to be an absolute Joseph either! Hark'ee, 'tis a little French milliner, a silly rogue that plagues me; and having some character to lose, on your coming, sir, she ran behind the screen.

Sir Peter. Ah, you rogue—— But, egad, she has overheard all I have been saying of my wife.

Joseph Surface. Oh, 'twill never go any farther, you may depend upon it!

Sir Peter. No! then, faith, let her hear it out.—Here's a closet will do as well.

Joseph Surface. Well, go in there.

Sir Peter. Sly rogue! sly rogue!　*(Goes into the closet.)*

Joseph Surface. A narrow escape, indeed! and a curious situation I'm in, to part man and wife in this manner.

Lady Teazle. (Peeping.) Couldn't I steal off?

Joseph Surface. Keep close, my angel.

Sir Peter. (Peeping.) Joseph, tax me home!

Joseph Surface. Back, my dear friend!

Lady Teazle. (Peeping.) Couldn't you lock Sir Peter in?

Joseph Surface. Be still, my life!

Sir Peter. (Peeping.) You're sure the little milliner won't blab?

Joseph Surface. In, in, my dear Sir Peter!—'Fore gad, I wish I had a key to the door!

Enter CHARLES SURFACE.

Charles Surface. Holla! brother, what has been the matter? Your fellow would not let me up at first. What! have you had a Jew or a wench with you?

Joseph Surface. Neither, brother, I assure you.

Charles Surface. But what has made Sir Peter steal off? I thought he had been with you.

Joseph Surface. He was, brother; but, hearing you were coming, he did not choose to stay.

Charles Surface. What! was the old gentleman afraid I wanted to borrow money of him!

Joseph Surface. No, sir: but I am sorry to find, Charles, you have lately given that worthy man grounds for great uneasiness.

Charles Surface. Yes, they tell me I do that to a great many worthy men. But how so, pray?

Joseph Surface. To be plain with you, brother, he thinks you are endeavoring to gain Lady Teazle's affections from him.

Charles Surface. Who, I? O lud! not I, upon my word.— Ha! ha! ha! ha! so the old fellow has found out that he has got a young wife, has he?—or, what's worse, Lady Teazle has found out she has an old husband?

Joseph Surface. This is no subject to jest on, brother. He who can laugh——

Charles Surface. True, true, as you were going to say—then, seriously, I never had the least idea of what you charge me with, upon my honor.

Joseph Surface. (In a loud voice.) Well, it will give Sir Peter great satisfaction to hear this.

Charles Surface. To be sure, I once thought the lady seemed to have taken a fancy to me; but, upon my soul, I never gave her the least encouragement. Besides, you know my attachment to Maria.

Joseph Surface. But sure, brother, even if Lady Teazle had betrayed the fondest partiality for you——

Charles Surface. Why, look'ee, Joseph, I hope I shall never deliberately do a dishonorable action; but if a pretty woman was purposely to throw herself in my way—and that pretty woman married to a man old enough to be her father——

Joseph Surface. Well!

Charles Surface. Why, I believe I should be obliged to borrow a little of your morality, that's all. But, brother, do you know now that you surprise me exceedingly by naming me with Lady Teazle; for i'faith, I always understood you were her favorite.

Joseph Surface. Oh, for shame, Charles! This retort is foolish.

Charles Surface. Nay, I swear I have seen you exchange such significant glances——

Joseph Surface. Nay, nay, sir, this is no jest.

Charles Surface. Egad, I'm serious! Don't you remember one day when I called here——

Joseph Surface. Nay, prithee, Charles——

Charles Surface. And found you together——

Joseph Surface. Zounds, sir, I insist——

Charles Surface. And another time, when your servant——

Joseph Surface. Brother, brother, a word with you! *(Aside.)* Gad, I must stop him.

Charles Surface. Informed, I say, that——

Joseph Surface. Hush! I beg your pardon, but Sir Peter has overheard all we have been saying. I knew you would clear yourself, or I should not have consented.

Charles Surface. How, Sir Peter! Where is he?

Joseph Surface. Softly, there!   *(Points to the closet.)*

Charles Surface. Oh, 'fore Heaven, I'll have him out. Sir Peter, come forth!

Joseph Surface. No, no——

Charles Surface. I say, Sir Peter, come into court.—(*Pulls in* SIR PETER.) What! my old guardian!—What!—turn inquisitor and take evidence incog.?

Sir Peter. Give me your hand, Charles—I believe I have suspected you wrongfully; but you mustn't be angry with Joseph—'twas my plan!

Charles Surface. Indeed!

Sir Peter. But I acquit you. I promise you I don't think near so ill of you as I did. What I have heard has given me great satisfaction.

Charles Surface. Egad, then, 'twas lucky you didn't hear any more. Wasn't it, Joseph?

Sir Peter. Ah! you would have retorted on him.

Charles Surface. Ah, ay, that was a joke.

Sir Peter. Yes, yes, I know his honor too well.

Charles Surface. But you might as well have suspected him as me in this matter, for all that. Mightn't he, Joseph?

Sir Peter. Well, well, I believe you.

Joseph Surface. (*Aside.*) Would they were both out of the room!

Sir Peter. And in future, perhaps, we may not be such strangers.

Enter SERVANT *and whispers* JOSEPH SURFACE.

Joseph Surface. Gentlemen, I beg pardon—I must wait on you downstairs; here's a person come on particular business.

Charles Surface. Well, you can see him in another room. Sir Peter and I have not met a long time, and I have something to say to him.

Joseph Surface. (*Aside.*) They must not be left together.—(*Aloud.*) I'll send Lady Sneerwell away, and return directly. —(*Aside to* SIR PETER.) Sir Peter, not a word of the French milliner.

Sir Peter. (*Aside to* JOSEPH SURFACE.) I! not for the world!—(*Exit* JOSEPH SURFACE.) Ah, Charles, if you associated more with your brother, one might indeed hope for your reformation. He is a man of sentiment. Well, there is nothing in the world so noble as a man of sentiment.

Charles Surface. Psha! he is too moral by half; and so apprehensive of his good name, as he calls it, that I suppose he would as soon let a priest into his house as a wench.

Sir Peter. No, no,—come, come,—you wrong him. No, no, Joseph is no rake, but he is no such saint either, in that respect.—(*Aside.*) I have a great mind to tell him—we should have such a laugh at Joseph.

Charles Surface. Oh, hang him! he's a very anchorite, a young hermit!

Sir Peter. Hark'ee—you must not abuse him: he may chance to hear of it again, I promise you.

Charles Surface. Why, you won't tell him?

Sir Peter. No—but—this way.—(*Aside.*) Egad, I'll tell him. (*Aloud.*) Hark'ee, have you a mind to have a good laugh at Joseph?

Charles Surface. I should like it of all things.

Sir Peter. Then, i'faith, we will! I'll be quit with him for discovering me. He had a girl with him when I called.

Charles Surface. What! Joseph? you jest.

Sir Peter. Hush!—a little French milliner—and the best of the jest is—she's in the room now.

Charles Surface. The devil she is!

Sir Peter. Hush! I tell you. (*Points to the screen.*)

Charles Surface. Behind the screen! S'life, let's unveil her!

Sir Peter. No, no, he's coming. You shan't, indeed!

Charles Surface. Oh, egad, we'll have a peep at the little milliner!

Sir Peter. Not for the world!—Joseph will never forgive me.

Charles Surface. I'll stand by you——

Sir Peter. Odds, here he is!

JOSEPH SURFACE *enters just as* CHARLES *throws down the screen.*

Charles Surface. Lady Teazle, by all that's wonderful!

Sir Peter. Lady Teazle, by all that's damnable!

Charles Surface. Sir Peter, this is one of the smartest French milliners I ever saw. Egad, you seem all to have been diverting yourselves here at hide and seek, and I don't see who is out of the secret. Shall I beg your ladyship to inform me? Not a word!—Brother, will you be pleased to explain this matter? What! is Morality dumb too?—Sir Peter, though I found you in the dark, perhaps you are not so now! All mute! Well—though I can make nothing of the affair, I suppose you perfectly understand one another; so I'll leave you to yourselves. (*Going.*) Brother, I'm sorry to find you have given that worthy man grounds for so much uneasiness.— Sir Peter! there's nothing in the world so noble as a man of sentiment!   *Exit.*

They stand for some time looking at each other.

Joseph Surface. Sir Peter—notwithstanding—I confess— that appearances are against me—if you will afford me your patience—I make no doubt—but I shall explain everything to your satisfaction.

Sir Peter. If you please, sir.

Joseph Surface. The fact is, sir, that Lady Teazle, knowing my pretensions to your ward Maria—I say, sir, Lady Teazle, being apprehensive of the jealousy of your temper—and knowing my friendship to the family—she, sir, I say—called here—in order that—I might explain these pretensions—but on your coming—being apprehensive—as I said—of your jealousy—she withdrew—and this, you may depend on it, is the whole truth of the matter.

Sir Peter. A very clear account, upon my word; and I dare swear the lady will vouch for every article of it.

Lady Teazle. For not one word of it, Sir Peter!

Sir Peter. How! don't you think it worth while to agree in the lie?

Lady Teazle. There is not one syllable of truth in what that gentleman has told you.

Sir Peter. I believe you, upon my soul, ma'am!

Joseph Surface. (*Aside to* LADY TEAZLE.) 'Sdeath, madam, will you betray me?

Lady Teazle. Good Mr. Hypocrite, by your leave, I'll speak for myself.

Sir Peter. Ay, let her alone, sir; you'll find she'll make out a better story than you, without prompting.

Lady Teazle. Hear me, Sir Peter! I came here on no matter relating to your ward, and even ignorant of this gentleman's pretensions to her. But I came, seduced by his insidious arguments, at least to listen to his pretended passion, if not to sacrifice your honor to his baseness.

Sir Peter. Now, I believe, the truth is coming, indeed!

Joseph Surface. The woman's mad!

Lady Teazle. No, sir; she has recovered her senses, and your own arts have furnished her with the means. Sir Peter, I do not expect you to credit me—but the tenderness you expressed for me, when I am sure you could not think I was a witness to it, has penetrated so to my heart, that had I left the place without the shame of this discovery, my future life should have spoken the sincerity of my gratitude. As for that smooth-tongued hypocrite, who would have seduced the wife of his too credulous friend, while he affected honorable addresses to his ward—I behold him now in a light so truly despicable that I shall never again respect myself for having listened to him. *Exit.*

Joseph Surface. Notwithstanding all this, Sir Peter, Heaven knows——

Sir Peter. That you are a villain! and so I leave you to your conscience.

Joseph Surface. You are too rash, Sir Peter; you shall hear me. The man who shuts out conviction by refusing to——   *Exeunt*, JOSEPH SURFACE *talking*.

ACT V

SCENE I: *The Library in* JOSEPH SURFACE'S *House*.

Enter JOSEPH SURFACE *and* SERVANT.

Joseph Surface. Mr. Stanley! and why should you think I would see him? you must know he comes to ask something.

Servant. Sir, I should not have let him in, but that Mr. Rowley came to the door with him.

Joseph Surface. Psha! blockhead! to suppose that I should now be in a temper to receive visits from poor relations!—Well, why don't you show the fellow up?

Servant. I will, sir.—Why, sir, it was not my fault that Sir Peter discovered my lady——

Joseph Surface. Go, fool!—(*Exit* SERVANT.) Sure fortune never played a man of my policy such a trick before! My character with Sir Peter, my hopes with Maria, destroyed in a moment! I'm in a rare humor to listen to other people's distresses! I shan't be able to bestow even a benevolent sentiment on Stanley.—So! here he comes, and Rawley with him. I must try to recover myself, and put a little charity in my face, however.   *Exit*.

Enter SIR OLIVER SURFACE *and* ROWLEY.

Sir Oliver. What! does he avoid us? That was he, was it not?

Rowley. It was, sir. But I doubt you are coming a little too abruptly. His nerves are so weak that the sight of a poor relation may be too much for him. I should have gone first to break it to him.

Sir Oliver. Oh, plague of his nerves! Yet this is he whom Sir Peter extols as a man of the most benevolent way of thinking!

Rowley. As to his way of thinking, I cannot pretend to decide; for, to do him justice, he appears to have as much speculative benevolence as any private gentleman in the kingdom, though he is seldom so sensual as to indulge himself in the exercise of it.

Sir Oliver. Yet he has a string of charitable sentiments at his fingers' ends.

Rowley. Or, rather, at his tongue's end, Sir Oliver; for I believe there is no sentiment he has such faith in as that "Charity begins at home."

Sir Oliver. And his, I presume, is of that domestic sort which never stirs abroad at all.

Rowley. I doubt you'll find it so;—but he's coming. I mustn't seem to interrupt you; and you know, immediately as you leave him, I come in to announce your arrival in your real character.

Sir Oliver. True; and afterwards you'll meet me at Sir Peter's.

Rowley. Without losing a moment.   *Exit.*

Sir Oliver. I don't like the complaisance of his features.

Enter JOSEPH SURFACE.

Joseph Surface. Sir, I beg you ten thousand pardons for keeping you a moment waiting.—Mr. Stanley, I presume.

Sir Oliver. At your service.

Joseph Surface. Sir, I beg you will do me the honor to sit down—I entreat you, sir.

Sir Oliver. Dear sir—there's no occasion.—*(Aside.)* Too civil by half!

Joseph Surface. I have not the pleasure of knowing you, Mr. Stanley; but I am extremely happy to see you look so well. You were nearly related to my mother, I think, Mr. Stanley?

Sir Oliver. I was, sir; so nearly that my present poverty, I fear, may do discredit to her wealthy children, else I should not have presumed to trouble you.

Joseph Surface. Dear sir, there needs no apology: he that is in distress, though a stranger, has a right to claim kindred with the wealthy. I am sure I wish I was one of that class, and had it in my power to offer you even a small relief.

Sir Oliver. If your uncle, Sir Oliver, were here, I should have a friend.

Joseph Surface. I wish he was, sir, with all my heart: you should not want an advocate with him, believe me, sir.

Sir Oliver. I should not need one—my distresses would recommend me. But I imagined his bounty would enable you to become the agent of his charity.

Joseph Surface. My dear sir, you were strangely misinformed. Sir Oliver is a worthy man, a very worthy man, but avarice, Mr. Stanley, is the vice of age. I will tell you, my good sir, in confidence, what he has done for me has been a mere nothing; though people, I know, have thought otherwise; and, for my part, I never choose to contradict the report.

Sir Oliver. What! has he never transmitted you bullion—rupees—pagodas?[33]

Joseph Surface. Oh, dear sir, nothing of the kind! No, no; a few presents now and then—china, shawls, congou tea,[34] avadavats,[35] and Indian crackers[36]—little more, believe me.

Sir Oliver. (*Aside.*) Here's gratitude for twelve thousand pounds!—Avadavats and Indian crackers!

Joseph Surface. Then, my dear sir, you have heard, I doubt not, of the extravagance of my brother; there are very few would credit what I have done for that unfortunate young man.

Sir Oliver. (*Aside.*) Not I, for one!

Joseph Surface. The sums I have lent him! Indeed I have been exceedingly to blame; it was an amiable weakness; however, I don't pretend to defend it—and now I feel it doubly culpable, since it has deprived me of the pleasure of serving you, Mr. Stanley, as my heart dictates.

Sir Oliver. (*Aside.*) Dissembler!—(*Aloud.*) Then, sir, you can't assist me?

Joseph Surface. At present, it grieves me to say, I cannot; but, whenever I have the ability, you may depend upon hearing from me.

Sir Oliver. I am extremely sorry——

Joseph Surface. Not more than I, believe me; to pity, without the power to relieve, is still more painful than to ask and be denied.

Sir Oliver. Kind sir, your most obedient humble servant.

Joseph Surface. You leave me deeply affected, Mr. Stanley.—William, be ready to open the door.

Sir Oliver. Oh, dear sir, no ceremony.

Joseph Surface. Your very obedient.

Sir Oliver. Sir, your most obsequious.

Joseph Surface. You may depend upon hearing from me, whenever I can be of service.

Sir Oliver. Sweet sir, you are too good.

Joseph Surface. In the meantime I wish you health and spirits.

Sir Oliver. Your ever grateful and perpetual humble servant.

Joseph Surface. Sir, yours as sincerely.

Sir Oliver. (*Aside.*) Charles!—you are my heir.   *Exit.*

Joseph Surface. This is one bad effect of a good character; it invites application from the unfortunate, and there needs no small degree of address to gain the reputation of benevolence without incurring the expense. The silver ore of pure charity is an expensive article in the catalogue of a man's good qualities; whereas the sentimental French plate I use instead of it makes just as good a show, and pays no tax.

Enter ROWLEY.

Rowley. Mr. Surface, your servant: I was apprehensive of interrupting you, though my business demands immediate attention, as this note will inform you.

Joseph Surface. Always happy to see Mr. Rowley.—(*Reads.*) Sir Oliver Surface!—My uncle arrived!

Rowley. He is, indeed: we have just parted—quite well, after a speedy voyage, and impatient to embrace his worthy nephew.

Joseph Surface. I am astonished!—William! stop Mr. Stanley, if he's not gone.

Rowley. Oh! he's out of reach, I believe.

Joseph Surface. Why did you not let me know this when you came in together?

Rowley. I thought you had particular business. But I must be gone to inform your brother and appoint him here to meet your uncle. He will be with you in a quarter of an hour.

Joseph Surface. So he says. Well, I am strangely overjoyed at his coming.—(*Aside.*) Never, to be sure, was anything so damned unlucky!

Rowley. You will be delighted to see how well he looks.

Joseph Surface. Oh! I'm overjoyed to hear it.—(*Aside.*) —Just at this time!

Rowley. I'll tell him how impatiently you expect him.

Joseph Surface. Do, do; pray give my best duty and affection. Indeed, I cannot express the sensations I feel at the thought of seeing him.—(*Exit* ROWLEY.) Certainly his coming just at this time is the cruellest piece of ill fortune. *Exit.*

SCENE II: SIR PETER TEAZLE'S *House.*

Enter MRS. CANDOUR *and* MAID.

Maid. Indeed, ma'am, my lady will see nobody at present.

Mrs. Candour. Did you tell her it was her friend Mrs. Candour?

Maid. Yes, ma'am; but she begs you will excuse her.

Mrs. Candour. Do go again; I shall be glad to see her, if it be only for a moment, for I am sure she must be in great distress.—(*Exit* MAID.) Dear heart, how provoking! I'm not mistress of half the circumstances! We shall have the whole affair in the newspapers, with the names of the parties at length, before I have dropped the story at a dozen houses.

Enter SIR BENJAMIN BACKBITE.

Oh, dear Sir Benjamin! you have heard, I suppose——

Sir Benjamin. Of Lady Teazle and Mr. Surface——

Mrs. Candour. And Sir Peter's discovery——

Sir Benjamin. Oh, the strangest piece of business, to be sure!

Mrs. Candour. Well, I never was so surprised in my life. I am so sorry for all parties, indeed.

Sir Benjamin. Now, I don't pity Sir Peter at all: he was so extravagantly partial to Mr. Surface.

Mrs. Candour. Mr. Surface! Why, 'twas with Charles Lady Teazle was detected.

Sir Benjamin. No, no, I tell you: Mr. Surface is the gallant.

Mrs. Candour. No such thing! Charles is the man. 'Twas Mr. Surface brought Sir Peter on purpose to discover them.

Sir Benjamin. I tell you I had it from one——

Mrs. Candour. And I have it from one——

Sir Benjamin. Who had it from one, who had it——

Mrs. Candour. From one immediately——But here comes Lady Sneerwell; perhaps she knows the whole affair.

Enter LADY SNEERWELL.

Lady Sneerwell. So, my dear Mrs. Candour, here's a sad affair of our friend Lady Teazle!

Mrs. Candour. Ay, my dear friend, who would have thought——

Lady Sneerwell. Well, there is no trusting to appearances; though indeed, she was always too lively for me.

Mrs. Candour. To be sure, her manners were a little too free; but then she was so young!

Lady Sneerwell. And had, indeed, some good qualities.

Mrs. Candour. So she had, indeed. But have you heard the particulars?

Lady Sneerwell. No; but everybody says that Mr. Surface——

Sir Benjamin. Ay, there; I told you Mr. Surface was the man.

Mrs. Candour. No, no: indeed the assignation was with Charles.

Lady Sneerwell. With Charles! You alarm me, Mrs. Candour.

Mrs. Candour. Yes, yes: he was the lover. Mr. Surface, to do him justice, was only the informer.

Sir Benjamin. Well, I'll not dispute with you, Mrs. Candour; but, be it which it may, I hope that Sir Peter's wound will not——

Mrs. Candour. Sir Peter's wound! Oh, mercy! I didn't hear a word of their fighting.

Lady Sneerwell. Nor I, a syllable.

Sir Benjamin. No! what, no mention of the duel?

Mrs. Candour. Not a word.

Sir Benjamin. Oh, yes: they fought before they left the room.

Lady Sneerwell. Pray let us hear.

Mrs. Candour. Ay, do oblige us with the duel.

Sir Benjamin. "Sir," says Sir Peter, immediately after the discovery, "you are a most ungrateful fellow."

Mrs. Candour. Ay, to Charles——

Sir Benjamin. No, no—to Mr. Surface—"a most ungrateful fellow; and old as I am, sir," says he, "I insist on immediate satisfaction."

Mrs. Candour. Ay, that must have been to Charles; for 'tis very unlikely Mr. Surface should fight in his own house.

Sir Benjamin. 'Gad's life, ma'am, not at all—"giving me immediate satisfaction."—On this, ma'am, Lady Teazle, seeing Sir Peter in such danger, ran out of the room in strong hysterics, and Charles after her, calling out for hartshorn and water; then, madam, they began to fight with swords——

Enter CRABTREE.

Crabtree. With pistols, nephew—pistols! I have it from undoubted authority.

Mrs. Candour. Oh, Mr. Crabtree, then it is all true!

Crabtree. Too true, indeed, madam, and Sir Peter is dangerously wounded——

Sir Benjamin. By a thrust in *seconde*[37] quite through his left side——

Crabtree. By a bullet lodged in the thorax.

Mrs. Candour. Mercy on me! Poor Sir Peter!

Crabtree. Yes, madam; though Charles would have avoided the matter, if he could.

Mrs. Candour. I knew Charles was the person.

Sir Benjamin. My uncle, I see, knows nothing of the matter.

Crabtree. But Sir Peter taxed him with the basest ingratitude——

Sir Benjamin. That I told you, you know——

Crabtree. Do, nephew, let me speak!—and insisted on immediate——

Sir Benjamin. Just as I said——

Crabtree. Odds life, nephew, allow others to know something too! A pair of pistols lay on the bureau. (for Mr. Surface, it seems, had come home the night before late from Salthill where he had been to see the Montem[38] with a friend who has a son at Eton) so, unluckily, the pistols were left charged.

Sir Benjamin. I heard nothing of this.

Crabtree. Sir Peter forced Charles to take one, and they fired, it seems, pretty nearly together. Charles's shot took effect, as I tell you, and Sir Peter's missed; but, what is very extraordinary, the ball struck against a little bronze Shakespeare that stood over the fireplace, grazed out of the window at a right angle, and wounded the postman who was just coming to the door with a double letter[39] from Northamptonshire.

Sir Benjamin. My uncle's account is more circumstantial, I confess; but I believe mine is the true one for all that.

Lady Sneerwell. (*Aside.*) I am more interested in this affair than they imagine, and must have better information.   *Exit.*

Sir Benjamin. Ah! Lady Sneerwell's alarm is very easily accounted for.

Crabtree. Yes, yes, they certainly do say—but that's neither here nor there.

Mrs. Candour. But, pray, where is Sir Peter at present?

Crabtree. Oh! they brought him home, and he is now in the house, though the servants are ordered to deny him.

Mrs. Candour. I believe so, and Lady Teazle, I suppose, attending him.

Crabtree. Yes, yes; and I saw one of the faculty[40] enter just before me.

Sir Benjamin. Hey! who comes here?

Crabtree. Oh, this is he: the physician, depend on't.

Mrs. Candour. Oh, certainly! it must be the physician; and now we shall know.

Enter SIR OLIVER SURFACE.

Crabtree. Well, doctor, what hopes?

Mrs. Candour. Ay, doctor, how's your patient?

Sir Benjamin. Now, doctor, isn't it a wound with a smallsword?

Crabtree. A bullet lodged in the thorax, for a hundred!

Sir Oliver. Doctor! a wound with a smallsword! and a bullet in the thorax?—Oons! are you mad, good people?

Sir Benjamin. Perhaps, sir, you are not a doctor?

Sir Oliver. Truly, I am to thank you for my degree, if I am.

Crabtree. Only a friend of Sir Peter's, then, I presume. But, sir, you must have heard of his accident?

Sir Oliver. Not a word!

Crabtree. Not of his being dangerously wounded?

Sir Oliver. The devil he is!

Sir Benjamin. Run through the body——

Crabtree. Shot in the breast——

Sir Benjamin. By one Mr. Surface——

Crabtree. Ay, the younger.

Sir Oliver. Hey! what the plague! you seem to differ strangely in your accounts: however, you agree that Sir Peter is dangerously wounded.

Sir Benjamin. Oh, yes, we agree there.

Crabtree. Yes, yes, I believe there can be no doubt in that.

Sir Oliver. Then, upon my word, for a person in that situation, he is the most imprudent man alive; for here he comes, walking as if nothing at all was the matter.

Enter SIR PETER TEAZLE.

Odds heart, Sir Peter! you are come in good time, I promise you; for we had just given you over!

Sir Benjamin. *(Aside to* CRABTREE.*)* Egad, uncle, this is the most sudden recovery!

Sir Oliver. Why, man! what do you do out of bed with a smallsword through your body and a bullet lodged in your thorax?

Sir Peter. A smallsword and a bullet?

Sir Oliver. Ay; these gentlemen would have killed you without law or physic, and wanted to dub me a doctor, to make me an accomplice.

Sir Peter. Why, what is all this?

Sir Benjamin. We rejoice, Sir Peter, that the story of the duel is not true and are sincerely sorry for your other misfortune.

Sir Peter. *(Aside.)* So, so; all over the town already.

Crabtree. Though, Sir Peter, you were certainly vastly to blame to marry at your years.

Sir Peter. Sir, what business is that of yours?

Mrs. Candour. Though, indeed, as Sir Peter made so good a husband, he's very much to be pitied.

Sir Peter. Plague on your pity, ma'am! I desire none of it.

Sir Benjamin. However, Sir Peter, you must not mind the laughing and jests you will meet with on the occasion.

Sir Peter. Sir, sir! I desire to be master in my own house.

Crabtree. 'Tis no uncommon case, that's one comfort.

Sir Peter. I insist on being left to myself. Without ceremony, I insist on your leaving my house directly!

Mrs. Candour. Well, well, we are going; and depend on't, we'll make the best report of it we can.   *Exit.*

Sir Peter. Leave my house!

Crabtree. And tell how hardly you've been treated!   *Exit.*

Sir Peter. Leave my house!

Sir Benjamin. And how patiently you bear it.   *Exit.*

Sir Peter. Fiends! vipers! furies! Oh! that their own venom would choke them!

Sir Oliver. They are very provoking indeed, Sir Peter.

Enter ROWLEY.

Rowley. I heard high words: what has ruffled you, sir?

Sir Peter. Psha! what signifies asking? Do I ever pass a day without my vexations?

Rowley. Well, I'm not inquisitive.

Sir Oliver. Well, Sir Peter, I have seen both my nephews in the manner we proposed.

Sir Peter. A precious couple they are!

Rowley. Yes, and Sir Oliver is convinced that your judgment was right, Sir Peter.

Sir Oliver. Yes, I find Joseph is indeed the man, after all.

Rowley. Ay, as Sir Peter says, he is a man of sentiment.

Sir Oliver. And acts up to the sentiments he professes.

Rowley. It certainly is edification to hear him talk.

Sir Oliver. Oh, he's a model for the young men of the age! But how's this, Sir Peter? you don't join us in your friend Joseph's praise, as I expected.

Sir Peter. Sir Oliver, we live in a damned wicked world, and the fewer we praise the better.

Rowley. What! do you say so, Sir Peter, who were never mistaken in your life?

Sir Peter. Psha! plague on you both! I see by your sneering you have heard the whole affair. I shall go mad among you!

Rowley. Then, to fret you no longer, Sir Peter, we are indeed acquainted with it all. I met Lady Teazle coming from Mr. Surface's so humbled, that she deigned to request me to be her advocate with you.

Sir Peter. And does Sir Oliver know all this?

Sir Oliver. Every circumstance.

Sir Peter. What, of the closet and the screen, hey?

Sir Oliver. Yes, yes, and the little French milliner. Oh, I have been vastly diverted with the story! ha! ha! ha!

Sir Peter. 'Twas very pleasant.

Sir Oliver. I never laughed more in my life, I assure you: ha! ha! ha!

Sir Peter. Oh, vastly diverting! ha! ha! ha!

Rowley. To be sure, Joseph with his sentiments! ha! ha! ha!

Sir Peter. Yes, yes, his sentiments! ha! ha! ha! Hypocritical villain!

Sir Oliver. Ay, and that rogue Charles to pull Sir Peter out of the closet: ha! ha! ha!

Sir Peter. Ha! ha! 'twas devilish entertaining, to be sure!

Sir Oliver. Ha! ha! ha! Egad, Sir Peter, I should like to have seen your face when the screen was thrown down: ha! ha!

Sir Peter. Yes, yes, my face when the screen was thrown down: ha! ha! ha! Oh, I must never show my head again!

Sir Oliver. But come, come, it isn't fair to laugh at you neither, my old friend; though, upon my soul, I can't help it.

Sir Peter. Oh, pray don't restrain your mirth on my account: it does not hurt me at all! I laugh at the whole affair myself. Yes, yes, I think being a standing jest for all one's acquaintance a very happy situation. Oh, yes, and then of a morning to read the paragraphs about Mr. S——, Lady T——, and Sir P——, will be so entertaining!

Rowley. Without affectation, Sir Peter, you may despise the ridicule of fools. But I see Lady Teazle going towards the next room, I am sure you must desire a reconciliation as earnestly as she does.

Sir Oliver. Perhaps my being here prevents her coming to you. Well, I'll leave honest Rowley to mediate between you; but he must bring you all presently to Mr. Surface's where I am now returning, if not to reclaim a libertine, at least to expose hypocrisy.

Sir Peter. Ah, I'll be present at your discovering yourself there with all my heart; though 'tis a vile unlucky place for discoveries.

Rowley. We'll follow.   *Exit* SIR OLIVER.

Sir Peter. She is not coming here, you see, Rowley.

Rowley. No, but she has left the door of that room open, you perceive. See, she is in tears.

Sir Peter. Certainly a little mortification appears very becoming in a wife. Don't you think it will do her good to let her pine a little?

Rowley. Oh, this is ungenerous in you!

Sir Peter. Well, I know not what to think. You remember the letter I found of hers evidently intended for Charles!

Rowley. A mere forgery, Sir Peter! laid in your way on purpose. This is one of the points which I intend Snake shall give you conviction of.

Sir Peter. I wish I were once satisfied of that. She looks this way. What a remarkably elegant turn of the head she has! Rowley, I'll go to her.

Rowley. Certainly.

Sir Peter. Though, when it is known that we are reconciled, people will laugh at me ten times more.

Rowley. Let them laugh, and retort their malice only by showing them you are happy in spite of it.

Sir Peter. I'faith, so I will! and, if I'm not mistaken, we may yet be the happiest couple in the country.

Rowley. Nay, Sir Peter, he who once lays aside suspicion——

Sir Peter. Hold, Master Rowley! if you have any regard for me, never let me hear you utter anything like a sentiment. I have had enough of them to serve me the rest of my life.

Exeunt.

SCENE III: *The Library in* JOSEPH SURFACE'S *House.*

Enter JOSEPH SURFACE *and* LADY SNEERWELL.

Lady Sneerwell. Impossible! Will not Sir Peter immediately be reconciled to Charles, and of course no longer oppose his union with Maria? The thought is distraction to me.

Joseph Surface. Can passion furnish a remedy?

Lady Sneerwell. No, nor cunning either. Oh, I was a fool, an idiot, to league with such a blunderer!

Joseph Surface. Sure, Lady Sneerwell, I am the greatest sufferer; yet you see I bear the accident with calmness.

Lady Sneerwell. Because the disappointment doesn't reach your heart; your interest only attached you to Maria. Had you felt for her what I have for that ungrateful libertine, neither your temper nor hypocrisy could prevent your showing the sharpness of your vexation.

Joseph Surface. But why should your reproaches fall on me for this disappointment?

Lady Sneerwell. Are you not the cause of it? Had you not a sufficient field for your roguery in imposing upon Sir Peter, and supplanting your brother, but you must endeavor to seduce his wife? I hate such an avarice of crimes; 'tis an unfair monopoly, and never prospers.

Joseph Surface. Well, I admit I have been to blame. I confess I deviated from the direct road of wrong, but I don't think we're so totally defeated neither.

Lady Sneerwell. No?

Joseph Surface. You tell me you have made a trial of Snake since we met, and that you still believe him faithful to us?

Lady Sneerwell. I do believe so.

Joseph Surface. And that he has undertaken, should it be necessary, to swear and prove that Charles is at this time contracted by vows and honor to your ladyship, which some of his former letters to you will serve to support?

Lady Sneerwell. This, indeed, might have assisted.

Joseph Surface. Come, come; it is not too late yet. *(Knocking at the door.)* But hark! this is probably my uncle, Sir Oliver: retire to that room; we'll consult further when he's gone.

Lady Sneerwell. Well, but if he should find you out too.

Joseph Surface. Oh, I have no fear of that. Sir Peter will hold his tongue for his own credit's sake—and you may depend on it I shall soon discover Sir Oliver's weak side!

Lady Sneerwell. I have no diffidence⁴¹ of your abilities! only be constant to one roguery at a time.   *Exit.*

Joseph Surface. I will, I will! So! 'tis confounded hard, after such bad fortune, to be baited by one's confederate in evil. Well, at all events, my character is so much better than Charles's that I certainly—hey!—what—this is not Sir Oliver, but old Stanley again. Plague on't that he should return to tease me just now! I shall have Sir Oliver come and find him here—and—

Enter SIR OLIVER SURFACE.

Gad's life, Mr. Stanley, why have you come back to plague me at this time? You must not stay now, upon my word.

Sir Oliver. Sir, I hear your uncle Oliver is expected here, and though he has been so penurious to you, I'll try what he'll do for me.

Joseph Surface. Sir, 'tis impossible for you to stay now, so I must beg——Come any other time, and I promise you, you shall be assisted.

Sir Oliver. No: Sir Oliver and I must be acquainted.

Joseph Surface. Zounds, sir! then I insist on your quitting the room directly.

Sir Oliver. Nay, sir——

Joseph Surface. Sir, I insist on't!—Here, William! show this gentleman out. Since you compel me, sir, not one moment— this is such insolence!   *(Going to push him out.)*

Enter CHARLES SURFACE.

Charles Surface. Heyday! what's the matter now? What the devil have you got hold of my little broker here? Zounds, brother, don't hurt little Premium. What's the matter, my little fellow?

Joseph Surface. So! he has been with you, too, has he?

Charles Surface. To be sure he has. Why, he's as honest a little——But sure, Joseph, you have not been borrowing money too, have you?

Joseph Surface. Borrowing! no! But, brother, you know we expect Sir Oliver here every——

Charles Surface. O gad, that's true! Noll mustn't find the little broker here, to be sure.

Joseph Surface. Yet, Mr. Stanley insists——

Charles Surface. Stanley! why his name's Premium.

Joseph Surface. No, sir, Stanley.

Charles Surface. No, no, Premium.

Joseph Surface. Well, no matter which—but——

Charles Surface. Ay, ay, Stanley or Premium, 'tis the same thing, as you say; for I suppose he goes by half a hundred names, besides A. B. at the coffee-house.[42]   (*Knocking.*)

Joseph Surface. 'Sdeath! here's Sir Oliver at the door. Now I beg, Mr. Stanley——

Charles Surface. Ay, ay, and I beg, Mr. Premium——

Sir Oliver. Gentlemen——

Joseph Surface. Sir, by heaven you shall go!

Charles Surface. Ay, out with him, certainly!

Sir Oliver. This violence——

Joseph Surface. Sir, 'tis your own fault.

Charles Surface. Out with him, to be sure!

(*Both forcing* Sir Oliver *out.*)

Enter Sir Peter *and* Lady Teazle, Maria, *and* Rowley.

Sir Peter. My old friend, Sir Oliver—hey! What in the name of wonder!—here are dutiful nephews—assault their uncle at first visit!

Lady Teazle. Indeed, Sir Oliver, 'twas well we came in to rescue you.

Rowley. Truly it was; for I perceive, Sir Oliver, the character of old Stanley was no protection to you.

Sir Oliver. Nor of Premium either: the necessities of the former could not extort a shilling from that benevolent gentleman; and now, egad, I stood a chance of faring worse than my ancestors and being knocked down without being bid for.

Joseph Surface. Charles!

Charles Surface. Joseph!

Joseph Surface. 'Tis now complete!

Charles Surface. Very!

Sir Oliver. Sir Peter, my friend, and Rowley too—look on that elder nephew of mine. You know what he has already received from my bounty; and you also know how gladly I would have regarded half my fortune as held in trust for him? judge, then, my disappointment in discovering him to be destitute of truth, charity, and gratitude!

Sir Peter. Sir Oliver, I should be more surprised at this declaration, if I had not myself found him to be mean, treacherous, and hypocritical.

Lady Teazle. And if the gentleman pleads not guilty to these, pray let him call me to his character.

Sir Peter. Then, I believe, we need add no more: if he knows himself, he will consider it as the most perfect punishment that he is known to the world.

Charles Surface. (Aside.) If they talk this way to Honesty, what will they say to me, by-and-by?

Sir Oliver. As for that prodigal, his brother, there——

Charles Surface. (Aside.) Ay, now comes my turn: the damned family pictures will ruin me!

Joseph Surface. Sir Oliver—uncle, will you honor me with a hearing?

Charles Surface. (Aside.) Now, if Joseph would make one of his long speeches, I might recollect myself a little.

Sir Oliver. (To JOSEPH.*)* I suppose you would undertake to justify yourself entirely?

Joseph Surface. I trust I could.

Sir Oliver. (To CHARLES.*)* Well, sir!—and you could justify yourself too, I suppose?

Charles Surface. Not that I know of, Sir Oliver.

Sir Oliver. What!—Little Premium has been let too much into the secret, I suppose?

Charles Surface. True, sir; but they were family secrets, and should not be mentioned again, you know.

Rowley. Come, Sir Oliver, I know you cannot speak of Charles's follies with anger.

Sir Oliver. Odd's heart, no more I can; nor with gravity either. Sir Peter, do you know the rogue bargained with me for all his ancestors; sold me judges and generals by the foot, and maiden aunts as cheap as broken china.

Charles Surface. To be sure, Sir Oliver, I did make a little free with the family canvas, that's the truth on't. My ancestors may rise in judgment against me, there's no denying it; but believe me sincere when I tell you—and upon my soul I would not say so if I was not—that if I do not appear mortified at the exposure of my follies, it is because I feel at this moment the warmest satisfaction at seeing you, my liberal benefactor.

Sir Oliver. Charles, I believe you. Give me your hand again: the ill looking little fellow over the settee has made your peace.

Charles Surface. Then, sir, my gratitude to the original is still increased.

Lady Teazle. Yet, I believe, Sir Oliver, here is one whom Charles is still more anxious to be reconciled to.

(Pointing to MARIA.)

Sir Oliver. Oh, I have heard of his attachment there; and, with the young lady's pardon, if I construe right—that blush——

Sir Peter. Well, child, speak your sentiments.

Maria. Sir, I have little to say, but that I shall rejoice to hear that he is happy; for me, whatever claim I had to his attention, I willingly resign to one who has a better title.

Charles Surface. How, Maria!

Sir Peter. Heyday! what's the mystery now? While he appeared an incorrigible rake, you would give your hand to no one else; and now that he is likely to reform I'll warrant you won't have him.

Maria. His own heart and Lady Sneerwell know the cause.

Charles Surface. Lady Sneerwell!

Joseph Surface. Brother, it is with great concern I am obliged to speak on this point, but my regard to justice compels me, and Lady Sneerwell's injuries can no longer be concealed. (Opens the door.)

Enter LADY SNEERWELL.

Sir Peter. So! another French milliner! Egad, he has one in every room in the house, I suppose!

Lady Sneerwell. Ungrateful Charles! Well may you be surprised, and feel for the indelicate situation your perfidy has forced me into.

Charles Surface. Pray, uncle, is this another plot of yours? For, as I have life, I don't understand it.

Joseph Surface. I believe, sir, there is but the evidence of one person more necessary to make it extremely clear.

Sir Peter. And that person, I imagine, is Mr. Snake. Rowley, you were perfectly right to bring him with us, and pray let him appear.

Rowley. Walk in, Mr. Snake.

Enter SNAKE.

I thought his testimony might be wanted; however, it happens unluckily, that he comes to confront Lady Sneerwell, not to support her.

Lady Sneerwell. A villain! Treacherous to me at last! Speak, fellow, have you too conspired against me?

Snake. I beg your ladyship ten thousand pardons: you paid me extremely liberally for the lie in question; but I unfortunately have been offered double to speak the truth.

Sir Peter. Plot and counterplot, egad!

Lady Sneerwell. The torments of shame and disappointment on you all!

Lady Teazle. Hold, Lady Sneerwell—before you go, let me thank you for the trouble you and that gentleman have taken in writing letters from me to Charles, and answering them yourself; and let me also request you to make my respects to the scandalous college, of which you are president, and inform them that Lady Teazle, licentiate, begs leave to return the diploma they granted her, as she leaves off practice and kills characters no longer.

Lady Sneerwell. You too, madam!—provoking—insolent! May your husband live these fifty years!   *Exit.*

Sir Peter. Oons! what a fury!

Lady Teazle. A malicious creature, indeed!

Sir Peter. Hey! not for her last wish?

Lady Teazle. Oh, no!

Sir Oliver. Well, sir, and what have you to say now?

Joseph Surface. Sir, I am so confounded, to find that Lady Sneerwell could be guilty of suborning Mr. Snake in this manner, to impose on us all, that I know not what to say: however, lest her revengeful spirit should prompt her to injure my brother, I had certainly better follow her directly.
                                                              Exit.

Sir Peter. Moral to the last drop!

Sir Oliver. Ay, and marry her, Joseph, if you can. Oil and vinegar—egad, you'll do very well together.

Rowley. I believe we have no more occasion for Mr. Snake at present?

Snake. Before I go, I beg pardon once for all, for whatever uneasiness I have been the humble instrument of causing to the parties present.

Sir Peter. Well, well, you have made atonement by a good deed at last.

Snake. But I must request of the company, that it shall never be known.

Sir Peter. Hey! what the plague! are you ashamed of having done a right thing once in your life?

Snake. Ah, sir, consider—I live by the badness of my character; I have nothing but my infamy to depend on; and, if it were once known that I had been betrayed into an honest action, I should lose every friend I have in the world.

Sir Oliver. Well, well—we'll not traduce you by saying anything in your praise, never fear.   *Exit* SNAKE.

Sir Peter. There's a precious rogue!

Lady Teazle. See, Sir Oliver, there needs no persuasion now to reconcile your nephew and Maria.

Sir Oliver. Ay, ay, that's as it should be; and, egad, we'll have the wedding tomorrow morning.

Charles Surface. Thank you, dear uncle.

Sir Peter. What, you rogue! don't you ask the girl's consent first?

Charles Surface. Oh, I have done that a long time—a minute ago—and she has looked yes.

Maria. For shame, Charles!—I protest, Sir Peter, there has not been a word——

Sir Oliver. Well, then, the fewer the better: may your love for each other never know abatement.

Sir Peter. And may you live as happily together as Lady Teazle and I intend to do!

Charles Surface. Rowley, my old friend, I am sure you congratulate me; and I suspect that I owe you much.

Sir Oliver. You do, indeed, Charles.

Rowley. If my efforts to serve you had not succeeded, you would have been in my debt for the attempt—but deserve to be happy—and you overpay me.

Sir Peter. Ay, honest Rowley always said you would reform.

Charles Surface. Why as to reforming, Sir Peter, I'll make no promises, and that I take to be a proof that I intend to set about it. But here shall be my monitor—my gentle guide. —Ah! can I leave the virtuous path those eyes illumine?

Though thou, dear maid, shouldst wave thy beauty's sway,
Thou still must rule, because I will obey:
An humble fugitive from Folly view,
No sanctuary near but Love—and you: *(To the audience.)*
You can, indeed, each anxious fear remove,
For even Scandal dies, if you approve.

EPILOGUE

By Mr. Colman.

Spoken by Lady Teazle.

I, who was late so volatile and gay,
Like a trade-wind must now blow all one way,
Bend all my cares, my studies, and my vows,
To one dull rusty weathercock—my spouse!
So wills our virtuous bard—the motley Bayes[43]
Of crying epilogues and laughing plays!
Old bachelors, who marry smart young wives—
Learn from our play to regulate your lives:
Each bring his dear to town, all faults upon her—
London will prove the very source of honor.
Plunged fairly in, like a cold bath it serves,
When principles relax, to brace the nerves.
Such is my case; and yet I must deplore
That the gay dream of dissipation's o'er.
And say, ye fair! was ever lively wife,
Born with a genius for the highest life,
Like me untimely blasted in her bloom,
Like me condemned to such a dismal doom?
Save money—when I just knew how to waste it!
Leave London—just as I began to taste it!
Must I then watch the early-crowing cock,
The melancholy ticking of a clock;
In a lone rustic hall for ever pounded,[44]
With dogs, cats, rats, and squalling brats surrounded?
With humble curate can I now retire,
(While good Sir Peter boozes with the squire,)
And at backgammon mortify my soul,
That pants for loo, or flutters at a vole.[45]
Seven's the main![46] Dear sound that must expire,
Lost at hot cockles[47] round a Christmas fire;
The transient hour of fashion too soon spent,
Farewell the tranquil mind, farewell content![48]
Farewell the pluméd head, the cushioned tête,
That takes the cushion from its proper seat!
That spirit-stirring drum—card drums I mean,
Spadille—odd trick—pam—basto—king and queen!

And you, ye knockers that with brazen throat
The welcome visitors' approach denote;
Farewell all quality of high renown,
Pride, pomp, and circumstance of glorious town!
Farewell! your revels I partake no more,
And Lady Teazle's occupation's o'er!
All this I told our bard; he smiled, and said 'twas clear,
I ought to play deep tragedy next year.
Meanwhile he drew wise morals from his play,
And in these solemn periods stalked away:—
"Blessed were the fair like you; her faults who stopped.
And closed her follies when the curtain dropped!
No more in vice or error to engage,
Or play the fool at large on life's great stage."

THE COUNTRY WIFE
by William Wycherley

The first performance of *The Country Wife,* by the King's Company at Lincoln's Inn Fields sometime between the early spring of 1672 and that of 1674, was a brilliant success. Though later, in more sedate times, the bawdiness of its plot was generally condemned, its literary qualities were still highly praised. Macaulay, writing in the 19th century, said of *The Country Wife,* "Though one of the most profligate of human compositions, it is the elaborate performance of a mind ingenious, observant, quick to seize hints, and patient of the toil of polishing."

1. *Castril*—A character in Ben Jonson's *The Alchemist.* Bayes is the author in *The Rehearsal* by George Villiers.

2. *Passe-partout*—Master key, pass-key.

3. *Probatum est*—It is approved.

4. *Orange wenches*—Prostitutes.

5. *Vizard-masks*—Masks were frequently worn in public; in this instance, a woman wearing such a mask; more specificially, a prostitute.

6. *"Sir Martin Mar-all"*—A comedy by Dryden. Sir Martin goes through the motions of serenading his lady, while a man concealed behind him is actually singing and playing the lute.

7. *Chateline's*—A fashionable French restaurant in Covent Garden. The Cock Tavern, in Bow Street, was frequented by Wycherley.

8. *Pox*—Syphilis.

9. *Basilisk*—A mythical beast whose breath, or even look, was fatal.

10. *French wether*—A ram gelded before maturity. A eunuch.

11. *New Exchange*—A building opened in 1609 which became a fashionable lounge after the Restoration. It was partially copied from the plan of the Royal Exchange, with a long paved arcade and rows of shops occupied by milliners, seamstresses, publishers, and perfumers.

12. *Bubbled*—Duped, cheated.

13. *Hictius doctius topsy turvy*—Terms used in juggler's patter. Shifty dealings, trickery.

14. *Covent Garden Drollery*—A collection of songs and poems published in 1672. *Tarugo's Wiles* is a comedy by Thomas St. Serle; *The Slighted Maid*, a comedy by Robert Stapleton.

15. *Eclaircissement*—Explanation, clarification.

16. *Pulvillio*—Scented powder.

17. *Megrim*—Variously: migrain, melancholia, or vertigo.

18. *Lincoln's Inn Fields, St. James's Fields, Pall Mall*—Residential areas of London, fashionable at this time.

19. *Canonical hour*—The hours of legal marriage.

20. *Fadges*—Succeeds.

21. *Out of Italy*—This refers to the practice of emasculating boys with good soprano voices. A castrato.

22. *Roll-wagon*—A low truck or van.

23. *Lombard Street*—The residential section where many wealthy goldsmiths had their homes. Locket's is a fashionable tavern.

24. *Paw*—Naughty.

25. *Pother*—Fuss, bother.

26. *Picquet, ombre, loo*—Fashionable card games.

35. *St. Bartholomew and his fair*—The Smithfield annual St. Bartholomew Fair.

36. *The Revolution*—The Glorious Revolution of 1688.

37. *Smoke him*—Make fun of him.

38. *Rekin*—Wrekin, a hill in Shropshire.

39. *Flap-dragon*—A raisin snatched from burning brandy and eaten hot; here, something of little value.

40. *Hare's scut*—Tail.

41. *Inns o' Court*—The four societies which controlled the legal profession.

42. *Salop*—Shropshire.

43. *Shrewsbury cake*—A rich, sweet biscuit.

44. *Call of sergeants*—The summoning of sergeants-at-law, or lawyers of special rank, to appear at the bar.

45. *Out of your time*—Finished serving as an apprentice.

46. *Dawks's Letter*—A weekly newsletter. *The Weekly Bill* was a mortality list.

47. *Shill I, shall I*—Shilly-shally.

48. *Citizen's child*—A bastard.

49. *Furnished like a deputy-lieutenant's hall*—Covered with the horns and antlers of numerous trophies.

50. *Cap of maintenance*—A symbol of high office, frequently bearing two elongated horn-like points.

51. *Pam in her pocket*—The knave of clubs, the highest card in loo.

52. *Set his hand in*—Start him playing the game.

53. *Pulvilled*—Sprinkled with a scented powder.

54. *Levee*—Arising.

55. *There never yet was . . .*—Quoted from Sir John Suckling.

56. *Thyrsis, a youth . . .*—Waller, *The Story of Phoebus and Daphne Applied.*

57. *I prithee . . .*—These lines are from a song by Suckling.

58. *Anan?*—What do you say?

59. *L'etourdie*—The giddy, foolish.

60. *Like Phoebus . . .*—From the poem by Waller cited previously. Mirabell adds the fourth line.

61. *Pragmatical*—Opinionated, dogmatic.

62. Ye *douceurs,* ye *sommeils du matin*—Sweet indulgences, mid-morning naps.

63. *Imprimis*—First of all.

64. *Fop-scrambling*—To chase a fop.

65. *Vizards*—Masks.

66. *Atlas*—A rich, imported satin.

67. *Clary*—These are all variously flavored brandies or cordials.

68. *Camlet*—Originally an imported, costly, satin-weave fabric made of Angora or camel's hair. Presumably a cheap European imitation is referred to here.

69. *Noli prosequi*—To drop charges.

70. *Decimo sexto*—A very small book size (sixteenmo).

71. *Lacedmonian*—Spartan. The Spartans are supposed to have spoken very briefly and to the point.

72. *Baldwin*—The name of an ass in folk lore.

73. *Gemini*—The twins; hence, a pair.

74. *Rantipole*—Wild, unruly.

75. *Borachio*—Spanish for drunkard; literally, wine bag.

76. *In vino veritas*—In wine there is truth.

77. *Pimple*—A jovial companion.

78. *Antipodes*—Parts of the globe which are diametrically opposite.

79. *Sophy*—Probably the shah.

80. *Tantony . . . pig*—St. Anthony was the patron saint of swine herds.

81. *Save-all*—A holder which permits the stub-end of a candle to be burned.

82. *Gauze and weaving of dead hair*—Making wigs.

83. *Frisoneer gorget*—A large, woolen collar. Colberteen is a coarse lace.

84. *Clergy.*—"Benefit of clergy." Medieval ecclesiastical courts —which could not inflict the death penalty—claimed jurisdiction over any member of the clergy accused of a crime by a temporal court. Subsequently this was extended to clerks in orders for any felony, but not for high treason. At the time of the play it had been further extended to anyone who could read.

85. *Abigails and Andrews*—Servants.

86. *Bridewell*—A prison.

87. *Naught*—Naughty, immoral. Sophisticated: seduced.

88. *Babies*—Dolls.

89. *Cantharides*—An aphrodisiac prepared from the blister beetle or Spanish fly.

90. *Cow-itch*—The pods of the cowhage plant are covered with barbed hairs which cause intolerable itching.

91. *Non compos*—Mentally deranged.

92. *Pylades and Orestes*—Pylades accompanied Orestes during his flight from the Furies. Hence; loyal friends.

93. *Mouth glue*—Saliva.

94. *Fox*—Sword.

95. *Ram vellum*—Legal documents.

96. *Mittimus*—A warrant.

97. *Messalina*—The notorious Roman empress. It is also possible that Mincing is mispronouncing *Miscellany*.

SHE STOOPS TO CONQUER

by Oliver Goldsmith

The leading theatrical figures of 18th century London had strong misgivings about the possible success of *She Stoops to Conquer*. However, through the influence of Samuel Johnson, it was prepared for production. Rehearsals were hectic and two of the leading comic actors of the time, Woodward and Smith, withdrew from the cast, saying they did not wish to be associated with a failure. Despite these difficulties the play opened at Covent Garden on March 15, 1773. A claque of Goldsmith's friends, led by Dr. Johnson, helped direct the enthusiasm of the audience and *She Stoops to Conquer* scored a deep and lasting success.

1. *Mr. Woodward*—A popular London actor. Woodward declined the part of Tony and hence does not appear in the original cast.

2. *Shuter*—"Ned" Shuter played Hardcastle in the original production of *She Stoops to Conquer*. He also appeared as Croaker in Goldsmith's *The Good-Natured Man*.

3. *Darby and Joan*—Traditionally, the happy old couple, as in eighteenth century ballads.

4. *Jorum*—A drinking bowl.

5. *"Water Parted"*—A song from Arne's opera *Antaxerxes*. *Araidne* is an opera by Handel.

6. *Duchess of Drury Lane*—A prostitute.

7. *Us that sell ale*—Ordinary people.

8. *Ally Cawn*—Hyder Ali and Ali Khan were Indian Sultans. "Ally Croaker" was a popular Irish song.

9. *Florentine*—A meat pie. Shaking pudding is a jelly; taffety cream a rich creamy dessert.

10. *India Director*—An officer of the East India Company.

11. *St. James and Ranlegh are fashionable resorts of the nobility*—Tower Wharf is in a thoroughly disreputable section of London. The same disparity is found in Mrs. Hardcastle's allusions.

12. *Tête-à-tête*—Biographical sketches of people involved in society scandals published in *Town and Country* or similar magazines.

13. *Inoculation*—Smallpox inoculation was introduced in 1718.

14. *Quincy*—Dr. John Quincy was author of the *Complete English Dispensatory*.

15. *Mauvaise honte*—Self-consciousness.

16. *Bully Dawson*—A notorious ruffian.

17. *Cracker*—Fire cracker.

18. *Morrice*—A Morrice Dance; hence, "dance away."

19. *Marcasites*—Iron pyrites or fool's gold.

20. *Rose and table cut*—Relatively unfaceted gems, so cut because they are too small to be cut into the more highly faceted brilliants.

21. *Catharine wheel*—A revolving piece of fireworks; a pinwheel.

22. *Cherry in "The Beaux Stratagem"*—The innkeeper's daughter in Farquhar's play.

23. *Lion, Angel, Lamb*—Imaginary names of inn-rooms.

24. *Tablets*—A memo pad.

25. *Seven, ames ace*—In hazard, winning and losing throws of dice. Ames ace, or both aces, is the lowest throw; American colloquialism-"snake eyes."

26. *"The Rake's Progress"*—One of Hogarth's famous series of engravings.

27. *Dullissimo Maccaroni*—A dull-witted dandy.

28. *Haspicholls*—Harpsichord.

29. *Baskets*—Basket-hilted rapiers; swords with shielded handles.

30. *But you know . . . her own disposal*—Early editions give this speech to Mrs. Hardcastle or omit it entirely. "Ay, but he's not of age . . ." was assigned to Mr. Hardcastle.

31. *Nancy Dawson*—A popular song.

32. *Che Faro*—An aria from Gluck's opera *Orfeo*.

33. *Heinel*—A fashionable German dancer.

34. *Spadille*—The ace of spades, in ombre or quadrille.

35. *Bayes*—The author in *The Rehearsal* by George Villiers.

NOTES TO

THE SCHOOL FOR SCANDAL
by Richard Brinsley Sheridan

The first production of this comedy was the result of many years of painstaking work. Using his well developed skills, Sheridan cleverly combined elements of two of his earlier plays, *The Slanderers* and *The Teazles* and composed *The School for Scandal*. The staging was also done with the greatest possible care. The first performance at Drury Lane on May 8, 1777 was acclaimed as a superb performance of a brilliant comedy.

1. *Quantum sufficit*—Plenty.

2. *Poz*—Positively.

3. *Sir Toby Bumper*—This character was omitted from the original cast of characters. In some later editions he is identified as Sir Harry Bumper.

4. *Tête-à-tête in the Town and Country Magazine*—Sketches of people involved in society scandals.

5. *City knight*—A knighted merchant.

6. *Diligence*—A public stagecoach.

7. *Laura*—The lady of Petrarch's sonnet cycle. Sacharissa is the name which Waller used to address Lady Dorothy Sidney.

8. *Tontine*—Annuities sold by act of the Irish parliament. The system was named for its originator, Lorenzo Tonti.

9. *Doubt*—Doubt not.

10. *Pantheon*—A fashionable concert hall.

11. *Fête champêtre*—A garden party.

12. *Tambour*—Embroidery frame.

13. *Pope Joan*—An unfashionable game of cards.

14. *Vis-à-vis*—A stylish carriage in which the occupants face each other.

15. *White cats*—Ponies.

16. *Macaronies*—Elegantly groomed ponies.

17. *Ring*—A drive in Hyde Park.

18. *French fruit*—Artificial fruits containing maxims printed on slips of paper; similar to the modern Chinese "fortune cookies."

19. *Law Merchant*—Mercantile law, under which endorsers assume responsibility for debts if the principals fail to pay.

20. *Cicisbeo*—A married woman's lover.

21. *Bluff*—Firm, staunch.

22. *a tear for pity. . . .* "Henry IV," Part II, IV, iv, 31-32.

23. *Annuity Bill*—Designed to protect minors against unscrupulous sellers of annuities.

24. *Bags and bouquets*—Footman's livery. The bag wig, which used a small pouch to hold the hair, was fashionable at the time.

25. *Post-obit*—To take effect after death.

26. *Quean*—A harlot.

27. *Bough pots*—Window boxes.

28. *Race cups, corporation bowls*—Trophies and testimonial awards.

29. *Malplaquet*—Marlborough defeated the French forces, but suffered twice as many casualties as his opponents.

30. *Kneller*—Sir Godfrey Kneller, a fashionable portrait painter.

31. *Wool sack*—A symbol of the law. The Lord Chancellor's seat is the Woolsack—originally chosen as the emblem of Britain's wealth.

32. *Birthday clothes*—Elegant garments worn at the king's birthday celebration.

33. *Rupees, pagodas*—Coins of India.

34. *Congou tea*—A black Chinese tea.

35. *Avadavats*—Small Indian songbirds.

36. *Indian crackers*—Fire-crackers.

37. *Seconde*—A position in parrying.

38. *Montem*—A carnival, called the Montem, is held every third year on Whit-Tuesday, by the boys of Eton. The festivities take place on Salthill.

39. *Double letter*—An overweight letter requiring extra postage.

40. *Faculty*—The medical profession.

41. *Diffidence*—Doubt.

42. *A. B.'s at the coffee-houses*—Appointments made under fictitious initials or concealed names.

43. *Bayes*—The author in *The Rehearsal* by George Villiers.

44. *Pounded*—Confined.

45. *Loo*—A fashionable card game of the eighteenth century; vole: to win all the tricks in a deal.

46. *Seven's the main*—In the game of hazard, seven is one of the easiest "points" to throw.

47. *Hot cockles*—A juvenile game.

48. *This and the next ten lines parody "Othello,"* III, iii, 347-357.

The text of this Bantam Classic is set in the
famous TIMES ROMAN type, used, because of
its legibility and simplicity, by *The Times*
of London.
The art work on the cover reproduces a
detail from panel III of William Hogarth's
famous work, THE RAKE'S PROGRESS.

BANTAM CLASSICS

are chosen from the whole span of
living literature. They comprise
a balanced selection of the best
novels, poems, plays and stories by
the writers whose works and thoughts
have made an indelible impact on
Western culture.

...L FRENCH DRAMA
...ace Fowlie, editor   HC135 / 60¢

...s volume are five plays representing the diversity, the traditions and ...style of Classic French Theatre: Corneille's *The Cid*, Racine's ...*haedra*, Moliere's *Intellectual Ladies*, Marivaux's *The Game of Love and Chance*, Beaumarchais' *The Barber of Seville*. Wallace Fowlie has translated and edited the text, and provided biographies of the dramatists.

CLASSICAL GERMAN DRAMA
Victor Lange, editor   SC170 / 75¢

A collection of works by late 18th and early 19th century German dramatists: *Nathan the Wise*, by G. E. Lessing, *Egmont* by Johann Wolfgang von Goethe, *Mary Stuart* by Friedrich Schiller, *The Prince of Homburg*, by Heinrich von Kleist, *Danton's Death* by Georg Büchner. Translation by Theodore H. Lustig. Introduction to this volume by the editor, Victor Lange. Bibliography.

NINETEENTH CENTURY RUSSIAN DRAMA
John Gassner, general editor   SC168 / 75¢

The drama of this period introduced a quality of realism unknown in more formalistic European theatre. *The Stone Guest* by Pushkin, *The Inspector General* by Gogol, *A Month in the Country* by Turgenev, *The Thunderstorm* by Ostrovsky, *The Power of Darkness* by Tolstoy. Translated by Andrew R. MacAndrew, with an introduction by Marc Slonim.

TWENTIETH CENTURY RUSSIAN DRAMA
John Gassner, general editor   SC174 / 75¢

Five outstanding works showing the brilliant range of Russian creativity during this era. *The Three Sisters* by Chekhov, *The Lower Depths* by Gorky, *He Who Gets Slapped* by Andreyev, *The Bathhouse* by Mayakovsky, *A List of Assets* by Olesha. Translated and with an introduction by Andrew R. MacAndrew.

SPANISH DRAMA   Angel Flores, editor   SC113 / 75¢

Important Spanish plays from the 16th to the 20th century, including: *The Olives* by Lope de Rueda, *The Vigilant Sentinel* by Cervantes, *Fuente Ovejuna* by Lope de Vega, *The Rogue of Seville* by Tirso de Molina, *The Truth Suspected* by Alarcon, *Life is a Dream* by Calderon, *When a Girl Says Yes* by Moratin, *The Great Galeoto* by Echegaray, *The Bonds of Interest* by Benevente, and *Blood Wedding* by Lorca. Introduction, bibliography and prefatory remarks to each play by Angel Flores.